GROUP IDENTITY IN THE RENAISSANCE WORLD

This book argues that the Renaissance, an era long associated with the historical development of individualism, in fact witnessed the emergence of radically new concepts of group identity. From the end of the fifteenth century, rapidly accelerating globalization intensified cross-cultural encounters, destabilized older categories of large- and small-group identity, and contributed to the rise of new hybrid group concepts. Drawing on insights from psychoanalysis, linguistics, and Simmelian social network theory, this book advances a theory of "group subjectivity" – perceptions, fantasies, and patterns of belief that guide the behaviors of individuals in groups and of groups themselves. Considering not only Europe but also South Asia, Africa, the Sugar Islands of the Atlantic, the Caribbean world, and Brazil, Hannah Chapelle Wojciehowski reconsiders the Renaissance in global context, presenting micro-histories of group identity formation, and persuasively argues that we think of that transformational era as a "re-networking" of the world and its peoples, rather than a "rebirth."

Hannah Chapelle Wojciehowski is Associate Professor of English at the University of Texas (UT) at Austin and an Affiliate of UT's Program in Comparative Literature as well as the South Asia Institute. A specialist in the history of subjectivity and group-identity formation, she is the author of *Old Masters, New Subjects: Early Modern and Poststructuralist Theories of Will*, as well as numerous essays on medieval and Renaissance authors and on the history and practice of literary theory.

GROUP IDENTITY IN THE RENAISSANCE WORLD

HANNAH CHAPELLE WOJCIEHOWSKI

University of Texas, Austin

CAMBRIDGE
UNIVERSITY PRESS

CAMBRIDGE
UNIVERSITY PRESS

32 Avenue of the Americas, New York, NY 10013-2473, USA

Cambridge University Press is part of the University of Cambridge.

It furthers the University's mission by disseminating knowledge in the pursuit of
education, learning, and research at the highest international levels of excellence.

www.cambridge.org
Information on this title: www.cambridge.org/9781107649323

© Hannah Chapelle Wojciehowski 2011

First published 2011
First paperback edition 2014

Printed in the United States of America

A catalog record for this publication is available from the British Library.

Library of Congress Cataloging in Publication data
Wojciehowski, Hannah Chapelle, 1957–
Group Identity in the Renaissance World / Hannah Chapelle Wojciehowski.
    p.   cm.
Includes bibliographical references and index.
ISBN 978-1-107-00360-6
1. Group identity – Europe – History.   2. Group identity – History.
3. Renaissance.   I. Title.
HM753.W65   2011
305.09′031–dc22   2010044853

ISBN 978-1-107-00360-6 Hardback
ISBN 978-1-107-64932-3 Paperback

To my parents

Betty Joan Cotter Wojciehowski

and

James Philip Wojciehowski

CONTENTS

Color plates follow page xxxiv.

vii

ACKNOWLEDGMENTS

Writing this book was an arduous journey and a great adventure. Many people guided me along the way, and without their help the project would not have been completed. The ideas for this book emerged during a trip to India in December of 1999. Supported by a research award from the University of Texas (UT), I visited the Historical Archives of Goa, where I was aided by Director S. K. Mhamai, and by associates M. L. Dicholkar and Arvind Yalagi. I also had the opportunity to work at the Xavier Centre of Historical Research in Porvorim, where I benefited immensely from the insight of Charles Borges, S. J., then Director of the Centre, as well as Lilia Maria d'Souza, the Centre's Librarian. Conversations with Michael N. Pearson, P. P. Shirodkar, and Pedro Moura Carvalho sent me off in new directions, as I began to understand the Renaissance in more global terms.

In the summers of 2000 and 2001, I received a K. Garth Huston and Fletcher Jones Foundation Fellowship and an Andrew W. Mellon Foundation Fellowship from the Henry E. Huntington Library in San Marino, California. There I was able to continue my research for this project with the guidance of Robert Ritchie, W. M. Keck Foundation Director of Research at the Huntington; and of Susi Krasnoo, Christopher Adde, and especially Jill Cogan of Reader Services. The opportunity to converse with groups of scholars at the Huntington was an unforgettable experience and a great boost to my own understanding of creative social collectives.

In the spring of 2002, I had the good fortune to work at the Virginia Foundation for the Humanities (VFH), thanks to a Rockefeller Resident Fellowship at the Institute for the Study of Violence, Survival, and Culture. I owe my lasting gratitude to James Garrison, then chair of the English Department at UT; Robert Vaughan, President of the VFH; Roberta Culbertson, Director of the Institute; and Ann Spencer, Program Associate. I would also like to thank Claudia Ferman, Susan Pennybacker, Victoria Sanford, and Leonard Smith, my fellow fellows that spring, and Jean Maria Arrigo. Many others inspired me that season, especially Vamik Volkan, Director of the Center for the Study of Mind and Human Interaction at the University of Virginia School of Medicine. Volkan's studies of ethnic conflict and large-group behaviors had a powerful influence on the shape of this book.

I would like to thank my own institution, the University of Texas, and especially Elizabeth Cullingford, Chair of the Department of English at UT, for her continued support of this project, particularly in its final stages. A University Research Institute Faculty Research Award in the fall of 2008 made it possible for me to complete the manuscript on which I had worked for many years.

The one thing that most of us never have enough of is time. Hence, I am enormously grateful to all those who made time to read the manuscript or various chapters, sometimes in multiple drafts, and to provide suggestions for improvement. I owe my deepest thanks and appreciation to three mentors – Albert Ascoli, Sidney Monas, and Leah Marcus – who went over the manuscript carefully and helped to bring it to its final form. Eric Chapelle, Betty Wojciehowski, and Kati Wojciehowski also read the entire manuscript and commented extensively on it. My friends Marilyn Migiel and Jeffrey Kahan, and my brother Jim Wojciehowski read and also helped to conceptualize the Freudian Foreword and the Introduction. Karen Pagani helped with translations from the French in these chapters and throughout the book.

Chapter 1 of this book began to take shape after a 2003 Telluride Summer Association Program course at the University of Texas. D'Arcy Randall, the co-teacher of the course, and our group of eighteen remarkable students taught me an enormous amount about the mystery of creativity in groups. Marilyn Migiel, Susan Gaylard, Dan Birkholz, Jorie Woods, Doug Biow, and the European Studies group at the University of Texas provided highly useful advice on the chapter. Philippe Dambournet and Robert Corum assisted with translations from the French, as did Marilyn Migiel from the Italian.

Jorge Cañizares-Esguerra, Alida Metcalf, and Miguel Santos-Neves suggested several improvements to Chapter 2. Sam Wilson provided useful anthropological information on the history of Caribbean peoples, and Jeffrey Chipps Smith helped me to sort out some art historical conundrums in that chapter. Marsilio Publishing extended permission to republish portions of the David Jacobson translation of Amerigo Vespucci's *Letters from a New World*, edited by Luciano Formisano (New York: 1992). Miguel Santos-Neves provided assistance with translations from the Portuguese, both here and in Chapter 4.

Doug Bruster, Jeffrey Kahan, Daniel Lochman, and Su Fang Ng read versions of Chapter 3, suggesting useful ways to frame the material. Ria Vanderauwera and Su Fang Ng provided translations from the Flemish. Conversations with James Hammond also improved the chapter.

Chapter 4 has the longest history of all those included in this book. The story of the tooth relic was first relayed to me by Michael Pearson during my initial trip to Goa. Members and fellows of the Virginia Foundation for the Humanities helped me to shape the chapter in its earliest stages. Madhu Kishwar published a short version of the essay in the June 2004 issue of *Manushi*, and João Camilo published a longer version in the 2007 issue of *Santa Barbara Portuguese Studies*. Gerry Heng, Jorie Woods, Alison Frazier, Judith Kroll, K. David Jackson, Susantha Goonatilake, Susan Glenn, Don Stadtner, Michael Pearson, and Pamila Gupta read drafts of the essay as it evolved, and provided many helpful suggestions on how to extend and improve it. Marcella Rossman and Paul Harford provided guidance on translations from the Spanish. Ishan Chakrabarti provided input on Pali and Sanskrit transliterations, here and in Chapter 6, and also helpful commentaries on Chapters 4–6.

Krystyna Kujawinska Courtney published the kernel of what would ultimately become Chapter 5 in *On Page and Stage: Shakespeare in Polish and World Culture* (Krakow: 2000). Kathleen Perry Long provided many helpful insights into the material for this chapter when we collaborated on a 2007 Telluride Summer Association Program course at Cornell University on the Renaissance Body (as did the remarkable students in that group). Daniel Lochman, Eric Mallin, and Noel Radley read recent versions of the chapter, offering their very useful feedback.

A number of friends and colleagues helped me with Chapter 6, including Virendra K. Jain, Manish Modi, Babu Suthar, Jerry Bump, Judith Kroll, Antonio dell'Andrea, Nathalie Hester, and Matthew Reilly.

Securing the permissions for use of the images in this book was no small task. A generous University Co-operative Society Subvention Grant awarded by the University of Texas at Austin made possible the use of color images in this book. Administrative Associate Donetta Dean-Gibbs processed endless paperwork concerning rights and permissions, for which I am truly appreciative.

Thanks to W. W. Norton & Company, Inc., for granting me permission to quote from *UTOPIA: A Norton Critical Edition*, Second Edition by Sir Thomas More, translated by Robert M. Adams (1992, 1975).

I would like to thank Thomas Staley, the Director of the Henry Huntt Ransom Humanities Research Center at the University of Texas, as well as Associate Director Richard Orem, Librarian Margaret Tanney, and Library Assistant Patricia Fox for all their help over the years in the creation and production of this book. I would also like to thank the staff of the Benson Latin American Collection at UT, especially Jorge Salinas, who helped me many times over the years.

I would also like to acknowledge the assistance of the following people: Dirk Imhof and Patricia Kolsteeg of the Museum Plantin-Moretus/Prentenkabinet – UNESCO World Heritage in Antwerp; Cynthia Franco of the DeGolyer Library at Southern Methodist University in Dallas; Sinead Ward of the Chester Beatty Library in Dublin; Lou Stancari of the National Museum of the American Indian in New York; Giema Tsakugi-now of the Philadelphia Museum of Art in Philadelphia; John Henry Rice and Howell Perkins of the Virginia Museum of Fine Arts in Richmond, Virginia; Katie Holyoak of the Royal Collection in London; Tânia Olim and Claudia Sequeira of the Instituto dos Museus e da Conservação in Lisbon; Pieter Muys of the Royal Museum of Fine Arts of Belgium in Brussels; Ruth Janson of the Brooklyn Museum in Brooklyn; Dominik Hunger of the Universitätsbibliothek in Basel; Erin Schleigh of the Boston Museum of Fine Arts; the staff of the Bayerische Staatsbibliothek in Munich; Glen Worthey of Special Collections at Stanford University in Palo Alto; Rita Apsan of the Freud Museum in London; John Powell of the Newberry Library in Chicago; Qamar Banerjee of the Asian Art Museum in San Francisco; Tricia Smith and Michael Slade of Art Resource in New York; Thomas Haggerty of the Bridgeman Art Library in New York; and David Corson of Cornell University's Carl A. Kroch Library in Ithaca, New York.

Adoration is how I would describe my feelings about the staff at Cambridge University Press, including the Publishing Director, Humanities & Social Sciences, Beatrice Rehl; Assistant Editor, Humanities and Social Sciences, Emily Spangler; and Senior Production and Design Controller, James Dunn; and about Shana Meyer, Senior Project Manager at Aptara, and copy editor Mary Ruff. My two readers for the Press provided exceptionally helpful advice and feedback about the manuscript, guiding it to its final form. It has been a privilege to work with such a professional team.

I would also like to thank the friends, family, and fellow travelers who provided their support over the years, listened to my ongoing litany of complaints about the writing process, helped me persevere, and gave me great ideas and inspiration all along the way: Sidney Monas, Albert Ascoli, Xianchun Vendler, David Vendler, Leah Marcus, Marilyn Migiel, Eric Mallin, Jeffrey Kahan, Cathy Caruth, Daniel Lochman, Gerry Heng, Helena Woodard, Jorie Woods, Alison Frazier, Carol MacKay, Dan Birkholz, Julia Mickenberg, Janice Inskeep, Marcella Rossman, Charles Rossman, Sandy Dunn, Paul Harford, Liz Cullingford, Su Fang Ng, John Rumrich,

Susan Glenn, Molly Campbell, Charles McClelland, Brent Turnipseed, Jacque Webster, John Rowley, Arlen Nydam, Kazel Morgan, Emma McClelland, Luanne Electra McKinnon, Daniel Reeves, Vittorio Gallese, Bart Wojciehowski, Dana Milne, and Cathy and Steve Lyders. What would I do without you? The remarkable students of the University of Texas also helped and inspired me. I would especially like to thank four students who magically changed my life from 2005 to 2008, and who inspired me with my own work: Ishan Chakrabarti, Kevin Cloud, Ann Terrill, and Michelle Ty.

There is one person I wish to thank again and again. My husband Eric Chapelle was with me every step of the way, showing me, quite literally, a whole new world and sharing the creative process with me. You are the music in my life.

To each and all of you, and to those I do not mention here, but who helped bring this work into being, you have my gratitude, love, and appreciation.

And, finally, to the reader of these lines and of this book: thank you and welcome!

LIST OF ILLUSTRATIONS

DREAMING THE GROUP: A FREUDIAN FOREWORD

Communities are to be distinguished, not by their falsity/genuineness, but by the style in which they are imagined.

> – Benedict Anderson, *Imagined Communities*

At the turn of the twentieth century, Sigmund Freud investigated the underlying structures of dreams, seeking to locate within them a hidden logic governing our unconscious lives. In *The Interpretation of Dreams* (1900), he proposed that while certain elements of dreams may appear strange or random, in fact they are not. Even in dreams – or rather, especially in dreams – things go together for a reason. To illustrate their combinatory logic and their relation to the subtending thoughts and fantasies from which dreams emerge, Freud proposed the following pictorial analogy:

> In the first place, dreams take into account in a general way the connection which undeniably exists between all the portions of the dream-thoughts by combining the whole material into a single situation or event. They reproduce *logical connection* by *simultaneity in time* [*Gleichzeitigkeit*]. Here they are acting like the painter who, in a picture of the School of Athens or of Parnassus, represents in one group all the philosophers or all the poets. It is true that they were never in fact assembled in a single hall or on a single mountain-top; but they certainly form a group in the conceptual sense.

> Dreams carry this method of reproduction down to details. Whenever they show us two elements close together, this guarantees that there is some specially intimate connection between what correspond to them among the dream-thoughts.[1]

---

[1] *On the Interpretation of Dreams*, in *Standard Edition*, 4: 314. *Die Traumdeutung*, in *Gesammelte Werke*, 2–3: 319.

In this account of how dreams work – and also, implicitly, of how groups work – Freud refers his readers to two frescos painted by the Renaissance artist Raphael on the walls of the Vatican's Stanza della Segnatura between 1509 and 1511 (Figures F. 1 and F. 2). Freud suggests that these two paintings demonstrate by analogy the associative properties of dream-work. In *The School of Athens*, Raphael had depicted the great philosophers of classical antiquity in conversation with each other. At the center of the painting, where the perspectival lines of the cavernous hall converge, the artist positioned the two founding fathers of western philosophy, Plato and his disciple Aristotle. They are rapt in speculation. Around them other legendary thinkers congregate, including Socrates, Zeno, Epicurus, Pythagoras, Euclid, Parmenides, Diogenes, and numerous others.[2] To explain the principle of *Gleichzeitigkeit*, or "simultaneity," in dreams – that is, the phenomenon of unexpected temporal and/or spatial conjunctions – Freud evokes Raphael's painterly fabrication of a "single situation or event:" *The School of Athens*, an imagined dialogue between philosophers who lived in widely different historical periods and geographic regions, yet who nevertheless appear together on the vaulted stage of Raphael's philosophical fantasy.

Similarly, in the *Mount Parnassus* fresco, Apollo, god of poetry and music, together with the nine Muses, presides over a gathering of renowned poets – nine ancient and nine contemporary. The artist envisioned a meeting of literary minds transcending time and space. In one grouping to the left of Apollo and the Muses, the poets Dante, Homer, Virgil, and Statius stand (Figure F.3). In art, as in dreams, such conjunctions are possible. Here the honored poets gather under the auspices of their patron god, perhaps to converse, perhaps to compete, perhaps to share poetry, ideas, and inspiration. Viewers are left to speculate on the nature of their engagements or even to imagine themselves joining the group. Similar to Raphael, who placed together in these frescos persons from different historical periods, as well as imaginary beings (Apollo and the Muses), Freud suggests, so does the dreamer combine diverse memories, experiences, and ideas organized into a narrative structure. These seemingly arbitrary juxtapositions within dreams reveal, on deeper examination, a guiding intentionality at work.

[2] From Vasari's time down to our own, the identities of the figures in Raphael's *School of Athens* have been much debated. See, for example, Vasari, *Lives*, 4: 216-218; Passavant, *Raphael of Urbino*, 89–99; Garello, Rossi, and Salomone, *Raffaello: La Scuola di Atene*; Bell, "New Identifications," 638–646; Rowland, "The Intellectual Background of the *School of Athens*," 131–175; and Joost-Gaugier, *Raphael's Stanza della Segnatura*.

The principle of simultaneity extends still more deeply within Raphael's composition, however, because several images of the philosophers are thought to be portraits of the artist's contemporaries. Michelangelo might have served as the model for the brooding figure draped in purple who dominates the center foreground of the painting, thought to be Heraclitus, ancient philosopher of change and flux. On the extreme right, Raphael painted himself, possibly as the sharp-eyed Apelles, and the androgynous figure in a white robe could represent Pico della Mirandola or Francesco della Rovere, or, according to popular speculation, Hypatia, as Raphael's mistress. Leonardo, bearded and magisterial, is said to appear as Plato (see Figures F.4–F.7).[3] In one painted figure, two (or perhaps more) historical persons converge, just as in dreams one person can stand in for another, or multiple meanings may be condensed within a single symbol. In this pivotal passage in *The Interpretation of Dreams*, Freud paves the way for his famous analysis of condensation and displacement, the twin mechanisms employed by the unconscious to distort, displace, compress, or magnify the image-text of the dream – namely, the feelings or impulses that are given expression in dream-work.

Although Raphael's two frescos appear at first glance to be limpid illustrations of Freud's concept of *Gleichzeitigkeit*, or simultaneity in dreams, we may well ask why he chose these two images in particular. There would, of course, have been any number of ways to analogize the placing together of disparate persons, objects, or themes in dreams. Was there a deeper logic driving this choice, which appears at the crux of Freud's explanation of dream-work, and which serves in a sense as the vanishing point of his own argument?

It is probably not a coincidence that Freud explains the phenomenon of *Gleichzeitigkeit* through the previously discussed visual analogies to two

---

[3] Michelangelo is generally thought to have served as the model for the figure of Heraclitus. See Rowland, 157. Similarly, Plato's image is frequently taken to be a portrait of Leonardo da Vinci. See Garello, v–vi, and Redig de Campos, *Raffaello nelle Stanze*, 17. Vasari may have been the first to identify the Raphael portrait in the painting. See *Lives*, 4: 217.

The image of the striking young blond in the white cape may be a portrait of Francesco Maria della Rovere, Duke of Urbino, as suggested by Redig de Campos (13) and Passavant (92). More recently, Joost-Gaugier has argued that the figure may represent the Florentine philosopher Pico della Mirandola (93–96). The popular notion that this image portrays the ancient philosopher Hypatia, modeled on the features of Raphael's mistress Margarita, has not been accepted by art historians. Because of its polysemy, this particular figure provides an interesting example of dreamlike simultaneity, since there is little agreement on the identity of this figure, its doubleness, or even its sex.

F.1. Raphael, *School of Athens*, ca. 1509–1510. Fresco, Stanza della Segnatura, Vatican Palace, Vatican State. Photo Credit: Scala / Art Resource, New York. Freud's first example of *Gleichzeitigkeit* (simultaneity) in *The Interpretation of Dreams*. (See color plate.)

F.1

F.2. Raphael, *Parnassus*, ca. 1510–1511. Fresco, Stanza della Segnatura, Vatican Palace, Vatican State. Photo Credit: Erich Lessing / Art Resource, New York. Freud's second example of *Gleichzeitigkeit*.

F.2

F.3. Raphael, *Parnassus*, detail of Dante, Homer, Virgil, and Statius. Photo credit: Erich Lessing / Art Resource, New York.

F.4. Raphael, *School of Athens*, detail of Heraclitus/Michelangelo. Photo credit: Alinari / Art Resource, New York.

well-known works of art from the Renaissance.[4] That period of history extending from the late fourteenth century in Italy to the early seventeenth

[4] Freud would return to these two frescos in his 1915 essay "Thoughts for the Times on War and Death." Describing a time before WWI, he wrote,

> Nor must we forget that each of these citizens of the civilized world had created for himself a "Parnassus" and a "School of Athens" of his own. From among the great thinkers, writers

F.5. Raphael, *School of Athens*, detail of Zoroaster, Ptolemy, Apelles/Raphael, and possibly the painter Sodoma or Raphael's mentor Perugino. Photo credit: Alinari / Art Resource, New York.

century has long been celebrated – or disparaged – as an era of extravagant individualism. This book explores how that era also heralded the transformation of the group, and of the community, because one change could not have occurred without the other. This transformation and reorganization of collective identities took place for the first time on a truly global scale. In his two telling analogies explaining the logic of dreams, Freud inadvertently highlights an aspect thereof – the combination of people in new, unexpected, and unconventional groupings, organized by choice and by fantasy. In doing so, he suggests another significant feature of collectives: namely, that groups do

and artists of all nations he had chosen those to whom he considered he owed the best of what he had been able to achieve in enjoyment and understanding of life, and he had venerated them along with the immortal ancients as well as with the familiar masters of his own tongue. None of these great men had seemed to him foreign because they spoke another language – neither the incomparable explorer of human passions, nor the intoxicated worshipper of beauty, nor the powerful and menacing prophet, nor the subtle satirist; and he never reproached himself on that account for being a renegade towards his own nation and his beloved mother-tongue.

Standard Edition, 14: 271–302, pp. 277–278.

F.6. Raphael, *School of Athens*, detail of Pico della Mirandola and/or Francesco della Rovere; alternately, Hypatia/Margarita. Photo credit: Scala / Art Resource, New York.

not have to be real – historical, concrete entities – to exert a powerful influence on cultures. Through these illustrations in *The Interpretation of Dreams*, Freud throws into relief the virtual group, the group as fantasy. It is possible not just in dreams but also in our imaginative lives to create new groupings of people, as well as animals, objects, and concepts.

Perspectival tour de force that it is, *The School of Athens* can be said to illustrate yet another conceptual phenomenon of which it serves as visual analogy: the unconscious lives of groups. Mastering the art and science of perspective, a new development of the Renaissance,[5] Raphael organized his

---

[5] See, for example, Kubovy, *The Psychology of Perspective and Renaissance Art*; Kemp, *The Science of Art*; and Damisch, *The Origin of Perspective*.

F.7. Raphael, *School of Athens*, detail of Plato/Leonardo da Vinci and Aristotle. Photo credit: Scala / Art Resource, New York.

fantasy around a vanishing point at the center of the painting, a point where multiple lines of perspective converge. That vanishing point has been carefully, perhaps ironically, obscured by the artist, who positions the two leading

As Kubovy notes, "The most obvious function of perspective was to rationalize the representation of space: With the advent of perspective, it became much easier to stage, as it were, elaborate group scenes organized in a spatially complex fashion" (1).

F.8. Raphael, *School of Athens*, with perspectival lines superimposed. Photo credit: Scala / Art Resource, New York.

figures of the group, Plato and Aristotle, on top of it (Figure F.8). Although Aristotle and Plato vie for center stage, the vanishing point implicitly lies somewhere behind the partially juxtaposed torsos of the two men. These philosophers compete to hold the center stage of Western metaphysics, not to mention the mysterious vanishing point of Raphael's great masterpiece – as of Freud's later on. They conceal something (the spatial point of convergence) while revealing something else (an interpretive dilemma or struggle).

A similar organizational phenomenon can be observed in the *Mount Parnassus* fresco. Although the great Renaissance artist situated his imaginary gathering of poets and Muses on a mountaintop rather than within an architectural space, there are implicit perspectival lines in this painting, as well. Lines of sight and other diagonals converge on Apollo or on an implicit vanishing point at the center of the painting. In this fresco, too, the center point remains obscured – here, by the body of the god. Raphael plays with the vanishing point in both of these works, drawing the viewer, who watches from his or her vantage, into that spatial and conceptual convergence.

In an earlier chapter of *The Interpretation of Dreams*, Freud had remarked, apropos of his dream of his patient Irma: "There is at least one spot in every dream at which it is unplumbable – a navel, as it were (*gleichsam einen Nabel*), that is its point of contact with the unknown."[6] This "navel" umbilically links the manifest content of the dream to the unconscious matter beneath it. It also marks the point beyond which the interpreter cannot proceed – a point of ultimate resistance or unknowability beyond which the dreamer cannot see or imagine further. Freud's visual analogies for simultaneity in dreams, *Mount Parnassus* and *The School of Athens*, hearken back to his earlier observation concerning the "navel of the dream." Together they function as an important counterpart to that observation. In one of these paintings, the navel, or vanishing point, is obscured by the appearance of a god; in the other, that point recedes behind a dreamlike staging of one of the great metaphysical debates of Western civilization, echoing all the way forward to the time of Freud's writing: Platonic idealism versus Aristotelian realism, the *Timaeus* versus the *Ethics*. Freud might well have noted that Raphael stages this encounter between Plato and Aristotle as a father-son contest.[7] Meanwhile, the navel of the painting remains concealed, as it were, by an interpretive struggle of signal import: "up there" or "right here," the directions – at once spatial and philosophical – indicated by the two central characters in this metaphysical drama (Figure F.7). Freud too had a stake in that contest, into which he sought to place himself by means of his materialist and archaeological theory of mind, behavior, and sexuality. Writing *The Interpretation of Dreams*, Freud was simultaneously writing himself into those groups.[8]

Freud presents the Raphael frescos as visual analogues of the dream-work – the unconscious logic governing unlikely combinations of persons, objects, and places within our dreams. Freud's brief discussion of *The School of Athens* and *Mount Parnassus* in *The Interpretation of Dreams* can also be taken to illustrate not only the groups within dreams but also *dreams within groups*, or *dreams about groups* – that is, the unconscious wishes, beliefs, and fantasies that exist alongside the more intentional, conscious, and deliberate modes of social organization. By analyzing Freud's paired examples, we can extract

---

[6] *On the Interpretation of Dreams*, Chapter 2, n. 1, in *Standard Edition*, 4: 111. The German reads: "Jeder Traum hat mindestens eine Stelle, an welcher er unergründlich ist, gleichsam einen Nabel, durch den er mit dem Unerkannten zusammenhängt." *Die Traumdeutung*, in *Gesammelte Werke*, 2–3: 116, n. 1.

I am indebted to Marilyn Migiel's essay "Faltering on Demand: Freud's Dream of Irma," 20–39, for insights into this crucial passage, and to Tom Conley's theorization of the navel in *The Self-Made Map*, 9 ff.

[7] Leonardo the materialist, father to the Italian Renaissance, perplexingly appears as Plato, as if to deconstruct the idealist position from within itself.

[8] See, Fara, "Freudian Snaps," 48–49, which analogizes *The School of Athens* and a famous 1922 photo of Freud and six disciples who formed what he called "the analytic brotherhood." See also Chapter 1, 17 and 19, Figure 1.2.

the notion, also Freudian, that social groups possess and are organized by certain qualities that must be considered dreamlike. All groups, Freud would later remind his readers, have an unconscious life – a subject to be explored at length in the present study. The vanishing point, or navel, of *The School of Athens* remains hidden by the group, its point of origin neither visible nor fully knowable.

Freud himself noted that groups have an unconscious, as well as a conscious life, and that the wishes of a group often revolve around their leaders or something behind their leaders. He would develop this point in *Group Psychology and the Analysis of the Ego* (1921), his principal and all-too-brief statement on social psychology.[9] The dreams and desires of persons in groups are also directed toward other members, and toward the group itself, which can easily become an object of love. The dreamlike quality of groups also extends to the "simultaneities" of group organization – their sometimes hidden or unconscious principles, like those that govern the operations of dream-life. These principles enable disparate individuals to form collectives, the whole being larger than the sum of its parts and also more mysterious.

As the chapters that follow elaborate, Freud's examples also draw attention to the unconscious lives of groups *in the Renaissance*. Contained within his transhistorical model of dream-work is a set of insights that today we may bring to bear on our understanding of that pivotal epoch in relation to our own. The Renaissance was an era in which the group was "re-networked" – an era in which multiple forms and rules of social life reorganized on a genuinely global scale. It can be argued that the momentous changes analyzed in the chapters that follow represent less a categorical break from earlier modes of collective identification and organization, than an intensification and acceleration of changes that had been under way for a long time. Whether changes of degree or of kind, or likely some combination thereof, these social changes reorganized the world of the Renaissance, poised on the threshold of what we think of as modernity. In his discussion of *Gleichzeitigkeit*, or simultaneity, Freud offered a refracted image of these transformations, suggesting a new approach for interpreting not just the past but also the early modern past in particular.

As we move further and further away from Freud's own era, many aspects of his model of the psyche seem increasingly anachronistic, because that model has been largely superseded by newer theories of mind and consciousness, some of which will also be considered in this book. Within

---

[9] *Group Psychology and the Analysis of the Ego*, in *Standard Edition*, 18. See especially Chapter V, "Two Artificial Groups: The Church and the Army," and Chapter X, "The Group and the Primal Horde."

literary studies, my own discipline, certain Freudian ideas still remain useful, however, along with those of several of his successors. In particular, his
analyses of language and of the seemingly arbitrary links between words and
ideas, or words and images – as for example, within dreams – are closely
related to metaphor, metonymy, and other rhetorical figures, the study of
which has remained a staple form of training in the literary and oratorical
arts for more than 2,400 years.

The present work has been inspired in part by Freud's concept of
Gleichzeitigkeit, and by his attention to strange or unexpected associations
in general. These ideas have been subsumed here into a methodology for
exploring the formation of groups in the early modern age, notions of collective identities, and the group words, concepts, and fantasies that helped
to define them. Taken together, the chapters that follow constitute not so
much a history of the Renaissance, as a "dream-analysis" of certain modes
and representations of group life in that epoch. Each of the following case
studies pursues several associations, understood both as concrete social relations within and between groups; as words and images that circulate within
groups and that pass from one collective to another, and that solidify into
new group concepts; and finally as speculative connections that lead into
the vanishing point of each tableau – that is, the limits of a group's visi-
bility and knowability. Each chapter explores the *Gleichzeitigkeit* of real and
imagined social arrangements, their strange and unexpected simultaneities,
their temporal recursions, and their often obscure relations to actual historical events. With this method, I aim to throw into relief certain principles
of social transformation not easily detected or revealed by more empirical
modes of analysis (and hence, complementary to the work of historians,
historical sociologists, and anthropologists). I also re-theorize the roots of
modern subjectivity along the axis of collective, rather than individual identity formation. As I hope to demonstrate, it is possible to analyze by these
associative means the real and imagined global communities of the Renaissance, and to trace the circulation of certain shared fantasies that helped
give shape to the networked world as we know it today. The results will, I
hope, be as surprising and revealing about the past – and the present – as the
simultaneities of any dream.

PLATES

F.1. Raphael, *School of Athens*, ca. 1509–1510. Fresco, Stanza della Segnatura, Vatican Palace, Vatican State. Photo Credit: Scala / Art Resource, New York. Freud's first example of *Gleichzeitigkeit* (simultaneity) in *The Interpretation of Dreams*.

F.1

2.1. *Adoration of the Magi*, Studio of Grão Vasco (1501–1506), oil on wood, 131 cm. × 81 cm. Museo de Grão Vasco; Viseu, Portugal. Divisão de Documentação Fotográfica – Instituto dos Museus e da Conservação, I.P. Photo: José Pessoa, 1999. This painting by Grão Vasco and his workshop for the Cathedral of Viseu is considered the first representation of a native American as one of the three Magi.

3.3. Master of the Morrison Triptych, *Adoration of the Magi* (1504), Oil on panel, 65 3/4 × 42 3/4 inches (167 × 108.6 cm). Image courtesy of The John G. Johnson Collection, Philadelphia Museum of Art. Such images had become a studio specialty of Antwerp at the turn of the sixteenth century.

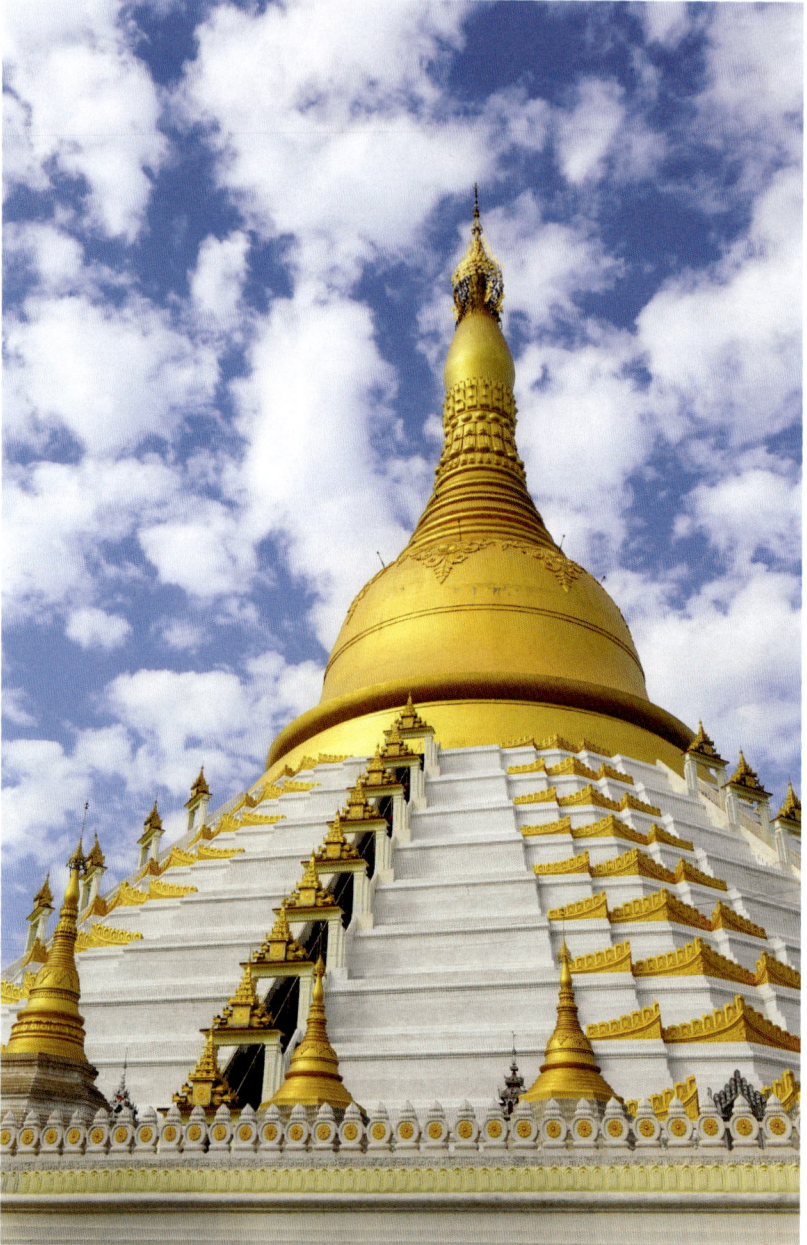

4.3. The Mahazedi Pagoda; Bago (Pegu), Myanmar. Construction of the Mahazedi was begun by Bayinnaung in 1559, and eventually housed the tooth relic received from Dhammapāla, King of Kōttē, as well as the alms bowl of the Buddha. Damaged by earthquakes in the twentieth century, the temple was rebuilt in the 1950s. Shutterstock Photos.

6.5. Ganadharavālaya Yantra. India, Gujarat, possibly Cambay, 1600–1650. Opaque watercolor on cloth. 26″H × 26 1/8″W, 66 cm × 66.4 cm. Jain painting in the Western Indian Style. Virginia Museum of Fine Arts, Richmond. Nasli and Alice Heeramaneck Collection, Gift of Paul Mellon. Photo: Travis Katherine Wetzel. © Virginia Museum of Fine Arts. This *yantra* (mystical diagram) was intended for meditations by a Jain spiritual aspirant. The sixth concentric circle features the twenty-four Tīrthaṅkaras. The central figure is unidentified.

6.6. Narsingh, illustration from *The Akbar nāmā*: Akbar, Abu-l-Fazl, author of the *Akbar nāmā* (on his immediate right), Jesuit missionaries and other courtiers debate religious beliefs at Fatehpur Sikri (1605). Akbar's two young sons Murad and Daniyal stand to his left. © Trustees of the Chester Beatty Library, Dublin. Painting on paper (detail), folio size 43 × 26 cm.

INTRODUCTION
THE GROUP AND THE INDIVIDUAL:
RECOLLECTING BURCKHARDT'S
RENAISSANCE

[T]he human being can never be fully understood apart from his or her relation with others.

> – Martin Buber, *I and Thou*

[H]istorical change, even at its most radical, takes place not in the form of absolute 'epistemic' rupture, but rather as the dynamic reconfiguration of words, categories, [and] concepts within pre-established forms. . . .

> – Albert Ascoli, *Dante and the Making of a Modern Author*

An Altogether Wild Plant

WRITING FROM BASEL, SWITZERLAND, ON THE FIRST OF AUGUST, 1860, to his friend Heinrich Schreiber, the cultural historian Jacob Burckhardt (Figure I.1) described the impending release of a new book:

> As soon as the printing is completed, I will send you a copy. My dear old friend will no doubt smile and shake his head at such dilettante work, but will surely concede that the author has not spared trouble and sweat. It is an altogether wild plant dependent upon nothing whatever already existing. One eulogy I should like to receive from your lips, namely, that the author firmly resisted many opportunities to let his fancy wander, and virtuously stuck to his sources.[1]

That "altogether wild plant" was Burckhardt's *Die Cultur der Renaissance in Italien* (*The Civilization of the Renaissance in Italy*), a cultural history of a transformative era in world history – an era that Burckhardt would play a significant role in defining for later generations. Burckhardt's appraisal of his own book as "an altogether wild plant" is doubly striking when held up

---

[1] "[E]ine *durchaus wildgewachsene Pflanze*." Burckhardt, *Letters*, 125; *Briefe*, 4: 53.

against the book's central hypothesis: namely, that the Renaissance in Italy was an age of flamboyant individualism. New modes of self-perception and desire, together with a seismic shift in subjectivity, marked the onset of an era that seemed to Burckhardt distinctively modern and secular in its contours, and that also represented a clear break with the medieval past. Obsessed with fame, status, appearances, and other modes of self-distinction, the men and women of Burckhardt's Italian Renaissance, unlike their medieval forebears, wanted to be unique and believed themselves to be so. Their art and their politics, insistently driven by the creative will to self-expression, told a very particular story, and for the Swiss cultural historian, a compelling one.

Burckhardt's story, like many great imaginative works, still attracts new audiences and new responses. His hypothesis concerning Renaissance individualism remains foundational in many ways, despite the fact that it has often been challenged by historians and cultural critics. For these reasons, Burckhardt's work might be called, in Foucauldian terms, a "transdiscursive" work, producing the possibilities and "rules" for the formation of other texts.[2] Although later theorizations of the Renaissance often diverge significantly from that of Burckhardt, many interpretations of the era still remain situated within the discourse that he established a century and a half ago. As the historian Joseph Mali has argued, *The Civilization of the Renaissance in Italy* remains a genuine classic work of historiography, even though "the application of new methodologies, such as cultural anthropology, psychology, and narratology in historical studies has of course extended Renaissance scholarship well beyond the conventional categories and boundaries of Burckhardt's study."[3]

To Wake or Dream: The Veil of the Group

Before reviewing some of the principal critiques of the nineteenth-century historian's work, let us first recall Burckhardt's most influential and also problematic claim – namely, that "the individual" was reborn during the

---

[2] Foucault, *What is an Author?*" in *The Essential Foucault*, 387. Foucault's prime examples of modern "founders of discursivity" are Marx and Freud.

[3] *Mythistory*, 108. In his assessment of the continuing endurance of Burckhardt's theory of the Renaissance, Mali concurs with earlier such assessments by Paul Kristeller ("Changing Views, 29) and Denys Hay ("Historians and the Renaissance," 1–2). Mali also notes challenges to Burckhardt's work, including Brown's edited collection, *Language and Images of Renaissance Italy*; Baron's essay, "The Limits of the Notion of 'Renaissance Individualism'" in *In Search of Florentine Civic Humanism*, 2: 155–181; and Kerrigan and Braden's book, *The Idea of the Renaissance*, 3–35.

See also Sigurdson, *Jacob Burckhardt's Social and Political Thought*, 254, n. 60, for a list of key discussions of Burckhardt's individualist hypothesis.

I.1. Jacob Burckhardt, 1892. *Universitätsbibliothek Basel*, Basel.

Renaissance. In *The Civilization of the Renaissance in Italy*, Burckhardt describes the emergence of individualism at the end of the European Middle Ages with the curious metaphor of *unveiling* – specifically, the unveiling of a group that is half-asleep or dreaming. For many centuries, he held, the dampening force of collective consciousness inhibited individuals from recognizing themselves as such. Over time, however, that "veil" of shared identity began to lift. In what might be the most quoted paragraph ever written about the Renaissance, Burckhardt stated exuberantly,

> In the Middle Ages, both sides of human consciousness – that which was turned within as that which was turned without – lay dreaming or half awake beneath a common veil (*wie unter einem gemeinsamen Schleier träumend oder halbwach*). The veil was woven of faith, illusion, and childish prepossession, through which the world and history were seen clad in strange hues. Man was conscious of himself only as member of a race,

people, party, family, or corporation – only through some general category (*in irgendeiner Form des Allgemeinen*). In Italy this veil first melted into air; an *objective* treatment and consideration of the State and of all the things of this world became possible. The *subjective* side at the same time asserted itself with corresponding emphasis; man became a spiritual *individual*, and recognized himself as such (*der Mensch wird geistiges* Individuum *und erkennt sich als solches*). In this same way the Greek had once distinguished himself from the barbarian, and the Arabian had felt himself an individual at a time when other Asiatics knew themselves only as members of a race. It will not be difficult to show that this result was owing, above all, to the political circumstances of Italy.[4]

In Burckhardt's conception of the European Middle Ages, a dreamlike state (*träumend oder halbwach*) consisting of "faith, illusion, and childish prepossession" had long veiled a more objective view of the world and of history, which would soon emerge in the Renaissance. More specifically, Burckhardt contended, medieval men and women were trapped in the "general categories" of collective identity. Unaware of themselves as possessing, either actively or potentially, individual subjectivity, they perceived themselves solely as "member[s] of race, people, party, family, or corporation." Burckhardt defined individualism as a form of waking up from the slumber of collective identity. For him, the principal feature of the Renaissance was not only individualism but also, implicitly, the condition of being awake.

In this crucial passage, Burckhardt linked the dynamics of groups to what Freud would a few decades later call *das Unbewußte*, "the unconscious." Here Burckhardt seems to suggest, in anticipation of Freud, that group processes – the behaviors, functions, and organizing principles of groups – are not identical to those of individuals. To be in a group, he implied, was to remain trapped in a dream; however, persons might escape from that communal dream-state by individuating, by unbinding themselves from the group and thereby transcending the categories of collective identity.

Arguing more, perhaps, against the Basel of his day than against the purportedly conformist Middle Ages,[5] Burckhardt perceived the rise of individualism as not only indicative of dramatic historical changes but also as highly desirable: "The Italians of the fourteenth century knew little of false modesty or of hypocrisy in any shape; not one of them was afraid of singularity, of being and seeming unlike his neighbours."[6] Within his formulation, the condition of nonindividualism – that is, the sense of belonging to a

[4] *Civilization of the Renaissance in Italy*, 1: 143; *Die Cultur der Renaissance in Italien*: 1: 131.
[5] See, for example, Gossman, *Basel in the Age of Burckhardt*, 223ff.
[6] *Civilization of the Renaissance*, 1: 144.

group – would be regarded as a problem indicative of misplaced modesty, conformity, or even hypocrisy. Significantly, Burckhardt held that Renaissance men and women were not the first individualists in history; he noted that the ancient Greeks and "Arabians" were also individualistic – that is, advanced – civilizations. Burckhardt viewed the rise of individualism as a developmental stage of certain great civilizations, of which the Renaissance in Italy was a comparatively recent instance.

What did this supposed rebirth of individualism enable in Burckhardt's model of early modernity? Rather than serving as an end in itself, individualism was instead the condition facilitating the free thought, creative expression, and cosmopolitanism that so mesmerized the Basel aesthete. For Burckhardt, to remain ensconced in one's group identifications meant to hide one's light under a veil, and thereby to suppress the sublime creative gifts likely to be expressed through highly individuated forms of human behavior. Individualism was at the root of what Burckhardt admired most about the Renaissance and also what he celebrated – its art and culture.

Even the state (i.e., the Italian political sphere) was, in his view, a work of art.[7] Although Burckhardt linked individualism with the despotism of Italian city-states during this transitional era, he insisted on a generative vision of those states and the dynamic between a people and its ruler: "Despotism, as we have already seen, fostered in the highest degree the individuality not only of the tyrant or *condottiere* himself, but also of the men whom he protected or used as his tools – the secretary, minister, poet, and companion." What trickled down from despotic power in Renaissance Italy was something of great value, in the Swiss historian's view: "These people [the right-hand men of the despot] were forced to know all the inward resources of their own nature, passing or permanent; and their enjoyment of life was enhanced and concentrated by the desire to obtain the greatest satisfaction from a possibly very brief period of power and influence."[8]

It is striking that in this passage at least, Burckhardt minimized the pronounced violence of Italian Renaissance culture while foregrounding it in other parts of his book. In a later chapter of the book entitled "Morality," however, he argued that, "the fundamental vice of this character [of men and women of the Italian Renaissance] was at the same time a condition of its greatness – namely, excessive individualism."[9] Burckhardt's powerful impulse to aestheticize violence as a significant, even as the defining aspect of that

---

[7] Part I of *Civilization of the Renaissance* is entitled "The State as a Work of Art." The title of my first chapter tropes on that title.
[8] *Civilization of the Renaissance*, 1: 144.
[9] *Ibid.*, 2: 442.

culture entailed that his assessment ultimately focus on the *collective* effects – as well as the individual and particular ones – of that great sea change he chose to characterize as a rebirth. The fears, traumas, and anxieties that individual men and women might have suffered under a particular despot (e.g., Cesare Borgia or Sigismondo Malatesta, tyrant of Rimini[10]), or that they might have experienced in the wake of intermittent warfare and invasion, internecine violence, crisis, and upheaval, mattered less to Burckhardt than the sum total of the effects of such transformations. In balance, he took these to be markers of civilization. Although the Italian Renaissance witnessed certain depths of human depravity, as he frequently noted, Burckhardt also found much to celebrate: the pinnacles of intellectual and creative achievement that were reached, and the passionate extremes of that era, as well: "By the side of profound corruption appeared human personalities of the noblest harmony and an artistic splendour which shed upon the life of man a luster which neither antiquity nor medievalism either could or would bestow upon it."[11]

Burckhardt's account of the Renaissance is highly ambiguous, as the political scientist Richard Sigurdson has observed, because it "wavers between a horrified condemnation of unfettered subjectivism and a fascinated admiration for the vitality and creativity of even the most wicked men of that period" – men whose actions he often appeared to glamorize.[12] In later life, Burckhardt sought to draw a moral to his story of the Renaissance, partly against his critics, by claiming that such tyrants were *Flagella Dei*, or scourges of God – men whose bad behavior must have served some higher, providential purpose. In an 1896 letter to Ludwig von Pastor, written half a lifetime after the publication of *Civilization of the Renaissance*, Burckhardt sought not only to defend his earlier work but also to distinguish his views from those of his former friend and protégé, Friedrich Nietzsche. He wrote,

> I for my part have never been an admirer of *Gewaltmenschen* and *Outlaws* in history, and have on the contrary held them to be *Flagella Dei*, willingly leaving their precise psychological construction to others, a point on which

---

[10] *Ibid.*, 2: 442.

[11] *Ibid.*, 2: 443.

[12] Sigurdson explains that this is one reason why many see Burckhardt's tyrants as perhaps the principal models for Nietzsche's theory of the *Übermensch*. *Jacob Burckhardt's Social and Political Thought*, 213, *et passim*.

In *Jacob Burckhardt and the Crisis of Modernity*, John R. Hinde offers a different view of *Civilization*, which follows that of Wolfgang Hardtwig (*Geschichtskultur und Wissenschaft* [1990]). Both historians argue that Burckhardt sought to underscore the amorality of the Renaissance, although in no sense validating the ruthless behaviors of *condottieri* and other seekers of power, including the humanists (220–226).

one can be most astonishingly mistaken. I really interested myself more in the creative aspect of things and that which makes people happy, the vitalizing aspect, which I thought was to be found elsewhere.[13]

In Burckhardt's retrospective view, creativity and its wellsprings had always been the primary focus of his research. Despite such late-life attempts at recuperating the ethical ambiguities of his earlier historiography – ambiguities rendered still more unsettling through Nietzsche's adaptations of his mentor's ideas – Burckhardt's perspective on his own material was and remains difficult to determine at times. This is perhaps because he emphasized the individual at the expense of the group, or some individuals at the expense of others. Meanwhile the history of the Renaissance group, or collective, remained largely hidden, at least in the historian's account, seemingly cast aside with the "common veil" of medieval group consciousness, which was implicitly nonvitalizing.

One of the great ironies of *The Civilization of the Renaissance* is that it reinscribed a general category of man – that majoritarian grouping of Renaissance individuals who flourished privately, notwithstanding their "political impotence" – in place of the other categories (i.e., race, people, party, family, or corporation) that were supposed unveiled or dismantled. In so doing, Burckhardt inadvertently raised an important question: can one talk about individuals as a group? Conversely, can one talk about groups individually, or about individual groups? Assuming that one can, then Burckhardt himself might have been amenable to such a project, not least because it squarely rests on the historiographic foundation that he laid a century and a half ago. Burckhardt did not deny the importance of the social, yet neither was it the emphasis of his book.[14] Nevertheless, the dynamics of group identity remain veiled in *The Civilization of the Renaissance in Italy*, perhaps because of Burckhardt's own deep distrust of groups, especially large ones. His anti-egalitarian politics are as well known as his fear of the

[13]Letter to Ludwig von Pastor, January 13, 1896, in *Letters*, 234–235. Dru leaves *Gewaltmenchen* in the original German, but we might translate it as "power-mongers" or "brutes." It is a word Nietzsche uses in *Die fröhliche Wissenschaft* (*The Gay Science*), for example ("Joke, Cunning, and Revenge," 17). Here Burckhardt seems to turn up his nose not only at the *Gewaltmenchen* of history but also the preoccupations of his former friend, which he would distinguish from his own.
    For an excellent analysis of the Burckhardt/Nietzsche divide, see Mali, 115ff.
[14]Sigurdson explains, "Burckhardt spends little time discussing the actual structures and processes of government ('one could die memorizing the constitutions of Florence,' he once said) but points out that Florentine politics involves 'a supreme political consciousness as well as the participation of a large proportion of the citizens in public life and in constitutional questions.' Yet the main factor in Florence's greatness is not so much that its politics determined its civilization, but that its politics did not impede culture." *Jacob Burckhardt's Social and Political Thought*, 185.

mass movements of his time, which he believed could pave the way toward totalitarianism.[15]

Some Critiques of Burckhardtian Individualism

Whether medieval or modern, groups seem to have inspired in the Swiss historian a certain anxiety; hence, his aestheticized portrait of the Italian Renaissance leaves groups more or less out of the picture – or rather, consigns them to the distant background, like the hilltop villages that appear in numerous paintings of that era. Perceiving the limitations of Burckhardt's position, however, many later historians, particularly since the late 1960s, have sought to factor the social back into their accounts of the Renaissance. In light of recent social histories of the early modern age, Burckhardt's views seem increasingly old-fashioned, although they have not gone away. Rather, they remain important reference points in our collective attempts to understand the history of subjectivity, a field of research that has expanded exponentially since Burckhardt's time.[16]

Among the objections to Burckhardt's individualist thesis are the following, summarized by historian Gene Brucker: Burckhardt's insistence on a radical break from the medieval past; his focus on the high-ranking and the renowned at the expense of other groups; his problematic insistence on the secularism of the Renaissance; and above all, his perception of individual freedom and autonomy as the credos of the age.[17] As Brucker explains,

> [Burckhardt] believed that the unique historical conditions in thirteenth- and fourteenth-century Italy had fostered the creation of a new type of man: free and independent, detached from the traditional social and psychological bonds of kinship and solidarity; above all, self-conscious, acutely aware of himself and his world, and capable of ordering and controlling his life. Burckhardt's concept thus has a social and a psychological dimension.[18]

Burckhardt's view of Renaissance man as free and independent has long functioned as a stereotype of the period. Meanwhile, Brucker draws attention

---

[15] On Burckhardt's conservatism, see, for example, *ibid.*, 52–53, and Hinde, 113–136, *et passim*.

[16] See Lukes, *Individualism*, and Taylor, *Sources of the Self*. On the many studies of individualism and individual subjectivity, see Martin, *Myths of Renaissance Individualism*, Chapter 1 (1–20), which surveys the extensive literature on this topic, and Ascoli's ground-breaking book *Dante and the Making of a Modern Author*, especially Chapter 1, "The Author in History," 3–64.

[17] "The Italian Renaissance," in *A Companion to the Worlds of the Renaissance*, 23–38. Brucker points out that Burckhardt was relying on a narrow set of sources – primarily literary works – and that he lacked "a solid scholarly edifice that has since been constructed by the labor of thousands." In sum, we know more today than in the nineteenth century. *Ibid.*, 24.

[18] *Ibid.*, 25.

to what Burckhardt had relegated to the background – the elaborate networks of communal relations in that era. The notion of Renaissance individualism becomes harder to sustain, Brucker maintains, when we take into consideration the highly complex relations of persons to groups during that period (indeed, in any period).[19] Renaissance men and women generally held a complicated set of perspectives about their own destinies, which few would have viewed as within their control or personal choosing.[20] In these ways, Brucker contends, Burckhardt's hypothesis concerning Renaissance individualism cannot be sustained.

In his recent book, *The Myth of Renaissance Individualism*, historian John Jeffries Martin has offered a further revaluation of Burckhardt's legacy. While acknowledging that the Renaissance was an era of profound social changes, Martin holds that the birth of the individual at the end of the European Middle Ages must be considered a myth. Not coincidentally, Burckhardt's concept of the *"geistiges Individuum,"* of Renaissance man or woman as free-thinking, autonomous, and exuberantly creative, was more a feature of nineteenth-century German Romanticism than of the Italian Renaissance.[21]

Martin contrasts this Romantic notion of subjectivity with that of post-structuralist scholarship on the Renaissance, especially Stephen Greenblatt's groundbreaking book *Renaissance Self-Fashioning* (1980). In this book, Greenblatt offered a influential revision of Burckhardt's thesis.[22] Where Burckhardt had seen evidence of powerful agency on the part of the individual, Greenblatt perceived a more determinist and socially oriented view of early

---

[19] For an outstanding introduction to that topic, see Trexler's edited collection *Persons in Groups*. In his introduction to the work, Trexler wrote, "The subject matter of this book, social behavior as it relates to individual and group identity formation in human beings, has as yet no discrete location in the academic division of labor" (3). The current work is very much inspired by and related to the impulse Trexler describes – the desire to determine what it is that makes a group a group. My thanks are due to Albert Ascoli for drawing my attention to this important work.

[20] Along this line, see also my book *Old Masters, New Subjects*, which discusses how the debate over free will versus predestination was not simply a theological conundrum, but an ideological struggle that affected many other areas of late medieval and Renaissance intellectual and cultural life.

[21] Martin is not the first to do so. Martin and many other contemporary historians hold that Burckhardt's concept of Renaissance individualism had more to do with the politics and culture of the nineteenth century than with the fifteenth or sixteenth. The Swiss cultural historian lived in a century, Martin writes, that was "largely defined by the growing recognition that traditional solidarities – communal, familial, and religious – had broken down. The rush of workers into the cities in the midst of the Industrial Revolution – and the demands for democratic institutions in the wake of the American and French revolutions – made the question of the individual and his or her role in society one of the most pressing issues of the day." *Myths of Renaissance Individualism*, 10.

[22] Greenblatt, *Renaissance Self-Fashioning*, 256–257, discussed in Martin, 6, *et passim*.

modern identity. Although some Renaissance men might have cultivated a belief in their own power to determine the course of their own lives – and sometimes those of others – their fantasies of autonomy were in Greenblatt's view by-products of the cultural institutions in which they found themselves.[23]

Navigating between the theories of Burckhardt and of Greenblatt, Martin proposes a *via media*, exploring the interface between the internal and the external selves as they were then understood. Martin writes,

> In the end, the selves I portray are not the apparently modern or postmodern figures that we often assume were the norm in this age.
>
> Sixteenth-century selfhood was, in fact, something far more elusive – indeed it is something tantalizingly difficult to grasp. To be sure, for many, one's identity was largely prescribed by the larger social groups (family, guild, community) to which one belonged. Nonetheless, European culture in the fifteenth and sixteenth centuries was shaped to no small degree by struggles over questions of identity, even questions of collective identity.[24]

According to Martin's model of subjectivity, the self is not a thing (e.g., soul, heart, mind, *res cognitans*) but a *relation* between "those dimensions of experience that people describe as *internal* (conscious or unconscious thoughts, feelings, beliefs, emotions, desires) and those they describe as *external* (speaking or writing, hating or loving, praying or blaspheming, laughing or crying, stealing or buying, and so on)."[25] Through his concept of the relational self, Martin offers an important reformulation of the interface between the individual and the collective that takes both into account.

Analyzing the Group: Some Methodological Questions

While Martin moves beyond poststructuralist readings of Renaissance identity such as Greenblatt's, his point of departure for the relational theory of selfhood nevertheless depends on a central tenet of both structuralism and poststructuralism: that is, the differential nature of the sign. According to Ferdinand de Saussure, one of the founders of structuralism, linguistic signs do not have meaning in themselves but rather in relation to what they are

---

[23] As Martin explains, "[W]hen we think about the history of Renaissance identities, we tend to hold them up as mirrors to ourselves, and what we see depends almost entirely upon where we stand. For Burckhardt, the Renaissance witnessed the birth of the modern individual; for Greenblatt, glimmerings of the postmodern self" (7).

[24] *Ibid.*, 19.

[25] *Ibid.*, 14.

not – all the other signs in the system.[26] Using a similar logic, we might say that an individual "signifies" only in relation to other individuals, as well as groups. To the extent that an individual can be said to *emerge*, he or she does so relationally, differentially, redefining each encompassing social tie or network in the process. Likewise for an *individual group*: group identity is defined by what it is presumed not to be – namely, some other group. It is the fundamental dynamic of a group to define itself against every other collective, including those that it resembles or with which it identifies most strongly. It is essential, then, to pull social networks into the foreground to study possible alterations of individual *and* group subjectivity – as social historians have done for some time – and to examine them in broader context.

Increasingly, scholars have recognized that the network of social relations that gave rise to the phenomenon called the Renaissance was not confined to Italy or even to Europe, but encompassed much of the globe. This far-reaching network comprised what the sociologist Immanuel Wallerstein has called the modern world-system.[27] During that watershed epoch, extending from approximately 1450 to 1640, the modern capitalist world-economy first developed.[28] There were innumerable factors that caused individuals and groups, whether small or large, to evolve and change, to reimagine themselves, and to reorganize within this emergent world-system. Proximate causes, as well as more distant and diffuse ones, helped to shape those transformations in personal and collective subjectivity.

[26] The notion of the differential nature of language, the fundamental insight of linguist Ferdinand de Saussure, became the central topos not only of structuralism but also of its offshoots, especially deconstruction. Saussure explains,

> Everything that has been said up to this point boils down to this: in language there are only differences. Even more important: a difference generally implies positive terms between which the difference is set up; but in language there are only differences *without positive terms*. Whether we take the signified or the signifier, language has neither ideas nor sounds that existed before the linguistic system, but only conceptual and phonic differences that have issued from the system. The idea or phonic substance that a sign contains is of less importance than the other signs that surround it.

Course in General Linguistics, 120.
Martin also notes that his theory of the relational self has its roots in object relations theory (137, n. 36).
[27] See *Modern World-System*, I. This was not the first world-system in history, but it had and continues to have particular features that distinguish it from precursor systems. It is, according to Wallerstein, the one that has developed into the modern world.
On the extensive challenges to Wallerstein's Eurocentric thesis, as well as recent syntheses of the original and its critiques, see Fernández-Armesto's discussion in "Empires in Their Global Context," 107–108, n. 14, *et passim*.
[28] Wallerstein, after Braudel, describes this time frame as the long sixteenth century. *Modern World-System*, I, 67–68.

Wallerstein's world-systems analysis, although useful for conceptualizing early modern globalization, has nevertheless been challenged, not least for its Eurocentrism. Historians and critics such as Donald Lach, Janet Abu-Lughod, Jack Goody, John M. Hobson, Su Fang Ng, and Charles H. Parker, to name a few, have highlighted the contributions of China, India, Malaysia, the Near East, and Africa to Western science, technology, economics, and culture during the medieval and early modern eras.[29] Since Burckhardt's time and well before, the European Renaissance and its accomplishments were thought to have been essentially self-generated, as Europe rediscovered its classical roots and underwent an extraordinary cultural renewal. In contrast to that older view, these and other historians have argued that most of the breakthroughs of the Renaissance – particularly scientific and technological discoveries such as the printing press – likely derived from precursor inventions from the East.[30] Moreover, the so-called Age of Exploration, pioneered by Portuguese and Spanish mariners who sailed to Africa, India, East Asia, and the Western hemisphere, was made possible by earlier navigational technologies and expertise hailing primarily from the Islamic world.[31]

In similar fashion, recent cultural histories of the New World have foregrounded the deep impact of indigenous knowledges on European cultures during the early modern era.[32] These revisionary studies call into question the notion of the Renaissance as it has traditionally been understood while also pointing to the existence of extensive knowledge and economic networks that linked many parts of the globe long before the fifteenth and sixteenth centuries. Recent historiography of imperialism has focused on peripheries rather than on metropolitan centers, and on subject communities rather than colonial elites, as historian Felipe Fernández-Armesto has noted. This shift in focus makes it possible to recognize how "the balance of cultural exchange tilted surprisingly: Europeans absorbed as much as or more than they transmitted."[33]

---

[29] Lach, *Asia in the Making of Europe*; Abu-Lughod, *Before European Hegemony*; Goody, *The East in the West* and *Renaissances: The One or the Many*; Hobson, *The Eastern Origins of Western Civilisation*, 161–189; Ng, "Global Renaissance," and Parker, *Global Interactions in the Early Modern Age*.

[30] On this point see, for example, *The Eastern Origins of Western Civilisation*, 161–189.

[31] *Ibid.*, 131–157. Hobson has shown the extraordinary impact of the Eastern world on the West, from antiquity to the Renaissance and well beyond.

[32] See, for example, Bauer, *The Cultural Geography of Colonial American Literatures*; Cañizares-Esguerra, *Nature, Empire, and Nation*; Barrera-Osorio, *Experiencing Nature: The Spanish American Empire and the Early Scientific Revolution*; Portuondo, *Secret Science: Spanish Cosmography and the New World*; and Bleichmar et al., eds., *Science in the Spanish and Portuguese Empires*.

[33] "Empires in Their Global Context," 94.

The era that Burckhardt characterized as a rebirth is now being reimagined through a different subtending metaphor: the network.[34] Indeed, the globalization, postnationalism, and informatics of our own historical moment have thrown into relief a particular aspect of the early modern period that was more difficult to observe before now.[35] The metaphor of the network is primarily a spatial and synchronic one, as opposed to the earlier temporal and diachronic metaphor of the Renaissance (imagined as the rebirth of classical antiquity). Both of these metaphors, together with the historiographic paradigms that grew out of them, describe and trace flows of energy, ideas, goods, cultures, and peoples, but they do so in different ways. The latter paradigm encompasses a much larger geographic area (e.g., the world, or much of it), and locates the sources of transformation, however imagined, within an accelerating process of exchanges. As literary historian Jyotsna Singh writes, "while the terms 'Renaissance' and 'global' traditionally would be considered anachronistic if yoked together, recent globally oriented scholarship of the past decade has led the way in creating a more expansive, shifting Renaissance world-picture."[36] It is to this global network and its complex relation to questions of social and cultural identity that we shall now turn.

Put simply, the thesis of the present book is that the pivotal era in history extending from the fifteenth to the seventeenth centuries can be redefined by and as a fundamental reorganization of collective identities that occurred globally. If identity is formed differentially, then the European Renaissance can be viewed as the result of a massive influx of difference, which also radiated outward again and circulated in global feedback loops.[37] Still more

[34] For a recent instance of this metaphor applied to the Renaissance, see Burke, *The European Renaissance*, 10–12; Singh, "Introduction: The Global Renaissance," 17; and Fernández-Armesto, *1492*, 3, *et passim*.

[35] The nationalistic paradigm of most previous scholarship on the Renaissance – even the comparative – is now giving way to a different paradigm in keeping, not surprisingly, with the political and social transformations of our own era. Thus it has become possible to see a different view of the past, as Linda Darling has suggested. "The old view of the Renaissance as a strictly European affair deleted from the story some important elements of the intellectual and cultural transformation that went under that name," she argues in a recent essay. Moreover, this limited view "distorted our perception of the economic and geopolitical interconnections of the period. If those elements are restored, we may be able to see the European Renaissance as in some sense a global event." "The Renaissance and the Middle East," 65–66.

[36] "Introduction: The Global Renaissance," in *A Companion to the Global Renaissance*, 5. For related instantiations of this paradigm, see Jardine, *Worldly Goods*; Brotton, *The Renaissance Bazaar*; Ng, "Global Renaissance"; Fernández-Armesto, *1492*, Charry and Shahani, ed., *Emissaries in Early Modern Culture*; and Parker, *Global Interactions in the Early Modern Age*.

[37] In *The Eastern Origins of Western Civilisation*, John Hobson also describes the differential nature of identity formation – notably in his chapter on Islam and the invention of Christendom (99–115).

significantly, the accelerating awareness of other cultures, ideas, and belief systems, other technologies, and other histories, precipitated the formation not only of new groups but also new conceptions of groups or new metaphors of "groupness," as we shall see in the chapters that follow. It was not only the individual but also the group that was reinvented or reconfigured during the early modern age, for one change inevitably necessitated the other.

Group concepts can vary significantly from one era to another; I consider such paradigm shifts in group identity to be a useful way to describe or define a historical period. To understand the evolution in subjectivities that accompanied the rise of the modern world-system, it is essential to understand how groups, as well as individuals, functioned in that evolving global network, and in the artificial memory of print culture, which allowed for the storage, retrieval, and dissemination of information on a previously unprecedented scale – information above all about identity.[38]

The "subjectivity" of Renaissance groups, as opposed to and distinct from 1) the subjectivity of individuals, and 2) the social and cultural histories of specific collectives, has been largely untheorized.[39] To do so might seem an impossibly large task, especially if one chooses to explore group subjectivity in a global rather than a European context. One must establish, first of all, what a group is or how it might be defined. Second, one must consider whether it is even possible to speak of subjectivity and groups in the same sentence, given that the former term is readily applied to individuals but rarely to collectives. Third, one must identify and define the groups to be considered – for example, family, neighborhood, guild, village, nation, or people; groups of female friends, groups of people standing together in a painting, groups of people who like pomegranates, or grapes, or both. Possible combinations of groups are essentially limitless. How might one arrive, then, at a representative sampling of that vast number of combinations that would enable one to talk about such changes in a meaningful way? Moreover, which general principles of early modern group identity could be extrapolated from such an exploration, if any? Which kinds of evidence concerning the subjectivity of groups would be considered most valid

A highly useful discussion of differential identity formation may also be found in the psychoanalyst Vamik Volkan's book, *The Need to Have Enemies and Allies*, 17–34, *et passim.*

[38] Of the cultural importance of the invention of the printing press, the historian Lewis Mumford has written, "The enrichment of the collective human mind, through the printing and circulation of books, is comparable only to that linking together of individual brains and experiences through the invention of discursive language." *The Myth of the Machine*, 1: 285.

[39] Cp. n. 19, *supra*, for a notable exception.

or convincing, and for whom? How might one understand and interpret the vectors of change – the social and psychological, intellectual, political, artistic, economic, and technological forces at work in the long sixteenth century – that might shed light on the emergence, evolution, continuity, or disappearance of groups in the early modern world-system?

To contemplate these questions and to begin to answer them, I shall return to Freud's theories, especially his influential treatise on group psychology, as well as the ideas of sociologist Georg Simmel and psychoanalyst Didier Anzieu. Together these theories offer some purchase on the complex question of group identity formation. Although they are by no means the only approaches to analyzing groups – far from it – I consider these theories particularly useful for the investigation of groups that follows. They also serve as a bridge between the age of Burckhardt and our own epoch, a time in which the understanding of groups and their behaviors continues to evolve rapidly across many fields and disciplines.

The Mind of the Group: A Freudian Perspective

Sixty-one years after Burckhardt described the lifting of the "common veil" and the individuation of Renaissance man, Sigmund Freud (1856–1939) presented his own meditation on the behaviors of persons in groups. In *Group Psychology and the Analysis of the Ego* (1921), Freud's approach to social psychology demonstrates some unexpected affinities with that of Burckhardt in *The Civilization of the Renaissance*. Elaborating on the theory of crowd psychology earlier proposed by Gustave Le Bon, an influential French sociologist of the time,[40] Freud wrote,

> A group is impulsive, changeable and irritable. It is led almost exclusively by the unconscious. The impulses which a group obeys may according to circumstances be generous or cruel, heroic or cowardly, but they are always so imperious that no personal interest, not even that of self-preservation, can make itself felt (*ibid.*, 41).[41] Nothing about it is premeditated. Though it may desire things passionately, yet this is never so for long, for it is incapable of perseverance. It cannot tolerate any delay between its desire and the fulfillment of what it desires. It has a sense of omnipotence; the notion of impossibility disappears for the individual in a group.[42]

[40] Freud devotes the initial pages of his essay *Massenpsychologie und Ich-Analyse* to summarizing and critiquing Le Bon's influential 1895 work *La psychologie des foules*.

[41] Here Freud again cites and paraphrases Le Bon. *Standard Edition*, 18: 77.

[42] In a note to this section, Freud directs the reader to Chapter 3 of his own *Totem and Taboo* (13: 85 ff). *Ibid.*, 18: 77.

Here and elsewhere in *Group Psychology*, Freud ratified many of Le Bon's assertions, together with those of other social psychologists of the day.[43] These included the tractable behavior of persons in groups, and the emergence of a type of "group mind," a form of shared consciousness that supersedes that of individuals and seems to dissolve individual autonomy and will. Freud considered these to be genuine phenomena of collectives, which he linked to the powerful desires of their constituents.[44] The theory of group mind, elaborated on by Freud, provides a useful means of conceptualizing the subjectivity of the group.[45]

The libidinal ties that bind the members of a group to their leaders and to each other tend to make them hostile to those outside of the group. "Therefore a religion, even if it calls itself the religion of love, must be hard and unloving to those who do not belong to it," Freud wrote.[46] The generally destructive attitude of groups toward nonmembers, he held, is directly proportional to the strength of the emotional bonds within the collective – a phenomenon characteristic of religions, armies, and other groups as well. Doubting that the negative aspects of the group mind could easily be transcended through the forces of human enlightenment and progress, Freud hypothesized,

> If to-day [sic] that intolerance no longer shows itself so violent and cruel as in former centuries, we can scarcely conclude that there has been a softening in human manners. The cause is rather to be found in the undeniable weakening of religious feelings and the libidinal ties which depend upon them. If another group tie takes the place of the religious one – and the socialistic tie seems to be succeeding in doing so – then there

[43] Among others, Freud references Wilfred Trotter, *Instincts of the Herd in Peace and War* (London, 1916), and William MacDougall, author of *The Group Mind* (Cambridge, 1920).

[44] Freud notes, however, that he uses the term *unconscious* (*das Unbewußte*) in a somewhat different sense than Le Bon does. "Le Bon's unconscious more especially contains the most deeply buried features of the racial mind, which as a matter of fact lies outside the scope of psycho-analysis. We do not fail to recognize, indeed, that the ego's nucleus, which comprises the 'archaic heritage' of the human mind, is unconscious; but in addition to this we distinguish the 'unconscious repressed,' which arose from a portion of that heritage. This concept of the repressed is not to be found in Le Bon." *Standard Edition*, 18: 75, n. 1.

[45] Variations on this concept continue to evolve to this day; for example, the theory of collective intelligence within cognitive science and communications. For an excellent discussion of the history of the group mind concept from the nineteenth century forward, see Robert A. Wilson, *Boundaries of the Mind*, especially Chapters 11 and Chapters 12, "Group Minds in Historical Perspective" and "The Group Mind Hypothesis." Wilson, although offering a superb analysis of strong and weak versions of the group mind concept, never mentions Freud in his text or notes. This may be taken as an indication of how low Freud's stock has fallen among those who seek to differentiate their views from his. It may also be taken as a problem.

[46] *Standard Edition*, 18: 98.

will be the same intolerance towards outsiders as in the age of the Wars of
Religion; and if differences between scientific opinions could ever attain
a similar significance for groups, the same result would again be repeated
with this new motivation.[47]

Burckhardt could not have said it better; the veil of the group can indeed be
blinding as well as binding, preventing members from seeing or accepting
outside points of view.

Freud also noted, however, that groups, although potentially barbaric,
violent, and dangerous, can and often do demonstrate *higher* moral standards
than do individuals. Groups are also capable of selflessness and devotion (here
Freud follows, once again, Le Bon's assessment of the positive potentials of
the group mind experience). Furthermore, groups can enable individual
people to achieve greater things than they might otherwise accomplish on
their own. Freud clarifies,

> As regards intellectual work it remains a fact, indeed, that great decisions in
> the realm of thought and momentous discoveries and solutions of problems
> are only possible to an individual working in solitude. But even the group
> mind is capable of creative genius in the field of intelligence, as is shown
> above all by language itself, as well as by folk-song, folklore, and the like. It
> remains an open question, moreover, how much the individual thinker or
> writer owes to the stimulation of the group in which he lives, and whether
> he does more than perfect a mental work in which the others have had a
> simultaneous share.[48]

Here Freud acknowledges that that the intellectual and creative lives of
individuals in no small part could be a product of a stimulating group environment – an appraisal with which Burckhardt might well have agreed.
What Freud defines here is the phenomenon of *collective creativity*, of which
the Italian Renaissance was one important example, as Burckhardt happily
noted. Freud also knew the creative potential of groups from his own experience, including his own "analytic brotherhood," the leaders of the group
and movement that he headed (Figure I.2).[49]

If Burckhardt imagined that men and women *woke up* from the dreamlike
state of medieval collective consciousness, giving rise to the Italian Renaissance through their individuation process, Freud probably would have dis-
agreed. The phenomenon of group consciousness cannot be done away with

[47] *Ibid.*, 18: 98–99.
[48] *Ibid.*, 18: 83.
[49] On the famous 1922 photo of Freud and six disciples who formed the so-called analytic brotherhood, see Fara, "Freudian Snaps," 48–49.

so easily, for the simple reason that humans are social animals, ensconced in group identifications. In Freud's view, a person does not readily or automatically transition from the group mind into individual conscious awareness.[50]

Freud's ideas concerning the individual in relation to the group, and vice versa, open an interesting window onto Burckhardt's views. As the preceding discussion has suggested, Freud would not have dismissed the notion of the "common veil" of the group outright, nor would he have denied that persons are capable of thinking and acting in more or less individuated ways. In these positions he seems implicitly to side with Burckhardt's earlier views. Within the Freudian schema, however, individuated behavior may or may not involve conscious awareness of one's actions, or an understanding of the sources of one's desires, thoughts, and affects.

Moreover, Freud held, what an individual does not understand about his or her own mental processes and personal formation can under certain conditions give rise to spectacular artistic or intellectual expressions. Like Burckhardt, Freud was captivated by the creative accomplishments of certain "Renaissance men," including da Vinci, Michelangelo, Shakespeare, and Descartes.[51] The play of the unconscious within individual creative life and its impact on conscious expressions of many forms clearly fascinated him. The play of the unconscious within *group* life was something that Freud considered rather less often, although later psychologists and sociologists have had much to add to the conversation, as we shall see.

In the chapters that follow, I shall return to the theory of "group mind," underscoring its relation to the conscious and unconscious lives of individual members and suggesting how certain patterns of thought, affect, behavior, and fantasy characterize that period.[52] To some extent, group mind can be

[50] The difference between individual and group behaviors posed a complex problem for the Viennese doctor of the mind. Freud made a provisional distinction in *Group Psychology* between so-called social and narcissistic mental acts. The former category comprises the feelings, responses, and behaviors that one experiences in response to others. The latter category, which he also calls *autistic*, represents those mental acts in which "the satisfaction of instincts is partially or totally withdrawn from the influence of other people." This difference, he suggests, is more one of degree than of kind, however. Freud doubted that individual psychology was categorically different from that of collectives, despite his awareness of the group mind phenomenon. Both individual and group behaviors, he argued, arise from the same or from similar unconscious processes that originate within the family structure. *Ibid.*, 18: 69.

[51] "Leonardo da Vinci and a Memory of his Childhood" (1910), in *Standard Edition*, 11: 63–137; "The Moses of Michelangelo" (1914), in *SE*, 13: 210–238; "The Theme of the Three Caskets" (1913), *SE*, 12: 291–301; "Some Dreams of Descartes': A Letter to Maxime Leroy" (1929), *SE*, 21: 203–204.

[52] Robert Wilson has argued that groups cannot be said to have full-blown minds; rather, he sees the group mind as a cognitive metaphor, a projection of a feature of individuals onto the group (*Boundaries of the Mind*, 266). He also discusses the social manifestation thesis – that is, the notion that certain features of individual psychic states appear in social contexts. While giving rise to the

I.2. The Committee at the Seventh International Psychoanalytic Congress, Berlin, 1922. Left to right: seated – Sigmund Freud, Sándor Ferenczi, and Hanns Sachs; standing – Otto Rank, Karl Abraham, Max Eitingon, and Ernest Jones. Freud Museum, London.

considered a transhistorical phenomenon; that is, regardless of when people live, they are likely to behave differently in groups than they would on their own. There were, however, habits of mind, desires, and fantasies that were specific to the Renaissance, the sometimes brilliant yet paradoxically cruel epoch when the modern world-system first came into being. In each case study, I shall trace some of those collective fantasies that characterized particular group interactions and that were described by one or more members of the group. Writings, paintings, performances, ritual actions – these and other modes of representation reveal how certain group fantasies, specific to a time and place, were articulated within and between groups, revealing a shared or distributed group consciousness, as well as its transformations.

Social Network Theory: Simmel's Foundation

In his influential analysis of the evolution of social groups in the West, Georg Simmel (1858–1918), sociologist and pioneer of social network

appearance of group mind, such states originate in the individual person (301). I accept Wilson's argument for reasons that become clear in my discussion of Anzieu below, 24–28.

theory, developed a historically based theory of individual and group networks. In "The Web of Group Affiliations,"[53] a chapter in his 1908 study
Soziologie, Simmel held that groups might in some circumstances actually cause persons to individuate (rather than merely "veiling" them, as
Burckhardt had suggested). Simmel explained,

> As the person becomes affiliated with a social group, he surrenders himself
> to it. A synthesis of such subjective affiliations creates a group in an objective
> sense. But the person also regains his individuality, because his pattern of
> participation (*die . . . Kreuzung der sozialen Kreise*) is unique; hence the fact
> of multiple group-participation creates in turn a new subjective element.
> Causal determination of, and purposive actions by, the individual appear
> as two sides of the same coin.[54]

In the Renaissance, Simmel contended, the possibilities for group affiliation
expanded considerably. A given individual might represent the nexus, or
point of intersection, between multiple groups, representing through his or
her affiliations a unique "pattern of participation."

[53] It should be noted that while Simmel is often considered the father of social network theory, the
primary metaphor of this chapter – the "web" – is actually a *mistranslation*, as E. V. Walter has
explained. Walter proposes a more literal translation of "Die Kreuzung sozialer Kreise": namely,
"the intersection of social circles," rather than "the web of group-affiliations." He writes:

> [A]n accurate rendering of Simmel's thought would convey that a "web" stretches out
> and connects, whereas a circle closes off and excludes. Simmel's sociological constructs are
> not clusters of organismic issues but architectonic structures, and his "circles" are closed
> perimeters which separate one area from another. His social forms are not expressions of
> organismic vitality but mechanical structural devices which place limits on life to keep its
> fluctuating elements under control, and there is no point in imposing organismic prejudices
> on an architectonic system.

It is intriguing to consider the possibility that the most popular metaphor of our time may be
related in a circuitous way to this mistranslation of Simmel. Such is the powerful draw of organic
metaphors where group bodies, even at their most loosely defined, are concerned. "Sociology of
Power," 153.

I have elected to use Bendix's 1955 translation, rather than the more literal 2009 translation,
which renders the title of the sixth chapter of *Sociology* as "The Intersection of Social Circles,"
precisely because the later history of sociology and social network theory seems to have been
profoundly influenced by the earlier organicist mistranslation.

[54] *Conflict and the Web of Group-Affiliations*, 134–140; *Soziologie*, 11, 467. Regarding the larger implications of the individual's relation to the group(s), Simmel adds,

> The genesis of the personality has been interpreted as the point of intersection for innu-
> merable social influences, as the end-product of heritages derived from the most diverse
> groups and periods of adjustment. Hence, individuality was interpreted as that particular
> set of constituent elements which in their quality and combination make up the individual.
> But as the individual becomes affiliated with social groups in accordance with the diversity
> of his drives and interests, he thereby expresses and returns what he has 'received,' though
> he does so consciously and on a higher level (141).

In the European Middle Ages, individuals also belonged to multiple groups, but did so in a manner that was typical of that historical stage of social development and different from that of later periods. Simmel held that medieval group affiliations were characterized by a concentric structure (*Konzentrische Bau von Kreisen*).[55] For example, a person might simultaneously belong to a village, town, or city; a league of cities (e.g., the Hansa League); guilds, armies, and other organizations. Simmel contended, "These patterns [of group affiliation] had the peculiarity of treating the individual as a member of a group rather than as an individual, and of incorporating him thereby in other groups as well."[56]

Simmel also argued that although the concentric pattern of medieval group affiliations might appear simple when viewed from a modern perspective, nevertheless, it was a "great social invention," simply because men and women could affiliate with larger groups without becoming alienated from their affiliations with their original localities. "This form could be serviceable as long as men had not invented purposive associations, which made it possible for persons to work together by impersonal means for impersonal ends, and thereby to leave the personality of the individual inviolate."[57]

Simmel contrasted these concentric group circles with the nonconcentric circles of the postmedieval world. These, he argued, were characterized by "juxtaposed" and intersecting patterns of group affiliation, which created through their conflicting demands proliferating possibilities of individuation. He explained,

> As the individual leaves his established position within *one* primary group, he comes to stand at a point at which many groups "intersect" (*in den Schnittpunkt vieler Kreise tritt*). The individual as a moral personality comes to be circumscribed in an entirely new way, but he also faces new problems. The security and lack of ambiguity in his former position gives way to uncertainty in the conditions of his life.[58]

Like Burckhardt, Simmel believed that the European Renaissance fostered more individuated forms of social organization, not only because that more complex society consisted of a considerably larger number of subgroups but also because these groups were no longer organized in concentric fashion. They therefore were more likely to be in conflict with each other, to work for different ends, and to place different requirements and demands on

---

[55] *Soziologie*, 11, 474.
[56] *Conflict and the Web of Group-Affiliations*, 139.
[57] *Ibid.*, 149. Simmel's "progressive" Hegelian model of history has been challenged on many fronts.
[58] *Ibid.*, 141. *Soziologie*, 11, 467.

people, who would in turn individuate further in response to the conflicting demands and requirements of their multiple group affiliations.

Attempting to isolate some of the variables that gave rise to a notable shift in group life during the early modern age, as well as the phenomenon of individualism itself, Simmel foregrounded the humanist movement in his analysis. He observed that in humanism, the Renaissance witnessed a new phenomenon – namely, the formation of collectives that consisted of like-minded people hailing from otherwise quite different groups (e.g., gender, social, national, or ethnic). Whereas earlier in European history, group structures and social differentiation had been based either on criteria of economic, military, or political self-interest, new social groups began to form in Renaissance Europe around intellectual and rational interests – specifically, humanist circles, in which individual members found themselves in a "colorful variety of life-situations."[59] Simmel explained, "This way of life was symbolic of the movement of Humanism, which embraced the poor scholar and the monk, the powerful General and the brilliant Duchess, in a single framework of intellectual interests."[60] Perhaps the differences between medieval and Renaissance groups in Europe were not as categorically different as Simmel suggested, or perhaps such differences would have varied from place to place (e.g., remote villages remaining more concentric in their social networks than large metropolises).[61] Despite these qualifications, however, Simmel's argument remains useful today because it highlights the reorganization of social networks in the European Renaissance.

Simmel's theorizing of Renaissance social networks enables us to hypothesize that such changes occurred in at least five ways: (1) at a certain general point, the combinatory possibilities of groups increased, although not necessarily to the same degree in all places. Persons could join or be assimilated into multiple, nonconcentric groups. Far from serving as a "veil," (2) this expanding web of group affiliations, actual and potential, enabled or enhanced (at least for some) the process of individuation. Simmel's model of group affiliation, then, can be used to defend Burckhardt's thesis, at least up to a point, by suggesting how new patterns of group affiliation that arose during the early modern era might have resulted in greater individuation among group members. Clearly the degree of individuation, predicated on an access to nonconcentric social circles as described by Simmel, would

---

[59] Ibid., 134–140.

[60] Simmel continues: "Thereby the way was opened for a most important, further differentiation of the social structure, though there are precedents for such a development in antiquity." Ibid., 137.

[61] Simmel's argument rested on an uncomplicated view of both the Middle Ages and the Renaissance (e.g., by insisting that the social organization of the latter was substantially more complicated than the former). On this point he would likely be challenged today.

depend on a person's location, gender, age, social class, and mobility of various sorts, as well as many other variables. The Simmelian model also suggests (3) increased possibilities of conflict. Such conflict might manifest externally as the differences between groups, or internally as psychic divisions resulting from the competing demands imposed by an individual person's nonconcentric group affiliations; (4) the accelerated flow of intellectual and cultural capital throughout the expanding global economy of the sixteenth century produced widespread exposure to different ideas, worldviews, and modes of being in the world – especially religious modes. Individual and group confrontations with difference generated cognitive dissonance on a global scale, as well as an accelerating transformation, hybridization, and reconceptualizing of collectives, actual and potential. Finally, (5) in the non-concentric pattern of group analysis, groups as they are usually understood are de-emphasized, as are individuals themselves. Indeed, neither can be considered the basic social unit; rather, it is the unexpected ties between people that must be foregrounded.[62]

Indeed, Simmel's theory of group affiliations, although limited to the European Middle Ages and Renaissance, gains strength when expanded outward into a global context. Individual and group points of contact expanded exponentially as the European maritime empires arose, and as they interacted with other empires, such as the Ottoman, the Safavid, the Mughal, the Russian, the Qing, the Tokugawa, the Aztec, and the Inca, as well as numerous smaller collectives, such as the coastal trading kingdoms of west Africa or the colonized Atlantic island communities of Madeira, the Canary Islands, or São Tomé.[63] Hence it is essential for scholars of the period to look beyond Europe to bring into view the emerging "world-wide web" of group affiliations. The unprecedented encounters between disparate groups during the age of exploration and conquest had social, economic, and psychological effects that continue to reverberate to this day. Simmel's theory of juxtaposed group affiliations provides a highly useful framework for studying group affiliations in the early modern age, and for analyzing how multiple group affiliations may have created particular difficulties and possibilities

---

[62] This insight is actually a later development in the history of social network theory, which I only touch on here. See, e.g., Wellman and Berkowitz, *Social Structures: A Network Approach*. This fifth and final notion recalls Martin's notion of the relational self, discussed above.

It should also be noted that the phrase "group-affiliation" does not appear in the German, nor does it appear in the 2009 translation, which renders the phrase as "social circles" (see n. 53, *supra*). Thus it is not actually groups that Simmel emphasizes in this chapter, but rather the ties between individuals that can, in the case of nonconcentric social circles, disrupt or "decenter" the role and power of groups as we usually understand them.

[63] On the scope of these empires, see Fernández-Armesto's concise and informative discussion in "Empires in Their Global Context," 100–106.

for persons within these juxtaposed or intersecting social networks. The present book explores a sampling of such early modern networks, locating points of contact between individuals and between groups and tracing their connections to persons and collectives far away.

The Group Envelope: Anzieu's Contribution

In puzzling over the behavior of groups, Freud noted the marked tendency of individuals to form collectives, a point made earlier by the social psychologist Wilfred Trotter.[64] Freud explains,

> Trotter derives the mental phenomena that are described as occurring in groups from a herd instinct ('gregariousness'), which is innate in human beings just as in other species of animals. Biologically, he says, the gregariousness is an analogy to multicellularity and as it were a continuation of it. (In terms of the libido theory it is a further manifestation of the tendency which proceeds from the libido and which is felt by all living beings of the same kind, to combine in more and more comprehensive units.) The individual feels incomplete if he is alone.[65]

Following Trotter's language, Freud introduces an organic metaphor (*multicellularity*) to describe persons in groups. This metaphor suggests that in some sense groups have bodies as well as minds of their own.

In the 1970s and 80s, the French psychoanalyst Didier Anzieu (1923–1999) would develop the theory of the group's body implicit in Freud's work and that of others, as well – the third framing theory to be applied in the present study. Unlike individuals, Anzieu notes, groups do not have bodies.[66] In fact, groups suffer from not having a body, ergo they must invent or imagine one.[67] Members of groups often use metaphors of the body and its parts to describe group activities, functions, feelings, and divisions. Unlike that of an individual person, the group's relation to its skin or "envelope" is not

---

[64] See n. 43, *supra*.

[65] *Group Psychology and the Analysis of the Ego*, Standard Edition, 18: 118.

[66] Anzieu was a disillusioned analysand of Jacques Lacan. After his break with Lacan, he helped to found in 1964 the French Psychoanalytic Association in Paris. Anzieu's research provided new inroads into the psychoanalytic study of groups.

Inquiring minds may want to read Anzieu's deeply critical account of his analysis with Lacan in *A Skin for Thought*, 15–32.

[67] In *Philosophy in the Flesh*, George Lakoff and Mark Johnson describe "primary metaphors," fundamental abstract concepts that derive from our early sensory-motor experiences. The metaphor of the organization as a physical structure is one example of a primary metaphor (51). Anzieu's "group envelope" must be considered a special subset of this category of primary metaphor. I will return to Lakoff and Johnson in my Conclusion.

real, but imaginary and metaphoric. In *The Group and the Unconscious* (1975), Anzieu explains,

> This organic metaphor is both tenacious and insidious. Familiar words convey it without our having to think: member, body, corporation, organ, organism, nucleus, cell, symbiosis, etc. However, the difference[s] between the human group and a living organism are essential. In a living organism there are several quite specific functions: nutrition, breathing, circulation, digestion, excretion, reproduction, locomotion. These functions have no group parallel. Furthermore man does not behave like an organ or a cell belonging to a larger unity: he seeks first what is in his interest, what gives him pleasure, he belongs simultaneously to several groups or groupings; he does not necessarily die if cut off from his group; he may change groups or functions in a group, or create new groups.[68]

Here Anzieu underscores the differences between the actual bodies of individuals and the imagined bodies of groups, which serve a different purpose: namely, the coming into being and the survival of the group. This imagined group body corresponds, Anzieu argues, to a dream of symbiosis between members of a collective. Anzieu holds that "what tends to dominate in the psychic organization of the group tends to be not so much the centre, the nucleus, but rather the enveloping 'ego skin,' which guarantees its unity, its continuity, its integrity, the differentiation between inside and outside, in which one finds areas of selective exchanges, implications and things forgotten."[69] The corporeal experience of each participant is fundamental to the collective projection of a protective envelope, the group's "body." Anzieu also argues that groups are experienced, at least initially, as quite threatening to their individual members. According to his psychoanalytic reading – a more embodied view of the social than that developed by his mentor Lacan[70] – the group may activate archaic corporeal fantasies within the individual – specifically the frightening fantasy of bodily dismemberment. Indeed it is very difficult to function in or as a group until that fear has been managed or dispelled.[71]

---

[68] *The Group and the Unconscious*, 125. We must note that Anzieu's description of juxtaposed group allegiances is postmedieval in the Simmelian sense.

[69] *Ibid.*, 243.

[70] Although many have turned to Lacan's theories – specifically his notion of the Symbolic order – to theorize the social realms of experience, I choose instead to draw from Anzieu, who provides a more "embodied" and concrete theory of group identity.

[71] It is worth quoting at length Anzieu's theory of a group's formation:

> A group is born when a number of individuals bound together by, and anxious over, the omnipresent image of the dismembered body, manage to overcome this anxiety, to reassure themselves and see and feel themselves as human beings, to feel pleasant, common, positive feelings. These feelings may then give rise to concerted actions and thoughts, enabling them

Groups come into being when individuals, often not yet connected, form a 'body.' One need only imagine the experience of walking into a room full of strangers not yet constituted as a group to call to mind the uneasiness or anxiety that people may often feel, at least initially. Anzieu argues that in such situations people tend to imagine, consciously or unconsciously, that they are being fragmented, torn apart, or devoured.[72] To address those anxieties, individuals may withdraw into themselves completely, or they may cluster together, provided they are allowed to gather where they choose.[73] Empty spaces, incompleteness, absences can provoke very unsettling fantasies among members of groups; hence, they must in some way be addressed, often through spatial reorganization. The physical creation or imagining of an envelope is one of many possible strategies by which a group manages to surmount the collective fragmentation anxiety; sharing a meal, a good laugh, or another activity that binds people together through a shared emotion

> to describe the changes that have overcome them. When they come to feel themselves as 'us,' when a unit superior to each individual, but in which each has a part, comes into being, then the group is born, like a living 'body.' Each person recognizes himself as a 'member.' The group that at last functions as such becomes differentiated and organized; the biological metaphor remains all-powerful: it gives itself 'organs' of decision-making, executive functions and control. It reaches its apotheosis when it is recognized by the state, institutionalized, acquires a legal status, and is funded: it has become an official body, like the large state 'bodies,' themselves organs of the social 'body,' as a whole. *Ibid.*, 123.

[72] *Ibid.*, 122. These fantasies of dismemberment he considers regressive – that is, they represent the anxieties of early childhood. Anzieu further explains, "The fact that the unified group calls itself a 'body' and those who compose its 'members' seems to us to be the survival, in everyday language, of the fragmentation anxiety aroused by the group situation." *Ibid.*,139.

Otto Kernberg confirms the regressive tendencies promoted by both large and small group experiences: "Impressive clinical evidence indicates that regardless of the individual's maturity and psychological integration, certain group conditions tend to bring on regression and activate primitive psychological levels.... The potential for this regression exists within us all." *Ideology, Conflict, and Leadership in Groups and Organizations*, 7.

[73] People generally make visual, verbal, or sometimes physical contact with other members of the group in formation – most likely with their neighbors. They may fill up the chairs around the room or a table, leaving no empty spaces.

Following the research of P. M. Turquet and others, Anzieu has argued that these attempts to plug the holes in a group are unconscious collective attempts at creating a protective envelope that binds the group together and creates a gratifying sense of comfort and safety. Describing "the relational frontier of the I with my neighbor's skin," Turquet explains the agitation and anxiety of persons in groups, who feel threatened by continuity, as it were, with his or her neighbors. By establishing contact – visual, verbal, or physical – a person can become a subject within a group, emerging from alienation and solitude. See "Menaces à l'identité personnelle dans le groupe large," 135–158; discussed by Anzieu in *The Skin Ego*, 28–31.

Anzieu interprets Turquet's theory in terms of the attachment drive: "the search for contact (in the double sense, bodily and social, of the term) ... ensures a dual protection both against external dangers and against an internal psychical state of distress, and ... enables signs to be exchanged in a reciprocal process of communication in which each partner feels himself recognized by the other." *The Skin Ego*, 29–30.

or positive experience – these are also mechanisms for restoring, and also constituting, the group's unified "body."[74]

According to Anzieu, individual members of groups often experience their initial (and sometimes ongoing) anxiety, as well as their possible harmony with the collective, in embodied terms such as those described earlier. He argues that such somatic projections within groups are fundamental because they serve a defensive function in the minds of the individual members. Body metaphors counteract the archaic terror of dismemberment likely to be activated within the individual entering or working in a group.[75] "It is significant," he writes, "that we base supposedly objective knowledge of social groups on this biological metaphor, whereas the *function* of this metaphor is to overcome the anxiety of the dismembered body."[76] Thus the fantasy of the intact and well-functioning (organic) human body might be thought of as the "default setting," although other group fantasies are certainly possible, as we shall see in the chapters that follow.[77]

The Group Is a Dream

In the 1970s, Anzieu and his research team CEFFRAP, based at the University of Nanterre in Paris, produced a set of theses concerning the nature, purpose, and organization of groups.[78] Noteworthy among them are Thesis 15, *Le travail du fantasme* (the work of fantasy), and 15a: "*It is not the exchange of women that founds the social bond, but the exchange of fantasies. Moreover, the Levi-Straussian thesis is itself the symbolic expression of a phantasmic representation of group life.*"[79] Taking issue with the famous dictum of the great anthropologist and pioneer of structuralism, they asserted that groups exist because of – and

---

[74] *The Group and the Unconscious*, 118.

[75] "If the new-found unity of the group suggests comparisons with living bodies rather than other possible examples of unity (arithmetical, chemical, sexual, architectural), this is because this reconstituted body is the dialectical negation of the primal dismembered body. The metaphor may be factually erroneous, nevertheless it is persuasive and effective, as high-powered ideas often are, because it corresponds to the *phantasized* reality of the group, because it expresses, as do myths, the transformation of the images that govern the underlying forces." *Ibid.*, 123–124.

[76] *Ibid.*, 118.

[77] For a history of premodern and early modern uses of corporeal metaphors employed to describe social groups, see Hale, *The Body Politic*; see also the brief discussion in Allport, "The Historical Background of Modern Social Psychology," 45–46.

[78] In 1962, Anzieu founded CEFFRAP, the *Centre d'études françaises pour la formation et la recherche active en psychologie*, ultimately based at the University of Paris X-Nanterre (home of much of the political activism in Paris in the late 60s). Anzieu and his associates created early French experiments in group psychoanalysis and psychodrama.

[79] Anzieu et al., "The Thèses du C.E.F.F.R.A.P.," 16–21 (my translation, with refinements by Karen Pagani).

by means of – the exchange of fantasies. As Anzieu clarifies elsewhere, "the group is a dream."[80]

Guided by Freudian principles, Anzieu's research group sought to identify recurring patterns or templates of group fantasies – the dream of *rebirth* being a common one (also highly relevant to this project) – and to show how such fantasies develop and unfold within a particular context.[81] Generally regressive in nature, such fantasies incorporate early bodily perceptions and archaic memories and beliefs about one's own body and bodily functions, as well as those of others. Group fantasies may not be shared by all group members in exactly the same way, and they may not be brought into collective awareness. Nevertheless, they continually circulate within the group, help to define the subjectivity of each collective, and serve to mitigate the anxiety of individuals in the face of the group.

Their psychoanalytic approach is, of course, only one of many possible methods for analyzing group identity and organization; because of its focus on the generally unrecognized or unconscious aspects of group life, it may strike some contemporary readers as less concrete than other more empirical or quantitative approaches.[82] Nevertheless, CEFFRAP's notion of fantasy within group life – of the *group as a dream* – is a highly useful one for "recollecting" the Renaissance – truly an era of unusual and phantasmatic group encounters – and for expanding a modified version of the Burckhardtian paradigm into new territory. The chapters of this book throw into relief the fantastic, dreamlike, and storied qualities of many such encounters, the effects of which radiated like waves around the globe, engulfing other persons and groups and destroying social networks while simultaneously creating new ones.

Group Concepts

The stories and histories of groups unfold within language, art, and other semiotic forms. Their records appear as signs, which can be passed on as

[80] *The Group and the Unconscious*, 129. See also Anzieu's introduction to *Groupes: Psychologie sociale clinique et psychanalyse*, 6.
[81] The CEFFRAP researchers also built on the psychoanalytic work of Melanie Klein, W. R. Bion, and Elliot Jaques, as well as the social psychology of Kurt Lewin, to name but a few of their influences and precursors.
[82] For example, the recent field of dynamical social psychology seeks to explain social phenomena as higher order systems that arise from the interaction of a large – usually incalculable – number of individual variables. The goal of this approach is not to identify or quantify all the variables, but to interpret the patterns within the secondary system. The framework of dynamical studies of social psychology is nonlinear dynamics, a branch of physics (a.k.a. chaos theory) that has been successfully applied within numerous other disciplines. The fundamentals of dynamical social psychology are beautifully explained in Andrzej Nowak and Robin R. Vallacher's textbook, *Dynamical Social Psychology* (1998), and in their edited collection, *Dynamical Systems in Social Psychology* (1994).

narratives to later generations. Each chapter of the present book recounts one or more stories of encounter, interaction, or conflict between two or more groups, together with the collective transformations resulting from them. Within each of these stories, I identify and analyze the active metaphors – key words and images on which these narratives turn. Literally a "carrying from one place to another" (from the Greek *metapherein*, "to transfer"), a metaphor is also a rhetorical term designating the transference of the sense of one word to another. Figures of speech, metaphors are the building blocks of poetry, drama, and oratory. As we shall see, they are also constitutive markers of identity, whether of groups or individuals.

This book explores transcultural metaphors of collectives – what I call *group concepts* – showing how the sense of a word or concept within one language, culture, or group passed at a certain point in time into another language, culture, or group, sometimes acquiring a different set of meanings in the process. Those new meanings were sometimes close or approximate translations, or they were distant relations of their originals. Not infrequently, they were mutations of earlier concepts of group identity, as the stories and examples that follow suggest. The philological component of each analysis contained herein reveals how a given metaphor of the group, often introduced and circulated by one or more of its individual members, could develop into another, and another, and another, thereby creating a chain of meanings, images, and fantasies of one's own collective or of another. These "signifying chains" reveal much about the organization of groups, their operative fantasies, and their imagined relationship to the body.[83]

Drawing on the preceding theories of groups deriving from Simmel, Freud, and Anzieu, each chapter also traces (1) the ramifying networks of group affiliations, real or imagined, within a story of metaphoric exchange; (2) the group's dominant affects at different points in the narrative, which direct its behavior and its motives for actions taken, the "mind of the group"; (3) the group's imagined envelope, its somatic fantasy at a given time that sustains the collective and directs its energies; and finally (4) the group fantasy, expressed alternatively as an intolerable fear and as an impossible wish or dream. Although somewhat abstract in its summary form, this methodology will, it is hoped, become concrete in its applications. These essays also derive from and participate in scholarly conversations about the history of the body, which have been prominent in the field of early modern studies for some time. A theorizing of the imagined or projected bodies of groups in the sixteenth century, together with their relation to the body politic, is my

---

[83] Here I adapt Jacques Lacan's notion of the signifying chain, which he introduced in his 1957 essay, "The Instance of the Letter in the Unconscious, or Reason since Freud," in *Jacques Lacan: Écrits*: 412–441.

contribution to these conversations within the emerging discipline of global Renaissance studies.

This hybridized approach for studying groups in the Renaissance is not intended as a substitute for social history, historical sociology, or psychoanalysis. It is rather an adaptation, a grafting of useful concepts from the social sciences into my own disciplines, literary and cultural studies, for the purpose of understanding in a new, tropological way the powerful narratives of re-networking and transculturation that characterize the world of the Renaissance.

Although global in its scope, this book makes no systematic attempt at global coverage. Each chapter has crystallized around a topic – a unique image, event, and set of words or concepts that represent important aspects of group identity formation in the sixteenth century and that follow an internal logic that is in part narratological. It made sense to me to tell the stories that unfold in this particular way, for the very reason that they are stories to be told, as well as histories to be reconstructed, studied, and evaluated.[84]

This method of investigation, an inductive and associative one, helps to shed light on the fantasies – conscious and unconscious, and inevitably connected to the body – that shaped the early modern groups discussed in this book, giving them the unique stamp of their era. Together these essays open windows onto collective identities in the Renaissance, their continuities and discontinuities with the past, as well as the present, and finally their transformations during an era of unprecedented social mobility and global transculturation. These essays attest to the combinatory powers of minds and of cultures attempting to name the transformations of group identities then under way, or just as often giving rise to them. They are also templates for further studies of the elusive history of the Renaissance group, writ small or large.

Chapter Groupings

It was only in the Renaissance that the word *group* as a generic term for collectives began to appear within the Romance languages. As philological evidence demonstrates, there was no analogous word in the Indo-European

---

[84]Now more than ever, sociologists, psychologists, and historians are appreciating the value and complexity of storytelling in their own researches. Two recent works that demonstrate this developing trend are the historical sociologist Charles Tilly's *Stories, Identities, and Political Change*, and the narrative psychologist Dan P. McAdams' *The Redemptive Self: Stories Americans Live By*.

languages before that era – striking evidence of a major shift in group consciousness. Chapter 1, "The Group as a Work of Art," traces the evolution of that metaphor in the Renaissance and beyond. By the sixteenth century, the Italian word and concept *gruppo*, which evolved from the earlier word *groppo* ("knot"), came to mean a representation of persons, objects, or notes within a work of art. In variant spellings, *gruppo* would gradually enter the other languages of Europe, offering a new, highly aestheticized metaphor for social relations.

This chapter links the evolving word and concept *gruppo* to a renowned work of art that dominated the imaginations of Renaissance artists, humanists, and collectors: namely, the three-figured statue known as the *Laocoön*, which was famously recovered on a winter's night in 1506 from beneath a Roman vineyard. The recovery of this long-lost sculptural masterpiece of the Hellenistic age would have a defining impact on Renaissance cultural networks and ultimately on the very notion of the group itself. Partly through the *Laocoön*, the Renaissance witnessed not only the invention of a new, generic word for collectives but also an aestheticized one, the meanings and implications of which were unprecedented in cultural history.

If the late Middle Ages and Renaissance witnessed the rise of a new word for small, intentional clusters of persons, and a new set of accompanying social possibilities, it also saw the appearance of new metaphors for the large group, which arose in conjunction with colonialization and the rise of the modern world-system. Chapter 2, "Of Cannibals and Caraíbas: The New World and Large-Group Transformations," examines late fifteenth- and early sixteenth-century geographic and ethnographic writings about the New World by Christopher Columbus, Amerigo Vespucci, Martin Waldseemüller, Jean de Léry, José de Anchieta, and several others. This chapter analyzes the array of words, metaphors, and fantasies – generally oral in nature – that would play a powerful and enduring role in subsequent colonial encounters and in the emergent definitions of large groups. These included national, continental, ethnic, and racial fantasies – all of which were dramatically redefined in the sixteenth century.

This chapter focuses on a pair of keywords, *cannibal* and its cognates in the European languages (an anthropophagous person), and *caraíba* (a prophet of the Tupí-Guaraní people in South America).[85] These terms, which are closely related etymologically, if not semantically, reveal a great deal about the interactions of Europeans and American natives during the early colonial

---

[85] Here I use the term *keyword* in a sense similar to that of Raymond Williams in his book *Keywords*: words that "open up issues and problems, in the same general area, of which we all needed to be very much more conscious" (15).

period and well beyond, because they signal the rise of race as one of the fundamental categories of large-group identity and as a principal ideology of colonialism. English and American scholarship on New World colonialism has studied the first term intensively, but far less often its relation to the second. In the examples traced in this chapter – especially the gradual conversion of the word/concept *caraíba* from "native prophet" to "white European" in the *Lingua Geral* of Brazil – it is possible to study the colonizing role of language in gradually consolidating and incorporating smaller groups into larger, racialized ones during the sixteenth century: namely, "white men" and "Indians." By tracing the evolution and transculturation of these metaphors, we can perceive how these large groups redefined themselves in relation to each other during the Renaissance, demonstrating Didier Anzieu's thesis, "the group is mouth."

Where do the organizing concepts of groups come from, and how do they develop and circulate? Chapter 3, "Utopia: The Prenascent Group," analyzes a well-known fantasy that organized a generation of humanists around and within an imaginary space. Writing in response to Vespucci and other early geographers, Thomas More developed an alternative fantasy of a new world without cannibals or monsters. Through his mythic island society on the other side of the world, Utopia, More projected a dream of equality, organizational efficiency, and group harmony. Paradoxically, however, Utopian society relies on the labor of slaves, many of whom perform their roles voluntarily. Utopia, the quintessential Renaissance metaphor for the good group that is no group, is thus connected to another word and concept rarely conceptualized as a metaphor: *servus*, the Latin word for a servant or slave.

Offering a new context for locating and interpreting More's group fantasy and the place of those two metaphors within it, this chapter connects the *Utopia* to Antwerp, a city and a group that More had visited in 1515. In that center of the early sixteenth-century global economy, More would have witnessed the practice of slavery firsthand; his resultant fantasy presents the author's complicated response to the institution of chattel slavery, a practice officially outlawed in Antwerp but also sanctioned in various ways. Finally, this chapter explores the largely unrecognized place of Africa within More's celebrated fantasy and within the city that helped to inspire it.

Chapter 4, "The Buddha's Tooth Relic: The Group Mystery," explores a key principle of group organization: the ineffable essence of collective identity as symbolized by an object held sacred by the group. In 1560, Portuguese Goan forces, led by the Viceroy Constantino de Bragança, attacked the Tamil population of northeastern Ceylon. In Jaffna they seized a reliquary said to contain the most sacred relic of the island's denizens. The origin and history of the relic had been recorded in the *Dāṭhāvaṃsa*, the *Mahāvaṃsa*, and other Ceylonese Buddhist chronicles written in the Pali language. That sacred relic was known as the *daḷadā*, the tooth of the Buddha, said to have been carried to the island in the fourth century CE by an Indian princess.

In his *Da Ásia*, the official history of the Portuguese Indies, the sixteenth- and early seventeenth-century Goan historian Diogo do Couto refers to the artifact as the *dente do Bugio*, or "the monkey's tooth," as well as the tooth of *Budão*, the tooth of the Buddha (to Couto and the Portuguese, an unfamiliar native deity or holy man). Couto identifies the tooth as a sacred object while also calling it by a term that would ultimately become a racialized insult: *bogio*. The slippage between *Budão* and *bugio/bogio* provides a striking example of a violent intergroup conflict over collective identity, rival religious groups, and their group mysteries.

Word of the captured tooth relic spread quickly throughout the South Asian Buddhist world, and the King of Pegu offered a fortune to recover it. Religious authorities in Goa prevented the ransoming of the relic, however, and destroyed it in a flamboyant public ritual the following year. This chapter analyzes the group fantasy expressed by the auto-da-fé of the tooth: namely, the desire to destroy a rival group through the ritual "execution" of one of its most sacred objects. That fantasy was summarily challenged when in 1566 two other *daḷadās* appeared in Ceylon – one in Colombo, and the other in Kandy – and authenticity was claimed for each.

Such linguistic slippages had already played a significant role in extreme intragroup conflicts of that region – specifically, between Portuguese Old Christians and New Christians (persons of Jewish ancestry). The inflamma- tory incident resulting in the founding of the Goan Inquisition turned on the phrases *filho de Hamam* ("Son of Haman") and *filho de homem* ("Son of Man") supposedly invoked during a 1557 celebration of Purim among a group of New Christians and the Jewish community of Cochin, and a violent conflict afterward. The destruction of the tooth relic in Goa three years later was not an isolated incident but part of a larger program instigated by ecclesiastical and secular authorities in colonial Goa, in Lisbon, and in other parts of the Portuguese empire to enforce intragroup, as well as extragroup conformity. This chapter studies the dark history of the Inquisition in sixteenth-century India and beyond, and its impact on numerous ethnic and religious group identities in the region.

If European colonialism and the encounters that resulted from it produced a wide range of new group configurations and accompanying fantasies, there were other vectors of change in the early modern world that had an equally profound impact on the organization of groups. The scientific revolution gave rise to profound transformations of group subjectivity. The fantasy of the group as a machine is one of them, as discussed in Chapter 5, "Hamlet's Machine: The Inorganic Group."

While writing a new play about physical, psychic, and political vulnerability, Shakespeare helped to coin this new metaphor at the beginning of the seventeenth century. The character Hamlet writes to his soon-to-be estranged lover Ophelia: "Thine evermore, most dear lady, whilst this machine is to him." The novel use of the word *machine* to describe the human body presages a dramatic shift in how individuals would perceive their own corporeality: a mechanistic fantasy of the body that would be developed by Descartes and Enlightenment philosophers. This new metaphor would in turn be extended to group bodies, increasingly fantasized as inorganic and indestructible. The pre-modern metaphor of the body politic gradually gave way to the *group as machine* – a fundamentally modern metaphor of the collective (e.g., army, state, corporation, or colonial empire).

The mechanization of the social metaphor must also be regarded as an aspect of what sociologist Norbert Elias called the "civilizing process" – the collective repression and denial of the body and its drives, which began to take place at an ever-accelerating rate at the end of the Middle Ages. The rise of the metaphor of the group machine would project a vision of social collectives free of organicism, sexuality, and also, conveniently, of destabilizing individual or group affect, and, finally, individual autonomy and responsibility for the actions of the group. The fantasy of the group as machine must itself be understood as a form of technology implemented at a given point in history, serving as a means of regulating, for better and for worse, the functions of individual components of the social machine.

While mechanistic metaphors of the group would become increasingly entrenched, organic metaphors for collectives large and small also continued to circulate and to evolve during the late Renaissance and Enlightenment. Chapter 6, "The Animal Hospitals of Gujarat: The Collective Unbound," explores the remarkable history of one such metaphor. Certain cities of northwest India such as Cambay and Surat were renowned for their sanctuaries for sick birds, mice, cows, sheep, and other animals or insects. By the sixteenth century and even before, these unique institutions had become tourist attractions for European visitors to that region. They wrote about them extensively in their travel narratives, describing them in various European languages as "animal hospitals" – a concept and metaphor quite different in its connotations from their Gujarati name, *panjrapol*.

Gujarati animal sanctuaries, maintained by Jains, Hindus, and other religious groups, perplexed Europeans and other visitors, who struggled to make sense of a worldview in which animals have souls and in which the man–animal hierarchy fundamental to European thought was conceptualized in completely different ways. The increasing contacts between India and Italy, Asia, Africa, and Europe intensified the Renaissance exploration of the perplexing questions of identity and selfhood in relation to the natural world, as well as the conception of the metaphysical. This final chapter explores the transculturation that resulted from European travel writings about the "animal hospitals" of Gujarat, and the influence of Indian religious and cultural views on Western theories of the soul, the body, and the human–animal divide.

Transculturation and the Associative Principle

The associative principle of analysis adopted in this book – rooted in the Freudian and later psychoanalytic traditions, as well as the Simmelian theory of social networks – may in the seeming randomness of its connections call to mind *The Heavenly Emporium of Benevolent Knowledge*, the "Chinese encyclopedia" described by Jorge Luis Borges.[86] The imaginary encyclopedia evokes the problem of classification, which is simultaneously the problem of grouping. It de-familiarizes group concepts and what we believe we understand about them.

It is the goal of the present work to de-familiarize, as well: not to generate perplexity or laughter (nor to rule them out), but to rethink and relocate the categories of "groupness" that we typically use to think about the past as well as the present. It is from the recombinant potentialities of groups in the Renaissance, and from all that in any time or place resists or exceeds the will to systematize, that this method derives its impetus. If indeed collectives – persons in groups, as well as ideas, beliefs, or things held in common – were for a time unbound, set free or set loose, they would coalesce again in new formations, new identities, new distributions and organizations, and new knowledges. Through their metaphors, embedded in the silt of old stories, we can once again encounter them afresh.

---

[86] In that mythic book, animals are divided into the following categories: (a) those that belong to the emperor; (b) embalmed ones; (c) those that are trained; (d) suckling pigs; (e) mermaids; (f) fabulous ones; (g) stray dogs; (h) those that are included in this classification; (i) those that tremble as if they were mad; (j) innumerable ones; (k) those drawn with a very fine camel's-hair brush; (l) etcetera; (m) those that have just broken the flower vase; (n) those that at a distance resemble flies. "The Analytical Language of John Wilkins," in *Borges: Selected Non-Fictions*, 231.

  This organizational concept was much admired by Michel Foucault, who opens *The Order of Things* with a brief discussion of the passage.

I

LAOCOÖN:
THE GROUP AS A WORK OF ART
ROME, 1506

[N]o equivalent for "small group" existed in the ancient languages, which amounts
to saying that the concept did not exist.

— Didier Anzieu, *The Group and the Unconscious*

Because we are used to thinking that creativity begins and ends with the person, it
is easy to miss the fact that the greatest spur to it may come from changes outside
the individual.

Mihaly Csikszentmihalyi, *Creativity: Flow and the Psychology of Discovery and
Invention*

IN THE RENAISSANCE, THE CONCEPTUALIZING OF GROUPS ENTERED A NEW
phase. At least in part we can link this development to a particular event.
On a winter's evening on or about January 14, 1506, a small group of local
people and out-of-town visitors gathered near the outskirts of the city of
Rome. From the vineyard owned by Felice de' Freddi on the Esquiline
hill, an important artifact had come to light: a large statue of apparently
ancient origin. One by one, they lowered themselves into a recently opened
subterranean chamber beneath de' Freddi's dormant vines. From that hidden
space, they excavated the *Laocoön*, a long-lost masterpiece of classical statuary
that had been walled up for centuries in the baths of the Roman Emperor
Titus.[1] Sensing the importance of this discovery, which would soon have

---

[1] In the earliest known letter, written a day or so after the *Laocoön* was excavated, an anonymous
eyewitness describes the discovery as follows:

> Per questa intenderete, Joannes mi, che uno Romano a questi dì, in una sua vignia in
> Roma, in loco dicto le Capoçe, apresso la chiesa di S. Piero ad Vincula, non longe ab
> Amphitheatro, ha trovato tre figure ex lapide pario in una camera antiquissima subterranea
> bellissima pavimentata et incrustata mirifice et haveva murato lo usso.... Che queste siano
> quelle figure che tempore Plinii erano in domo Titi imperatoris est clarissimum signum,
> perché sono de mirabile excellentia.... Et quel loco vulgariter se chiama la Casa de Tito

a profound impact on the artistic microclimates of Renaissance Rome and Florence, these witnesses could scarcely contain their excitement.

The excavation of the *Laocoön* was observed by an eleven-year-old boy, Francesco da Sangallo, son of the renowned Florentine architect Giuliano da Sangallo. Many decades later, Francesco would recall the events of that evening:

> I was quite young when I was first in Rome. At that time the Pope was informed of the discovery of some very beautiful statues (*certe statue molto belle*) in a vineyard near Santa Maria Maggiore. The Pope dispatched one of his men to go get Giuliano da Sangallo and have him take a look right away. And so he went immediately. And since Michelangelo Buonarroti continually visited our house, because my father had bid him come, having given him the commission for the Pope's tomb, he wanted him to go, too. I also came along for the ride, and off we went. When we had descended to where the statues were, my father immediately said, "This is the Laocoön that Pliny mentioned." Then they opened up the hole in the ground more so that they could pull the statue out. After we saw it, we went back to eat, talking the whole time about ancient matters, as well as the latest news from Florence. . . . [2]

In the words of Leonard Barkan, this was a great narrative of discovery.[3] In his son's account, Giuliano da Sangallo played the decisive role in the evening's drama by immediately recognizing the statue as the ancient masterwork

imperatore et quelle Capoçe, che sono sale subterranee cum molte porte de prospectiva, erant Therme Titi imperatoris.

Discussed in Van Essen, "La découverte du Laocoön," 292–293, and quoted from Maffei's "La fama di Laocoönte nei testi del Cinquecento," 104–105.

According to this witness, Felice de' Freddi immediately received several lucrative offers for the statue, but Julius II insisted that the find would be his. De' Freddi's recompense for the statue appears to have been a complicated affair that dragged on for many years. The inscription on de' Freddi's tomb in Rome's Santa Maria in Aracoeli recalls his fifteen minutes of fame in the Renaissance, declaring that he "merited immortality on account of his own virtues, and for having found the divine image of Laocoön, which one can see almost breathing in the Vatican." Maffei, 114–115.

[2] [I]o era di pochi anni la prima volta ch'io fui a Roma, che fu detto al papa che in una vigna presso a Santa Maria Maggiore s'era trovato certe statue molto belle. El papa commandò a un palafreniere: "Va, e di' a Giuliano da S. Gallo, che subito là vadia a vedere." E così subito s'andò. Et perché Michelagnolo Bonarroti si tornava continuamente in casa, che mio padre l'haveva fatto venire, e gli haveva allogata la sepoltura del papa et volle che ancor lui andasse; ed io così in groppa a mio padre, et andammo. Et scesi dove erano le statue: subito mio padre disse: "Questo è Hilaoconte, che fa mentione Plinio," et si fece crescere la buca, per poterlo tirar fuora. E visto, ci tornamo a desinare e sempre si ragionò delle cose antiche, discorrendo ancora di quelle di Fiorenza. . . .

Letter from Francesco da Sangallo to Vicenzio Borghini dated February 28, 1567. Maffei, 110–111. My translation, with thanks to Susan Gaylard for improvements.

[3] *Unearthing the Past*, 3.

described by Pliny the Elder in his *Natural History*. Confirming the unique historical and artistic value of the sculpture, the elder Sangallo distinguished himself by his deep knowledge of classical sources.

Renaissance artists, collectors, and intellectuals also recognized the statue's relation to another famous classical text, Virgil's *Aeneid*. The statue grouping (Figure 1.1) depicts Laocoön, a Trojan priest of Neptune, flanked on either side by his two young sons. All three are trapped in a lethal tangle of enormous, biting snakes. This legendary monument of Hellenistic statuary may have been based on the Laocoön episode in Book II of Virgil's *Aeneid*, or perhaps on still earlier written or pictorial versions of the story.[4] In Virgil's account, Laocoön strenuously opposes the Trojans' decision to bring the wooden horse into the walled city of Troy. "Trust not the horse, ye Trojans," he urges his compatriots. "Whatever it be, I fear the Greeks, even when bringing gifts."[5] Laocoön hurls a spear into the side of the horse, which reverberates ambiguously. Unfortunately for the Trojans, the priest's prescient advice goes unheeded; later, however, the goddess Minerva, protectress of the Greeks, cruelly punishes Laocoön and his two sons for that act of resistance by dispatching two sea serpents to kill them.[6] The statue, reputedly the collaborative work of three sculptors from Rhodes — Hagesander, Polydorus, and Athenodorus[7] — depicts the agonizing final moments of Laocoön and his sons as the snakes bind, bite, and destroy their intended prey.

Although Francesco Sangallo's story of the statue's discovery could represent a certain secondary revision of the evening's events (his letter was written in 1567, more than sixty years after the discovery), this account provides important information about the discovery of the *Laocoön*: its chthonic hiding place beneath the Roman vineyard, its links to an earlier history, and its power to generate excitement among the luminaries of the age — including Michelangelo, the redoubtable Pope Julius II, and Francesco's own father

---

[4] Following epigraphical research into Rhodian inscriptions, Margarete Bieber argues that the statue dates from 80–20 BC, before the publication of the *Aeneid* after Virgil's death in 19 BC. *Laocoön: The Influence of the Group*, 12. More recently, Richard Brilliant has noted that most scholars currently consider the Laocoön and other statue groupings found at Sperlonga, Italy, to have been made by the same atelier, possibly for the villa of the Emperor Tiberius. He also notes that many consider the statue to be a second- or first-century BCE work. *My Laocoön*, 10–11, 44–45. Settis, while also acknowledging that specialists now date the statue between the middle of the second century BCE and the middle of the first century CE, or perhaps later, places the creation of the statue between 40 and 20 BCE (27, 75). The debate on the dating, origin, and creators of the *Laocoön* is far from settled.

[5] Virgil, *Aeneid* II, 48–49: "equo ne credite, Teucri./ quidquid id est, timeo Danaos et dona ferentis." 318.

[6] *Ibid.*, II, 201–233 (330–333).

[7] On the creators of the statue, mentioned by Pliny in his *Natural History*, see n. 55.

1.1. *Laocoön*, with restorations completed in 1960. Marble, 2nd c. BCE–1st c. CE (?). Museo Pio Clementino, Vatican Museums, Vatican State. Photo credit: Archive Timothy McCarthy/Art Resource, New York. In 1957–1960, the group was restored by Filippo Magi, who attached to the *Laocoön* a replacement arm that had been found in a Roman antique shop more than fifty years earlier.

Giuliano da Sangallo. Nothing begets fame more than fame itself, and the fame of the *Laocoön* had long since been established by Pliny, as Sangallo the Elder noted. How much more extraordinary, then, was the chance to reawaken that long-dormant fame, simply by extracting it from the ground,

1.2. Hendrik van Kleef, painting of the Antiquarium established by Julius II, 1589 (?). Musées Royaux de Beaux Arts, Brussels. Guests stroll about the private sculpture garden, which allowed the assembled sculptures and other antiquities to be viewed in a natural setting.

as if to resurrect the whole of antiquity by means of such an action. There were many such gestures in the Renaissance, sleights of hand attempted again and again in any number of ways, although the unique iconic status of the *Laocoön* in the collective imagination would remain secure for several centuries. As Barkan has astutely argued in his discussion of this event, "The unearthed object [became] the place of exchange not only between words and pictures but also between antiquity and modern times and between one artist and another" – that is, a "nexus point" within multiple networks of

1.2

exchange.[8] The statue also gave rise to fantasies, fears, and desires – many of them about the body, both of individuals and of groups – within the social networks partly precipitated by its discovery.

As soon as it was unearthed, the statue created a tremendous stir. Pope Julius II purchased the statue and ultimately placed it in what would become his Antiquarium, located between the north and east wings of the Belvedere Court and the hemicycle connecting it to the apostolic palace (Figure 1.2).[9] This private sculpture garden would become the site of an important

[8] Barkan, 4.
[9] Petrosillo, *The City of St. Peter*, 283; Christian, *Empire Without End*, 161–167, 265–275.

collection of classical statues and sarcophagi, including the *Laocoön*, the *Apollo Belvedere*, *Hercules and Antaeus*, the *Venus Felix*, and the *Commodus*, all acquired by 1510. The *Cleopatra* and the *Tiber* were added by 1512, and the *Nile* by 1513. The *Tigris* was probably also included in the statue collection at this early stage.[10] The statuary of the Antiquarium itself constituted a group that soon was recognized as one of the most important collections of classical antiquities in sixteenth-century Europe. Young artists employed by the papal court were invited by Julius to lodge in the adjacent Palazetto del Belvedere and to study the statuary in the garden below. This outdoor viewing space, inspired by Greco-Roman precedents, enabled the Pope and his guests to view and enjoy the statuary in an atmosphere of renewed classicism.[11] This collection later would form an important part of the Museo Pio-Clementino, created by Clement XIV (1769–1774) and Pius VI (1775–1799), and the core of the current Vatican Museums.[12]

The *Laocoön*, the centerpiece of Julius II's Antiquarium, was more or less intact at the time of its discovery, although the right arms of the father and the younger son were missing.[13] An early sixteenth-century engraving of the *Laocoön* by the artist Marco Dente depicts the statue in its unrestored form, before it had been installed in the Belvedere courtyard (Figure 1.3). The renowned architect Donato Bramante, original designer of the Belvedere, held a contest in 1510 and invited young artists in Rome to create a wax version of the *Laocoön* that supplied the missing limbs. Raphael judged this contest, awarding the first prize to Jacopo Sansovino.[14] In the 1530s, Giovanni Angelo Montorsoli, a protégé of Michelangelo, added an outstretched terracotta arm to the central figure, which was removed a decade later, although copies of these restorations still exist. Michelangelo may have played a role in creating a different, flexed version of the missing arm, which was left unfinished, although another extended arm, possibly sculpted by Bernini, was added to the statue in 1540.[15] The outstretched position of the replacement arm (Figure 1.4) was assumed by many to be accurate until the

---

[10] Other statues would be added later. See Brummer, *The Statue Court in the Vatican Belvedere*, 35 *et passim*. The statue initially identified as *Cleopatra* later came to be known as the *Sleeping Ariadne*.

[11] Petrosillo, 283.

[12] *Ibid.*, 284.

[13] Brummer, 80. The statue could have been broken in other ways at the time of its unearthing – a point that Brummer argues on the basis of some early engravings of the *Laocoön*, in which the figures are not mounted on the base. On this question, as well as the history and mystery of Laocoön's missing arm, the many attempts to restore it, and the probable recovery of the original arm in the mid-twentieth century, see *ibid.*, 84ff.

[14] This contest was documented by Giorgio Vasari. See *Vite*, VI: 178. See also Barkan, 9–10.

[15] Haskell and Penny, *Taste and the Antique*, 246.

MCVS·RAVENAS·

· LAOCHOON ·

· ROMAE·IN·PALATIO·PONT·IN·
· LOCO·QVI·VVLGO·DICITVR·
·BELVIDERE·

1.3. Marco Dente da Ravenna, *Laochoon*, (1522–1525), engraving. 47.9 cm × 32.9 cm. Photograph © 2011. Museum of Fine Arts, Boston. The arms of the father and younger son were missing at the time of the statue's discovery.

twentieth century, when what is now considered the definitive restoration –
a sharply bent arm found in a Roman antique shop – was put into place.[16]

The *Laocoön* would remain a central and compelling piece of the Belvedere
collection, inspiring numerous restorations, imitations, and adaptations in
many media. The statue garnered intense interest in the artistic and intellectual communities first of Italy, and then of other European countries,
creating a network of people drawn to the statue and its interpretation.[17]
For example, a late sixteenth-century drawing of the group by Federico
Zuccaro (Figure 1.5) depicts his brother Taddeo seated among the statues
of Julius II's Antiquarium and drawing the *Laocoön*. There were many reasons for the shared interest – for example, the statue's unique and powerful
representation of bodies in pain, its hyper-realistic depiction of the human
body, and its metonymic relation to the entire world of Greek and Roman
antiquity. There is, however, still another reason for the interest that it generated from the moment of its rediscovery. The *Laocoön* signaled not only
the renaissance of classical art but also, perhaps more profoundly, the rise of
the group as a work of art.

Regarding this fame, Barkan has observed that the *Laocoön* generated "a flood of correspondence within the first month [following its
recovery] and a series of poetic responses throughout the sixteenth century; scores of drawings, copies, and re-creations in the work of virtually every Renaissance artist; [and] instant political valorization as far
in the future as the time of Napoleon...."[18] Moreover, Barkan contends, the *Laocoön* was "not only the most famous of all antiquities
in the sixteenth century but also [came], through Gotthold Ephraim
Lessing and others, to be the very symbol of art as a subject."[19]

---

[16]In 1957–1960, the group was restored by Filippo Magi, who attached to the *Laocoön* a replacement
arm that had been found by the German archaeologist Ludwig Pollak in a Roman antique shop
in 1905 but was not recognized as belonging to the sculpture for several decades. *Il Ripristino del
Laocoonte*, 6ff.

    The aesthetic problem of reconstructing the sculpture also might have had a "group body"
component – that is, the shared desire to complete the group by plugging its "holes." See
Introduction, 26, n. 73.

[17]For a partial list of Renaissance engravings, drawings, castings, and copies of the *Laocoön*, see Bober
and Rubenstein, *Renaissance Artists and Antique Sculpture*, 154–155. See also Maffei's anthology of
prose, poetry, and epigrams inspired by the Laocoön (*op. cit.*).

[18]Barkan, 2.

[19]Barkan argues that modern critics and art historians often tend to overemphasize the importance
of the *Laocoön* on Renaissance and Baroque culture, while minimizing the impact of other classical
antiquities recovered during the same era. Nevertheless, Barkan persuasively demonstrates that the
famed serpentine sculpture was indeed at the center of the emerging "canon" of antique statuary
in the early modern era. *Ibid.*, 3.

1.4. Vatican *Laocoön* with Renaissance restorations, marble, sixteenth century to 1960. Photo Credit: Alinari/Art Resource, New York.

Over time this provocative sculpture would simultaneously emerge as an emblem of the work of art *as a group* – a catalyst, as well as an emblem, of the shifting social relations that characterized Renaissance Europe.

1.5. Federico Zuccaro, *Taddeo Zuccaro Copying Laocoön. Julius II's Antiquarium with Bramante Corridor, S. Peter's and Vatican Palace in background.* Pen and ink drawing, 7 3/16 in. × 16 3/4 in., detail (ca. 1595). Gabinetto dei Disegni e delle Stampe degli Uffizi, Florence. Photo credit: Scala/Art Resource. The dome of St. Peter's, under construction at the time the drawing was made, appears on the top right.

The Group as Word and Concept: A Philological Knot

To better understand the possible meanings of this event, let us turn from the story of the literal excavation of the *Laocoön* group to a philological excavation of the roots of the modern word *group*. The Italian word *gruppo*, with its cognates in many other European languages, has a fascinating history. To the long inventory of things purportedly invented by Italians (i.e., the individual; the Renaissance; the modern state, according to the historian Jacob Burckhardt) we must add the group – both as a *word* and as a *concept*. Toward the end of the Middle Ages, this important word developed a new range of meanings within the Italian language. The evolution of *gruppo* represents, quite literally, an original and artful way of thinking about gatherings or clusters, especially of people.

1.5

In the ancient world, no generic word for "small group" seems to have existed. [20] As the Indo-Europeanist linguist Carl Darling Buck states, "instead of any generic term, there is a wealth of individualistic terms, differentiated according to the object referred to."[21] For example, there are numerous words that designate specific categories or kinds of persons, animals, or objects (e.g., in English, *band* [armed men, robbers, musicians], *bevy* [girls, roes, certain types of birds], *bunch* [grapes, flowers, keys], *flock* [sheep, geese,

---

[20] I am indebted to the French psychoanalyst Didier Anzieu, whose work on individual and group psychology in many ways inspired this book. In *The Group and the Unconscious*, Anzieu writes: "[N]o equivalent for 'small group' existed in the ancient languages, which amounts to saying that the concept did not exist. There was only the individual on the one hand and society on the other, and this opposition became one of the major themes of sociology" (117). It might be safer to say, however, that no generic word for "small group" existed in the Indo-European languages. Moreover, there are many words describing certain kinds of small groups in antiquity, although these terms are nongeneric.

[21] *A Dictionary of Selected Synonyms in the Principal Indo-European Languages*, 930.

goats], *cluster* [flowers, stars, people]).[22] Buck notes that the Italian word *gruppo*, which was used as an art term (as in a group of sculpted or painted figures), later evolved into the most nearly generic term.[23] Notable medieval words for human collectives, such as Chaucer's *felaweshipe* or *compagnye*, or Boccaccio's *brigata*, although significant descriptors of early modern "associational forms," as David Wallace has termed them,[24] also should be distinguished from the word (and concept) *gruppo*, insofar as the former do not possess generic connotations but apply primarily to people. The aesthetic connotations of *gruppo* and its cognates give these words a unique place in the evolving lexicon of Renaissance metaphors for social concepts, as we shall see.

The emergent concept of the group must be further distinguished from words for *crowd* or *multitude*, which are abundant in linguistic history. In the Indo-European languages, such words often derive from terms meaning *much* or *many*. Frequently they carry a negative connotation by also denoting *turmoil* or *disorder*. Many words for *crowd* derive from verbs signifying *to press*, because they indicate a closely packed number of persons, while others stem from words for *people*. Words meaning *heap* or *pile* could also signify a large number. The Sanskrit *bāhulya-* derives, for example, from *bahu-*, meaning *much* or *many*. Similarly, the Greek πλῆθος comes from the same root as πολύς, meaning *much* or in the plural *many*; the Latin *multitūdō*, from *multus*; the Latin word *turba* is a loanword from or cognate with the Greek τύρβη, meaning turmoil or disorder. The Italian word *folla* and the French *foule*, backformations from the verbs *follare* and *fouler*, signify *full cloth*, hence *press* or *crowd*. These ultimately derive from the Vulgar Latin *fullō* (*fuller*). Spanish conveyed the concept in various ways: as *multitud* and *muchedumbre*, as well as *gentío* (from *gente*, meaning *people*). In addition to *mulțime*, the Romanian language acquired the word *gloată*, from the Slavic, late Church Slavonic, and Bulgarian *glota*, or *crowd*; the Irish *slūag*, meaning *crowd*, *host*, or *army*; and the Welsh *lliaws* (*more*) and *torf*, from the Latin *turma*, meaning *troop* or *throng*. Similarly, the Old Norse term *þröng*, the Old English *geþrang*, and Middle English *thrang*, with Old High German *githrengi* and the Dutch *gedrang*, all originally involved the concept of pressure.[25] Meanwhile, the

---

[22] *Ibid.*, 930–931.

[23] *Ibid.*, 930.

[24] See "The *General Prologue* and the Anatomy of Associational Form," in *Chaucerian Polity*, 65–103.

[25] Buck, 929–930. There are many such variants in the Germanic languages.

Danish *hob* and the Swedish *hop* derive from the Low German *hōp*, or *heap*. The list continues.[26]

Separate from this host of words used to denote the concept of a crowd emerged a new word as a generic term for collectives.[27] As noted above, this was the Italian *gruppo*, which derived from the earlier word for *knot* in Italian, *groppo*. In Dante, in Boccaccio, and in Petrarch, we find metaphoric variations on the theme of the knot, the *groppo*. This medieval term was a derivative of the Germanic word *kruppa*, meaning a *rounded mass* or *lump*.[28] In its primary sense, *groppo* signified a knot or tangle, as of thread or hair. Figuratively, it could also connote a problem or enigma – that is, a conceptual knot.

In the *Inferno*, Dante employs the word *groppo* in both of these senses. In *Inferno* XIII, a canto devoted to the suicides, he writes of the shade Lano, who impales himself on a bush as he tries to escape from the dogs that are chasing him:

> "Lano, sì non furo accorte
> le gambe tue a le giostre dal Toppo!"
> E poi che forse li fallia la lena,
> di sé e d'un cespuglio fece un groppo.

> "Lano, your legs
> were not so nimble at the jousts of Toppo!"
> And then, perhaps because he'd lost his breath,
> he fell into one tangle with a bush. (*Inferno* XIII, 120–123)[29]

Here Dante imagines a tangle, or knot, of human and shrub limbs. He could also have had in mind the Germanic etymology of the word, suggesting a pile or mass.

[26]For further examples, see *ibid.*, 929–930.

[27]*Ibid.*, 930. Buck notes, however, that even the generic *gruppo* did not apply to animals but to persons and objects.

[28]*Groppo* derives from a radical found in Germanic and Celtic languages that signifies *to reunite* or *to amass*. Ottorino Pianigiani, *Vocabolario etimologico della lingua italiana*, 2 vols. (Milano: Casa Editrice Sonzogno, 1937), 1: 650.

The *American Heritage Dictionary* traces the many variants back to the hypothetical Indo-European base *ger-*, signifying "curving, crooked." From this root, numerous Germanic words meaning curled, hooked, or bent can be traced. Additionally, words meaning rounded mass, collection, vessel, or container may also derive from the *ger-* base, including the Old English *cruma*, a fragment: crumb, and *cropp*, a cluster, a bunch, an ear of corn: crop; the Frankish *kruppa*, rump: croup; Middle Dutch *cruyse*, pot: cruse; the Italian *gruppo*, an assemblage: *gruppo*; and many more. *The American Heritage Dictionary of the English Language*, ed. William Morris (Boston: Houghton Mifflin Company, 1969), 1516.

See also Julius Pokorny, *Indogermanisches etymologisches Wörterbuch*, 3 vols. (Bern: Francke, 1959), 2: 382 ff.

[29]Dante Alighieri, *La divina commedia*, 123–124; *The Divine Comedy*, 114.

Two cantos earlier, in Dante's discourse on usury, the word *groppo* also appears, this time in a more metaphorical sense. Dante asks Virgil about a variety of sins, usury included:

> "Ancora un poco indietro ti rivolvi"
> diss'io, "là dove di' ch'usura offende
> la divina bontade, e 'l groppo solvi."

> "Go back a little to that point," I said,
> "where you told me that usury offends
> divine goodness; unravel now that knot." (*Inferno* XI, 94–96)[30]

We observe in Dante's writings, then, some of the medieval usages of this curious word; here, *groppo* connotes a puzzle or enigma.

Boccaccio offers yet another metaphor of the knot in the *Decameron*. In Novella Quarta on the second day, Lauretta describes the fortunes of the shipwrecked Landolfo Ruffolo, buffeted in the water by a *groppo di vento*, a gust of wind:

> Ma, come che il fatto s'andasse, adivenne che solutosi subitamente nell'aere un groppo di vento e percosso nel mare. . . .

> But, as luck would have it, suddenly the sea was struck by a strong gust of wind. . . .[31]

The use of the word *groppo* to describe a knot of air or wind, a thunderhead or cloudburst – namely, a meteorological phenomenon – is not unique to Boccaccio, because the word in this sense also has cognates in medieval Occitan and Catalan.[32]

Petrarch applies the concept of the knot or cluster to a gathering of people. In the *Trionfi*, Petrarch speaks of *un bel groppo* – a "knot" of persons: "Vidi. . . / i tre Teban ch' i' dissi, in un bel groppo" ("I saw the three Thebans that I described in a lovely knot").[33] By helping to push the metaphor in

---

[30] *La divina commedia*, 106; *The Divine Comedy*, 104.
[31] Boccaccio, *Decameron*, 4: 122; *The Decameron*, 83.
[32] The word *gropada* in medieval Catalan and the Occitan *groupado* had a similar connotation: "*nubarrón tempestuoso*"– a thunderhead. See "Grupo" in Joan Coromines and José A. Pascual, eds., *Diccionario crítico etimológico castellano e hispánico*, 6 vols. (Madrid: Editorial Gredos, 1980), 3: 228. Also in medieval Catalan and Occitan, the word *grop* indicates a "*nudo de madera*," or knot of wood, a sense that also existed in the Italian. "En conclusión, el vocablo es autóctono en italiano, lengua de Oc y catalán, y desde estos idiomas se extendió por una parte al francés y por la otra al portugués y castellano."
[33] *Trionfo della Fama* II, 16, in *Rime, trionfi, e poesie latine*, 537. The three Thebans in question are Epaminondas, Bacchus, and Hercules.

a new, anthropomorphic direction, Petrarch helped to redefine the *group* (a new word and concept for collectivity) at the same time.

The significance of this development would become manifest only gradually. The spelling of the word changed; a *u* substituted for the *o*, existing as an alternative spelling of the older word and gradually taking on a life of its own. In the fifteenth century, Politian could write humorously of a love relationship gone sour:

> Io ho rotto el fuscellino
> pure un tratto, e sciolto el gruppo;
> i' son fuor d'un gran viluppo,
> e sto or com'un susino.

> I have broken it off
> Once and for all, and loosened the ties;
> I am finally free of that huge tangle,
> And right now I'm doing just peachy.[34] (*Rime* CXVI)

Here the poet imagines loosening the ties (or untying the knots) of love between two people.[35] In a poem full of knots, snares, and sexual entanglement, Politian goes on to describe the end of a highly erotic but deeply frustrating relationship with a woman who had caught him in her web ("*fe' insaccarmi nella ragna*").[36]

Metaphoric variations on *groppo* and *gruppo*, a knotty pair of words, continue to appear throughout the sixteenth century. These words could signify doubt, difficulty, or complication. They could also refer to the climax or turning point of a dramatic action. Both Castelvetro and Tasso use *groppo* to describe the plot of a story or play – specifically, the complication, or knot, that must be resolved.[37] Meanwhile, in the *Orlando furioso*, Ariosto writes of the *groppo* used by the sorceress Alcina to trap hapless men: "Alcina ve li tien per muro e fossa/ a chi volesse uscir fuor del suo groppo" ("Alcina

---

[34] *Rime-Canzoni a ballo* CXVI, in *Poesie volgari*, 1:110. I am indebted to Marilyn Migiel for her improvements to this translation.

[35] So glossed by the editor: "*sciolto . . . gruppo*: "[ho] sciolto il vincolo, il legame" (*ibid.*, 2: 285).

[36] For fans of the word *gruppo*, this is a definitely a poem worth reading.

[37] In his commentary on Aristotle's *Poetics* (1570), Lodovico Castelvetro describes how authors create plausible resolutions to complications in the plot (i.e., by using the persons or things within the story, rather than outside of it). He cites an example of this technique in *Decameron* 7: 6: "S'usano quelle persone a sciogliere il groppo le quali l'avevano annodato nella novella di madonna Isabella appo il Boccaccio. . . . " *Poetica d'Aristotele vulgarizzata e sposta*, 433.

Similarly, Torquato Tasso wrote: "e tale per aventura è alcuna moderna tragedia in cui la materia ed i nomi son finti, ma 'l groppo è così tessuto e così snodato come presso gli antichi Greci si ritrova." *Discorsi dell'arte poetica* (1587), in *Scritti sull'arte poetica*, 6. Cited in *Grande dizionario della lingua italiana*, ed. Salvatore Battaglia, 21 vols. (Turin: UTET, 1961–), 7: 61.

holds there with walls and moats whosoever should want to escape from her snare" [6:56]).[38] In the same poem, however, Ariosto describes "un bello et amichevol groppo/ de li principi illustri l'eccellenza" (a fine and courteous band of stately princes [3:40]).[39] In this alternative context, the word approaches its more modern meaning of collectivity.

Such clusters could be animate or inanimate, as, for example, in Galileo's 1612 discussion of a "gruppo delle macchie [solari]" ("a group of sunspots").[40] Similarly, the seventeenth-century Jesuit historian Daniello Bartoli described Gotò in Japan as "un gruppo di cinque isole che tutte insieme formano un regno" ("a group of five islands that together form a kingdom").[41]

By the fifteenth and sixteenth centuries, the words would assume an additional connotation within the context of the musical and visual arts. A *groppo* or *gruppo* could designate a musical trill or ornament, as well as a ricercar or fantasia.[42] Moreover, in its new spelling and its earlier one, it came to designate a cluster of figures in a sculpture or painting.[43] For example, Leonardo da Vinci wrote of "Molti disegni di gruppi" ("many drawings of groups" – i.e., of people or objects).[44] Somewhat later in the sixteenth century, Giovanvettorio Soderini would employ the word in its new, artistic sense, writing of "gruppi di statue aggavignate insieme, come le forze d'Ercole o simili" ("groups of statues carved together, such as the labors of Hercules or the like").[45] Here Soderini describes the design of outdoor gardens and landscape design, recommending the strategic placement of statues and fountains for visual effect. The group, both word and concept, had become a work of art: that is, it had become an aesthetic representation of persons or objects in a composition.

In these examples, we can detect a striking development in the history of an idea. A group differs from a crowd, a throng, or even a multitude. By virtue of the intentional relation of its component figures, especially in this

[38] Ludovico Ariosto, *Orlando furioso e cinque canti*, 1: 233.

[39] *Ibid.*, 1:150.

[40] Galileo Galilei: "Nel gruppo delle macchie [solari] P, cominciate ad apparire il dì 25 di giugno, si vede conseguentemente gran mutazione ed augumento in numero." Letters on sunspots, 1612. Cited in Battaglia, 7: 83.

[41] *Istoria della Compagnia di Gesù. L'Asia descritta dal padre Daniello Bartoli, libri otto* (first published in 1650–1673), Vol. 8. Cited in Battaglia, 7: 83.

[42] Battaglia, 7: 85. See also *gruppo/groppo* and *ricercar* in J. A. Westrup and F. Ll. Harrison, *The New College Encyclopedia of Music*, rev. by Conrad Wilson (New York: W. W. Norton, 1976), 246, 457.

[43] Cp. Battaglia, 7: 85 (13): "Pitt. e sculpt. Rappresentazione artistica di cose o persone che insieme formano un episodio in sé compiuto o riproducono simbolicamente un'idea, un concetto."

[44] *Scritti scelti*, 51. Cited in Battaglia, 7: 85.

[45] *I due trattati dell'agricoltura e della coltivazione delle viti*, 1, 277. Cited in Battaglia, 7: 85.

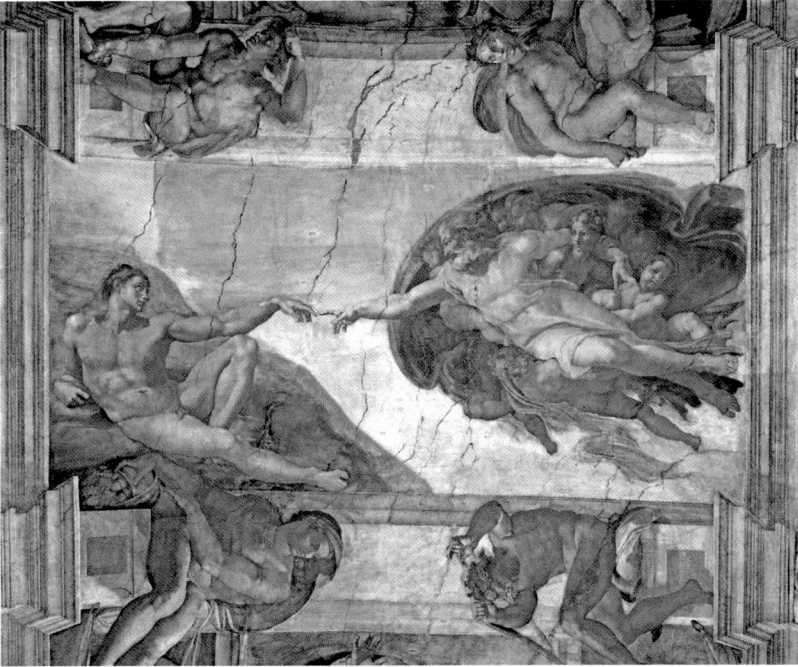

1.6. Michelangelo, "The Creation of Adam," fresco (1508–1512), Sistine Chapel, Vatican Palace, Vatican State. Photo credit: Scala/Art Resource, New York.

artistic context, a *gruppo* is by its nature more controlled, more composed, smaller, and more arranged than many of the aforementioned concepts of the collective. This new usage had novel – even radical – social and cultural implications, as we shall see.

Vasari's Groups

The conceptual transformation of the group as a knot into the group as a work of art also can be traced in the writings of the great art historian Giorgio Vasari, who employs the word not infrequently in his *Le vite de' più eccellenti pittori scultori e architettori* (*Lives of the Most Eminent Painters, Sculptors and Architects* [1550, 1568]). Interestingly, Vasari uses the term to describe paintings and two-dimensional art, rather than sculptures – for example, in his description of the *Creation of Adam* scene in Michelangelo's Sistine Chapel (Figure 1.6):

> [Michelangelo] then went on, beyond that scene, to the Creation of Adam, wherein he figured God as borne by a group of nude Angels of tender age [*un gruppo di Angioli ignudi e di tenera età*] which appear to be supporting

1.7. Michelangelo, "The Creation of Adam," detail of God and surrounding angels. Sistine Chapel, Vatican Palace, Vatican State. Photo credit: Scala/Art Resource, New York. Vasari described these figures as a *gruppo*.

> not one figure only, but the whole weight of the world [*i quali par che sostenghino non solo una figura, ma tutto il peso del mondo*]; this effect being produced by the venerable majesty of His form and by the manner of the movement with which He embraces some of the little Angels with one arm, as if to support Himself [*quasi che egli si sostenga*], and with the other extends the right hand towards Adam, a figure of such a kind in its beauty, in the attitude, and in the outlines, that it appears as if newly fashioned by the first and supreme Creator rather than by the brush and design of a mortal man.[46]

In Michelangelo's fresco, the soon-to-be-animate Adam is poised opposite God and his celestial host, an individual person defined by and against the

---

[46]"E così seguitò sotto a questo la Creazione di Adamo, dove ha figurato Dio portato da un gruppo di Angioli ignudi e di tenera età, i quali par che sostenghino non solo una figura, ma tutto il peso del mondo, apparente tale mediante la venerabilissima maiestà di quello e la maniera del moto, nel quale con un braccio cigne alcuni putti, quasi che egli si sostenga, e con l'altro porge la mano destra a uno Adamo, figurato–di bellezza, di attitudine e di dintorni–di qualità che e' par fatto di nuovo dal sommo e primo suo Creatore più tosto che dal pennello e disegno d'uno uomo tale." *Vite*, 6: 40–41; *Lives*, 9: 34.

1.8. Michelangelo, "The Creation of Adam," detail of Eve. Sistine Chapel, Vatican Palace, Vatican State. Photo credit: Scala/Art Resource, New York.

group. It is interesting that it is the group of angels, rather than God or Adam, that draws Vasari's initial attention. He describes to his readers the power of the angelic host: this group appears to support God, as well as "the whole weight of the world." The word *gruppo* seems especially apt here, because the angels seem knotted together, a solid yet sublime mass of bodies entwined under the encircling cloak of the Creator (Figure 1.7). To Vasari, their effect within the painting is to convey – literally, to *sustain* – the "venerable majesty" of the divinity stretching toward man. It is the dynamic of mutual support, of God encircling his angels, who in turn seem to sustain him, that captivates Vasari's imagination.

It is not clear why Vasari refers to these angels as *putti*, or cherubs, because the most prominent figure under God's arms appears to be an adult female – the unborn Eve, peering with interest at her future mate (Figure 1.8). Vasari does not articulate the thought that God is sustained in part by a female spirit, yet that enigmatic image could be what drew his attention to the group of angels.

Vasari uses the word *gruppo* several times to describe clusters of figures in paintings – for example, the Mount Parnassus wall of Raphael's Stanza della Segnatura (Figures F.2–F.3):

> There are portraits from nature of all the most famous poets, ancient and modern, and some only just dead, or still living in his day; which were taken from statues or medals, and many from old pictures, and some, who were still alive, portrayed from the life by himself. And to begin with one end, there are Ovid, Virgil, Ennius, Tibullus, Catullus, Propertius, and Homer; the last-named, blind and chanting his verses with uplifted head, having at his feet one who is writing them down. Next, in a group [*tutte in un gruppo*], are all the nine Muses and Apollo, with such beauty in their aspect, and such divinity in the figures, that they breathe out a spirit of grace and life. There, also, are the learned Sappho, the most divine Dante, the gracious Petrarca, and the amorous Boccaccio, who are wholly alive [*che vivi vivi sono*], with Tibaldeo, and an endless number of other moderns; and this scene is composed with much grace and executed with diligence.[47]

Intrigued by the manner in which Raphael captured the great poets of history, Vasari observes the lifelike quality of Sappho, Dante, Petrarch, and Boccaccio (*che vivi vivi sono*), or perhaps that they are alive together in the artist's extraordinary fresco. It is the Muses who form a *gruppo*, with Apollo (Figure 1.9). What Vasari emphasizes about this grouping, as with the other figures gathered around them, is the liveliness of its component figures, a quality that provides the painting with its aesthetic power.

The artistic properties attributed to the knot, the mass, and the cluster endow the Renaissance metaphor of the *gruppo* with new vitality. In Vasari's analysis of Raphael's fresco, it is not the representation of the individual figure that commands attention with its beauty and power but the dynamic relation of single figures in relation to others. The differential relation of the parts to the whole, and of the individual figure to the group, creates an energy in the painting that, he suggests, mirrors on a structural level what can be imagined on a thematic one – a convocation of poets and Muses. As in the previous example, *The Creation of Adam*, the figurative grouping depicts the gathering of unique and extraordinary energy not within but *between* figures (God arcs down to touch Adam – a plan and an activity supported by angels; Apollo and the nine Muses breathe forth their inspiration onto

---

[47] *Lives*, 4: 220; *Vite*, 4, 171.

1.9. Raphael, *Parnassus*, detail of Apollo and the Muses. Stanza della Segnatura, Vatican Palace, Vatican State. Photo Credit: Scala/Art Resource, New York. Vasari identified the cluster of Muses as a *gruppo*.

the poets assembled around them). Just beyond the frame of each fresco the viewer stands and watches, in some sense also touched by that energy.

During the late Renaissance and Baroque eras, the word *gruppo* in its artistic and compositional sense began to pass into other European languages. It entered the Dutch language as *groep* (also *groepe, groeppe, group*, and *grop*) near the beginning of the seventeenth century. The Flemish painter, poet, and biographer Karel van Mander introduced the word in his *Schilderboeck* (1604) to describe compositional groups within paintings.[48]

The word *groupe* appeared in the French language in the later seventeenth century, also in the emergent artistic sense. Molière used the word to describe the figures in a fresco painted in the cupola of the Parisian church of the Val-de-Grâce by his friend Pierre Mignard (Figure 1.10):

> N'ayant nul embarras; nul fracas vicieux,
> Qui rompe ce repos si fort ami des yeux:
> Mais où, sans se presser, le groupe se rassemble,

[48] A. Beets and J. W. Muller, *Woordenboek der Nederlandsche Taal*, 18 vols., Vol. 5 (Leiden: Martinus Nijhoff, A. W. Sijthoff, 1900). With thanks to Su Fang Ng for assistance with translation.

Et forme un doux concert, fasse un beau tout-ensemble,
Où rien ne soit à l'œil mendié, ni redit. . . .

The figures do not crowd together, and no inartistic clangor
Distracts the eye from a [welcome] sense of restful ease:
Rather, the [full] assembly gathers together unforced,
Creating sweet harmony, forming a lovely whole,
The eye wanting for no detail, and nothing being repeated. . . . [49]

In this encomium to his friend's artistry, Molière imports the word *groupe* from the Italian, using the term in its aesthetic sense and celebrating the compositional balance of Mignard's figures.

At the end of the seventeenth century, the word *group* appears in the English language for the first time, again signifying figures or objects organized in an artistic composition.[50] The word in its compositional sense also made its way into Spanish (*grupo*) and Portuguese (*grupo*) at approximately the same time.[51] By the seventeenth and eighteenth centuries, it entered the German language as *gruppe*, notably in connection with the *Laocoön*,[52] as well as the Swedish and Russian tongues, and many other languages.[53] Only after the aesthetic meanings of *gruppo* were absorbed into the other languages of Europe did the word in its more modern sense – that is, an assemblage or collective, especially of people – then take hold.

---

[49] *La Gloire du Val-de-Grâce* (1669), cited in *Le grand Robert de la langue française*, ed. Alain Rey, 6 vols. (2nd. ed., Paris: Dictionnaires le Robert, 2001), which gives as the primary signification of *groupe* the following: "Réunion de plusieurs personnages, de plusieurs éléments figurés formant une unité organique dans une oeuvre d'art (peinture, sculpture). *Un groupe sculpté. Le groupe des trois Grâces.*" 3: 1579. With thanks to Philippe Dambournet and Robert Corum for exegetical and translation advice.

[50] The first definition cited by the *Oxford English Dictionary* is the following: "An assemblage of (two or more) figures or objects forming in combination either a complete design, or a distinct portion of a design." The artistic senses of the word "group" emerged earliest in English, appearing toward the end of the seventeenth century. *The Compact Edition of the Oxford English Dictionary*, 2 vols. (Oxford: Oxford University Press, 1971), 1: 459.

[51] "Entraría como término de las bellas artes, hablando de grupos pictóricos y escultóricos, y después se generalizó." Coromines and Pascual, 3: 228.

[52] "[D]as *wort stammt aus der bildenden kunst*: 'groupe *wird in der mahlerey eine versammlung vielerhand leiber nahe an einander genennet, als etwan von tieren oder früchten; also ist der Laokoon eine zusammengesetzte* groupe *oder* groppo *von drey schönen figuren*' (Marperger, *kaufmannmagazin* (1708)." Jacob and Wilhelm Grimm, ed., *Deutsches Wörterbuch*, 33 vols., Vol. 9 (Leipzig, Verlag von S. Hirzel, 1935), 969.

[53] The word *grupp* is first recorded in Swedish in the late eighteenth century. Svenska Akademien, *Ordbok över Svenska Språket*, 33 vols, Vol. 10 (Lund: Lindstedts Univ. Bokhandel, 1929), 1057.

The word группа first occurs in Russian in the eighteenth century, later passing into Ukrainian and other Eastern European languages. See Jaroslav B. Rudyckyj, *An Etymological Dictionary of the Ukrainian Language* (Winnipeg, Ukrainian Free Academy of Sciences, 1962–), I, 8, 746.

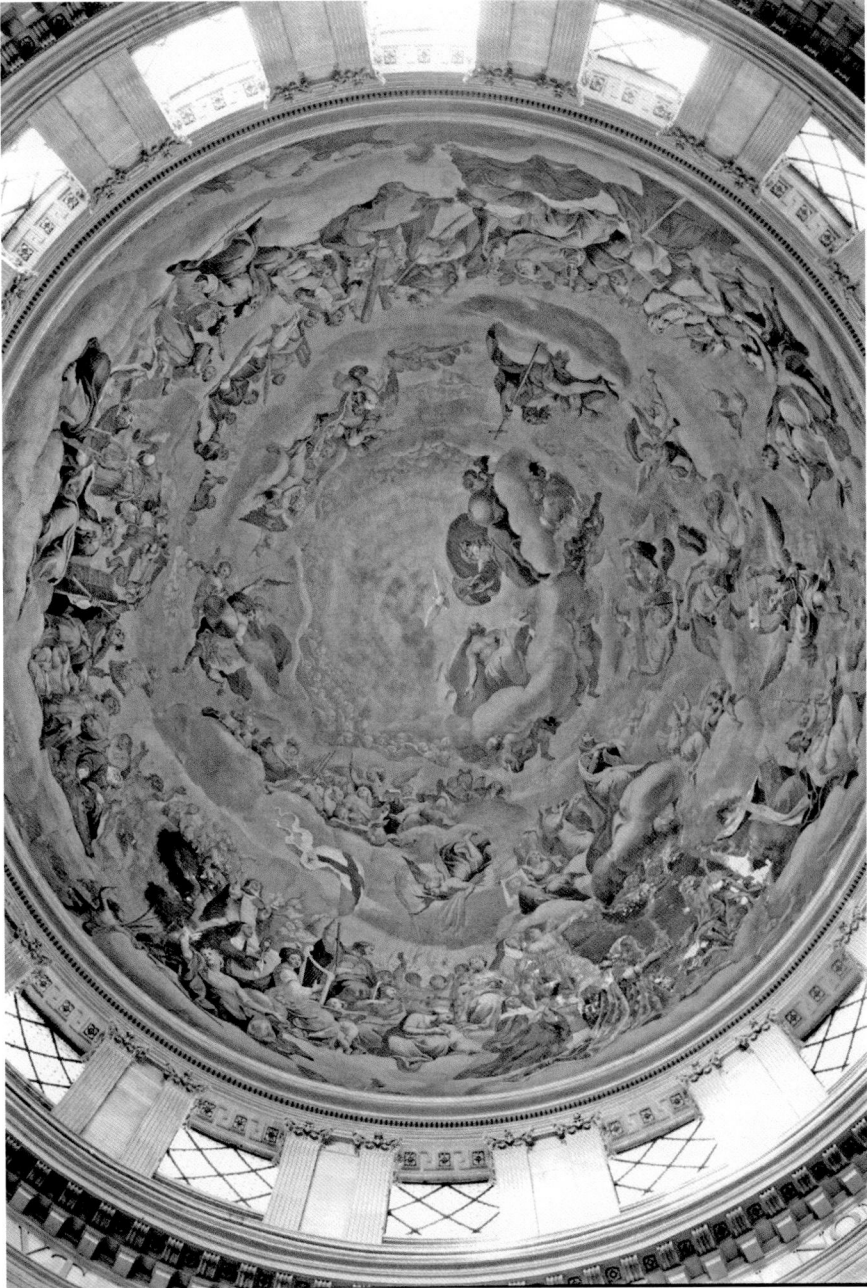

1.10. Pierre Mignard, cupola, Church of the Val-de-Grâce, fresco, 1662–1666, Paris.
Photo credit: Scala/White Images/Art Resource, New York. Molière introduces the
word *groupe* to the French language in his discussion of his friend's painting.

The word and concept of the group is such a familiar one today that it is difficult to imagine how and why it evolved from its multiple precursor metaphors (i.e., the mass, the knot, the tangle, the enigma or difficulty, the gust of wind, the erotic tie, the cluster or bunch, the musical composition, or the work of art) into our social understanding of this unique term. Today's word *group* is a pale version of its former self. Like Nietzsche's "coins which have lost their pictures and now matter only as metal, no longer as coins" (the philosopher's simile for dead metaphors),[54] most of its earlier stamp has been worn away. To study its evolution defamiliarizes not only the word itself but also the ideas connected to it. Why did the group, a new word and concept, emerge in the Renaissance? Was this an arbitrary or accidental mutation of language, or was it perhaps a more purposive development, a reflection of social change or cultural evolution? Arguably the many concepts of the knot that had developed since medieval times lent themselves to further elaboration, especially to describe rapidly evolving networks of associations – human or otherwise. The group, we must remember, is a metaphor for the associative itself.

The *Laocoön*: Visual and Verbal Metaphor of the Group

As we have observed, the notion of the differential relation of the individual to the collective can be traced in the evolution of the early modern word *gruppo*. The transition from undifferentiated knot to the relational artistic grouping began to emerge during the century and a half separating Petrarch from Leonardo. The idea of the group as a work of art would continue to evolve over the next two centuries. By the eighteenth century, this new aesthetic concept of the group would thoroughly penetrate the languages and epistemes of other European nations and beyond. This linguistic and conceptual shift was in part catalyzed by the recovery of the *Laocoön* – not just any old statue, but a powerful visual metaphor in which the various senses of *gruppo* were condensed: knot, tangle, enigma, cluster, connected figures, artistic composition. How was the statue put together, literally and figuratively? Was it made from one stone or many? How did its creators sculpt the statue? What did the group and its parts mean? Which stories did it suggest to its viewers?

In June of 1506, six months after the *Laocoön* was recovered, a man named Cesare Trivulzio described the archaeological discovery in a letter to his

---

[54] *On Truth and Lie in the Extra-Moral Sense*, in *The Portable Nietzsche*, trans. Walter Kaufmann (New York: Viking, 1967), 47.

brother, quoting the crucial passage from Pliny that describes the statue and its makers:

> I believe you will have heard how a few months ago the statue of Laocoön with his two sons was found here in Rome, among the ruins of the palace of the Emperor Titus, which Pliny describes . . . with these words: *"The reputation of some, distinguished though their work may be, has been obscured by the number of artists engaged with them on a single task, because no individual monopolizes the credit nor again can several of them be named on equal terms. This is the case with the Laocoön in the palace of Titus, a work superior to any painting and any bronze. Laocoön, his children, and the wonderful clasping coils of the snakes* [liberos draconumque mirabilis nexus] *were carved from a single block in accordance with an agreed plan by those eminent craftsmen Hagesander, Polydorus, and Athenodorus, all of Rhodes."*[55]

Pliny had claimed in his *Natural History* that the *Laocoön* had been carved from one stone (*ex uno lapide*), which, had it been true, would have been a spectacular sculptural accomplishment.[56] Artists who examined the statue, including Michelangelo and Giancristoforo Romano, soon disputed Pliny's claim, however. They perceived that the group consisted not of one single piece of marble but several; however, the jointures were so well hidden that it was difficult to see them.

Regarding the actual construction of this group, Trivulzio writes,

> [These sculptors] say that Pliny was deceived, or that he intended to deceive others, in order to make the statue even more admirable. That is because they could not carve three statues of this size, with so many intertwinings of snakes [*gruppi di serpenti*], so amazing to behold, from one piece of marble and have them hold together without additional supports.[57]

---

[55]   Io credo che avrete inteso come a' mesi passati è stata trovata qui in Roma, tra le rovine della casa dell'Imperator Tito, la statua di Laocoonte co' due suoi figliuoli; della quale fa menzione Plinio . . . con queste parole: *Deinde multorum obscurior fama est, quorundam claritati in operibus eximiis obstante artificum numero; quoniam nec unus occupat gloriam, nec plures pariter nuncupari possint, sicut in Laocoonte, qui est in Titi Imperatoris domo, opus omnibus picturae, et statuariae artis praeferendum: ex uno lapide eum et liberos draconumque mirabilis nexus de consilii sententia fecere summi artifices Agesander, Polydorus et Athenodorus Rhodii.*

In Bottari, *Raccolta di lettere sulla pittura, scultura,* 3: 474; Maffei, 108.

I have drawn the translation of Pliny from his *Natural History* 36, iv, ll. 37–38, 10: 29, 31. The Latin text in this edition reveals numerous corruptions or variations in Trivulzio's text of Pliny: for example, "nec deinde multo plurium fama est" and "mirabiles nexus" (28).

[56] As Leonard Barkan explains, "The object itself is the most complexly articulated of ancient statues; hence [Pliny's] notion that it is constructed out of a single piece of stone amounts to an assertion of almost magical status." *Unearthing the Past,* 5.

[57] "[D]icono che Plinio s'ingannò, o volle ingannare altri, per render l'opera più ammirabile. Poiché non si potevano tener salde tre statue di statura giusta, collegata in un sol marmo, con tanti e tanto mirabili gruppi di serpenti, con nessuna sorta di stromenti." Bottari, 475; Maffei, 108.

Here Trivulzio explores two of the enigmas concerning this statue: its identity and its composition. In one crucial respect, the classical description did not match the recovered artifact (agonistically pointed out by Michelangelo and other sculptors) – namely, the manner of its construction. Trivulzio eagerly confirms that this was indeed the same statue described by Pliny; to do so, however, he has to argue that the historian misrepresented the *Laocoön* – accidentally or on purpose – as having been carved from one piece of marble.[58]

In exploring this enigma of identity, Trivulzio also raises several conceptual problems about the construction of the piece: the relation of individual parts to the whole – hence, of the individual figures to the group – and also the relation of the sculpture to its three separate but collaborating creators. These questions had implications far larger than the *Laocoön* and its intriguing history. Among other things, the recovered *Laocoön* provided a visual metaphor for the evolving concepts of groups and of group identity in the Renaissance: the statue represents an aesthetic arrangement of figures circumscribed by a knot. Trivulzio's account is the first to employ the word *gruppo* to describe the *Laocoön*, although he uses the word in its earlier, medieval sense (i.e., a knot or tangle) as a translation of Pliny's term *nexus*.[59] These visual and verbal knots might have anticipated or helped to solidify the concept of the group in its emergent compositional sense. Only in the eighteenth century, however, would it become common to describe the *Laocoön* itself as a *gruppo* – that is, an arrangement of figures in space, a sculptural composition.

The Pain of the Group

Other contemporaries reflected on various aspects of the statue's knots, actual and implied – for example, its history, composition, realism, and raw emotion. In perhaps the most famous *Laocoön* poem, composed in Latin shortly after the excavation, the humanist Jacopo Sadoleto described the physical and emotional suffering represented by the artists:

---

[58] There is, of course, another possibility, which is that Pliny saw an earlier version of the statue. Brilliant, 68.

[59] Trivulzio's choice of words, "tanti e tanto mirabili gruppi di serpenti," echoes the phrase "*liberos draconumque mirabiles nexus*," which earlier in his letter he quotes from Pliny – *gruppi* being a translation of the Latin word *nexus*.

Early to mid–sixteenth-century commentators on the *Laocoön* did not use the word "gruppo" or "groppo" to describe the statue as a multifigured sculptural composition, as far as I can determine. The word in that sense would achieve wider currency during the Baroque era and eighteenth century, frequently in reference to the *Laocoön*.

Two gleaming snakes cover a vast space with their gathered coils, and
move in sinuous rings, and hold three bodies bound in a many-twisted
knot (*ternaque multiplici constringunt corpora nexu*). Eyes scarce can bear to
behold the cruel death and fierce sufferings. One gleaming [snake] seeks
Laacoon himself, winding him all about, above, below, and attacks his
groins at last with poisonous bite. The imprisoned body recoils, and you
see the limbs writhe and the side shrink back from the wound. Forced by
the sharp pain and bitter anguish, he groans; and, trying to tear out the
cruel teeth, throws his left hand upon the serpent's back. The nerves strain,
and the whole body in vain collects its strength for the supreme effort. He
cannot endure the fierce torture, and pants from the wound.[60]

The violence of the representation – horrifying yet compelling – emerges
in Sadoleto's ekphrastic description. Pain binds the figures together in "a
many-twisted knot." It also binds the viewers to the spectacle: "We see the
movement, the wrath and pain, and almost hear the groans," Sadoleto says
of the statue's intense realism.[61] His poem also shows us what we do not
actually see but what we might imagine with his help – for example, how
"the vitals grow tumid from the stopping of the pulses, and black blood
distends the livid veins."[62]

---

[60]
       ternaque multiplici constringunt corpora nexu.
       Vix oculi sufferre valent crudele tuendo
       exitium, casusque feros: micat alter et ipsum
       Laocoonta petit, totumque infraque supraque
       implicat et rabido tandem ferit ilia morsu.
       Connexum refugit corpus torquentia sese
       membra, latusque retro sinuatum a vulnere cernas.
       Ille dolore acri et laniatu impulsus acerbo,
       dat gemitum ingentem, crudosque evellere dentes
       connixus, laevam impatiens ad terga Chelidri
       obiicit: intendunt nervi, collectaque ab omni
       corpore vis frustra summis conatibus instat.
       Ferre nequit rabiem et de vulnere murmur anhelum est.

"De Laocoontis statua Jacobi Sadoleti Carmen," in Maffei, 118, 120.

    The modern prose translation that I cite appears in Gotthold Ephraim Lessing, *Laocoön: An Essay
upon the Limits of Painting and Poetry*, 209. This edition also includes the Latin text of Sadoleto's
poem, printed in full in Lessing's original essay.

[61] Lessing, 209. "aspicimus motumque iramque doloremque,/ et paene audimus gemitus. . . . Maffei,
120.

[62] Lessing, 209. "obsaepto turgent vitalia pulsu,/ liventesque atro distendunt sanguine venas." Maffei,
120.

    As Leonard Barkan explains, "Ekphrases are categorically different from the works of art they
supposedly describe; indeed, the poetic description of an imaginary sculpted Laocoön would
doubtless not resemble the statue in Rome any more than Virgil's narrative does. Yet this fabric of
texts tantalizes readers with the possibility that, together with the rediscovered works themselves,
it will reconstruct a complete visual antiquity." *Unearthing the Past*, 4–5.

Sadoleto describes the dire effects of this vicariously experienced pain on the viewer:

> With what part shall I begin as the greatest? the unhappy father and his two sons? the sinuous coils of the terrible serpents? the tails and the fierceness of the dragons? the wounds and real pains of the dying stone? These chill the mind with horror, and pity, mingled with no slight fear, drives our hearts back from the dumb image.[63]

For Sadoleto, the *Laocoön* represents the moments between life and death. The superlative art of the statue generates in the viewer the horror, pity, and fear,[64] while also perhaps inducing a shared form of embodied cognition relating to the experience of physical pain.[65] This empathy-inducing quality forges a bond between the sculptural group and the viewers, and the circle of the group expands to incorporate the witnesses in its pain.[66]

    Viewers' vicarious experience of suffering also binds them to the original artists and to classical antiquity itself: "Illustrious Rhodes begot you of old.

---

[63] Lessing, 209.

> Quid primum summumve loquar? Miserumne parentem
> et prolem geminam? An sinuatos flexibus angues
> terribili aspectu? caudasque irasque draconum
> vulneraque et veros, saxo moriente, dolores?
> Horret ad haec animus, mutaque ab imagine pulsat
> pectora non parvo pietas commixta tremori.

Maffei, 118.

[64] Sadoleto's notion of vicarious suffering uncannily anticipates Aristotle's theory of tragedy as outlined in the *Poetics*, soon to be recovered and widely reprinted in the mid-sixteenth century. Aristotle's concept of catharsis as a vicarious, strangely pleasurable experience of pity and fear, fits in well with a Renaissance aesthetic already in place at the time of the recovery.

[65] Recent research on the human Mirror Neuron System shows that when we witness the emotions and feelings of others, we do not imagine them but in some sense actually *have* them – a milder version, in general. See, for example, Rizzolatti, Sinigaglia, and Anderson, *Mirrors in the Brain*, and Gallese's essays "Before and Below Theory of Mind," "Embodied Simulation: From Neurons to Phenomenal Experience," and "The 'Shared Manifold' Hypothesis."

    These recent discoveries of the embodied nature of perception could in fact explain the impact of recovered classical statuary on Renaissance group identity in an entirely new way, as I discuss in the conclusion to this book. The renewed awareness of the body and its physical and emotional states – an awareness that we associate with Renaissance art and culture – would in such an account owe its existence to a shared set of embodied perceptions, such as those described by Sadoleto, radiating outward through new instantiations in various media, and gathering ever more people into a large group creatively energized by those embodied perceptions.

[66] Several early-modern commentators on the *Laocoön* attempted to derive a moral lesson from the statue, arguing that the viewer should not only empathize with the suffering represented but also *emulate* it. Ettlinger has noted that, "The history of the transformations of the *Laocoön* after its rediscovery is a long one which leads to many and often remote subjects. But some of them are direct and modern renderings of the old theme of suffering in stoic silence. That is why theologians during the Counter Reformation could recommend the *Laocoön* to those who had to make images of the Passion of Christ, of suffering saints and martyrs." "*Exemplum Doloris*," 126.

Long the glories of your art lay hid, but Rome beholds them again in a second
dawn, and celebrates them with many voices, in fresh acknowledgment of
the old labor."[67] For Sadoleto, as for numerous others, the *Laocoön* was
literally and figuratively a pathos-laden knot connecting the present to the
past and uniting the living and the dead through art. That imagined bond
with Troy, with Rhodes, and with the past was not a fully reassuring one. The
deaths of Laocoön and his sons, and the traumatic extinction of a family line,
represented by the statue, raised the question of the survival of the group – the
Trojans of ancient times, as well as the Romans, who considered themselves
their historical and cultural descendants.[68] The recovered *Laocoön* tapped
into some deeply felt anxieties about Roman group identity, its real and
imagined vulnerabilities, and its desires.

It is not a coincidence that a large number of Latin poems and epigrams
written about the *Laocoön* in the sixteenth century focus on the *nexus* or
nodi of snakes encircling the figures,[69] for these knots were not only visual
focal points but also conceptual ones. The most celebrated archaeological
find of the Renaissance, the *Laocoön* functioned as a metaphor for one of the
powerful transformations of European group consciousness then under way.
One well-known aspect of this transformation (and there were many others,
as we shall see) was the collective aspiration to revive, to reanimate, and to
re-embody the classical past. Discussions of the *Laocoön* gave voice to certain
shared anxieties about the annihilating but revivifying processes of cultural
transformation. This was a group enterprise more than an individual one, a
shared identification with dying heroes – or, more specifically, the masculine
bodies of dying heroes, which Sadoleto invites his readers to inhabit for a
time as their own.

Sadoleto's poem, along with many others about the famous statue, reveals
an important aspect of group organization. As the psychoanalyst and large-
group theorist Vamik Volkan has shown, national, ethnic, and religious
groups organize around their shared mental representations of historical

---

[67]Lessing, 209.
    The Latin reads:

> "vos extulit olim
> clara Rhodos, vestrae iacuerunt artis honores
> tempore ab immenso, quos rursum in luce secunda
> Roma videt, celebratque frequens: operisque vetusti
> gratia parta recens." Maffei, 120.

[68]This important insight was suggested to me by Professor Eugene Vance of the University of
    Washington, in response to a talk on which this chapter is based.

[69]On the recurrent use of the works *nexus* and *nodi*, see the poems and epigrams anthologized in
    Maffei, "Poesia: Roma e altro," in "La fama di Laocoonte nei testi del Cinquecento," 117–150.

events. For example, a heroic battle can induce a sense of triumph in the group, serving as its "chosen glory"; alternatively, a calamity befalling a group's ancestors can serve as the group's "chosen trauma."[70] Interestingly, a similar organizing fantasy plays out in Sadoleto's poem. By proposing a collective identification with the represented pain of Laocoön and his sons, linked to the tragic destruction of Troy, Sadoleto helped to reactivate a partly latent but available group identity: Romans, as heirs and descendants of ancient Troy. By the end of the poem, the pain of Laocoön and his sons – here represented as the chosen trauma – is transformed by the poet, becoming a chosen glory. Of the recovery of the statue group, Sadoleto effuses, "Rome beholds them again in a second dawn."[71] Death and rebirth – central motifs of the era – emerge in Sadoleto's poem as powerful fantasies of the newly reconstituted group. Sadoleto's was not the only version of such fantasies of vulnerability, death, and recovery provided by the *Laocoön*. These fantasies could be positively or negatively inflected, or often both at once.

The classical image of suffering evoked by the *Laocoön* could also be put to the service of an explicitly Christian agenda, thereby serving the interests of a somewhat different group of ancient Rome's heirs. Giovanni Andrea Gilio da Fabriano, Canon of San Venanzo, suggested in his *Due dialogi* (1564) that the *Laocoön* could serve as a model for artistic depictions of Christian martyrs. Helping to define a Counter-Reformation aesthetic for religious art, Gilio supported the idea of graphic representations of suffering and torment when religious instruction and inspiration were at stake, arguing that devotional painters of his day could learn much from their classical forebears:

> If ancient paintings could be found, many more secrets of the art could be seen in them that are not seen today; however, from statues we can extract a clear lesson about the skill of the ancient painters and sculptors – skill which each of you might have seen in Rome in many statues and especially in the *Laocoön* of the Belvedere. For Laocoön, so knotted up by the serpents (*così annodato dai serpenti*), shows, along with his sons, the anguish, the pain, and torment that he felt in that [mortal] act. Certainly it would be a new thing, and a beautiful one, to see a Christ on the cross so transformed by wounds, spittle, taunts, and blood; or Saint Blaise with

---

[70] Volkan presents example after example of how these collective memories and fantasies play out within ethnic groups: "Czechs hold on to the memory of the battle of Bila Hora in 1620 when the Czech nation became part of the Hapsburg monarchy and lost its freedom for nearly three hundred years. Scots keep alive the story of the battle of Colloden, precipitated by Bonnie Prince Charlie's vain attempt to restore a Stuart to the English crown in 1746. The Lakota people retain mental representation of the massacre of the Big Foot band at Wounded Knee in 1890." *Bloodlines*, 48–49.

[71] Lessing, 209.

his flesh torn off by iron combs; or Saint Sebastian so full of arrows that he looks like a porcupine; or Saint Lawrence on the grill – burned, seared, splitting apart, torn and disfigured.[72]

Like so many others of his day, Gilio was moved by the extraordinary depiction of pain conveyed by the *Laocoön*, which he and other commentators sought to translate into the Counter-Reformation tradition of religious artwork, in which bodily suffering would play an important meditative and inspirational function. Rather than simply identifying with the ancient groups connected to the statue and to the story it told, the Canon of San Venanzo highlighted the distinctions between groups – pagan versus Christian – and implicitly emphasized group rivalries and their comparative scenes of martyrdom. As Volkan's analyses of groups suggest, depictions of martyrdom, whether visual or verbal, can serve as powerful chosen traumas for both religious and ethnic groups.

The *Laocoön* remained a cultural touchstone for more than 300 years, as artists, critics, and philosophers continued to meditate on the meanings of that group and especially its representation of pain. From the time of its recovery until the eighteenth century, when the much-admired statue became a focus for the aesthetic philosophies of Winckelmann, Lessing, Herder, and Goethe, among others, the *Laocoön* remained a liminal image of evolving group consciousness at the threshold of modernity.[73] Like their predecessors, eighteenth-century commentators were fascinated by the paradox of beautiful pain. The brilliant antiquarian Ennio Quirino Visconti, cataloguer of the Museo Pio-Clementino at the Vatican (then recently founded), described the splendid beauty of the group in pain: "From this hardly moral fable there resulted the most perfect tragedy that sculpture had ever expressed. Thus one could call this group marvelous (*gruppo meraviglioso*), where a virtue that suffers so unjustly is represented in the most sublime manner that could be conceived."[74] For Visconti, the group had become not only a work of

---

[72] Maffei, 192–193. My translation, with improvements by Albert Ascoli.

[73] These three writers of the German classical age, like Sadoleto and countless others, were fascinated by the problem of pain represented by the *Laocoön*. See Johann Winckelmann's *Gedanken über die Nachahmung der griechischen Werke in der Malerei und Bildhauerkunst* (1755; trans. *Reflections on the Imitation of Greek Works in Painting and Sculpture*), as well as the *Geschichte der Kunst der Altertums* (1764; trans. *The History of Ancient Art*); Gotthold Ephraim Lessing, *Laokoon oder über die Grenzen der Malerei und Poesie* (1766; trans. *Laocoön: An Essay Upon the Limits of Painting and Poetry*); and Johann Wolfgang Goethe, "Über Laokoon" (1798; trans. *Upon the Laocoön*).

For treatments of these and other analyses of the *Laocoön*, see, for example, Bieber, *op. cit.*, and especially Richter, *Laocoön's Body*.

[74] "Da questa favola così poco morale è risultata la più perfetta tragedia che la scultura abbia espressa. Così può chiamare questo gruppo meraviglioso, dove la virtù che suffre ingiustamente

art, but also a marvel of sublime suffering. Significantly, he used the word *gruppo* to describe the composition itself, as well as its exquisite appeal, rather than the knots or tangles of the serpents.

In *The Expression of the Emotions in Man and Animals* (1872), even Charles Darwin commented briefly on the famous statue, noting that the contracted brow of Laocoön offered a realistic representation of human grief. Darwin observed that the ancient Greeks knew how to depict grief in their sculptures, as the facial expression of Laocoön clearly demonstrated.[75] The sculpture served for centuries as an *exemplum doloris*, an example or model of suffering.[76]

The Erotic Life of Groups

It was not only suffering that the *Laocoön* invited its viewers to contemplate but also eros. Pietro Aretino, noted libertine, satirist, and social critic, voiced his erotic fantasies for his Renaissance audience and for posterity, at least one of which was inspired partly by the *Laocoön*. In his 1534 *Ragionamento della Nanna e della Antonia*, an imagined dialogue between two courtesans, Nanna describes an orgy that she had witnessed at the convent that she had joined as a young woman. One erotic group in Nanna's convent included a bishop ("il generale"), four nuns, and three young friars. At a certain point in the festivities, she recounts, the bishop passionately fondled a young woman and a young man at the same time; in so doing, he "wore that

---

si è rappresentata nella più sublime guisa che mai potesse idearsi." Visconti, *Statue del Museo Pio-Clementino*, 2: 73.

[75] "The grief-muscles are not very frequently brought into play; and as the action is often momentary, it easily escapes observation. Although the expression, when observed, is universally and instantly recognized as that of grief or anxiety, yet not one person out of a thousand who has never studied the subject, is able to say precisely what change passes over the sufferer's face. . . .

The ancient Greek sculptors were familiar with the expression, as shown in the statues of the Laocoön and Arretino; but, as Duchenne remarks, they carried the transverse furrows across the whole breadth of the forehead, and thus committed a great anatomical mistake: this is likewise the case in some modern statues. It is, however, more probable that these wonderfully accurate observers intentionally sacrificed truth for the sake of beauty, than that they made a mistake; for rectangular furrows on the forehead would not have had a grand appearance on the marble. The expression, in its fully developed condition, is, as far as I can discover, not often represented in pictures by the old masters, no doubt owing to the same cause; but a lady who is perfectly familiar with this expression, informs me that in Fra Angelico's 'Descent from the Cross,' in Florence, it is clearly exhibited in one of the figures on the right-hand; and I could add a few other instances." Charles Darwin, *The Expression of the Emotions in Man and Animals*, 184–185.

[76] The recent discovery of the human Mirror Neuron System in the brain has given a new scientific basis for the experience of empathy described by Sadoleto and so many others after him. See, for example, Rizzolatti and Sinigaglia, *op. cit.* (n. 65), and Freedberg and Gallese, "Motion, emotion and empathy in aesthetic experience."

frowning look the marble statue at the Vatican Museum gives the snakes that are strangling him between his sons."[77] Rather than interpreting Laocoön's facial expression as simply or primarily one of pain, Aretino joked about its erotic overtones. The three figures of the sculpture, encircled and bitten by the phallic serpents, seem to have inspired – at least partly – Aretino's fantasy of an orgiastic threesome (ultimately an eightsome, as Nanna tells it).

In this titillating fantasy that incorporated the *Laocoön*, Aretino imagined what his contemporaries either did not consciously perceive or chose not to articulate in writing: the erotic or sensual qualities of the famous sculpture, and specifically fantasies of penetration as transgressive pleasure. Instead, they chose to express admiration for the artists' sensitive and realistic portrayal of the human body, or to focus on the nobility and pathos of human suffering, or to contemplate various concepts of justice or injustice implied by the famous work of art. The erotic charge of the statue also might have registered as reactions of embarrassment or disgust, as suggested by a famous anecdote regarding Pope Adrian VI (1522–1523). Paolo Giovio reports that when the Bolognese ambassador came to visit the Vatican and stood before the *Laocoön*, singing the statue's praises, the Pope "quickly withdrew his gaze and denounced the statue as an idol of an impious people."[78]

Adrian was but one in a long line of popes and other religious authorities who expressed their disdain for pagan art and its parts. According to a legend reported by Andrea Fulvio, Gregory the Great (ca. 540–604) had "ordered that all the most beautiful statues . . . should be thrown into the Tiber so that men, captivated by their beauty, should not be led astray from a religion that was still fresh and recent."[79] Shortly after his election, Pope Pius V (1566–1572), a later Renaissance pope, announced that "it was not suitable for the successor of St. Peter to keep such idols at home."[80] Despite his pious

---

[77] Disse il generale: "Facciamo tutti un'otta; e tu, pinchellon mio, basciami; così tu colomba mia," e tenendo una mano nella scatola dell'angeletta e con l'altra facendo festa alle mele dell'angelone, basciando ora lui e ora lei, *facea quell viso arcigno che a Belvedere fa quella figura di marmo ai serpi che l'assassinano in mezzo dei suoi figli* [my italics]. Alla fine le suore del letto e i giovincelli e il generale e colei alla quale egli era sopra, colui il quale gli era dietro con quella dalla pestinaca muranese, s'accordaro di fare ad una voce come s'accordano i cantori o vero i fabbri martellando: e così, attento ognuno al compire, si udiva un "ahi, ahi," un "abbracciami," un "voltamiti," "la lingua dolce," "dàmmela," "tòtela," "spinge forte," "aspetta ch'io faccio," "oimè fa," "stringemi," "aitami". . . .

    Maffei, 201. Rosenthal, *Aretino's Dialogues*, 22.

[78] "[A]versis statim oculis tanquam impiae gentis simulachra vituperaret." Paolo Giovio, *Vita di Adriano VI*, quoted in Maffei, 183.

[79] *Antiquitates urbis* (Rome: 1527), fol. lxxxi recto, quoted in Haskell and Penny, *Taste and the Antique*, 14. Fulvio argued that the story about Gregory was in fact not true.

[80] Pastor, *History of the Popes from the Close of the Middle Ages*, 17: 111, n. 1, discussed in Haskell and Penny, 14–15.

crusade against erotic art and against the widespread practices of prostitution and sodomy in sixteenth-century Rome, Pius kept the collection essentially intact. In doing so, he greatly disappointed European art collectors, who were hoping to acquire the Belvedere antiquities. Pius did, however, forbid access to the statues, which had already been partly obscured by protective shutters, as if to regulate the fantasies and the activities of his fellow Romans and of visitors to the Holy City.[81]

The attitudes of the scandalous and the scandalized toward the *Laocoön* attest to the spectacle of eros presented by that sculptural group, and by the larger grouping of recovered classical statuary. As the art historians Francis Haskell and Nicholas Penny have argued, "we need not doubt that it was often the nudity, at least as much as the 'purity' and 'simplicity,' of many antique statues that came as a relief to readers of Ovid after the bleak austerity of Calvinism or the elaborate imagery of so much of the art of the Counter-Reformation."[82]

Aretino's dialogue, as well as the moral crusade of Pius V, suggests that the accelerated recovery of classical art and culture stimulated a new curiosity among many of those who came in contact with artifacts of those earlier cultures – an erotic curiosity about the body. In the eyes of Renaissance viewers, the *Laocoön* presented a very particular spectacle of the body: penetrated and dying, but also dying in the orgasmic sense. These dissonant themes of eros and thanatos were difficult to contain in any one representational response, or any single fantasy of the group and its imagined body. This avid curiosity prompted by the recovery of the famous sculpture and many other classical masterpieces was one powerful variable leading to new understandings of the human body and new configurations of the group.

Elective Affinities: Principles of the Group as a Work of Art

Underlying the Renaissance concept of the group as a work of art are four organizing principles: 1) the intentional, 2) the aesthetic, 3) the historical, and 4) the creative. These principles indicate a collective shift in awareness – a shift toward new combinatory possibilities, new nodes of interest and interaction that intensified during that age of emergent groupism.

---

[81] Haskell and Penny note, "[W]hen the Pope finally died in 1572 it became apparent that fears and hopes alike had been exaggerated: not a single statue considered to be of the highest excellence had left the city, and, shuttered off though its contents were, the [Belvedere] courtyard with its *Venuses* and its *Antinous* survived intact despite a campaign of unprecedented violence against courtesans and sodomites" (15).

[82] *Ibid.*, 14.

The compositional arrangement of individual components that constitute each group implies a certain intentionality behind that spatial arrangement of figures – especially that of the artist. This concept was not built into earlier notions of the collective, such as the tribe, the family, the throng, or the horde. In fact, it can be said to emerge in the new notion of the group in the Italian Renaissance. As a concept, the *gruppo* was no longer associated primarily with accidental knots, tangles, and snarls but with deliberately constructed dramatic plots, musical motifs, and artful arrangements of figures in space. People, like words, notes, and objects, could be rearranged, shaped, and combined artistically. Such intentional combinations also imply a certain freedom of action or license – artistic or otherwise. Over time, this notion of intentionality within the group as a work of art would assume its full social dimension, alongside other less premeditated or freely chosen relationship possibilities among humans. The group as a work of art, with its underlying notions of intentionality and choice, can be considered an example of what the sociologist Georg Simmel described as the nonconcentric patterns of group affiliation characteristic of the postmedieval world.[83]

The three figures of the *Laocoön*, the angels under the cloak of God in Michelangelo's *Creation of Adam* in the Sistine Chapel, Apollo and the nine Muses of Raphaels' *Mount Parnassus* fresco of the Stanza della Segnatura – each of these groups of individual figures was carefully constructed and arranged for aesthetic effect. One purpose of such groupings was to please and delight, although sometimes paradoxically through the representation of pain or violence. The aesthetic pleasure afforded by exquisite sculptures or paintings was not new to the early modern era. Nevertheless, the gradual overflow of the aesthetic into reconceptualized social collectives was in fact a startlingly new development. Previous notions of the multitude did not conventionally incorporate an aesthetic dimension, often quite the contrary. Again it must be emphasized that the Dutch, French, Spanish, German, and English cognates for *gruppo* first entered these languages as descriptors of aesthetic arrangements of figures in sculpture, painting, and music.

Together these two organizational principles, the intentional and the aesthetic, would entail a revolutionary rethinking of social combinations, according to which the collective was no longer defined by the usual categories of belonging – kinship, fealty to a sovereign, military ties, shared belief, or trade. The group as a work of art does not possess the arbitrary and sometimes chaotic organization implied by terms such as *multitude, throng,* or *heap.* Notably absent in the emerging concept of the *gruppo* was a clear

[83] *Conflict and the Web of Group-Affiliations*, 146 ff. See also the Introduction to this book, 19–24.

notion of hierarchy – a point to which I shall return later. Instead, the word and concept of *gruppo* were, in the primary early modern sense, a function of aesthetic choice or desire – especially the artist's desire to place the figures or objects in a particular relation to each other. The implied knot, the knot drawn from the previous history of the word, became an intentional entwining of limbs, lines of sight, diagonals, or imagined pathways of energy linking individual elements into a unified composition – similar to the knotted serpents of the *Laocoön* group.

The temporal axis implicit in the examples of the *groppo* or *gruppo* analyzed previously must not be neglected in favor of the spatial – that is, the organization of forms or figures in space – because sculptures and paintings not only have a compositional history but also can *represent* a history, thereby evoking possible connections to a real or mythic past. This diachronic and also narrative element of Renaissance art and of Renaissance appropriations of classical works must be emphasized. Medieval art, too, self-consciously engages and reanimates a larger history, and so the diachronic dimension of the group as a work of art is not exclusively a Renaissance phenomenon, although its forms differ in some key respects. Notable among these would be the Renaissance representation of history, religion, mythology, and other narratives through comparatively more detailed depictions of embodied experience that in turn helped to reconfigure social identities. This change occurred in part through the word/concept of the *gruppo*, which would attach to and reshape the group envelope, the collective concept of the group's body.

The group as a work of art extended backward through time to connect present and past, the living and the dead. This was perhaps the privileged fantasy of Italian Renaissance culture, and a powerful myth of origin with classical and Christian variants (e.g., Apollo and the nine Muses; God, Eve, and the angels). Although it is probably true that every culture has its myths of collective origins, the innovation of the Renaissance was the addition of a new word and concept – *gruppo* – that literally named a shift in consciousness, and a gradual revolutionizing of collective identities that accompanied it.

Creativity, perhaps the most significant of the four organizing principles of the group as a work of art, pertains to the Renaissance makers of culture, rather than to their products. As the psychologist Mihaly Csikszentmihalyi has noted, "Because we are used to thinking that creativity begins and ends with the person, it is easy to miss the fact that the greatest spur to it may come from changes outside the individual."[84] As we continue to move away from individualist accounts of the Renaissance and its luminaries toward

[84] *Creativity*, 31.

a collectivist understanding of that age of transformations, more global in scope, we must contemplate the dynamic interactions of groups – for example, the collective outpouring of creativity directed toward the aesthetic transformation of public spaces: churches, libraries, gardens, museums, cities, and even entire countries.

Csikszentmihalyi analyzes the transindividual factors that led to the creative surge resulting in the transformation of Florence, "a new Athens," at the beginning of the fifteenth century. This transformation was marked especially by Brunelleschi's spectacular engineering feat of building a dome over the open apse of Santa Maria del Fiore, the city's cathedral. It was not only artists and architects like Brunelleschi who contributed their talents to the remaking of that city but also Florence's leading families, its bankers, churchmen, heads of guilds, and general citizenry, all of whom contributed their wealth, vision, encouragement, enthusiasm, and ambition to the goal of group transformation. Similar renaissances were undertaken in Rome, Antwerp, and many other cities in Europe and in other parts of the world, on large scales as well as small. These alterations of public space and culture resulted from the creative rivalries, collaborations, exchanges, mutual inspirations, and attachments to the well-being of the collective, and not simply the individual quest for fame and recognition.

To return to the principal group discussed in this chapter – the *Laocoön* – we can trace the effects of the discovery of an ancient piece of statuary, a catalyst emerging from outside the individual and the collective, that contributed to a shift in embodied group consciousness already under way. The discovery of the *Laocoön*, part of a larger obsession with the recovery of the Greco-Roman past and one of the greatest fulfillments of that desire, led to a statue collection and courtyard to contain it. More importantly, the discovery gave rise to hundreds of artistic responses in painting, sculpture, poetry, and fiction – that is, to a group's awareness of itself as a group, directing its creative energies toward the shared wish of reincorporating the past in order to reimagine and transform the present. "[C]reativity must, in the last analysis, be seen not as something happening within a person but in the relationships within a system," Csikszentmihalyi astutely observes.[85] A group comes alive to itself when its myriad relationships are activated toward constructive, collaborative, and creative ends. Such was the most positive manifestation of the Renaissance.

Because new words continually come into being, mutate, evolve, and then sometimes become obsolete, we must ask how much significance should be

---

[85] *Ibid.*, 36.

attached to the emergence of *gruppo* as word and concept. For example, can we assume from this new coinage that there was a concomitant reconfiguration of social relations? Indeed we must, although not simply because a fresh word and implicitly a fresh way to imagine collectives and collections moved across Europe and ultimately the world, radiating outward from Italy. If we accept, however provisionally, Burckhardt's thesis that a fundamental shift in consciousness took place at the end of the Middle Ages – a shift tied to the so-called rise of the individual in Italy – then it is reasonable to surmise that a shift in group consciousness must also have taken place.

There is still much to say about how and why this shift occurred. By analyzing the group as a work of art – in effect, a group that refuses to disclose its hierarchies, its active principles of power circulating within and among its members or components – one runs the risk of sublimating or ignoring the violence of the upheavals in Renaissance identities, both individual and collective. It is therefore worth keeping in mind Walter Benjamin's famous maxim: "There is no document of civilization which is not at the same time a document of barbarism."[86] Rather than aestheticizing violence to minimize or sublimate its impact – an identifiable tendency within Burckhardt's *Civilization of the Renaissance in Italy* and in many subsequent histories of the Renaissance – it is crucial to explore their interrelation. The chapters that follow begin to trace those connections.

A fifth organizing principle of the group as a work of art might also be added here (in addition to the intentional, the aesthetic, the historical, and the creative). This fifth principle is the *compensatory*. The stabilizing power of the group metaphor that this author has described perhaps marked the intense anxiety of an era of unprecedented and accelerating social change. The tearing apart and reweaving of the social fabric as a result of the Reformation and Counter-Reformation, the Wars of Religion, the rise of long-distance maritime colonies (fueled by chattel slavery and resource-appropriation), the decline of feudalism and emergence of capitalism, the many other developments and reorganizations that were global in nature, and the massive influx of information from other parts of the world – information *about* other groups and their own modes of embodiment – helped to generate the compensatory fantasy of control, beauty, and organization, or the group as a work of art.

On that memorable January evening in 1506, the small crowd that had assembled in Felice de' Freddi's vineyard and then beneath it witnessed the emergence not of the individual, but of the Renaissance group. Knot, tangle,

---

[86]"Theses on the Philosophy of History," in *Illuminations*, 256.

enigma, collective, and artistic composition, the *Laocoön* gathered into itself, as if by magic, the paradoxes of its age. Frozen in a moment between living and dying, between the present and remote antiquity, the *Laocoön* embodied possibilities still undreamt, perplexing and liminal, in the serpentine bonds connecting one individual to another.

2

OF CANNIBALS AND CARAÍBAS:
THE NEW WORLD AND LARGE-GROUP
TRANSFORMATIONS
VISEU, 1506

[T]he people on the previous islands were very afraid of the Carib and some called them 'Caniba', but 'Carib' on Espanola . . . they must be a daring people for they roam these islands eating anyone they can capture.

> – Christopher Columbus, *Journal of the First Voyage*

Let us return to our wild men of America, they bear great reverence to these Prophets, otherwise named *Pages* or *Charaïbes*, which is to say, half Gods.

> – Andre Thevet, *The New Found Worlde or Antarctike*

The group is a mouth.

> – Didier Anzieu, *The Group and the Unconscious*

The *Adoration of the Magi*

SOMETIME DURING THE YEAR 1506, THE PORTUGUESE PAINTER KNOWN as Grão Vasco and other members of his workshop completed a large altarpiece for the Cathedral of Viseu, a city in north-central Portugal.[1] The retable consisted of eighteen painted panels, sixteen of which remain in existence today. Among the panels attributed to Vasco is the *Adoração dos Magos*, or *Adoration of the Magi* (Figure 2.1), a painting noted for its original iconography. In that painting, one of the three Magi is depicted as a Brazilian

---

[1] 1506 is the presumed date of completion of the altarpiece, for on May 7th of that year, Vasco Fernandes, more commonly known as Grão Vasco, accepted another commission to paint an altarpiece for the Cathedral at Lamego, where he lived from 1506 until 1511. Rodrigues, "Vasco Fernandes, Esboço Biográfico," 78.

According to Dalila Rodrigues and others, Vasco painted the retable with a partner, Francisco Henriques. See also Palla, *Traje e Pintura*, 25; and Rodrigues, *Grão Vasco*, 210.

2.1. *Adoration of the Magi*, Studio of Grão Vasco (1501–1506), oil on wood, 131 cm. × 81 cm. Museo de Grão Vasco; Viseu, Portugal. Divisão de Documentação Fotográfica – Instituto dos Museus e da Conservação, I.P. Photo: José Pessoa, 1999. (See color plate.)

Indian. The panel is thought to present the first image of an American native in a European painting.[2]

The New World Magus appears in a feathered headdress and collar, gold bracelets, a shirt and doublet, tasseled short pants, and sandals. In his left hand he bears a gift: a silver-mounted vessel made from a coconut shell, which contains raw gold. In his right, he carries a long arrow. The feathered crown, collar, and arrow in Vasco's painting identify the central figure as a New World native, probably a Tupinambá Indian of coastal Brazil.[3]

In 1500, a Portuguese expedition led by Pedro Álvares Cabral had reached the Brazilian mainland.[4] Pêro Vaz de Caminha, a member of that expedition, wrote a letter to King Manuel I of Portugal, documenting their encounters with native peoples and describing the gift of a headdress of parrot feathers and collar of shells presented to Manuel by their hosts.[5] In addition to these and other gifts described by Caminha, one ship from Cabral's group may have also brought Brazilian natives back to Europe.[6] From the earliest voyages of Columbus, large numbers of natives of the Caribbean and the continents were transported back to Europe, principally as slaves.[7] The Italian cosmographer Amerigo Vespucci stated that his group returned from their

---

[2] From the end of the previous century, artists had often depicted one of the three kings as an African or Moor (Palla, 53). Rodrigues argues that the Tupinambá Magus occupies the place traditionally reserved for the African Magus, Balthasar. *Grão Vasco*, 91. Some have suggested, however, that the third king in the painting is of African descent. See Fernández-Armesto, *Amerigo*, 165.

On the novelty of the painting's iconography, see Bettencourt Pires, "A América no Imaginário Europeu," 427.

[3] Dalila Rodrigues, José Teixeira, and Ronald Raminelli, among others, identify the native figure as a Tupinambá Indian. See *Grão Vasco e a Pintura Europeia do Renascimento*, 91; "Adoration of the Magi," 152; and *Imagens da Colonização*, 152.

[4] The first landfall of the Portuguese on the southern continent took place on April 22, 1500, near the harbor of Porto Seguro.

[5] "E um deles lhe deu um sombreiro de penas de aves, compridas, com uma copazinha pequena de penas vermelhas e pardas, come de papagaio. E outro lhe deu um ramal grande de continhas brancas, miúdas, que querem parecer de aljaveira, as quais peças creio que o capitão manda a Vossa Alteza." "A Carta de Pêro Vaz de Caminha," 115. Noted by Faria, "Brasil: visões europeias da América Lusitana," 72.

On the history of this letter, and the possibility of earlier Portuguese voyages to the coast of South America, see Dias, "Brazil's Birth Certificate," 10–15.

[6] Cabral's fleet traveled on to India from Brazil, but one ship returned directly to Portugal, possibly with Tupí natives aboard.

[7] The enslavement and enforced prostitution of New World natives by Europeans was practiced from the first voyage of Columbus onward. Columbus reports the capture of natives in his letter to Ferdinand and Isabella, and also in his *Diario*, which would be transcribed and reworked by Bartolomé de las Casas and published much later. *Journal of the First Voyage*, 234–237.

On slavery as a motivating factor of Columbus's voyages, see Nicolás Wey Gómez' important new book, *The Tropics of Empire*, esp. Chapter 1, "Machina Mundi: The Moral Authority of Place in the Early Transatlantic Encounter," 61–106.

1497–1498 expedition to the New World with 222 slaves, who were sold in Spain on their return.[8] In 1501, Queen Isabella of Spain issued an edict licensing the enslavement and sale of Carib prisoners of war.[9]

Vasco's painting alludes to those first contacts between Europeans and American natives in several ways. The feathered Magus represents the New World in all of its perceived exoticism, incongruity, danger, and potential for exploitation or inclusion. Some art historians have suggested that the bearded figure kneeling in the right foreground is a portrait of Cabral himself, newly returned from the Americas.[10] The infant Jesus plays with a gold coin that the worshipper has given to him or that the infant offers his supplicant, possibly as a reward.[11]

This curious image of the Christ child with a coin evokes the motto of the Portuguese expansion since the time of Henry the Navigator: *Em nome de Deus e do lucro* (in the name of God and gold).[12] In a dreamlike fashion, the *Adoration of the Magi* condenses in a single, enigmatic representation a set of desires and fantasies engendered by the European discovery in 1500 of a new continent to the west: inclusion, assimilation, and financial and material gain, as well as the possession, domestication, and thrilling encounter with alterity itself, embodied in the native Magus. The panel also offers a fantasy of double birth, as Miguel Faria has perceptively noted: that of the Christ child and of the New World.[13]

Incorporation

As noted in the previous chapter, the recovery of an ancient sculpture, the *Laocoön*, helped to give rise to new artistic and cultural networks, to powerfully re-imagined bonds with artists and heroes of classical antiquity, and to a new aesthetic concept of the group itself. Vasco's *Adoration of the Magi* likewise presented an artistic *gruppo* – a small number of figures arranged in a carefully organized composition. Installed at Viseu in the very year that the *Laocoön* was pulled from Felice de' Freddi's vineyard, Vasco's painting

---

[8] "Letter to Piero Soderini," [also referred to below as the *Quattro viaggi*, or *Four Voyages*], in Luciano Formisano, ed., *Letters from a New World*, 76.

[9] Lestringant, *Cannibals*, 30, and Helminen, "¿Eran Canibales los Caribes?" See also n. 35.

[10] Faria, 72, and Teixeira, 153. Teixeira dates the painting to ca. 1501–1502. If this is indeed a portrait of Cabral, who would have been 35 at the time, the portrait appears to be age-advanced. Teixeira explains this as a function of Cabral's weathering activities as an explorer.

[11] Teixeira assumes the former – that is, that the coin has been presented by Cabral. *Ibid.*, 152.

[12] *Ibid.*, 152.

[13] Faria, 72. Birth, rebirth, resurrection: in various ways these themes recur as organizing fantasies within many varieties of groups as a means of imagining their origins.

offered other fantasies of the group as well – fantasies that would speak volumes to the world of the Renaissance. Among them was the fantasy of incorporation, of assimilating the stranger, the foreigner, the adversary, or newcomer into one's own group. An ancient and possibly universal fantasy – at times a utopian one – it would assume new forms and meanings in the age of nascent colonialism.

Vasco's painting reveals how individual figures within a small *gruppo*, such as the Magi and Holy Family, simultaneously could stand for larger groups – tribes, peoples, nations – allegorizing their interactions and power relations. The *Adoration* idealizes the colonial encounter between Portugal and the New World by depicting the peaceful incorporation of one or more ethnic groups into the Christian family. The painting also hints at large-group transformations under way at the beginning of the sixteenth century, when the modern world-system began to take shape. The Renaissance as it was once understood – namely, as a great leap forward in European cultural development – cannot be separated from its larger colonial matrices, as many historians and literary critics of the last several decades have argued, and also from a still larger network or world-system. Additionally, the perceived "rise of individualism" occurring in parts of Europe during the early modern age and first theorized by Burckhardt was itself a function of incorporative, large-group reorganizations that were taking place on the global stage.

To incorporate: the English verb and its cognates in French, Spanish, and other Romance languages derive from the postclassical Latin verb *incorporare*, and the noun *corpus*, "body." In its early modern and its contemporary senses, the verb *incorporate* signifies "to combine or unite into one body or uniform substance; to mix or blend thoroughly together (a number of different things or one thing *with* another)."[14]

The verb *incorporate* can also mean "to take or absorb into the body." Literally or figuratively, it can mean to make something one's own. The medieval Latin verb possessed strong ecclesiastical and Eucharistic connotations, as suggested by the author of the *Tractatus de sancta Eucharistia*: "Non igitur satis est nasci de Virgine Christum,/ Si suus esuriens homo non incorporet ipsum." ("It is not therefore enough that Christ was born of a virgin, if his hungry mankind did not incorporate him").[15] In this sense, one

[14]"Incorporate," *Oxford English Dictionary* 1: 1408.

[15]Cited in Ducange, *Glossarium mediae et infimae latinitatis* 4 (Graz, Austria: Akademische Druck-U. Verlagsanstalt, 1954), 333.

Encorporer appears in the late twelfth-century sermons of St. Bernard, meaning "to unite with the body of Christ." *Grande Larousse de la langue française*, 6 vols. (Paris: Librairie Larousse, 1973), 3: 2614.

The verb had passed from the Latin into the Spanish (*incorporar*) by 1386. "Cuerpo," in Coromines and Pasqual, *Diccionario crítico etimológico castellano e hispánico*, 2: 276.

incorporates by eating. Through the Eucharistic rite, communicants absorb Christ's substance into their own bodies.

This sense of the word would gradually be obscured by less overtly stomatic meanings. By the end of the Middle Ages, to incorporate would acquire new connotations, among them "to combine or form into a society or organization, *especially* to constitute as a legal corporation."[16] These economic and political connotations of the word had developed in English and the Romance languages by the fifteenth century, in conjunction with the rise of merchant capitalism; by the sixteenth, they also included the following: "To admit (a person) as member of a company or association; to receive or adopt into a corporation or body politic."[17]

Less commonly, the early modern verb could also mean "to furnish with a body; to give bodily shape to; to embody" or "to copulate."[18] In its various semantic contexts, the act of incorporation creates one from many, and by uniting or assimilating, neutralizes otherness or difference. As literary theorist Maggie Kilgour has explained, "The idea of incorporation . . . depends upon and enforces an absolute division between inside and outside; but in the act itself that opposition disappears, dissolving the structure it appears to produce."[19] Within groups, incorporation remains in some sense a fundamental and inevitable aim, as Didier Anzieu has suggested, because the creation of an imaginary body or envelope gives that which is *in-corporate*, or lacking a body, a sense of identity and wholeness.[20] A fundamental aspect of group identity formation in any era, the impulse to incorporate would become a veritable symptom of the large-scale conflicts of the Renaissance, a reaction formation to the crises of identity, both individual and collective, that resulted from the development of the modern world-system.

In a variety of senses, the desire to incorporate, together with the fear of incorporation by alien groups, propelled the colonizing process from its beginnings. These desires and fears were frequently expressed in oral terms – that is, with images and metaphors of eating or feeding on the one hand, and of being eaten on the other. The group, as Anzieu famously declared, is a mouth[21] – and never more openly, perhaps, than in the sixteenth century.

[16] *Oxford English Dictionary*, 1: 1408.

[17] *Ibid.*, 1: 1408.

[18] *Ibid.*, 1: 1408.

[19] See Kilgour's brilliant study of the concept of incorporation from Homer to Freud and Northrop Frye, *From Communion to Cannibalism*, 4, *et passim*. See, too, Dipesh Chakrabarty's *Provincializing Europe*, 97–113, which offers a related theory of incorporation from a post-colonial perspective.

[20] See Introduction, 25–27. For a related and highly useful perspective on this topic, see Turner, "Toward an Analysis of the Corporate Ego," 103–147.

[21] Following Freud, Melanie Klein, and others, Anzieu observed that oral fantasies inevitably circulate within groups, regardless of whether they are recognized as such. In his analysis, oral fantasies play a constitutive role in the formation of groups and emerge both as a means of expressing individual

From the time of the sixteenth-century historian Bartolomé de las Casas and the essayist Michel de Montaigne up to our own time, a vast amount of scholarship has been devoted to the European preoccupation with cannibals in the early modern age, along with Europe's "consumption" of the New World through its colonizing processes.[22] This chapter analyzes the complementary nature of such oral fantasies – of eating and of being eaten – within the writings of early explorers, missionaries, and travelers. Among these were Christopher Columbus and Amerigo Vespucci, who visited the New World in the late fifteenth and early sixteenth centuries; the French explorers André Thevet and Jean de Léry, who were associated with the short-lived Villegaignon colony founded in Brazil in the mid-sixteenth century; Hans Staden, the German traveler captured by Tupinambá cannibals at approximately the same time; and the Canarian Jesuit José de Anchieta, who sought to missionize Brazilian natives in the latter half of the sixteenth century.

This chapter also traces the powerful consolidating effects of these fantasies, which are recurrent topoi in colonial writings, on large-group identities in both Europe and the Americas. Whereas the previous chapter

---

and collective anxiety and of managing it. He argues, "The situation of the group in general, and of the free group in particular, provokes a regression to oral [pre-Oedipal] sadism, a correlative anxiety of loss of personal identity and a compensatory search for fusion with the imago of the good mother." *Group and the Unconscious*, 160.

[22] Fray Bartolomé de las Casas was one of the first to describe the "cannibalistic" behaviors of Europeans in the New World. As Jorge Cañizares-Esguerra notes, "it was the *encomienda* (the assignment of entire communities to serve a given conquistador) that Las Casas most detested, for it had sanctioned a form of institutionalized cannibalism in which all settlers were allowed to 'drink [the natives'] blood and eat their bodies.'" "The Devil in the New World," 27. Las Casas, *Historia de las Indias*, II: 1286, in Vol. 4 of *Obras completas*.

For a sampling of critical discussions of the early modern European preoccupation with cannibals, see, for example, O'Gorman, *The Invention of America* (1961); Lévi-Strauss, *The Savage Mind* ([1962] 1966); Galeano, *Open Veins of Latin America* (1973); Morison, *The European Discovery of America* (1971–1974); Arens, *The Man-Eating Myth* (1979); Todorov, *The Conquest of America* (1984); Palencia-Roth, "Cannibalism and the New Man of Latin America" (1985); de Certeau, *Heterologies* (1986); Hulme, *Colonial Encounters* (1986); Campbell, *The Witness and the Other World* (1988); Helminen, "¿Eran canibales los Caribes?" (1988); Greenblatt, *Learning to Curse* (1990); Combès, *La tragédie cannibale chez les anciens Tupi-Guarani* (1992); Grafton, *The Power of Tradition and the Shock of Discovery* (1992); Boucher, *Cannibal Encounters* (1992); Hulme and Whitehead, eds., *Wild Majesty: Encounters with Caribs from Columbus to the Present Day* (1992); Montrose, "The Work of Gender in the Discourse of Discovery" (1993); Zamora, *Reading Columbus* (1993); Rabasa, *Inventing A-M-E-R-I-C-A* (1993); Conley, *The Self-Made Map* (1996); Barker, Hulme, and Iversen, eds., *Cannibalism and the Colonial World* (1998); Guest, ed., *Eating Their Words: Cannibalism and the Boundaries of Cultural Identity* (2001); Llewelyn Price, *Consuming Passions* (2003); Cañizares-Esguerra, *Puritan Conquistadors* (2006); Bandiera, *Canibais no Paraíso* (2006); Lestrigant, *Cannibals* (op. cit.) and Kilgour, *From Communion to Cannibalism* (op. cit.).

identified a powerful new concept of small-group identity that arose at the end of the medieval period, this chapter explores the development and configuration of new large-group identities, some of them continental or transcontinental in scope. Investigating collective identity formation by a method both philological and psychoanalytic, this chapter examines certain oral metaphors and fantasies within the large-group incorporations of the sixteenth century and also studies their connections to the conceptual collapse or consolidation of smaller groups (e.g., linguistic, ethnic, religious, and cultural) into the progressively larger, racialized categories still in evidence today.

To analyze these early modern transformations in collective identities around the world, it is essential to consider the prevalent group concepts not only of sixteenth-century European peoples but also of other collectives around the world during that period. The second half of this chapter therefore investigates certain group concepts of New World natives, as well as they can be reconstructed, focusing on those of the Tupinambá natives of coastal Brazil. Also known as "cannibals," this group, and many other tribes of Central and South America, and the Caribbean, practiced ritual anthropophagy. Their group identities were defined largely by the practice of physically incorporating their enemies, or in some cultures, members of their own groups.[23] Within a few centuries of contact, the coastal Tupinambá and many other New World tribes would mostly disappear as a result of enslavement, genocide, disease, and creolization. Their displacement, vanishing, or merging with other groups is a testament to the ultimate dissolution of group identity. Despite their muted voices in that history, however, the Tupinambá cannibals were powerful catalysts, as well as objects, of group transformation. Quintessential emblems of the group as a mouth, their uncanny images proliferated in the sixteenth century, even, it would seem, on the altarpiece at Viseu.[24]

---

[23] The anthropologist Marvin Harris draws a distinction between warfare cannibalism, the consumption of one's enemies, and mortuary cannibalism, the consumption of the dead of one's own group. Mortuary cannibalism among some Native American tribes generally involved the consumption of ashes, powdered bones, or carbonized flesh. Harris considers it a phenomenon quite different from warfare cannibalism, on which the current chapter focuses. See *The Sacred Cow and the Abominable Pig*, 199–234.

[24] Although Rodrigues, Raminelli, and Teixeira identify the native Magus in Grão Vasco's painting as a Tupinambá native, to my knowledge, no one has drawn the further conclusion that the painter, almost certainly unwittingly, might have painted a cannibal into his adoration scene, or that later viewers might have made that association in any case. To identify the Magus as a cannibal could elide the fact that he has been, at least to some extent, integrated into the Christian group, however.

2.2. *Jar in the form of a woman or the Taíno Earth Mother Cahubaba.* Santiago Province;
Dominican Republic, Chicoid/Taíno (1200–1500 CE), ceramic, 15 × 9 × 18 cm.
Courtesy, National Museum of the American Indian, Smithsonian Institution, New
York (127442). Photo by Carmelo Guadagno.

The Renaissance of the Cannibal

When Columbus and his crew arrived at the densely populated islands of
the Caribbean, especially Cuba and Hispaniola, they encountered not one
but several primarily matrilineal societies with complex forms of social and
political organization, elaborate mythologies and religious practices, well-
developed agriculture, and distinctive traditions of arts and crafts (Figures 2.2
and 2.3).[25] Most of this group information was not readily apparent or
available to the Admiral, however, who essentially perceived the natives as
cultural blank slates. In his 1493 *Epistola de insulis nuper inventis* (Letter on the

[25]For a good introduction to Taíno art and culture, see Bercht et al., eds., *Taíno Pre-Columbian Art
and Culture from the Caribbean.*

2.3. *Mythological Figure.* Dominican Republic, Chicoid/Taíno (1200–1492 CE), ceramic, 41 × 21 × 19 cm. Courtesy, National Museum of the American Indian, Smithsonian Institution, New York (053753). Photo by Carmelo Guadagno. This image is thought to represent the *zemi* (demigod) Deminán Caracaracol, one of the four sons of primordial mother Itiba Cahubaba. Caracaracol discovers the secret of fire.

Newly Discovered Islands), Christopher Columbus wrote to Ferdinand and Isabella of his desire to convert these natives, whom he considered meek, receptive, and good-willed by nature, and also lacking religious beliefs of their own. Hence they could be readily incorporated into his own group. Not only Spain but also Christendom itself would reap the spiritual and temporal benefits afforded by the conversion of "so many souls of peoples hitherto lost."[26] Columbus also reports that the natives called the Europeans "*gentes ethereas,*" or celestial people.[27]

Columbus also relayed to the Spanish sovereigns native reports of another group that would probably be more difficult to assimilate: namely, the inhabitants of "Charis," who were "considered very warlike by their

[26] *Epistola,* 18.
[27] This topos of European superiority as a body fantasy that recurs throughout his writings. *Ibid.*, 4th facsimile page (unnumbered).

nature," and who were said to eat human flesh.[28] *Charis, Carib, Caniba, caníbales* – the name of that place and group appears in many forms in the Admiral's writings. As las Casas wrote in his redaction of Columbus's diary of the first voyage:

> The Indians enjoyed themselves very much with the Christians and brought them certain arrows belonging to the Caniba or Cannibals, and they are made from the stem of a reed with fire-hardened points inserted at the tip and are very long. They showed them two men with pieces of flesh missing from their bodies and gave them to understand the cannibals had eaten mouthfuls of them. The Admiral did not believe it.[29]

Initially skeptical of their existence, Columbus wondered whether the Caniba were "quite simply the people of the Great Khan who must be very close by."[30] He theorized that when these warlike people came in their boats and abducted members of neighboring tribes, their kinsmen imagined that they had been eaten. Later, however, when certain natives attacked his landing party after a trading dispute, Columbus concluded that they must be the Caribs, who were in fact "man-eaters."[31]

As Frank Lestringant has argued, Columbus can be credited with the creation of the Cannibal as word and concept.[32] This act of naming was in effect a rebirth or "renaissance" of the cannibal, for Columbus recoined the word *carib*, a word meaning *brave* or *powerful* in the native idiom (according to one derivation), and *bad* or *evil* (according to another).[33] With this name, Columbus would fuse an ambiguous New World root to a familiar Old World noun: *canis*, or dog, as Lestringant notes.[34] Hence the early modern cannibal is a hybrid group concept, a novel identity that would be assigned to multiple anthropophagous groups (first to the Caribs of the Lesser Antilles,[35]

[28] On his first voyage to the New World, Columbus heard reports of but did not meet the fearsome inhabitants of the isle of Charis, although everywhere the natives reported their terror of that group. Discussed by Lestringant, *Cannibals*, 15–17.

[29] *Journal of the First Voyage*, 135.

[30] The Spanish reads "Gran Can." *Ibid.*, 120–121.

[31] "[C]reya que eran los de Carib, y que comiesen los hombres. . . ." *Ibid.*, 194–195.

[32] Lestringant, 15.

[33] Philip P. Boucher also suggests "bitter manioc eater" as a possible meaning of the name *Carib. Cannibal Encounters: Europeans and Island Caribs*, 2. Later in this chapter I discuss the debates over the etymology of this word and concept.

[34] Lestringant analyzes the fusion of these two words and concepts in the writings of Columbus and others. Columbus seems to have conflated the Caribs with the legendary Cynocephali, dog-headed monsters described fancifully in earlier geographic literature. *Cannibals*, 15–22.

[35] Samuel M. Wilson has argued that the natives called *Caribs* by the Spanish and by many up to this day were actually a more heterogeneous group or set of groups than had previously been supposed, and that they were not fully distinct from the Taíno peoples of the Greater Antilles. It was Columbus who set up a dichotomy between good natives (Taínos) and bad Caribs – a

then the Brazilian Tupinambá and other Tupí-speaking tribes, and later to Africans). It would also serve as a generic designation for any group or person deemed subhuman or savage. Europeans would also use the partly fictional concept of the cannibal differentially, strategically redefining their own group identities against that concept.

It was not Columbus, however, but his contemporary Vespucci who would catapult the image of the cannibal into the collective consciousness of Europeans. In 1502 or 1503, Vespucci published in Florence the *Mundus novus* (*New World*), addressed to his former patron, Lorenzo di Pierfrancesco de' Medici.[36] Supposedly translated from lost Italian originals into Latin, German, Italian, French, Dutch, Flemish, and Czech, Vespucci's *Mundus novus* would become a runaway bestseller in Europe shortly after its publication.

In 1505, a second text appeared bearing Vespucci's name: the *Lettera delle isole nuovamente trovate in quattro suoi viaggi* (*Letter concerning the isles newly discovered on his four voyages*).[37] Addressed to a "Magnificent Lord" identified in later editions as Piero di Tommaso Soderini, Gonfalonier of Justice in the Florentine Republic, Vespucci describes his participation in four expeditions to the New World, providing sensational accounts of shipwrecks, friendly and unfriendly encounters with cannibals and giants, and discoveries of new lands of unearthly beauty and appeal.[38] Printed editions of the *Mundus novus* and the *Quattro viaggi* went through sixty editions before 1529, exceeding

dichotomy that would be relentlessly invoked as a justification for the enslavement of anyone who might be classified as the latter. "The Cultural Mosaic of the Indigenous Caribbean," 170–179, *et passim.*

[36] Formisano suspects that the *Mundus novus*, a Latin translation based on a lost Italian original, may have been published first in Florence at the end of 1502 or the beginning of the next year. It was reprinted many times within the space of a few weeks in Venice, Paris, Antwerp, and other cities. *Letters from a New World*, xix–xxi.

[37] On the dating and early editions of the *Quattro viaggi*, purportedly by Vespucci, I follow Formisano's introduction to *Letters from a New World*, xxii.

Certain accounts of his purported voyages were published in Vespucci's lifetime, whereas others circulated only in manuscript form. The earliest printed work is the *Mundus novus*, a Latin translation of a lost Italian original that was sent by Vespucci from Lisbon to his patron Lorenzo di Pierfrancesco de' Medici. This work describes a voyage to the New World that took place in 1501–1502. The *Mundus novus* was included in a 1507 Italian anthology of travel narratives, published in Vicenza as *Paesi novamente retrovati et Novo Mondo da Alberico Vesputio Florentino intitulato*.

Vespucci's second published account, the *Lettera di Amerigo Vespucci delle isole nuovamente trovate in quattro suoi viaggi*, appeared ca. 1505 in Florence, and documents two Spanish and two Portuguese voyages supposedly undertaken by him. A Latin translation of this text, *Quattuor Americi Vespuccij navigationes*, was incorporated by Martin Waldseemüller into a manual of geography and cosmography entitled *Cosmographie Introductio* (1507). See Formisano's excellent discussion of the textual history of works attributed to Vespucci in *Letters from a New World*, xix–xl.

[38] This letter sought to establish that Amerigo Vespucci, like Christopher Columbus, had completed four transatlantic voyages, while also claiming that the Florentine pilot, rather than Columbus, had discovered the new continent.

the published reports on Columbus's travels during that same period by a factor of nearly three to one.[39] These two published works, partly drawn from unpublished letters by Vespucci, are composite works, the publication of which might never have been authorized by the Italian cosmographer.[40] A curious blend of the facts as Vespucci interpreted them, as well as the fanciful "improvements" of unknown hands, Vespucci's published accounts were shot through with elements of the fantastic, improbable, horrific, and absurd. "Vespucci's" writings helped to define one of the most influential European fantasies of the sixteenth century – the fear of being devoured by cannibals of the New World, of being literally consumed by an alien group. This pair of travel narratives and others like them would help to forge new concepts of collective identity for several continents. Rather inadvertently, they would also give rise to a more functional approach to managing collective difference – the discipline of comparative ethnography.[41]

[39] Hirsch, "Printed Reports on the Early Discoveries and Their Reception," *First Images of America*, 2: 540–541.

[40] The "Vespucci question" (how many expeditions he actually participated in, where he actually went and what really happened, and what he himself wrote or others wrote in his name) has been intensely debated since the early sixteenth century. Fray Bartolomé de las Casas argued that it was Columbus rather than Vespucci who had first discovered the new continent. Because Vespucci received what many considered an undeserved honor, and because the two published narratives present inconsistent and contradictory information about the New World, Vespucci has often been reviled as a liar and a fraud.

    In 1924 and 1926, the brilliant Italian philologist Alberto Magnaghi analyzed the published writings, as well as the unpublished manuscripts on which the *Four Voyages* and the *New World* are based, to demonstrate that Vespucci made two, rather than four, voyages to the western hemisphere. Magnaghi held that only the unpublished manuscripts were authentic, and that other persons took possession of these documents after Lorenzo di Pierfrancesco de' Medici died, added their own embroidery, and published the works in Vespucci's name. See *Amerigo Vespucci: Studio critico*.

    Since Magnaghi's time, many have continued to debate the Vespucci question, but today most critics doubt the authenticity of the published texts, which are considered to be composite works published with or without Vespucci's consent. For a useful summary of the Vespucci debates, see Pereira, "A Problemática Vespuciana," 91ff. See also Formisano's brief discussion of the Vespucci question in *Letters from a New World*, xxviii ff., and Calderón de Cuervo, "Las cartas de Amerigo Vespucci: hacia la conceptualizacion discursiva del Nuevo Mundo," 91–107. Formisano, siding with Magnaghi and with later supporters Guiseppe Caraci and T. O. Marcondes de Souza, contends that in the *Mundus novus* and the *Quattro viaggi*, "we can discern the general outline of a cultural and political operation, exquisitely Florentine in character, which glorifies Vespucci by indirectly attacking Columbus . . . " (xxxii).

    Also following Magnaghi, Vespucci's recent biographer Felipe Fernández-Armesto argues that while Vespucci was in many ways a self-aggrandizing poseur, the *Quattro viaggi* "is a confection in which relatively little input can be traced to the alleged author. A reader can almost hear the slash of the scissors and the splash of the paste." *Amerigo*, 128.

[41] Warwick Bray contends that "[t]he emergence of comparative ethnography is just one aspect of a late sixteenth-century phenomenon, the transition from a medieval world view to a recognizably modern one." As an example of this new, more relativistic and open-minded approach to alterity, Bray cites Michel de Montaigne, who wrote later in the century, most famously in defense of

Vespucci's works, and pamphlets and printed news in general, seem to have held particularly strong appeal for German readers. As Thomas R. Adams has suggested, "The ferment and unrest of the people of the Holy Roman Empire in the pre-Reformation years apparently stimulated the avid reading of this type of ephemeral publication."[42] The recurrent phrase *mundus novus* in the Latin texts also presented an accidental pun that would not have been lost on learned readers in the German-speaking regions of Europe: the Latin *mundus* recalls the German word for mouth, stomach, or trap: *Mund* (plural *Münder*, genitive *Mundes*). Ironically or appropriately, as we shall see, the New World would become associated with "new mouths."

The *Mundus novus* described New World cannibalism in sensational detail, describing in an oft-quoted passage the prodigious appetites of the natives, sexual and otherwise:

> They take as many wives as they wish, and son may couple with mother, brother with sister, cousin with cousin, and in general men with women as they chance to meet. They dissolve marriage as often as they please, observing no order in any of these matters. Moreover, they have no temple and no religion, nor do they worship idols.... The peoples make war among themselves without art or order. The elders deliver orations to the young to sway their will, urging them on to wars in which they kill each other cruelly, and they take captives and keep them, not to spare them, but to kill them for food: for they eat each other, the victors eat the vanquished, and together with other kinds of meat, human flesh is common fare among them. This you may be sure of, because one father was known to have eaten his children and wife, and I myself met and spoke with a man who was said to have eaten more than three hundred human bodies; and I also stayed twenty-seven days in a certain city in which I saw salted human flesh hanging from house-beams, much as we hang up bacon and pork. I will say more: they marvel that we do not eat our enemies and use their flesh as food, for they say human flesh is very savory.[43]

For the purposes of this reading, it is essential to note that the *Mundus novus* describes a group without boundaries: moral or religious boundaries, as

---

the New World cannibals. See "European Impressions of the New World," in *The Meeting of Two Worlds*, 313.

　　To credit Vespucci with the development of comparative ethnography is as problematic as giving him credit for the discovery of the New World. Nevertheless, the Vespucci of the manuscript letters, rather than of the works published in his name, reveals a curiosity, skepticism, and openness toward the unfamiliar that can be said to anticipate the sophisticated reversals of perspective typifying the essays of Montaigne later in the century.

[42] Hirsch notes that of the thirty-seven vernacular editions of Vespucci's *Mundus novus*, nearly one-half were published in German or Germanic languages. "Printed Reports," 541.

　　See also Christine R. Johnson's excellent overview of Renaissance travel narratives in German-speaking lands, *The German Discovery of the New World*.

[43] Formisano, 49–50.

well as the boundaries uniting or separating families, ages, food groups, and other fundamental systems of classification. The perceived lack of boundaries among the people described in the *Mundus novus* presented to the European imagination a spectacle worthy of Greek tragedy: in Lestringant's words, "they embodied both Oedipus, lying with his mother, and Thyestes devouring his own children."[44]

Paradoxically, fear could be combined with desire, as suggested by the continuation of that passage. Vespucci (or his proxy) writes,

> Their women, as I said, although they go naked and are exceedingly lustful, still have rather shapely and clean bodies, and are not as revolting as one might think, because, being fleshy, their shameful parts are less visible, covered for the most part by the good quality of their bodily composition. It seemed remarkable to us that none of them appeared to have sagging breasts, and also, those who had borne children could not be distinguished from the virgins by the shape or tautness of their wombs, and this was true too of other parts of their bodies, which decency bids me to pass over. When they were able to copulate with Christians, they were driven by their excessive lust to corrupt and prostitute all their modesty. The people live to be 150 years old, seldom fall ill, and if they do happen to contract some sickness, they cure themselves with certain roots of herbs.[45]

As noted in the previous chapter, the spectacle of nudity had a profound effect on the "clothed" imaginations of Europeans – even more so in the flesh than in artistic representations. Sexuality and childbirth, imagined as Eve's punishment within the Judeo-Christian tradition, pose no burden for these women, who live inordinately long and healthy lives. "[I]f anywhere in the world there exists an Earthly Paradise," Vespucci writes a few pages later, "I think it is not far from those regions. . . ."[46] In this ambivalent description of the native women, the author hints at another more desirable type of engulfment – sexual exploration and consummation to be enjoyed without the usual punishments or stigmas generally attached to them within European Christian culture.

Vespucci's fantasies of a paradise of erotic freedom and earthly abundance did not readily square with his reports of cannibalism, incest, disfigurement, and other body- and boundary-shattering transgressions, nor did they for his readers. Collectively, Europeans would continue to hold these

[44]Lestringant, 30.
[45]Formisano, 50–51.
[46]*Ibid.*, 52.

divergent fantasies in mind at the same time. On the one hand, they feared the engulfment, fragmentation, or destruction of the Christian group body. On the other, they imagined and desired those whose bodies appeared to have been bestowed with mysterious, seductive, age-defying properties, and who acted on their desires with apparent impunity. As historian Hayden White has observed, these natives paradoxically violated "all of the taboos that should have rendered them 'unclean' and degenerate," yet they nevertheless enjoyed "the attributes formerly believed to have been possessed only by the Patriarchs of the Old Testament: robust health and longevity of life."[47]

Cannibals in Paradise: Vespucci's *Quattro viaggi*

Such paradoxes would be further elaborated in Vespucci's second pamphlet, the *Quattro viaggi*, published two years after the *Mundus novus*. Even more sensational than the first, this text contains a chilling tale of cannibalism not included in the earlier account and most likely fabricated.[48] In the account of his third voyage (his first with the Portuguese), members of Vespucci's own group are attacked by cannibals. After his fleet sailed from the African port of Bezeguiche across the Atlantic for sixty-seven days, the author writes, "It pleased God to reveal new lands to us on 17 August [1501], where we anchored half a league from shore...."[49] When they disembark somewhere on the mainland of the new continent, the crew observes a group of natives at the top of the mountain, who are also observing them. Two crewmembers volunteer to make contact. They leave the ship with the order to return within five days.

On the seventh day, the Portuguese return to shore. One of their men, a courageous youth, disembarks, approaches a group of women, who gather around him, "touching him and gazing upon him in admiration." Meanwhile, from the ship, the author writes,

[W]e saw a woman come from the mountain, carrying a big club in her hand; and when she reached our Christian, she stole up from behind and, raising this club, gave him such a blow that it knocked him dead on the ground. And immediately the other women grabbed him by the feet and

[47] "The Noble Savage Theme as Fetish," in *First Images of America*, 1: 125–126.
[48] The fact that such crucial events are excluded from the earlier account of Vespucci's 1501–1502 voyage provided by the *Mundus novus* certainly makes the second account highly suspect. These details might have been added to justify the Portuguese acts of violence against native populations, also described by Vespucci.
[49] Formisano, 87. Bezeguiche is the present-day Gorée, near Cape Verde.

dragged him toward the mountain, and the men leaped toward the shore to shoot at us with their bows and arrows; and they so frightened our men, who were in the boats resting with the shallow-water anchors by the land, that despite all the many arrows they were shooting into the boats, no one managed to pick up his weapons. Yet we fired four charges of mortar at them, and while none of the shots hit anyone, the very sound of them was enough to send them fleeing toward the mountain, where the women were already hacking the Christian up into pieces, and, in a great fire they had built, were roasting him before our eyes, showing us many pieces and then eating them; and the men, indicating by their gestures that they had killed and eaten the other two Christians: which weighed up on us heavily, and we believed them, having seen with our eyes the cruelties they committed upon the dead man.[50]

"All of us considered this an intolerable wrong," the author exclaims, "and more than forty of us prepared to land and avenge such a beastly and cruel death, but the captain general would not consent; and they remained unpunished for so great an offense."[51]

Noteworthy here is the repeated use of the word *Christian* (*Cristiani*), rather than *Portuguese* or *European*. Christian was a generic designation for the transnational crew, but it was not a neutral one. Rather, that group name and identity performed a consolidating function by alluding to a shared large-group identity transcending that of nation, region, or language group. This shared religious identity was a fragile one, soon to be shattered by the Reformation. Significantly, the violent divide separating Catholics and Protestants would arise in part from their irreconcilable views of the Eucharistic rite, turning on the literal incorporation of the body of Christ, with its cannibalistic overtones, or more figural ones proposed by the reformers.[52]

A 1509 Strasbourg edition of the *Quattro viaggi* provided a graphic illustration of this incident (Figure 2.4), condensing in visual form the conflicting elements of the story — namely, the convergence of sexuality and death in Vespucci's narrative of the third voyage. The woodcut depicts the young man

---

[50] *Ibid.*, 88–89.

It is not clear how it would have been possible for the Portuguese, who were moored in small boats at the shoreline or possibly had returned to their ships, to witness the butchering, cooking, and cannibalizing of the young Christian, one of many incongruous details of the text that suggest multiple hands.

[51] *Ibid.*, 89.

[52] As Lestringant has argued, the similarity between the cannibalism of some native tribesmen of the New World and the commemorative theophagy of the Christian rite – intolerable for some – would soon erupt into European consciousness, fueling at least in part the bitter sacramental debates of the Protestant Reformation. See *Cannibalism*, 8–9, *et passim*, as well as Kilgour, "The Reformation of the Host," *From Communion to Cannibalism*, 79–139.

Von der neuwen welt

daruß võ den völckern andere kaufftē/vñ sind võ vns gangen/mit dem geding/dz sy zü vns nach fünff tagen vff das höchst sorgten wider zekummen/wann wir ir so lang warteten/vnd also haßen sy den weg angriffen vñ nd wir die widerfart zü vnsern schiffen genen.

2.4. Vespucci, *Von der neuwen welt....* Folio E4 v of *Diss Büchlin saget wie die zwe herre Fernandus K. zü Castilien und herr Emanuel K. zü Portugal haben das weyte mör ersüchet unnd funden wie Insulen unnd ein Nüwe welt von wilden nackenden Leüten, vormals unbekant.* Engraving on wood, 1509, 12.2 × 9.7 cm. Reproduction from the 1902 facsimile edition courtesy of the Harry Ransom Humanities Research Center, University of Texas. This woodcut offers a suggestive image of New World female cannibals preparing to attack an unsuspecting European man. Many similar images of cannibals would appear in Europe over the course of the sixteenth century.

in the seductive embrace of three attractive nude women, while an older, more aggressive-looking female cannibal prepares to club the unsuspecting man from behind. Similarly graphic images of cannibals and their practices began to proliferate on the maps and illustrations of early sixteenth-century printed works.[53] Cannibalism would remain a powerful psychological threat to the European Christian group body, although not for the first time in their history, as Geraldine Heng has argued.[54] It would also become a central theme of early colonial ideology, as many scholars have noted.[55]

For the purposes of this study, it is important to reflect on how the practice of cannibalism, real and imagined, helped to transform European group identity, and how European perceptions of New World natives, projected back onto them, would result in the differential reconfiguration of their large-group identities. Psychoanalysts have long asserted that from our earliest years forward, the concept of cannibalism plays a powerful role in human fantasy life.[56] Fragmentation anxiety and the fear of being "devoured" are fundamental fantasies that people experience among a group of strangers.[57] Such ideations can be traced back to fears dating from infancy and early childhood – earlier states of existence and of mind to which adults may regress in certain threatening group settings. If the fantasy of being "eaten alive" can be considered – at least for some people – a standard reaction to unfamiliar groups, how much more intense must this sentiment have been in the sixteenth century, when Europeans discovered that cannibalism was a common practice in another part of the world.

Large-group regression – in psychoanalytic terms, the collective return to primitive mental mechanisms as a means of dealing with panic or terror – was one significant outcome of colonial encounters between Europeans and the tribal peoples of the Americas, especially, but not exclusively, with actual

[53] In *Canibais no Paraíso"* (*op. cit.*), Julio Bandiera presents a range of visual images of the cannibal – and of indigenous peoples of the Americas – made by early modern Europeans. See also Levenson, ed., *Circa 1492. Art in the Age of the Exploration* (op. cit.), and Kohl, ed., *Mythen der neuen Welt.*

[54] Heng discusses the intriguing discussion of cannibalism, the Crusades, and medieval romance in her book *Empire of Magic.*

[55] On the alignment of cannibalism, racism, and misogyny in protocolonialist ideology, see, for example, de Certeau, *La fable mystique*; Montrose, "The Work of Gender in the Discourse of Discovery"; Zamora, *Reading Columbus*; Rabasa, *Inventing A-M-E-R-I-C-A*; Conley, *The Self-Made Map*; Llewelyn Price, *Consuming Passions*; Wey Gómez, *The Tropics of Empire*; and Lestrigant, *Cannibals.* See also n. 22.

[56] Freud discussed the topic of cannibalism in *Totem and Taboo* (1912–1913), linking the practice to the mindset of some "primitive races." Having introduced the topic in the first edition of *Three Essays on the Theory of Sexuality* (1905), he extended his discussion in the 1915 edition, linking it to the oral stage in a child's development. See *Three Essays, Standard Edition*, 7. See also Laplanche and Pontalis, *The Language of Psychoanalysis*, 55.

[57] Anzieu, *Group and the Unconscious*, 76, 139, *et passim.* See also the Introduction to this book, 24–27.

cannibals.[58] Symptoms of large-group regression can include the surrendering of individual will, the collective dehumanization of perceived adversaries, the amplification of cultural identities, and magical thinking.[59] Some or all of these features can be observed in Vespucci's writings and in other European descriptions of the New World, which are replete with regressive group fantasies. Such fantasies would feed into an emerging, newly consolidated European group identity, to which we shall return later. The naming of America is a pivotal chapter in that history.

The Naming of America

In 1507, the German cartographer Martin Waldseemüller, with members of a learned society in St. Dié, Lorraine, published a treatise on world geography.[60] Entitled *Cosmographiae Introductio*, or "Introduction to Cosmography," this book also included a Latin translation of Vespucci's 1505 *Quattro viaggi*.[61] For the St. Dié group, Vespucci's text described nothing less than a world historical event. Despite their reliance on Ptolemy, the most famous cosmographer of antiquity, these humanists recognized that a monumental discovery had taken place.

   In that same year, Waldseemüller had published a globe and a large planar map of the world.[62] The latter, known as the *Universalis cosmographiae*, or World Map (Figure 2.5), was printed from woodblocks fitted with labels in metal as well as wooden type; the map was so large that it had to be printed

[58] On the nature and symptoms of large-group regression, see for example Volkan's insightful essay, "Large-Group Identity, Large-Group Regression and Massive Violence." In describing the regressions of ethnic, national, or religious large groups, Volkan defines collectives as ranging from the ten thousands to the millions. I use the term *large-group* more loosely, to encompass the regressions of a ship's crew, a tribal group, a nation of readers, or even a whole continent.

[59] *Ibid.*, 15ff.

[60] Under the patronage of René II, Duke of Lorraine, a type of Renaissance think-tank known as the Gymnasium Vosagense published classical and recent information on world geography.

[61] In the *Cosmographiae introductio*, Vespucci's *Quattro viaggi* bears the title *Quattuor Americi Vesputii navigationes*. This text was said to have been translated "de vulgari Gallico in Latinum," from French into Latin. The dedication, supposedly by Vespucci, is addressed to Duke René of Lorraine. Most likely Johannes Basinus translated the Italian text, which was dedicated to Pietro Soderini, Gonfalonier of Justice in Florence, into Latin, substituting René's name for Soderini's. See Fischer and Wieser, eds., *The Cosmographiae Introductio of Martin Waldseemüller*, 12–13; Formisano, xxiv.

[62] The globe is now lost, but globe gores printed from the original woodcut still exist. These gores can be pieced together like segments of an orange peel to form the skin of a globe approximately 3 inches in diameter. Harley, *Maps and the Columbian Encounter*, 67.
   Elizabeth Harris argues that the planar world map was produced and printed by a printer named Grüniger in Strasbourg, under the supervision of Waldseemüller and other members of the Gymnasium at St. Dié. "The Waldseemüller World Map: A Typographic Appraisal," 33.

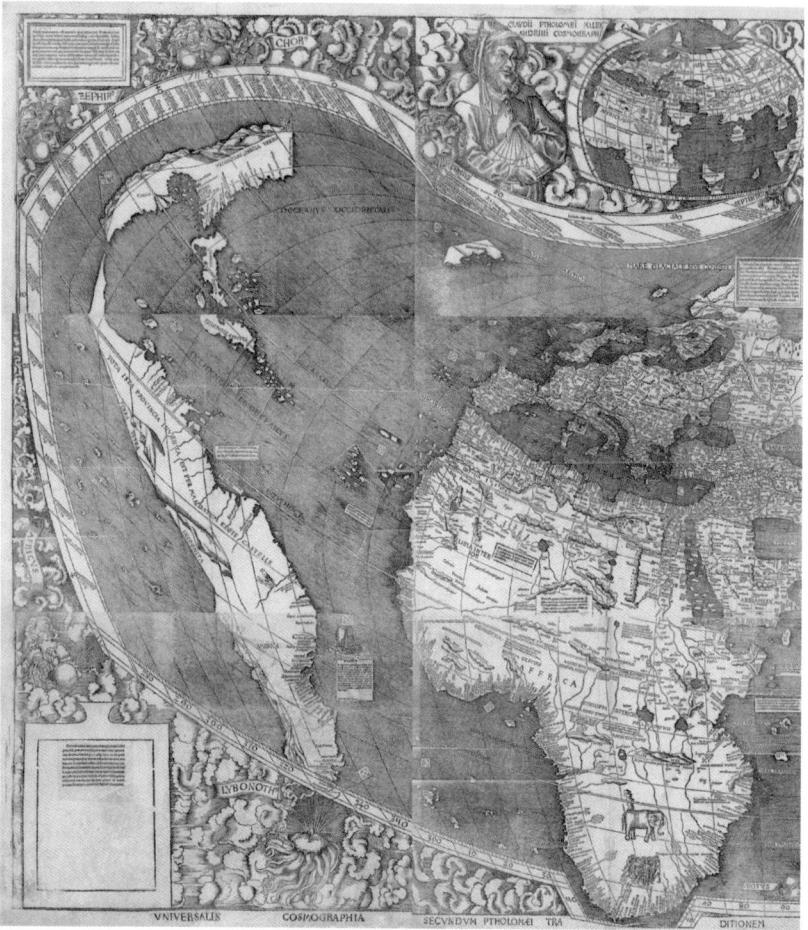

2.5. *Universalis cosmographia secundum Ptholomaei traditionem et Americi Vespucii alioru[m]que lustrationes*, [St. Dié], 1507. One map on 12 sheets; 128 × 233 cm., sheets 46 × 63 cm. or smaller. Courtesy of the Library of Congress, Geography and Map Division, g3200. This important map reflects European knowledge of world geography in the early sixteenth century. The continents of the Western hemisphere were at this time largely *terra incognita*, or "unknown land."

on twelve sheets of paper. Pieced together, these twelve prints formed a whole map approximately 8′ by 4′ in dimension; one thousand copies were printed. These maps were intended for display in the halls and libraries of the European elite in the early sixteenth century.[63]

[63] Harley, 67; Harris, 30.

2.5

Waldseemüller and his group sought to provide their audience with the most up-to-date information then available about the earth's geography and radically to revise previous conceptions about it. Portraits of the cosmographers Vespucci and Ptolemy adorn the top of the map. Europe is depicted in minute detail in contrast to the rest of the world. Africa dominates the central portion of their map, although it is not yet filled in. Asia appears with some notable distortions as well. Meanwhile, a new landmass appears to the west, bearing for the first time in history the name *America* (Figure 2.6). The author of the *Cosmographiae introductio* explains that formerly the world

had been divided into three parts: Europe, Africa, and Asia.[64] "Now,"
however,

> these parts of the earth have been more extensively explored and a fourth
> part [*quarta pars*] has been discovered by Amerigo Vespucci. . . . Inasmuch as
> both Europe and Asia received their names from women, I see no reason
> why any one should justly object to calling this part Amerige, i.e., the
> land of Amerigo, or America, after Amerigo, its discoverer, a man of great
> ability.[65]

Through this act of naming by the cosmographers of St. Dié,[66] the unknown
continent received the name *America*, defined differentially against Europe,
Africa, and Asia – continents, as well as large-group identities, in the process of being reconceptualized.[67] In 1507, the people of Europe, who were
divided into approximately 200 states, statelets, and statelike entities, had
barely begun to think of themselves as a large group, as the historical sociologist Charles Tilly has argued.[68] In fact, European identity became more

---

[64] The first edition of the *Cosmographiae introductio*, published on April 25, 1507, lists no author but
presents two dedicatory letters to the Emperor Maximilian, one by Philesius Vogesigena (a.k.a.
Matthias Ringmann, cartographer, humanist, and poet), and the other by Martinus Ilacomilus.
The name *Ilacomilus* is a Hellenized form of the name Waldseemüller. In a variant issue of
the work, as well as its second edition, which was printed on the 29th of that same month,
the Gymnasium Vosagense appears as the collective editor; however, the 1509 Strasbourg edition
published by Grüninger references "Ilacomilus" instead of the Gymnasium. Karrow, Jr., *Mapmakers
of the Sixteenth Century and their Maps*, 568–569, 574.
  Waldseemüller has most often received credit for writing this work, sometimes in tandem with
his friend Matthias Ringmann. More recently, however, Franz Laubenberger and Steven Rowan
conclude that Matthias Ringmann was the real author of that work, rather than Waldseemüller;
hence Ringmann was the actual namer of America – a view seconded by Karrow and others. See
Laubenberger and Rowan, "The Naming of America," 99 *et passim*.
[65] Fischer and Wieser, 70.
[66] See n. 64. The identity of the actual namer of America remains contested.
[67] O'Gorman argues that the real innovation of Waldseemüller's book and map was the breaking
free from the conceptual framework of the *orbis terrarum*, the island of the world imagined as a
single land mass. The new continent thus was conceived of as a distinct geographic entity that
would be placed on equal footing with the other three parts of the world. "America," he writes,
"was literally a 'new' world, which offered the possibility of enlarging man's old cosmic home by
adding a new portion of the universe conceived as capable of becoming another Europe." *The
Invention of America*, 121–131, 139.
[68] At the turn of the millennium, Charles Tilly has argued, Europe did not exist, for "the roughly
thirty million people who lived at the western end of the Eurasian land mass had no compelling
reasons to think of themselves as a single set of people." By 1490, however, that situation had begun
to change. At that point, Europe's 80 million people "divided into something like 200 states, would-
be states, statelets, and state-like organizations." Around the periphery of Europe there were many
large territories or kingdoms, such as the Ottoman Empire, Hungary, Poland, Lithuania, Muscovy,
the lands of the Teutonic Order, the Scandinavian Union, England, France, Spain, Portugal, and
Naples. Within that circle, in contrast, there existed numerous political entities much smaller in

2.6. *Universalis cosmographia*, detail of "America." Courtesy of the Library of Congress, Geography and Map Division, g3200. Europeans had charted relatively little of the continent by 1507, and the western portion of America remains a blank on this map.

size. South Germany included sixty-nine free cities in addition to multiple bishoprics, duchies, and principalities. The Italian peninsula also contained a large number of city-states – between 200 and 300 in 1200 CE. From Flanders to the borders of Hungary and Poland there were hundreds of independent state-like entities. Establishing the exact number of such states depends on the criteria for statehood that one uses; such definitions can yield as few as 80 independent regions or as many as 500. *Coercion, Capital, and European States*, 38–45.

The invention of Europe – and the chronology of that invention – is undoubtedly more complicated than Tilly suggests. In his essay "'Europe' in the Middle Ages," William Chester Jordan confirms that although the word *Europe* did not appear with frequency on medieval maps, the word *Christianitas* ("Christendom") was used by mapmakers from the eleventh century onward to indicate the larger collective (74–75).

easily conceivable as a result of visualizations such as this one, and other continental identities with it.[69]

On his 1513 world map, included in his Strasbourg edition of the Ptolemy Atlas, Waldseemüller seemed to have undergone a change of heart, for he redesignated the new continent *Terra Incognita*, or "unknown land." In 1516, Waldseemüller published his marine map, the first printed nautical chart of the world. This document also attempted to re-name the new continent, substituting the words *Terra Nova* and *Terra Papagalli*, or "Land of Parrots," for the earlier name *America*. In 1515, the name *America* appeared on the "Paris" or "Green" globe not once but four times. For the first time, the name was affixed to the continent of North America as well. In 1520, Peter Apian published a world map adapted from Waldseemüller's 1507 World Map; once again the name *America* appears on the southern continent. The name recurs on maps by Laurent Fries (Strasbourg 1522), Franciscus Monachus (Antwerp, ca. 1527), Peter Apian (Ingolstadt 1530), Johann Honter (Cracow 1530), Oronco Finé (Paris 1531), and Sebastian Münster (Basel 1532), again over the southern continent.[70]

The naming of America and the taking hold of that name were no mere accidents of history. Other more complex factors helped to forge the link between Amerigo Vespucci the traveler and the two continents that would ultimately bear his name.[71] America, the word and the concept, would have profound implications for collective identities during the course of the sixteenth century and beyond. Not one but several large groups were summoned into being by the 1507 continental naming, groups that did not exist before that seminal event.

Waldseemüller and his group were consumed by the cartographic debates and breakthroughs of their generation. In their mountainous enclave of St. Dié, they pondered fundamental questions: What did the world really look like? What were the edges of its landmasses? How might areas of the globe previously unknown to Europeans be further documented on the updated maps that they sought to create? How should they respond to and report on the rapidly changing information beginning to flow into Europe?

It was under the influence of Vespucci's writings that one or more members of the St. Dié group invented the name *America*, thereby seeking to

---

[69] On the consolidation of a European identity, see John Hale's superb chapter "The Discovery of Europe" in *The Civilization of Europe in the Renaissance*, 3–50.

[70] Schwartz, *The Mismapping of America*, 15.

[71] For an excellent overview of interpretations of that seminal act, see Whitney, "The Naming of America as the Meaning of America," 195–220.

underscore the achievement of the Florentine cosmographer. Because other continents (e.g., Europa, Asia, Africa) had already been named after females, why, the *Cosmographiae introductio* proposes, should this new continent *not* be named after a man – namely, the "man of great ability" who discovered it? Of note, however, the Latin name *America*, like the Hellenized name *Amerige*, is a feminized form of the masculine noun/name Amerigo. How might we understand this inaugural sex change of the continent, whereby Vespucci's name acquired its feminine ending?

Vespucci's biographer Frederick Pohl called the name *America* "a work of art," a "euphonious" name that was "such an excellent choice that once it had appeared in print, nothing could destroy it."[72] Psychogeographer William Niederland proposed a more Freudian interpretation, observing that within the name are various linguistic particles associated with the mother and the maternal body – specifically, the breast:

> The phonemic forms, AM, AME (in German: AMME – wet nurse; AMMA – in infantile linguistic pattern, MAMMA, MUTTER) AND MER, MÈRE (in French, sea and mother respectively), are apt to evoke orally- and maternally-tinged images or ideas. The linguistic equivalents of the same roots, AM, AME, MER, can be found in many other languages.[73]

Niederland theorized that the maternal associations suggested by the name helped give rise to Waldseemüller's projection, both cartographic and psychoanalytic. The name *America* is itself a metaphor of contact – a metaphor of "orally- and maternally-tinged images or ideas," of the soon-to-be colonized continent. "It is likely," he argued, "that the phonetic and onomatopoetic qualities of the name given to the area may have contributed to its rapid acceptance and spread."[74] In Niederland's view, the original readers of the *Cosmographiae introductio* and of Waldseemüller's 1507 map of the world would have been attuned to those nuances of meaning, to the metaphors of the maternal breast suggested by the word *America*.

Niederland further conjectured that the naming of America may represent "the return of the repressed," the emergence of meanings specifically negated by the authors' stated decision to name the continent after Vespucci – "its

---

[72] *Amerigo Vespucci, Pilot Major*, 174. On other interpretations of the name America, see also Jantz, "Image of America in the German Renaissance," 98–100, and Cook, "Ancient Wisdom, the Golden Age, and Atlantis," 38, n. 83; and Kadir, *Columbus and the Ends of the Earth*, 60–61.

[73] Niederland, "The Naming of America," 468.

Niederland adds, "From the every beginning, European immigrants settled in America, with the utopian image of a huge *Isle of Fortune* and its unconscious concomitants, that is, of sharing in the mother's magic powers and bounty" (469).

[74] *Ibid.*, 468.

discoverer, a man of great ability" (*inventore sagacis ingenii viro*). Consciously this name called to mind Amerigo Vespucci; unconsciously, Niederland held, it evoked the maternal body. This fantasy was in part elicited by the erotically provocative and at times sexually threatening descriptions of native women that are prominently featured in Vespucci's *Quattuor navigationes*, the narrative accompanying the *Cosmographiae introductio*.[75]

The New World as Breast

Niederland's view of the hidden breast of America will no doubt strike some contemporary readers as antiquated Freudianism. For that reason, it is worth recalling the other discovery of Christopher Columbus, one that was long ignored in standard treatments of his voyages yet that corroborates Niederland's theory: namely, his belief that the western hemisphere was shaped like a giant breast. In 1498, while contemplating the mouth of the great Orinoco River in what is today Venezuela, Columbus concluded that he had arrived at the Earthly Paradise, or close to it, as he would later write to the Spanish sovereigns in his account of this third voyage:

> I always read – in recorded testimonies and experiments by Ptolemy and all the others who wrote on and studied this subject regarding both the eclipses of the moon and other examples of movement from east to west, such as the elevation of the pole from north to south – that the world, both land and water, was spherical. Now, however, I have experienced a difference so great in these matters, as already stated, that I have begun to think that is about the world's shape, namely, that it is not as round as they described it, being rather shaped like a pear, very round all over but on its stem end having a protuberance, like one who has a perfectly round ball but for a spot which resembles a woman's breast, with the nipple being the highest part and closest to the sky; this spot is located under the equinoctial line and in this ocean sea, at the very end of the orient (I call the end of the orient the place where all the land and islands end).[76]

---

[75] Niederland is careless in certain portions of his argument. He seems to conflate the two published texts of Vespucci, and he focuses primarily their sexually threatening elements. Moreover, his discussions of the ethos of the St. Dié group seem both homophobic and reductive. Nevertheless, his basic insight into the phonemic content of the name seems to me important and also persuasive.

[76] Christopher Columbus, *Accounts and Letters of the Second, Third, and Fourth Voyages*, 83. This edition is based on a unique manuscript copy of Columbus's log, copied by Fra Bartolomé de las Casas, now housed in the National Library in Madrid. The account of the third voyage was not published until 1825, although it was somewhat known in its time. For example, Peter Martyr knew of it and ridiculed this idea in his *Decades* (Dec. 1, Bk. 6).

From this high point of the world, Columbus hypothesized, the four rivers of the world streamed forth. This was or could be the earthly paradise of which many had spoken previously but unfortunately had never managed to locate. He sought to draw proof that he had arrived at or near this sacred site from the many indicators around him:

> [T]he signs very much support this idea, for I never read nor knew of so much fresh water penetrating so far inland and so near salt water, and another strong proof is the extreme mildness of the climate. And if it does not come from there, from paradise, the wonder is even greater, because I do not believe that a river as big and deep is known anywhere else in the world.[77]

Attempting to explain this unique perspective of the great explorer, Jesús Varela Marcos and Maria Montserrat León Guerrero recently have suggested that Columbus was hard-pressed to justify the results of his third voyage to the Spanish crown. Hence he set reason aside and allowed himself to believe that he had found such a justification in his discovery of paradise – a mystical-geographical success that he dreamed he had obtained.[78] In Columbus's fantasy, the New World had developed a great, welcoming breast.

Vespucci too believed that the New World resembled an earthly paradise, although there is no evidence that he subscribed to Columbus's cosmography. Like Columbus, however, Vespucci linked the New World to fantasies about native breasts and childbirth, as the passages quoted previously suggest. As Niederland has observed, numerous beliefs and legends about paradise – specifically island paradises – tap into unconscious fantasies about birth, death, and the maternal body. Common to all such beliefs, he states, are

---

[77] *Account of the Third Voyage*, 89, 91. Greenblatt notes that Columbus was hesitant to claim that he had really discovered Eden in the New World. "In effect, the marvelous takes the place of the miraculous, absorbing some of its force but avoiding the theological and evidentiary problems inherent in directly asserting a miracle." *Marvelous Possessions*, 79.

[78] For their part, the *Reyes Católicos* appear to have recognized that Columbus needed to be relieved of his charge after the disastrous third voyage, which he was just a few months after his return. *Colón, su tesis "pezonoidal" del globo terráqueo y el itinerario del tercer viaje*, 35.

See also O'Gorman, *Invention of America*, 98ff., and Wey Gómez, *The Tropics of Empire*, 430–434. Wey Gómez offers a different but compelling explanation of Columbus's fantasy that the earth was not round: Columbus wanted to understand why temperature could vary so much along the same latitude; this fact seemed to disprove the theory of climactic zones prevalent at the time. It was also a theory of racial groupings that varied according to zone. Columbus sought to explain the relative coolness of the Orinoco River basin and the relative whiteness of the inhabitants there, both of which facts contradicted the zonal theory, by theorizing that they lived at a higher altitude.

Although it might have been Columbus's intention to explain what he took to be a geographic anomaly, the somatic fantasy that frames his theory is also significant, as we shall see.

"the infantile fantasies of returning to the early nursing situation of a 'blissful' state of plenty."[79] If Niederland is correct in his supposition, then it is no coincidence that both Columbus and Vespucci link their positive feelings about the New World and its inhabitants to fantasies about the breast.[80] Mapmakers, too, engaged fantasies of birth and origins as they recharted the world at the beginning of the sixteenth century.[81]

Columbus, Vespucci, and the St. Dié group released into European consciousness two complementary fantasies about the New World – both oral and both regressive. According to the first, the native group, implacably cannibalistic, threatened to devour the European Christian group. That fantasy, undoubtedly provoked by extremes of cannibalistic violence that some Europeans had witnessed or heard about, served as a powerful justification for colonialism and missionizing. As historian Jorge Cañizares-Esguerra has revealed through his extensive analyses of English Puritan and Spanish Catholic colonial writings, the two cultures shared a demonologic view of the New World, according to which, "cannibalism was a reflection of the hellish world Satan had instituted in America."[82] In that shared perspective on the New World, native rituals and institutions were perceived as demonic inversions of Christian Church structures. Natives themselves were collectively viewed as effeminate, a sign of their corruption to the colonizers. Both groups would increasingly describe the colonizing process as an epic act of liberation and as a form of mass exorcism of demons from the land.[83]

According to the second fantasy, seemingly a far cry from the first, the New World was conceived as a welcoming breast, self-replenishing and always available. This fantasy and other erotic wishes also served as a justification for taking possession of the continents to the west and their people and resources. Each of these fantasies could be mobilized in different contexts, or sometimes at the same time, as, for example, on a 1505 Augsburg broadsheet depicting Vespucci's cannibals (Figure 2.7). In that image, a Madonna-like native woman nurses her baby and caresses her older child, while a group behind her cannibalizes a fresh victim. Complementary fantasies, they represent the Janus face of orality in colonial representations of the New World, or the fear of being consumed and the desire to consume, which were most

---

[79] "The Naming of America," 467–468. Here Niederland follows the ideas of E. Jones in *Essays in Applied Psychoanalysis*, I: 98.

[80] Such fantasies lend support to Melanie Klein's theory of the good and bad maternal breasts, which elaborate on Freud's theory of the oral stage of development. See for example, "Mourning and its Relation to Manic-Depressive States," 146–174.

[81] See, e.g., Conley, *The Self-Made Map*, 7–12.

[82] Cañizares-Esguerra, *Puritan Conquistadors*, 83.

[83] *Ibid.*, 83.

2.7. Johann Froschauer, broadsheet representing Vespucci's cannibals, Augsburg (1505), woodcut, hand-colored, 10″ × 13 3/4″ (25.5 × 35 cm.) Bayerische Staatsbibliothek, Munich, Einblatt Sammlung V, 2. The broadsheet incorporates text from Vespucci's *Mundus novus*. These natives are depicted with feather crowns, as in Grão Vasco's *Adoration*.

visible in writings and artwork dating from the first encounters. Paradox-ically, both fantasies served the same end: the incorporation of the alien group.[84]

Tupí-Guaraní Group Identities

Still to be considered in this investigation are the group identities of sixteenth-century indigenous Brazilians as they themselves might have understood them. If for early modern Europeans the cannibal played the role of the ultimate alien, who or what constituted extreme alterity for the indigenous peoples of the New World, including the so-called cannibals?

---

[84] Merrall Llewelyn Price makes a similar point regarding Columbus in *Consuming Passions*: "Colum-bus's evident desire for origins reframes the imperial project as the impossible search for the nur-turing pre-Oedipal mother, but since such an encounter is unattainable, the colonizers find only the castrating general archetype. . . ." (97). I would argue in contrast that both fantasies remained operative during the colonial era, but that they effectively serve the same end.

Did the European colonizers perform a parallel function for them? Such
an assessment is very difficult to make on the basis of extant evidence,
most of which was recorded by persons outside of their cultural groups –
explorers, Jesuit missionaries, and other European observers writing during
the early centuries of colonization; and later on by non-native historians,
anthropologists, and linguists. Although outsiders (or border-inhabiters) to
those native South American groups, these recorders nevertheless provide
insights into the group identities of the Tupí-Guaraní peoples during the
Renaissance. In addition, native languages themselves contain intriguing
clues about the transformations of indigenous identities after Cabral's landfall
in 1500.

At the beginning of the sixteenth century, the Tupí-Guaraní people occupied a large portion of the southern continent, including Brazil. These
ethnically related tribes spoke similar languages that belonged to the same
linguistic family, Tupí-Guaraní. Their languages did not exist in written form
before the arrival of Europeans. The Tupí tribes had settled in the middle
and lower basin of the Amazon River and along its main tributaries of the
right bank. They also occupied much of the Atlantic coast, from the mouth
of the Amazon south to Cananea. The Guaraní people lived to the south of
the Tupí, from Cananea to the Rio do Sul, and to the west, in the region that
is present-day Paraguay. Another Guaraní people, the Chiriguano, lived farther west, near the borders of the Inca Empire.[85] These two large but related
groups were distinguished from the Caribs and Arawaks to the north, as well
as other indigenous groups of the Americas and the Caribbean.

There were certain native tribes of the Tupí-Guaraní with whom the
Portuguese and French interacted most frequently during the sixteenth century – namely, those tribes inhabiting the coastal regions of Brazil, where
Portugal and France sought to establish colonies. These were the Tupinambá,
Potiguara, Caetes, Tupiniquim, Temiminó, and Tamoios, among others.
These groups were united by a shared language and cultural heritage yet
were nevertheless divided by violent intergroup hostility and intermittent
warfare.[86] Of these coastal groups, the Tupinambá Indians in particular would
become the most familiar and most notorious to Europeans. As noted earlier, it was the Tupinambá and the Caribs to the north with whom Europeans would increasingly associate the word and concept *cannibal*.[87] In the

---

[85] Clastres, *The Land-Without-Evil*," 1.

[86] Balée, "Complexity and Causality in Tupinambá Warfare," 180–97.

[87] Anthropophagy was practiced by numerous Tupí-Guaraní tribes, as well as the Aztecs, Iroquois,
and many other New World groups; however, for Europeans it was the Tupinambá of coastal
Brazil who inherited the Caribs' mantle of infamy.

sixteenth century, a simplified version of the Tupinambá dialect would be adopted by the Portuguese as the *Lingua Geral*, or "common language," of colonial Brazil, which was used in interethnic communities in the northern part of the country. Later on, the *Lingua Geral* would become the basis of modern Tupí (Nheengatú).[88] In multiple ways, then, the Tupinambá stood metonymically for other peoples of South and North America in the minds of Europeans.

By the beginning of the eighteenth century, the indigenous communities of coastal Brazil had largely disappeared under the pressure of warfare, disease, and creolization.[89] Meanwhile, the *Lingua Geral* remained, conserving a partial record of its own history and evolution and of the persons and groups who spoke it. A keyword in that colonial lexicon was the word and concept *caraíba*. This important term, together with its many cognates and variant spellings, signified several things to the Tupí-Guaraní peoples, defining in part their notions of the sacred: ergo, the core structure of their group identities (a connection discussed at length in Chapter 4). The remainder of this chapter focuses on that word and concept, etymologically related to the European word *cannibal*. By tracing the evolution of the term *caraíba*, we can learn a great deal about indigenous group identities and their metamorphoses during the Renaissance, as well as group processes in general. In its many variant spellings, *caraíba* signified, inter alia, the "sacred" in the languages of the Tupí-Guaraní. Over time, however, it would come to mean *Christian*, and then *white man*. Embedded in the history of this keyword is the rapid transformation and loss of indigenous group identity, as well as the assimilation of these native groups into those of their colonizers.

A Problem of Translation: *Carabi*

When Europeans reached the coast of South America in the sixteenth century, they reported that the natives had referred to them as *carabi* or *caraíba*. Before we consider the possible meanings of this group appellation, we must note the similarity of that word to the constellation of terms reported by Columbus in his 1493 *De insulis nuper inventis* and in the journal of his first

---

[88] The Portuguese developed a simplified form of this language, based on the dialect spoken by the coastal Tupinambá, which became the *Língua Geral Amazônica*, or Amazonian general language, of colonial Brazil. Nheengatú, a version of that language, is still spoken today along the Rio Negro and in pockets in the Amazon region. A second form of colonial Tupí, the *Língua Geral Paulista*, based on the Tupí tribal dialect spoken near Sao Paulo, later died out. Campbell, *American Indian Languages*, 23.

[89] See, for example, Clastres, *The Land-Without-Evil*, 2.

voyage (i.e., *Charis, Carib, Caniba*, and, of course, *caníbales*). It might seem a remarkable coincidence that indigenous tribesmen of coastal South America called Europeans by a name strikingly similar, at least in sound, to the one that Europeans gave to them. In fact, it was no coincidence at all, as many linguists and lexicographers have noted, although the important implications of these related words and concepts for transformations in large-group identities merit further elaboration.

In the *Quattro viaggi*, Amerigo Vespucci provides the first European reference to this new name for his own group, which he interprets favorably. Describing his first voyage to the New World on the Spanish expedition (possibly that of Alonso de Hojeda and Juan de la Cosa [1499–1500]), Vespucci (or his editor) writes,

> Many tribes came to see us, and marvelled at our features and our whiteness; and they asked us whence we came, and we gave them to understand that we came from heaven, and that we were going to see the world, and they believed it. In this land we set up a baptismal fount, and baptized countless people; and in their language they called us *carabi*, which means 'men of great wisdom.'[90]

In this influential description of group difference, several markers of collective identity emerge, such as skin pigmentation (real/imagined), place of origin (real/fictitious), religion, and language. Noteworthy here is the racialized category of whiteness (*bianchezza*), which in this account takes precedence over Christianity as the premier mark of the newly arrived group. As in many later colonial texts, race in conjunction with religion emerges in this passage as that which differentiates Old World groups from New.[91] In the sixteenth century, this pairing of skin color and religion increasingly became the new mark of the European large group in relation to other large groups outside of Europe.

Because no human beings are literally white, it is important to recognize in Vespucci's report a somatic fantasy about his own group – not original to him but a fantasy nonetheless. In this passage, the concept of whiteness

---

[90] Formisano, 73 and 191, n. 31. The variant spelling "Caraiibi" appears in the early Italian edition possessed by the Biblioteca Nazionale Centrale di Firenze, B. R. 192, while "Caraibi" (?) appears in a manuscript copy, the Codice Vaglienti. See Vespucci, *Lettera al Soderini*, 2, 37. Waldseemüller's Latin edition reads "charaibi." Fischer and Wieser, lxvii.

[91] For a useful introduction to the evolution of notions of race in the early modern world, see Cañizares-Esguerra's essay, "Race, Theories of," and bibliography in *Europe 1450 to 1789*: 129–131. See, too, Cañizares-Esguerra's essay "Demons, Stars, and the Imagination," 313–325, as well as the other essays in this recent collection.

also attaches to a fifth marker of group identity, that of being "men of great wisdom," denoted by the native noun *carabi*. There is a certain double-voicing in Vespucci's report of this New World noun. The narrator implies that the natives apply the term *carabi* to the Europeans in a straightforward way; that is, they believe the story that the crew has descended from heaven. Although it might or might not be based on an actual historical incident, his report seems to align with Columbus's claim that natives called his crew *gentes ethereas*, or "heavenly people."[92]

In contrast, the Europeans know that they have not descended from heaven and that they are deceiving the natives to gain the upper hand. Their "great wisdom" rests in their ability to pull off this deception. Thus the fifth marker of the European group is the ability to deceive, which they do for a purportedly good cause – conversion – the ends justifying the means.

In proclaiming to understand native speech, Vespucci provides verification that his group has succeeded in their trick, demonstrating a kind of wisdom. We need not accept Vespucci's gloss of *carabi* at face value, however. What did the epithet mean to the natives who gave Europeans that new name, assuming that they actually used it in some form? Was it related etymologically or semantically to the name *Carib*, the designation for the often anthropophagous ethnic group(s) of the Antilles, Central America, and the northeastern shores of South America? Did Vespucci conflate encounters with several native groups in this portion of his narrative?[93] Who were these natives whom Vespucci supposedly met, and which language were they speaking?

These questions cannot be answered with any certainty. Vespucci's itinerary on that voyage remains the subject of intense debate. His expedition could have landed on the coastline north of the Amazon River, close to present-day Venezuela. Vespucci's group also could have traveled south of the Amazon, however. Their itinerary has some bearing on the potential meanings of *carabi*. For example, if Vespucci were describing Arawak-speaking natives living in coastal areas north of the Amazon, they might have been comparing Vespucci's group to the Caribs – that is, their anthropophagous enemies. That interpretation does not square with the native

---

[92]See n. 27.

[93]Where exactly Vespucci might have landed on that first voyage and how far south along the coast he traveled are subjects of considerable dispute. Vespucci's group might have traveled north of the Amazon River, close to present-day Venezuela, as Formisano believes (xiv). They might also have traveled south of that river, if Vespucci's group split off from Hojeda's fleet, as Fernández-Armesto has argued (147ff.). These questions cannot be answered with any certainty at present.

adulation reported in Vespucci's story, however, nor with the accompanying reports of cannibalism. Alternatively, if Carib Indians of Guyana were speaking, they might have recognized the Europeans as members of their own group during the baptismal episodes. A third scenario is that Tupinambá natives inhabiting the coastal regions south of the Amazon delta might have been comparing the Europeans to 1) their own native sachems, or 2) to their adversaries, the Carib Indians to the north.[94]

Luciano Formisano, the modern editor of Vespucci's works, takes the word *carabi* to be of Tupí-Guaraní origin. "[S]eers, prophets, or simply wise men, the *carabi* are first of all messengers of a word from the gods or the Beyond."[95] Here Formisano follows a standard interpretation that dates back to the sixteenth century, when the first European travelers to Brazil attempted to describe indigenous tribes and their religious beliefs, languages, and practices.

Among these ethnographers was the French Franciscan André Thevet. Thevet had traveled to coastal Brazil with the Villegaignon expedition in 1555, seeking to establish a French colony near present-day Rio de Janeiro. That ill-fated enterprise lasted only a few years before collapsing in 1560. In *Les Singularités de la France Antarctique* (The Singularities of Antarctic France; 1557), Thevet wrote an important account of native Brazilians living along the coast. He reported that when he and his French crew arrived in Cabo Frio, they were warmly greeted by the natives, who welcomed them, "one after the other, as was their custom, with the word *Caraiubé*, which means 'good life' [*bonne vie*] or 'be welcome' [*soyez le bienvenu*]."[96] Here the

---

[94]Each of these possibilities is predicated on the accuracy of "Vespucci's" reporting, which is of course highly questionable. There are other possible interpretations of the ambiguous term, as we shall see.

[95]Formisano, 191. Formisano also notes that Waldseemüller's Latin translation of the text presents a significantly different version of this scene. In that text, it is the natives who call themselves *carabi* as they perform baptisms. Waldseemüller's edition reads: "in hac tellure baptisteria fontesque sacros plures instituimus in quibus eorum infiniti seipsos baptisari fecerunt se eorum lingua charaibi hoc est magnae sapientiae viros vocantes." Waldseemüller could have altered the meaning of the (supposedly) French source text from which he was working, or perhaps his source really was different from the printed Italian versions. There are many Vespucci questions that simply cannot be answered. However we account for these textual variations, they open up two opposing perspectives on the encounter. In one case, the Europeans are called *carabi*; in the other, the natives refer to *themselves* by that term.

Incidentally, Fischer and Wieser translate this passage incorrectly, ignoring the reflexive pronouns "seipsos" and "se," and perhaps following the Italian: "We established in this land many baptismal fonts or baptisteries, in which they made us baptize countless numbers, calling us in their own tongue 'charaibi,' – that is to say, 'men of great wisdom.'" (lxvii, 112).

[96]Lestringant, ed., *Le Brésil d'André Thevet*, 113.

reported word *Caraiubé* has a meaning quite different from that assigned to it by Vespucci's crew, assuming that this greeting was in fact a variation of the word *carabi*, as reported by Vespucci.

In a later chapter, describing the religion of the Americans (based partly on Vespucci's text), Thevet introduces another word, *charaïbe*, meaning *prophet* or *demi-god*.[97] He states that the natives, who were initially astonished by the appearance and behavior of the Christians, applied that epithet to them. Once it became apparent that Christians could get sick and die, and that they were subject to the same passions that the natives were, however, they ceased calling them *charaïbes* and instead began to deride them. Moreover, in certain places ("especially among the Cannibals"), the natives thought no more of killing and eating Christians if they irritated them than they did their own enemies.[98] Thevet's definition of *charaïbes* as demi-gods seems to accord with the descriptions of Columbus and Vespucci, who report the native belief that the Christians had descended from the sky.[99] Noteworthy, however, is Thevet's statement that the Brazilian natives no longer use this epithet in praise of Christians (i.e., Europeans).[100]

In a later chapter, Thevet once again introduces the keyword, describing the native *pagés* or *charaïbes* as vagabond prophets who traveled from village to village and who claimed to communicate with the spirit world in exchange for food and other gifts.[101] These wandering prophets were greatly venerated by the people, who asked for their help and protection against sickness, death, or other harm. If the prophets failed to deliver, however, the people did not hesitate to kill and eat them, because they were considered unworthy of their title and standing.[102]

[97] *Ibid.*, 125.

[98] " . . . si on les irrite, ils ne font difficulté de tuer un chrétien et le manger, comme ils font leurs ennemies. Mais cela se fait en certains lieux et spécialement aux Cannibales, qui ne vivent d'autre chose: comme nous faisons ici de bœuf et de mouton." *Ibid.*, 125. With thanks to Karen Pagani for clarifications of the French.

[99] Thevet's gloss is not unproblematic, however, because he closely follows Vespucci's account in this chapter and echoes many of his assumptions and claims. On certain parallels between the two authors, see Lestringant, *Cannibals*, 46.

The term *caraiba* in reference to Europeans also appears in numerous Portuguese writings of the period.

[100] Instead, he says, they call them "Mahire," a name for one of their "ancient prophets, whom they detest and abhor." *Le Brésil d'André Thevet*, 125.

[101] Thevet conflates *pagés*, who were village shamen, with the wandering *charaïbes*, who roamed from village to village, having no fixed abode. The *charaïbes* had far greater standing than the local healers. *Le Brésil d'André Thevet*, 144.

[102] *Ibid.*, 147.

A *Caraïbe* Ceremony

Jean de Léry, a French Huguenot and a member of the first Protestant mission to the Americas, also documented the role of the native *caraïbes*, the wandering prophets discussed by Thevet. In his *Histoire d'un voyage faict en la terre du Brésil* (*History of a Voyage to the Land of Brazil*; 1578), Léry describes his flight from the Villegaignon colony (having nearly escaped death at the hands of his fellow Frenchmen), and his two months' stay at an outpost on the Brazilian mainland near a Tupinambá encampment. Having witnessed the arrival of ten or twelve *caraíbas* at a nearby native village and their ceremonies, Léry compared them to "popish indulgence-bearers, [who] would have it believed that by their communication with spirits they can give to anyone they please the strength to vanquish enemies in war, and, what is more, can make grow the big roots and the fruits... produced by this land of Brazil."[103]

Léry also witnessed a Tupinambá ceremonial dance led by visiting *caraíbas*. To perform this dance, the village men formed three nonconcentric circles, enclosing three or four of the *caraíbes* in each. The visiting prophets wore robes, headdresses, and bracelets made of brightly colored feathers, holding in each hand a *maraca*, a ritual rattle through which the spirits were thought to speak (Figure 2.8).[104] While the village men danced, the prophets blew tobacco smoke over them, saying, "So that you may overcome your enemies, receive all of you the spirit of strength."[105] Léry's eyewitness account of this ritual merits quoting at length:

> These ceremonies went on for nearly two hours, with the five or six hundred men dancing and singing incessantly; such was their melody that – although they do not know what music is – those who have not heard them would never believe that they could make such harmony. At the beginning of this witches' Sabbath, when I was in the women's house, I had been somewhat afraid; now I received in recompense such joy, hearing the measured harmonies of such a multitude, and especially in the cadence

---

[103] *History of a Voyage to the Land of Brazil*, 140.

    The Portuguese Jesuit Fernão Cardim offered a similar explanation of the *caraíba* in his *Origem dos Indios do Brasil* (1584): they were native shamans who claimed to make the crops grow and to raise the dead. "Do principio e origem dos indios do Brasil," *Tratados da terra e gente do Brasil*, 105, 145.

[104] On the cult of the maraca among the Tupinambá and other Tupí tribes, see Métraux, *La religion des Tupinambá et ses rapports avec celle des autres tribus Tupi-Guarani*, 68–78; Clastres, *The Land-Without-Evil*, 38–39; Combès, *La tragédie cannibale chez les anciens Tupi-Guarani*, 149–151; and Tomlinson, *The Singing of the New World*, 110–120.

[105] *History of a Voyage to the Land of Brazil*, 142.

2.8. *Caraïbes* (image of a dancer and a maraca player). Woodcut from Léry's *Histoire d'un voyage . . .*, Geneva, 1611. Courtesy of the Newberry Library, Chicago. These two *caraïbes* perform a ritual dance, while a parrot and monkey placidly look on.

and refrain of the song, what at every verse all of them would let their voices trail, saying *Heu, heuraure, heura, heuraure, heura, heura, oueh* – I stood there transported with delight. Whenever I remember it, my heart trembles and it seems their voices are still in my ears. When they decided to finish, each of them struck his right foot against the earth more vehemently than before, and spat in front of him; then all of them with one voice uttered hoarsely two or three times the words *He, hua, hua, hua,* and then ceased.

Since I did not understand their language perfectly at that time, they had said several things that I had not been able to comprehend, and I asked the interpreter to explain them to me. He told me that at the beginning of the songs they had uttered long laments for their dead ancestors, who were so valiant, but in the end, they had taken comfort in the assurance that after their death they would go join them behind the high mountains, where they would dance and rejoice with them. Likewise, they had pronounced violent threats against the Ouetaca (a nation of enemy savages who, as I have said elsewhere, are so warlike that they have never been able to subdue them), to capture and eat them, as their *caraïbes* had promised. . . . [106]

From Léry's description, together with several others like it, we learn that the *caraíbas* did not live in any single village but wandered from one to the next, living on the offerings made to them. They were thought to make the spirit world speak to the living, and they incited the villagers to war against their enemies. Although outsiders, the *caraíbas* unified members of each tribal village that they visited through their ritual performances. These wandering prophets of the Tupinambá, and of the Tupí-Guaraní peoples in general, were uncanny visitors whose function in part was to bring the living in contact with their dead. [107]

Tupinologists have long analyzed the relation of the *caraíbas* to the practice of cannibalism. Although they did not directly participate in cannibalistic rituals (as far as we know), these native prophets sanctioned and incited the practice through the performance of their ritual functions.

From the sixteenth century onward, observers and theorists have debated the possible motives or reasons for cannibalism among some native tribes of South America. These motives include food, revenge, appeasement of the dead, and the ritual incorporation of the enemy, including his/her strength, identity, and name. In his essay "Of Cannibals," the French philosopher Michel de Montaigne explained the logic of Tupinambá cannibalism as the

[106] *Ibid.*, 143–144; the French reads "*Caraïbes.*" Histoire *d'un voyage,* 403 *et passim.*
[107] Clastres describes the presence of these wandering great shamans (*karai,* in Guaraní) throughout Tupí-Guaraní tribes. See *The Land-Without-Evil,* esp. 25–42.

recovery through ingestion of one's own dead.[108] Similarly, the twentieth-century sociologist Florestan Fernandes analyzed the ritual cannibalism of the Tupinambá as a "restoration of the collective We."[109] In this sense, to cannibalize would be to recover one's own dead through the incorporation of the other, and in so doing to reappropriate the sacred into one's one body, and into the "body" of the group. The liminal *caraíbas*, both outside and inside the system, bridged the gap between the living and the dead, as well as the geographic distance between tribal groups. They defined the boundary enclosing amicable tribal groups and separating them from their enemies, thereby clarifying who could and could not be incorporated through ritual violence.[110]

The *caraíbas* also performed another important group function for their people, which was to lead tribes across the South American continent in search of the legendary Land-Without-Evil. This was a separate but related quest for the sacred and for unity with the departed. These mass migrations, which could have begun before the arrival of Europeans, greatly intensified during the sixteenth and seventeenth centuries, as native populations sought to escape the sphere of European influence – a subject to which we will return shortly.

Given the complicated role of the *caraíbas* within Tupí-Guaraní culture, as best as anthropologists can reconstruct it, the conceptual link between Europeans and these native prophets is not easy to specify. If Europeans were initially called *carabi*, as Vespucci claimed, it was not simply a matter of their

---

[108] Describing the situation of captive warriors about to be eaten, Montaigne writes:

> I have a song composed by a prisoner which contains this challenge, that they should all come boldly and gather to dine off him, for they will be eating at the same time their own fathers and grandfathers, who have served to feed his body. "These muscles," he says, "this flesh and these veins are your own, poor fools that you are. You do not recognize that the substance of your ancestors' limbs is still contained in them. Savor them well; you will find in them the taste of your own flesh." An idea that certainly does not smack of barbarity.

"Of cannibals," in *The Complete Essays of Montaigne*, 150–159, p. 158.

[109] Fernandes, *A função social da guerra na sociedade Tupinambá*, 332, 336, 339, discussed by Eduardo Viveiros de Castro in *From the Enemy's Point of View: Humanity and Divinity in an Amazonian Society*, 275 ff.

Castro offers a still more subtle, depersonalized thesis regarding Tupinambá cannibalism: "The virtue of enemies that was necessary to incorporate was precisely that of being enemies: this is what was eaten. Instead of a 'magical superiority' obtained by the dissolution of the enemy's identity in the belly of the society of eaters, such a superiority would be derived from a determination *by* the enemy, a cannibal transformation *into* the enemy. The contrary of an identification – literally, an identification *to the contrary*" (*From the Enemy's Point of View*, 286).

[110] These concentric group alliances and oppositions have been analyzed by Combès, among others. See *La Tragédie cannibale chez les anciens Tupi-Guarani*, 70–75.

being "men of wisdom" in the eyes of the natives, or, as Thevet describes it, half-gods. Rather, they might have been perceived as powerful go-betweens, moving between groups and realms like the native *caraíbas*.[111]

Later on, as Thevet and others report, Europeans were often viewed as dangerous adversaries, enemies to be avoided, vanquished, or eaten, rather than sacred emissaries, nor were they necessarily perceived as a homogeneous group. In a short time, the natives began to distinguish between nations of Europeans, either forming alliances with them against their native enemies, or waging war against them. The testimony of Hans Staden, which he offered in the *Warhaftige Historia und Beschreibung* (*The True Story of His Captivity*; 1557), provides intriguing information about these native perceptions of European group identities and differences. Staden, a German seafarer who traveled to Brazil with the Portuguese, was captured by the Tupinambá in the early 1550s.[112] Assuming that Staden was Portuguese and hence one of their mortal enemies, the Tupinambá let him know in no uncertain terms that he would be eaten.

While admitting that he worked for the Portuguese as a gunner, the terrified Staden insisted that he was not of that group but that he was actually French. The skeptical Tupinambá had him language tested by a young Frenchman living nearby, who quickly determined that Staden knew no French.[113] Staden then argued that he had forgotten his native language as a result of his long absence from his homeland. Whereupon the chief replied, not without a certain cruel humor, "that he had already helped to capture and eat five Portuguese who all said they were Frenchmen, and had lied about this."[114]

---

[111] On the many instantiations of this concept in sixteenth-century Brazil, see Alida Metcalf's exceptional book, *Go-betweens and the Colonization of Brazil*, esp. 195–234. This chapter owes much to Metcalf's analysis, to which I shall return shortly.

[112] Staden was captured by the Tupinambá near the coastal fort of San Vincente and carried off to the village of Uwattibi. See *Hans Staden's True History*, 47 ff. The full German title of his captivity narrative is *Warhaftige Historia und Beschreibung eyner Landtschafft der wilden, nacketen, grimmigen Menschfresser Leuthen in der Newenwelt America gelegen*.

[113] The Frenchman, an ally of that tribe against both the Portuguese and Tupiniquim, stated, "Kill him and eat him, the good-for-nothing. He is a real Portuguese, your enemy and mine." Staden had been banking on that fact that the Frenchman, a Christian, would help him and "put in a good word" for him. The Christian large-group bond proved useless in that conflict, however. *Ibid.*, 60.

 Later the Frenchman returned to the village, surprised to find that Staden was still alive. Staden reproved him in Tupí for betraying a fellow Christian, without thought of his own eternal future. Whereupon the Frenchman felt ashamed, stating that he really did think that Staden was a Portuguese. He later intervened with the Tupinambá, explaining that Staden belonged to a third group, the Germans, but the natives refused to give up a slave whom they had captured in enemy territory. *Ibid.*, 71–73.

[114] *Ibid.*, 62.

Fortunately Staden was saved by other circumstances. (The natives judged him to have certain powers of healing and prophesy; moreover, he reports that his singing impressed them.) Still divided over whether he was French or Portuguese, they observed that he had a red beard like the Frenchmen. Because in their experience the Portuguese almost always had black beards, they decided to err on the side of caution and keep him alive, although he remained enslaved.[115] Staden's captivity narrative provides information on how the Tupinambá differentiated two separate European groups – one, an enemy group; the other, sometime allies. Although Staden does not use the word caraíbas or a variant, he states that his captors came to attribute sacred powers to him, powers that gave him a certain ambiguous standing within their group.

The Tupí Uncanny

As we shall see, linguistic analysis of this keyword complicates the puzzle still further – a puzzle that encompasses native projections onto European groups and of their own shifting group identities in relation to them. With its apparent connections to the sacred as well as the dead, the keyword carabi used by Vespucci and its relation to the Tupí word caraíba present a fascinating linguistic enigma. Lexicographers have proposed sharply contrasting meanings and derivations of the evolving Tupí word caraíba (noun and adjective, also spelled karaíua and caraíua by Europeans). These include the following:

1. a) something sacred or holy
   b) an (indigenous) shaman
   c) a Christian
   d) a white man.[116]
2. a) powerful, evil
   b) white, civilized.[117]

---

[115] Ironically, Staden was eventually ransomed by the captain of a French ship, who traded knives, axes, mirrors, and combs for the German, who lived to tell about his brush with the cannibals. Ibid., 99.

[116] Antônio Geraldo da Cunha, Dicionário histórico das palavras portuguesas de origem tupi (São Paulo, Brasil: Edições Melhoramentos, 1977), 102. Cunha's excellent entry on caraiba explains the modern Brazilian word and its likely Tupí derivations.

[117] "Caraíua," Octaviano Mello, Dicionário tupi-português / português-tupi (Manaus: Edições Governo do Estado, 2003), 34. According to Mello, the words caraíba and caráiba, names given to the Indian tribe (in English, Caribs), derive from the adjective caraíua, meaning powerful or evil. This adjective, frequently contracted to cariba or caríva, is frequently used today in the sense of "white" or "civilized."

3. a) stranger; foreigner
   b) white man or European.[118]

According to Antônio Geraldo da Cunha, compiler of the first set of definitions, the Brazilian word *caraíba* originally derived from a Tupí word meaning *sacred* or *holy*. *Caraíba* referred to the spiritual guides of the Tupí-Guaraní people, the prophets who announced the Land-Without-Evil and to their concept of the sacred.[119] After colonization, however, this name came to be applied to Europeans. According to Cunha, *caraíba* appears to be etymologically linked to the word *Caribe*, a designation given by Europeans to ethnic groups of the Antilles and the mainland. *Caribe*, in turn, derived from the Arawak and Carib word *caribe*, meaning *brave or courageous man* or *hero*.[120]

In modern Tupí, the ancient shamanistic or sacred connotations of the word have completely fallen away, as suggested by Octaviano Mello's definitions (2), although the connotation of evil accreted to it. When did the word acquire that negative connotation, and what clues does that shift provide about native group identities in the sixteenth century?

Luiz Caldas Tibiriçá proposes an alternative derivation for the modern Tupí word *caraíba* in (3), meaning *stranger* or *foreigner*: namely, that it is a contraction of *cari-aíba*, or *bad stranger*. This was an Old Tupí name for the Arawaks. In the language of the Arawak Indians, *cári* signified *man*. *Aíba* is a Tupí adjective meaning *bad* or *evil*. According to Tibiriçá, the word *caraíba* has no etymologic relation to the word *Caribe*, the name of the native ethnic group, stemming from their ancient word for brave. *Caraíba* is, however, etymologically connected to the contracted Tupí adjective *cariba* or *caríua*, meaning *powerful* yet also *bad* – a name given to the European invaders. It

---

[118] Luiz Caldas Tibiriçá, *Dicionário tupi-português* (São Paulo, Brasil: Traço Editora, 1984), 82.
    Other dictionaries present a similar range of meanings. In his *Vocabulário tupi-guarani português* (São Paulo: Editora Gráfica Nagy Ltda, 1983), Francisco da Silveira Bueno defines *caraiba* as "adj. Strong, brave, intelligent, sacred, holy. White man, European" (80, my translation).
    In his *Dicionário: A língua tupi na geografia do Brasil* (Campinas, SP: Gráfica Muto Ltda., 1983), Orlando Bordoni presents three separate entries for *caraiba*: 1) Foreigner, white, or European (Tibiriçá); 2) contraction of "cari-aiba," evil stranger (Tibiriçá); and 3) those of Bueno, above (150, my translation).
[119] See also Clastres, *The Land-Without-Evil*, 25–42, and Navarro, *Método moderno de tupi antigo*, 607. "Karaíba – profeta que anunciava Terra sem Mal; + homem branco; + cristão."
    Clastres offers yet another derivation of *carai/caraíba*: "Montoya's *Tesoro* recalls that *carai* was the title given to great shamans and the name given to Spaniards, and proposes the following etymology: the word would be formed by binding *cara* (skill, shrewdness) and *y*, which indicates perseverance." (30).
[120] Cunha, *Dicionário histórico*, 102. Variants on *caribe* include *cariba, caniba,* and *galibi* among the Caribs and Arawaks.

was the Jesuits, Tibiriçá argues, who distorted the word *caraíba* by assuming that it signified *Christian, saint,* or *holy* (these missionaries did not realize that they were being insulted).[121] Strangely, Tibiriçá does not mention in his dictionary the Tupí word for *shaman* or *prophet* in any of its variant spellings or pronunciations (i.e., *caraíba, carai, caraiva*), a word recorded in numerous European colonial texts of the sixteenth and seventeenth centuries.[122]

As we have seen, the range of possible meanings and derivations of the word *caraíba*, versions of which appear in several indigenous languages both early modern and modern, runs the gamut from sacred/holy to bad/evil. One is reminded of Freud's analysis of the word *heimlich*, a word that encompasses both the homely and familiar, as well as the secret, unfamiliar, and unsettling. "Thus *heimlich* is a word the meaning of which develops in the direction of ambivalence, until it finally coincides with its opposite, *unheimlich*," Freud observed in his essay "The Uncanny."[123] This analogy between the *unheimlich*, or uncanny, and the *caraíba*, words that can convey essentially opposite meanings, can be extended even further. The Tupí word/concept *caraíba* may be an indigenous version of the uncanny, both pre- and post-contact, because it is closely connected to the concept of the stranger – that is, one who crosses the boundaries of the group. According to this logic, we could retranslate Vespucci's reported term *carabi* as "uncanny strangers," rather than "men of great wisdom" – or at least factor the uncanny into his description. The *caraíba* is a concept that ramified in many directions, particularly as native cultures began to transform, assimilate, or disappear with the arrival of the Europeans. Christian missionaries continued to redefine the native uncanny, assimilating the sacred and the profane of indigenous peoples to a new set of religious and cultural norms.

Anchieta's Mission

The writings of the Jesuit missionary José de Anchieta (1553–1596), who lived among the native Tupí-speaking tribes of Brazil for many decades, provide important evidence on the evolution of the word and concept *caraíba* in sixteenth-century Brazil, together with its relation to the uncanny. Anchieta instructed the natives in Latin and also learned their language, compiling a grammar and dictionary of Old Tupí. He, too, recorded the use of *caraíba* as a name for the Portuguese and also helped to solidify that nomenclature.

[121] Tibiriçá, 82.
[122] Ibid., 82–83.
[123] *Standard Edition*, 17: 226.

In a 1584 document, Anchieta described the local shamans (*pagés*), who performed a variety of rituals and healings to manipulate the people, or so he thought. He considered their practices mendacious and even demonic. "All of these inventions [of the *pagés*] are described by a single word, *caraíba*, which means something holy or supernatural; and for that reason they gave that name to the Portuguese, after they arrived, taking them for something great (*cousa grande*), as if from the other world, because they came so far hovering above the waters."[124]

With this explanation, written nearly a century after the first contact, Anchieta provides further evidence of the collective transformations then under way. He suggests that the native word *caraíba* was applied to the Portuguese shortly after their arrival in the New World. Like Columbus, who claimed that the Indians of the Caribbean called his crew *gentes ethereas* ("heavenly people"),[125] and like Thevet, Anchieta suggests that Brazilian natives almost reflexively acknowledged the Europeans as otherworldly.

A few pages later, however, Anchieta presents a very different view of the Portuguese in his own day, and the natives' responses to them:

> What terrifies the Indians most and makes them flee the Portuguese, and as a result, the churches, are the tyrannies performed against them, forcing them to serve all their lives as slaves, separating wives from husbands, parents from children, wounding them, selling them, etc., and if any Native, accustomed to his liberty, goes to the churches where his relatives are Christians, the Portuguese do not consent to have him there, wherefore many times the Indians, so as not to return to their control, flee into the forests, and when they can no longer do that, they give themselves up to be eaten by their enemies; these injustices and irrationalities are thus the cause of the destruction of churches that had been assembled and the perdition of many who under Portuguese power.[126]

In effect, Anchieta presents a split perception of his own group, consisting of good colonizers (missionaries) and bad ones (enslavers and abusers).[127] He also shows the split that had opened up in the native groups: some converted to Christianity, whereas others remained in their tribal groups or reverted to their cannibalistic mores after partly assimilating.

[124] "Informação do Brasil e de suas capitanias," 340. Translation by Miguel Santos-Neves.
[125] See n. 27.
[126] "Informação do Brasil e de suas capitanias," 342.
[127] This split perception was, in fact, not new to Anchieta but was a common reaction among the Jesuits and other missionaries, who observed the failure of the colonists to maintain Christian norms. My thanks to Alida Metcalf for pointing out that this was a wider phenomenon.

It is possible that the connotations of the word *caraíba* might have depended in part on the group that one was in and on that group's degree of assimilation or resistance to European collectives. Depending on that proximity or distance, Christianity could have represented the *new* sacred, rather than the old, or alternatively, the rival or enemy culture – that is, the new profane.

As a missionary, linguist, and prolific writer, Anchieta was deeply involved in the process of redefining the sacred and profane for the Brazilian natives. His 1587 drama *Na festa de S. Lourenço* (At the Feast of St. Lawrence) offers a case in point. This remarkable piece of theater was composed in three languages – Tupí, Portuguese, and Spanish – for the festival of San Lourenço and was performed in the *aldeia*, or missionary settlement of that name.[128] The *auto*, or play, which might be dubbed a devotional comedy, dramatizes the struggle of the martyred Christian saints Lawrence and Sebastian against three demons, Guaixará, Aimbirê, and Saravaia, for control of the town and its people. Anchieta's play moves nimbly between cultures and languages, offering spiritual counsel to recent converts and to long-established members of the Christian fold.[129]

The play opens with the martyrdom of St. Lourenço, who is being roasted alive on a grill. The historical St. Lawrence was martyred in this fashion in 258 CE, under the Roman Emperor Valerian. Anchieta may have been aware that his opening scene resonated with Tupí mythology, because Maira-Monan, a demigod of the Tupinambá, was said to have been roasted by humans on a pyre.[130] Lourenço dies a courageous death and later returns as the patron saint and protector of the village. Meanwhile, Guaixará, Aimbirê, and Saravaia plot to corrupt the villagers, tempting them to ancient vices, such as excessive drinking of cauim (the native alcoholic beverage), waging war on other tribes, and killing and eating prisoners.[131]

The historical Guaixará was a Tamoio chief, an ally of the French and mortal enemy of the Portuguese; his memory remained sacred among certain segments of the indigenous community.[132] In Anchieta's play, he is recast as

[128] Today part of Niterói, S. Lourenço was situated across the bay from Rio de Janeiro. It was founded by the native chief Araribóia, who later converted to Christianty.
[129] For excellent discussions of this play, see Cafezeiro and Gadelha, *História do teatro brasileiro*. 44–55; Fernández, "José de Anchieta and Early Theatre Activity in Brazil"; Prado, *Teatro de Anchieta a Alencar*, 22–30; Wasserman, "The Theater of José de Anchieta and the Definition of Brazilian Literature."
[130] If so, this would represent a sophisticated use of intertextuality on Anchieta's part. On the myth of Maira-Monan, see Clastres, 19, and Métraux, 10–11.
[131] *Teatro de Anchieta*, 3: 146.
[132] *Ibid.*, 145.

the chief of the demons. In Act II, when questioned by St. Lourenço in Tupí about his identity, Guaixará replies, also in Tupí

> Guaixará, kaguára, ixé,
> mboitiningusú, jaguára,
> moruára moroapyára,
> andirá-guasú bebé,
> añánga morapitiára.
>
> I am Guaixará, the drunkard,
> The great rattlesnake,
> The jaguar of the bush,
> I am the flying bat,
> The cannibal, the avenging demon.[133]

Cannibalism, quite literally demonized in this scene, remains a significant threat within the play. The saints prevent Guaixará and his minions from wreaking havoc in S. Lourenço and inciting a return to native ways. In Act III, however, the demons gleefully roast and torment the Emperors Decius and Valerian, who have been condemned to eternal fire for their nefarious roles in Lourenço's martyrdom. Anchieta's play reinforced the idea that cannibalism was a practice that needed to be forsworn, although he treats the subject with a certain dark humor.[134]

While the demons in the play are presented as shape-shifting cannibals, the play describes the Christian people of Rio as *karaíba* in a scene recounting the failed canoe raid on that city by the historical Guaixará and his men.[135] Describing the battle, Aimbirê reminds Guaixará that

> Karaíba nasetái.
> *São Sebastião*, aé,
> omondyk tatá sesé,
> imondya. Nopytái
> amó abá maranápe.
>
> Few were the Christian people,
> But Saint Sebastian

---

[133] *Ibid.*, 154. My translation from the accompanying modern Portuguese.

[134] Although certain elements of Anchieta's play suggest humor, it is essential for modern readers to recognize that this was a scary play as well. As the work of Cañizares-Esguerra has demonstrated, European colonizers and missionaries took their demonology very seriously. See *Puritan Conquistadors*.

[135] *Ibid.*, 151. In 1566, Guaixará led an attack on Rio, commanding a force of 180 Indian canoes. Fire was used to drive off the attackers, and the flight of the Tamoio was attributed to the intercession of Saint Sebastian.

> Set the ships on fire,
> And frightened them ever since,
> No one remained in the battle.[136]

Na festa de S. Lourenço offers an early instance of the word *karaíba* used in its more modern sense of Christian and possibly Portuguese, having been almost fully detached from its earlier connotation of shaman or prophet, and from Tupí culture in general. In Anchieta's play, the keyword *karaíba* functions as an indicator of group transformation at a time when the Tupí-speaking tribes of coastal Brazil were being assimilated, decimated, or driven inland. The changing uses of the word *karaíba* clearly reveal a loss of consensus among the indigenous people regarding the nature of the sacred. Anchieta, missionary and founding father of Brazilian letters, would play a defining role in that process, helping to shift the Tupí concept of the sacred away from its native contexts and appropriating it to his own group. Ironically, the very hybridity of a play that actually licenses cannibalism but only in hell conserves an element of the native uncanny, still closely connected to the sacred and the dead.

Apiába and *Índios*

Anchieta's play offers a clear example of how *karaíba*, a word closely linked to the Tupí concepts of the sacred and the afterlife, as well as their priestly caste, gradually took on a radically different meaning: that is, the Christian, the person of European descent, the white man. These were not simply the Jesuit's idiosyncratic reformulations of Tupí words but examples of larger linguistic and cultural changes that had been under way for nearly a century.

It is also useful to note the various ways in which Anchieta refers to native groups in the play *Na festa de S. Lourenço*. At times his characters mention specific tribes, such as the Tapuia, the Tupinambá, the Tamoio, and the Temiminó.[137] At other times, they refer to natives in general with the Tupí words *abá* and *apiába* (people).[138] *Abá* is a fundamental word in the Tupí lexicon. Its meanings include the following: man (in contrast to woman), human (in contrast to animal), people, or person.[139] *Apiába* (also

---

[136] *Ibid.*, 151.

[137] *Ibid.*, 149–150.

[138] *Ibid.*, 152, 154, 160, 161.

[139] Tibiriçá, 43; Navarro, *Método moderno de tupi antigo*, 600; C. Baptista de Castro, *Vocabulario Tupy-Guarany* (Rio de Janeiro, Ariel Editora Limitada, 1936), 16. *Abá* can also mean "excess" or "a lot." Cp. etymologies on p. 48.

apyaba) is a closely related word, also meaning man.[140] After the arrival of the Europeans, these words were gradually translated as *Indian* as well. Those generic Tupí nouns for man or mankind were redefined in the early colonial era to mean 1) the group of people who lived in the Indies, – that is, the new western continent; and by the latter part of the sixteenth century 2) the group of people who were not *caraiba* in the revised sense – that is, Christian, white, and European. These semantic developments and changes reveal how the Tupí-Guaraní notions of the sacred and of collective identity itself were appropriated or redefined by Old World groups.

Later a new word would appear in the lexicon of the *Lingua Geral*, marking a fusion of these two large-group identities, the Indian and the European. That word was *caraiboca*. According to Tibiriçá, this new word can mean *mestizo, servant,* or *one who works for the white man*. He suggests a derivation from *caraib* (white man) + *oca* (house).[141] The term *caraiboca* indicated the rise of a third group, both hybridized and subjected, and bridging European and American collectives. All of these words – *caraíba, abá, apiába, caraiboca* – reveal the loss or transformation of large-group identities among the New World peoples after 1500. Distant relations of the European term *cannibal*, these signifiers reveal paradoxically the swallowing up of indigenous cultures by more powerful groups.

Grão Vasco's altarpiece at Viseu, with its unique and unsettling image of the Tupinambá Magus, encoded the beginning of that long process of large-group incorporation. Armed conflicts with Europeans eventually resulted in death or assimilation, or in the mass religious migrations inland during the sixteenth and seventeenth centuries.

The first recorded migration took place in 1539, when a group of 12,000 Tupí natives walked from Brazil to Peru. Ten years later, 300 members of that original group arrived in Peru, where they were promptly captured by the inhabitants of the town of Chachapoyas.[142] Thousands of others died along the way or were left behind, their fates unknown.

Many subsequent migrations were also recorded. In 1562, 3,000 Tupinambá Indians of Bahia followed two *pagés*, or shamans, into the bush, although this exodus was stopped through Jesuit intervention.[143] In 1609, a group of Potiguara Indians from Pernambuco, perhaps 60,000 in number, was convinced by a prophet to travel to "a beautiful land, where all things

---

[140] Tibiriçá, 47; Navarro, 607; Castro, 23 (*apiaba*).

[141] Tibiriçá, 82. Variations include *cariboca, cariboco,* and *caboclo*. The contracted form *carioca* today refers to denizens of Rio de Janeiro.

[142] Clastres, *The Land-Without-Evil*, 49–51.

[143] *Ibid.*, 51. On the distinction between *pagés*, or village shamen, and *charaíbes*, see n. 101.

would come abundantly and naturally, without any difficulty or labor."[144] They died in large numbers on the island of San Luiz de Maranhão. A few years prior to that migration, 8,000 to 10,000 Tupinambá villagers from that same region followed a *karai* [*caraiba*] who was half-native and half-Portuguese into the interior. The prophet told his followers that "he was not a man born of a father or mothers, as others were, and that he had come from the mouth of God the Father." That prophet was killed by the French, and the survivors returned to Pernambuco only to undertake the journey again a few years later, again unsuccessfully.[145]

As Hélène Clastres has argued in her influential study of these mass migrations, natives who ventured on their impossible journeys to the mythic Land-Without-Evil "chose willingly to break away from the too-human burden of collectivity."[146] We might also say that these largely forgotten quests represent the slow dissolution of their groups.[147] Whereas Clastres' account highlights the futility of these mass migrations, Alida Metcalf's research throws into relief another crucial aspect – namely, resistance to colonization and enslavement.[148] Metcalf underscores the hybridity of the movements (natives, *mamelucos* [persons of white European and Amerindian descent], Africans, mulattoes, and occasionally whites and others), and of the belief systems subtending them. Called *santidades* (after "sanctity" or "holiness"), some of these millenarian messianic movements fused the native notion of the Land-Without-Evil with the Christian concept of the Second Coming of Christ and with Central African practices of ancestor worship and spirit possession, all in an eclectic and volatile mix. Indian and African slaves, as well as free persons, often joined forces in these *santidades*, because resistance to slavery and to European hegemony seems to have been their primary driving force.

Describing the famous 1585 Santidade de Jaguaripe in Bahia, Metcalf explains the threat posed by the movement, both because it was a new form of resistance to colonial power, and because it was in fact a new religion.[149] The leaders of the Santidade de Jaguaripe were Antônio, Aricute, and Mãe de Deus – figures who combined the native role of the *caraíba* with elements of Christianity and African religious beliefs into new hybrid forms. Antônio,

---

[144] *Ibid.*, 51–52.

[145] *Ibid.*, 53–54.

[146] *Ibid.*, 56.

[147] Brazil's native population, possibly as high as 5,000,000 before the Conquest, has dwindled to an estimated 600,000 today. Ricardo, ed., *Povos indígenas no Brasil. 2001/2005*, 17.

[148] Metcalf, 211 ff.

[149] *Ibid.*, 233. Also see Vainfas, *A heresia dos indios*.

also known as "the pope," was a baptized Christian Indian who was raised in a Jesuit mission village and a leader of one congregation of the Santidade. He claimed to have descended from heaven and to have created all of the animals in the world. Aricute, an Indian known as the "second pope," and his prophetess wife Mãe de Deus (Mother of God), possibly a recently arrived African slave, led a second congregation of the Santidade, which for a time found a home on the sugar plantation and estate of Fernão Cabral de Taíde, situated on the Jaguaripe River.[150] More and more people joined the two groups and performed their rituals, and additional congregations began to appear.

The powerful threat created by the movement can be inferred from the records relating to its suppression the following year. In 1585, the Jesuit provincial states in his annual letter that the leader of the Santidade, who may have been Antônio, was captured by Indians, dragged through the villages, and mocked. Sentenced to death by the Governor, he was then hanged by the Indians. The provincial also notes in his letter that the Church was still attempting to suppress the sect. Meanwhile, Aricute, Mãe de Deus, and a third leader were dispatched to Lisbon for punishment, and their church was burned to the ground. The remaining leaders were murdered in front of their followers.[151] Disavowed or even partial assimilation could have fatal consequences, as Metcalf's examples demonstrate, as could subverting the new system with a hybrid concept of the caraíba.

A Digestive: Three Conclusions

By tracing the evolution of the intricately related words/concepts cannibal and caraíba over the course of the sixteenth century and into our time, we can identify certain elements of early modern psychic life relating to the formation, transformation, and expansion of new large-group identities. We can detect in these paired metaphors and in other colonial keywords such as America what Anzieu identifies as the regressive oral and digestive fantasies subtending group dynamics. Such fantasies are manifestly present in the writings of early modern explorers, missionaries, and protoethnographers who documented the actual practices of New World cannibalism. Anzieu considers such fantasies to be an immutable and transhistorical feature of collective life, residing in the unconscious minds of persons in groups and in the myths of all cultures, whether ancient or modern.

[150] Metcalf, 218–220, 224.
[151] Ibid., 232–233.

From the competing oralities of groups in conflict we can extract three general principles: 1) the struggle to define one's own collective and that of others can become, among other things, a linguistic battle over control of a culture's dominant metaphors. The evolution of the morpheme *carib* into the word/concept *cannibal*, designating the Indian (and later African) man-eater, and *caraiba*, designating the white man, provides an interesting case in point. The dominant group may succeed in appropriating the sacred of the dominated, converting it to its own ends. As a consequence, the dominated group can potentially be redefined as its own profane.

2) The somatic reference points for good and bad group names/concepts can be the mouth, teeth, breast, or other body parts, consumed or consuming, or connected to digestion and ultimately excretion. The human body and its functions are never far removed from group concepts and fantasies. For example, the verbal and visual imagery employed by Europeans to describe New World natives presents a Janus face. On the one hand, male and female natives were depicted as demonic, devouring cannibals; on the other, natives, the land itself, and even the name of the continent were feminized, evoking in the minds of at least some European colonizers the regressive fantasy of the good breast. This association might not always have been made consciously, as Niederland contended about the naming of America.

3) If "the group is a mouth," as Anzieu has argued, then ultimately the only good mouth is that of one's own group. The oralities of other groups are likely to be perceived as monstrous or threatening, as we shall see in a quite different context in Chapter 4. Other groups are likely to become nonthreatening when they are incorporated, assimilated, or able to be consumed in some fashion – or imagined to be so, as in the case of Columbus's fantasy of the New World Eden as the nipple of the globe. When another group is partly absorbed or introjected into one's own, hybridization results. From this neither/nor or both/and emerges the stranger within, a familiar reminder of the perpetual instability and porosity of all group boundaries. Like the Tupinambá Magus on the high altar of the Cathedral of Viseu, the hybrid exposes the paradox of edibility: through its acts of consumption, the group must of necessity become another, for group identity perpetually consumes and transforms itself through its contacts with others.

As the preceding principles and examples suggest, orality in some sense guides and defines the psychic lives of all groups, for the simple reason that the body is the fundamental reference point for humans; its nourishment and survival drive not only the social world but also the metaphorizing capacities of individuals and collectives residing in it.[152] We must also remember, however, that not all oral histories are the same. Indeed, the study of metaphors allows us to recognize the particular histories of particular groups in particular times and places, and to theorize their possible impact on the present. In the examples traced in this chapter – especially the conversion of the Tupí-Guaraní word/concept *caraíba* from native prophet to white European – it is possible to understand the colonizing role of language in gradually consolidating and incorporating smaller groups into larger ones: white men and Indians.

The rise of race as a fundamental category of large-group identity in the early modern world is perhaps the most significant development in group identity formation during that era, the impact of which is still felt today. Paradoxically, race was and remains a comparatively static concept of collective identity quite at odds with the micro- and macro-transformations of groups that accelerated during the Renaissance, and with the pan-hemispheric, pan-Atlantic, and/or global forging of new groups, whether ethnic, religious, cultural, and/or linguistic.[153] The next chapter continues to explore the idea of race as a preeminent group fantasy of the Renaissance, by analyzing its obscure relation to another foundational group concept of that epoch: Utopia.

---

[152] "It is noteworthy," the eighteenth-century Italian historian Giambattista Vico stated in *The New Science*, "that in all languages the greater part of the expressions relating to inanimate things are formed by metaphor from the human body and its parts and from the human senses and passions." *The New Science of Giambattista Vico*, 116.

This tendency to use somatic metaphors may be linked to what neuroscientists now call embodied cognition. See notes 65 and 76 in Chapter 1, as well as the Conclusion to this work.

[153] As Jorge Cañizares-Esguerra and James Sidbury have argued in a recent essay, group identity is very much a moving target during the colonial period, and indeed in any period. They state,

> To understand the processes of cultural change experienced by the peoples of the Atlantic basin – whether called creolization, ethnogenesis, Anglicization, or the growth of nationalism – requires that we step back from typologies based upon generalizations about various national-imperial Atlantic experiences; the processes that matter were indeed pan-hemispheric and pan-Atlantic but they were fundamentally driven by local variables (contingency, geography, demography and other local material conditions) as they modified the beliefs that peoples from all three continents brought to their interactions. They did not follow reliable patterns; instead they changed relentlessly over time and space.

"Mapping Ethnogenesis in the Early Modern Atlantic."

3

UTOPIA:
THE PRENASCENT GROUP
ANTWERP, 1515

Amaurot lies at the navel of the land, so to speak, and convenient to every other
district, so it acts as a capital.

> – Thomas More, *Utopia*

A world-economy always has an urban centre of gravity, a city, as the logistic heart of
its activity. News, merchandise, capital, credit, people, instructions, correspondence
all flow into and out of the city. Its powerful merchants lay down the law, sometimes
becoming extraordinarily wealthy.

> – Fernand Braudel, *The Perspective of the World*

[T]he utopia may well be a sensitive indicator of where the sharpest anguish of an
age lies.

> – Frank Manuel, "Toward a Psychological History of Utopias"

Realizations of the Group

AS THE PREVIOUS TWO CHAPTERS HAVE SUGGESTED, GROUP METAPHORS
frequently contain an identifiable somatic component. They do so
because the human body serves as the site of cognition and in general as the
premier reference point for the envelope of the social organism as imagined
and instantiated by its members. Group metaphors (i.e., fantasies that have
become fixed in language) come into being in a given time and place,
although sometimes their origins are shrouded in the mists of a remote and
inaccessible past. By contrast, others have a more recent and identifiable
origin. All of the chapters of this book identify social metaphors that date
from the late Middle Ages or Renaissance. Recognizing such metaphors
allows us to re-theorize the social changes of those centuries more globally.
We might think of this approach as the psychosomatic history of groups, by
which I mean the study of projected shapes or envelopes of social collectives.

These shapes can evoke a full human body, certain body parts or functions, stages of human development, or other metaphors still more complex or obscure. The somatic element of such metaphors often lingers just below the surface of the shared discourses in which they circulate. This chapter explores the relation of the individual person to the group – specifically, the individual writer's power to coin new metaphors for one or more collectives and in so doing to reimagine the social world and its possibilities.

In the case of the aestheticizing metaphor of the *gruppo*, the group as a work of art, it was not one person but many who gave the word creative new meanings that were associated with developments in the visual and plastic arts, as well as music, and to the embodied responses of individual people and groups to recovered works of art such as the *Laocöon*. The idea of the Renaissance as an explosion of artistic and creative expression can be linked to this phenomenon of group reorganization, along an axis of shared embodied perception that disseminated outward in progressively larger circles of contact.

The bifurcating metaphors of cannibals and *caraíbas* – metaphors as foundational to the social world of the global Renaissance as that of the *gruppo* – direct our gaze toward a still wider horizon of large-group political and economic encounters during the age of expansion and colonization. Although Christopher Columbus coined the metaphor of the cannibal, the later evolution of that word, together with that of its cognate *caraíba*, reveals an intensely complex history of large-group identity transformations. *Caraíba* was one of the principal New World metaphors of the sacred within the social body, a metaphor extending throughout the Tupí-Guaraní languages. Gradually this developed into a racialized metaphor for the "white" envelope of the dominant group, and was projected back in an altered form onto the subordinated group, as another racialized metaphor of demonic orality. It is the symmetrical and bidirectional transformation of this metaphor, which took place over the first century of colonization, that makes it such a noteworthy example of Renaissance regrouping – the realization of colonial social orders organized in part around oppositional large-group words and concepts.

The present chapter examines another highly influential group metaphor of the Renaissance: *utopia*. Coined by Thomas More in the year 1515, the word *utopia* came to signify the ideal society or commonwealth. This metaphor circulated first among a small group of humanist intellectuals in Europe and then gradually radiated outward across the globe over the course of the next several centuries. As a group metaphor, utopia also contains a somatic component – that of *prenascence*, the corporeal fantasy of group gestation. Like all regressive fantasies, the word/concept possesses a strongly defensive and compensatory element, as we shall see. At the same time, however, utopia must be considered a progressive fantasy, because it provided a highly useful technology (if we may call it that) for re-theorizing the collective during moments of crisis, and projecting the group back into a scene of its imagined origins to imagine giving birth to itself again.

This chapter speculates on the origins of More's fantasy by connecting his literary fiction to the concrete social, political, and economic environments that helped to shape it. One catalyzing context was More's 1515 trip to the Netherlands and to Antwerp. In contrast to most previous interpretations of More's great work, this reading focuses on possible material context for the *Utopia* – that is, a city and its people – rather than for example on More's intellectual formation as a humanist thinker. By speculating on a different set of variables that informed More's writing, this chapter intends to serve as a supplement to earlier readings of the *Utopia*. Those readings generally place More's ideas within western political and philosophical traditions from Plato forward; the intent of this reading is to open out discussions of *Utopia* onto global questions of group identity formation circa 1515 – what I call the *Prenaissance* of the modern world.

The Merchants' Emporium

Sometime during the year 1515, an unknown artist created a panoramic engraving that depicts the city of Antwerp from the left bank of the Scheldt River (Figures 3.1 and 3.2). Several ships move about the city's harbor or wait at the docks to load or unload their cargos. A Venetian galley, armed with a bombard and maneuvered by the labor of convicts or slaves, appears on the left of the image; another galley is already moored at a pier. A Portuguese caravel, heavily armed with cannons, also appears near the left while others are unloaded at the central dock. Anchored on the right is a sailing ship preparing to carry pilgrims to the Holy Land; workers are busy stocking the ship with provisions for that voyage.[1] A few bystanders watch the traffic on the river while dozens of others are shown hard at work in and around the city. Numerous steeples and towers, especially those of the Cathedral, still under construction, soar over houses that nestle on narrow streets and suggest the city's expansive self-confidence.

Wheeling flocks of birds convey a sense of freedom and prosperity. An immense banner floats above the town, bearing the legend: *Antverpia mercatorum emporium* – "Antwerp, the Merchants' Emporium." Two titanic figures

[1] Discussed by Voet in *Antwerp: The Golden Age*, 130.

3.1. Anonymous, *Antverpia mercatorum emporium*, Antwerp (1515), woodcut, 53 cm. × 220 cm. Image courtesy of Museum Plantin-Moretus/Prentenkabinet, Antwerp – UNESCO World Heritage. Photo credit: Peter Maes. This remarkable image dates from the same year that Thomas More visited the city.

stand protectively above the city: on the left, Mercury, god of communication and eloquence, trade and prosperity; and on the right, Vertumnus, patron of the changing seasons and the products of trade. Their joint presence attests to the city's proud and unambivalent love of commerce.

The engraving shows a permeable city – open to earthly or heavenly visitors, open to merchants and to trade, open to the world. Traffic in many forms circulates in and around Antwerp. From the vantage point across the Scheldt, the viewer does not see the half-moon shape of the city extending behind the waterfront, concealed from this perspective; the medieval walls surrounding the city are not visible.[2] The geographic accessibility of Antwerp made possible its rise – first as a commercial center, and then as the capital of the global economy in the early to mid-sixteenth century – just as it would contribute to its conquest and decline a few decades later.[3]

---

[2] Medieval walls punctuated by towers surrounded the city. Recognizing the vulnerability of these walls to attack, city planners decided to tear down these older walls in 1542 and to build a bastioned system of fortifications that would take twenty years and two million guilders to implement. These fortifications would be redesigned and rebuilt multiple times thereafter. Antwerp boasted state-of-the-art fortification and high-tech military engineering. See Lombaerde, "Antwerp in its golden age," 102.

[3] Antwerp's geographic location was central to its economic prominence at the beginning of the sixteenth century. Situated on the estuary of the Scheldt River, 50 miles from the North Sea,

·GEZICHT OP DE REEDE VAN ANTWERPEN IN 1515·

3.1

In 1515, Antwerp was rapidly becoming the cosmopolitan center of an expanding global economy – a role that in the recent past had been played by Venice and Bruges. "Antwerp did not set out to capture the world," economic historian Fernand Braudel wrote; "on the contrary, a world thrown off balance by the great discoveries, and tilting towards the Atlantic, clung to Antwerp, *faute de mieux*. The city did not struggle to reach the visible pinnacle of the world, but woke up one morning to find itself there."[4]

There were many reasons for Antwerp's spectacular rise as a center of trade and finance. Since the latter decades of the preceding century, the Brabant trade fairs helped to fuel the commercial expansion of Antwerp, partly at the expense of cities in Flanders.[5] The trade in English wool was beginning to relocate to Antwerp from Bruges and the markets of Flanders; hence, the finishing and dyeing industries took hold in Antwerp, as did

---

Antwerp had an exceptional port at its disposal. A series of dramatic floods during the fifteenth century had reconfigured the estuary, improving the channel between Antwerp and the sea and facilitating travel to the city. Voet, *Antwerp: The Golden Age*, 56.

[4] On Antwerp as the capital of the global economy during the early to mid-sixteenth century, see Braudel, *The Perspective of the World*, 27–31 and 143–157. See also Limberger's more recent essay "'No town in the world provides more advantages,'" 39–62; and Van der Wee's seminal study, *The Growth of the Antwerp Market and the European Economy (14th–16th Centuries)*.

Limberger finds Braudel's theory about European economic poles somewhat reductive (41), but he nevertheless accepts the claim that Antwerp enjoyed a spectacular rise and fall in the sixteenth century. See also Wegg, *Antwerp 1477–1559*, 60ff.

[5] Van der Wee, 2: 98–123.

the trade and redistribution of cloth. From the mid-fifteenth century on, southern Germans brought to Antwerp much of the copper, silver, and mercury mined in central Europe. In turn, the availability of these metals brought the Portuguese to Antwerp, who traded metal products in Africa and Asia for spices and slaves.[6] Raw sugar from Madeira and other Atlantic islands began arriving in Antwerp in significant quantities at the beginning of the sixteenth century, where it would be refined and sold to other parts of Europe and the world.[7] The French imported products such as salt, wine, and dye-stuffs, as well as writing paper, glasses, pitch, clothwork, and other small wares. German and Italian banking houses – for example the Fugger, Welser, Hochstetter, Imhof, Frescobaldi, Gualterotti, and Affaitadi – controlled the sale of Portuguese spices, made vast profits, and contributed heavily to the development of Antwerp as an international center of finance. Antwerp became the leading European center for short-term commercial and government credit and also the site from which Spain transferred its gold and silver to northern Europe to serve the goals of Hapsburg global politics. It was the seat of major innovations in the theory and practice of finance.[8]

When Antwerp became the principal money market of the Netherlands in the early sixteenth century, the printing industry also began to develop rapidly there.[9] Whether as a cause or an effect of the exchange of money, goods, and ideas there, for at least a few decades, citizens of Antwerp would enjoy a degree of freedom and tolerance unusual in sixteenth-century Europe. In painting and printmaking, in music, in architecture, in book

[6] For a more precise list of items traded by Europeans in Africa, see Alpern, "What Africans Got for Their Slaves: A Master List of European Trade Goods," 5–43.

[7] A superb nineteenth-century mural by Piet Verhaert in the Antwerp *Stadthuis*, or city hall, depicts the arrival of the first loads of sugar from the Canary Islands in 1508.

[8] Voet, *Antwerp: The Golden Age*, 148–149; Murray, *Antwerp in the Age of Plantin and Brueghel*, 59–60; Van der Wee, 2: 26. Van der Wee notes, however, that the Italian banking firms gradually began losing their preeminence in the Low Countries, a fact illustrated by the bankruptcy of the Frescobaldi house in 1518 and the liquidation of the Gualterotti in 1523. 2:131.

[9] The expansion of the Antwerp book trade was also a consequence of the Protestant Reformation. Just months after Luther posted his theses, the Augustinian monk Jacob Proost was disseminating these ideas in Antwerp, which became the first city in the Netherlands where the Reformation took root. William Tyndale, the great translator of the New Testament into English and future nemesis of Thomas More, settled in Antwerp in 1527. There he would live and work until 1536, when he was executed for heresy in Vilvoorde (ironically surviving More, but only by a year).

From 1500 to 1540 there were 120 printers in the Low Countries, and 56 of them operated in Antwerp; of the 4600 editions printed in those decades, 2500 – more than half – came from the presses of that city. These printers published works in Flemish, the local language, but also English, French, Spanish, Italian, Latin, Hebrew, and Greek. See Voet, *Antwerp: The Golden Age*, 150–151; de Nave, "William Tyndale and the Antwerp Printers," 3–9; and Johnston and Gilmont, "Printing and the Reformation in Antwerp," 188–213.

3.2 *Antverpia mercatorum emporium*, detail of the Onze-Lieve-Vrouwekathedraal (Cathedral of Our Lady). Image courtesy of Museum Plantin-Moretus/Prentenkabinet, Antwerp – UNESCO World Heritage. Photo credit: Peter Maes. This image shows the second tower of the Cathedral under construction. More's first meeting with Giles and Hythloday in the *Utopia* takes place near this building.

publishing, and in the decorative arts of sixteenth-century Antwerp, economic and material prosperity fueled an outpouring of creative expression.[10] For the prosperous, the city offered a culture of abundance, defined in part by the availability of luxury goods and a thriving artisanal culture. Antwerp artists catered to the middle and upper-middle classes, who sought to decorate their homes with portraits, landscapes, and devotional art. Many sixteenth-century painters of renown lived and worked in Antwerp at various times, including Lucas Cranach, Albrecht Dürer, Hans Baldung Grien, Lucas van Leyden, Quentin Matsys, Frans Floris, and Pieter Bruegel the Elder.[11] The premier European metropolis of the early sixteenth century, Antwerp was unapologetically affluent.

In 1515, the nightmare that would unfold in Antwerp during the Wars of Religion – a nightmare of sectarian violence and destruction shared by much of Europe in varying degrees – was still undreamt. Meanwhile, other dreams of the group – utopian dreams – would take shape there. For Thomas More, who visited the city in the summer or fall of that year, the mercantilism of Antwerp would provide material inspiration for an unforgettable vision of its antithesis: a place beyond the known regions of the world and beyond the reaches of physical and material desire as well. More, the visiting Under-Sheriff of London, would call this mysterious place, marked by the unusual communalist practices of its natives, Utopia. One of the premier group fantasies of the sixteenth century, More's masterwork exerted – and continues to exert to this day – a powerful pull on the real and imagined lives of collectives.

Business had first brought More to the Netherlands in 1515.[12] He and others had been commissioned by Henry VIII to pursue a trade agreement

---

[10] The excellent collection *Urban Achievement in Early Modern Europe* discusses the creative outpouring in all of these fields. Lombaerde discusses architecture and urban space in "Antwerp in its golden age" (99–127); Vlieghe, "The fine and decorative arts in Antwerp's Golden Age" (173–185); Waterschoot, "Antwerp: books, publishing, and cultural production before 1585" (233–248); and Vanpaemel, "Science for sale: the metropolitan stimulus for scientific achievements in sixteenth-century Antwerp" (287–304).

See also Vermeylen's study of the Antwerp art market during the sixteenth century: *Painting for the Market*, esp. 15–34.

[11] Vlieghe, 174; Murray, 152 ff.

Numerous lesser-known artists resided in Antwerp as well; in the first two decades of the sixteenth century, 293 new masters were registered with the artists' and craftsmen's Guild of St. Luke, compared with 303 for the period between 1454–1500. Voet, *Antwerp: The Golden Age*, 152–153.

[12] J. H. Hexter theorizes that More left Bruges for Antwerp shortly after negotiations were suspended sometime before July 21, 1515. He may have stayed there for some time, or he may have gone away and come back before his return to London in the fall. See "More's Visit to Antwerp in 1515," Appendix A of *Utopia*, in *Complete Works* 4, edited by Surtz and Hexter, 573–576.

with envoys of the future Holy Roman Emperor Charles V. In May of that year, More traveled to Bruges with a group of negotiators who were hoping to forestall a trade war with the Netherlands and who were seeking more favorable terms for the overseas English wool market.[13] The Bruges negotiations were suspended in July, but More remained abroad for another three months, returning home to London in October of 1515. Although he was not well compensated by the Crown for his diplomatic efforts,[14] More found other aspects of his travel far more profitable. Through his connections with the humanist scholar Desiderius Erasmus, More was invited to visit the home of Peter Giles, the *griffier*, or town registrar, of Antwerp.[15] It is not known how long More remained in Antwerp during his free months in 1515, but sometime during or after his visit to the city, More began writing what would become Book II of *Utopia*, with Antwerp as its backdrop.[16]

More's literary masterpiece was probably begun in Antwerp in 1515[17] and published in Louvain the following year. By proposing a radically different set of relations between the individual and the group, the work challenged the social and political realities of the era. Book I includes a harsh critique of More's England, described as a nation of brutal inequalities and social injustice. Book II, probably written first, describes life on the faraway island of Utopia – a Greek pun of More's invention that fuses two

[13] The trade commission to Flanders included More, Cuthbert Tunstall, Richard Sampson, Thomas Spinelli, and John Clifford. The specific purpose of the mission was to dispute Dutch import duties, which the English protested by putting an embargo on all their wool exports to Holland. Charles, Regent of the Netherlands and soon to become the Holy Roman Emperor, threatened to retaliate, impelling certain diplomatic efforts by Henry VIII. Marius, *Thomas More*, 62; Ackroyd, *The Life of Thomas More*, 165.

[14] Marius puts More's wages for this business trip in context. In July 1515, More received 20 pounds for the embassy to Flanders, while Tunstall and Sampson, two of the other emissaries, received 30 pounds. In that same month, Sir Richard Wingfield, the Ambassador to France, received over 333 pounds. When More returned, he received 60 pounds for his "diets" in Flanders, which did not cover the per diem he had been promised. "Why did More get so little? Perhaps Henry thought he was wealthy enough to give his service to the state. If so, More did not agree." *Thomas More*, 190–191.

[15] The name "Peter Giles" was the Anglicized version of Pieter Gilles, also known as Petrus Aegidius. For a brief biography of Giles and his friendship with More and Erasmus, see Bernstein, "Erasmus and Pieter Gillis," 131.

On the responsibilities and status of the position of *griffier*, or registrar, see Kint, *The Community of Commerce*, 327–331.

[16] "Meanwhile, as my business led me, I made my way to Antwerp," More would write in the opening pages of that work; "Ego me interim (sic enim res ferebat) Antverpiam confero." We do not know what business, if any, brought More to Antwerp. *Thomas More: Utopia: Latin Text and English Translation*, edited by Logan, Adams, and Miller, 42, 43.

[17] See Hexter, "More's Visit to Antwerp in 1515," 573–576, and Logan, Adams, and Miller, *Utopia*, xx–xxii.

distinct and contradictory meanings: *ou-topos*, or "no place," and *eu-topos*, or "good place." In that imaginary society – the good place impossible to locate – property and resources are distributed equally among the citizenry, and individual striving for wealth, status, and power has largely been eliminated. Differences between individual Utopians – differences in appearance, temperament and personality, beliefs, opinions, and taste – have also been downplayed, whereas the differences between groups – that is, between the Utopians and other polities on earth – are foregrounded within the narrative.

If the *geistiges Individuum*, or "spiritual individual," cast off the "common veil" of the group during the Renaissance, as Jacob Burckhardt argued, we might say that Thomas More imagined putting the common veil back on, because *Utopia* is quintessentially an anti-individualist fantasy. Regardless of whether the author himself advocated the end of private property and the rise of a proto-socialist state – questions still debated today – More articulated an important fantasy for his group – that is, for the circle of European humanists who served as the immediate audience for the work and for an expanding circle of future readers as well. What could have been the wish behind his fantasy of subduing individual voices and wills in favor of those of the group? This fantasy was not unique to More but was voiced by many political philosophers of the era.[18] More broadly still, what might Thomas More's *Utopia* tell us about the larger transformations of group identity in the Renaissance?

Antwerp and the Conception of *Utopia*

Walking through the affluent city of Antwerp in 1515, down to its busy docks along the Scheldt River, More would have encountered numerous citizens, resident aliens, and foreign visitors like himself, engaged in work or leisure. Toward the beginning of Book I of *Utopia*, the character More describes a meeting with one such foreigner, Raphael Hythloday, in Antwerp. This imagined contact sets the story in motion:

> One day after I had heard Mass at Notre Dame, the most beautiful and most popular church in Antwerp, I was about to return to my quarters when I happened to see [Peter Giles] talking with a stranger, a man of quite advanced years, with a sunburned face, a long beard, and a cloak hanging loosely from his shoulders; from his face and dress, I took him to be a ship's captain. (43)[19]

---

[18] For additional examples, see Skinner, *The Foundations of Modern Political Thought*, 1: 211–243.
[19] All page references are to the Logan, Adams, and Miller edition of the *Utopia*.

Concerning this stranger, Giles reports to More, "there is no mortal alive today can tell you so much about unknown peoples and unexplored lands; and I know that you're always greedy for such information" (43). This man, named Raphael Hythloday, traveled extensively with none other than Amerigo Vespucci, says Giles:

> Being eager to see the world, he left to his brothers the patrimony to which he was entitled at home (he is a Portuguese), and joined Amerigo Vespucci. He was Vespucci's constant companion on the last three of his four voyages, accounts of which are now common reading everywhere. . . . (45)

By foregrounding Hythloday's connections to the Italian cosmographer, as well as the popular *Mundus novus* and *Quattro viaggi* attributed to Vespucci, More presents his protagonist as a bona-fide world traveler. Hythloday's Portuguese nationality indicates his membership in the most successful community of European seafarers at that time.

More's interest in the Portuguese, as well as "unknown peoples and lands," was most likely stimulated or intensified by at least three factors relating to his 1515 travels abroad. The first is that Antwerp was rapidly becoming one of the primary publishing centers of Europe – a role that would intensify in the decades after the Reformation.[20] Columbus's *De insulis nuper inventis*, his first letter on the New World, had been published there in 1493.[21] In addition, several editions of Vespucci and Vespucciana were published in Antwerp prior to More's visit.[22] For example, a Flemish translation of Vespucci's *Mundus novus*, addressed to Lorenzo di Pier Francisco de Medici, was published by the Antwerp publisher Jan van Doesborch in 1507.[23] Through Peter Giles, More may have become acquainted with this publisher and his works, given that, as his host observes, he was "always most greedy to hear" about travel and exploration.

Doesborch also published in 1508 *Die reyse van Lissebone* (The Journey from Lisbon), which incorporated another letter purportedly by Vespucci that describes a Portuguese voyage around Africa to India – "the island of

[20] See n. 9.

[21] Hirsch, "Printed Reports on the Early Discoveries and Their Reception," 553. Also see the discussion of Columbus's letter in Chapter 2.

[22] It is not certain which texts and editions of Vespucci that More might have read prior to his writing of the *Utopia*. Likely More saw a Latin translation of the *Quattro viaggi* entitled *Quattuor Americi Vespuccij navigationes* that had been incorporated into Waldseemüller's 1507 *Cosmographie introductio*. An English summary of Vespucci called *Of the Newe Lands* was published in Antwerp in 1510. Numerous other editions circulated throughout Europe at the beginning of the sixteenth century (see Chapter 2, n. 37).

[23] A single copy of this Flemish Vespucci, entitled *Van der nieuwer werelt*, can be found in the John Carter Brown Library in Providence, RI, and in facsimile.

Nagore which lieth in Great India, beyond Calicut and Cochin."[24] Although "Albericus" dates his trip as having occurred in 1500, the details of the narrative seem to describe the actual 1505–1506 voyage of Dom Francisco de Almeida's fleet to Southeast Asia. If More read this text or heard about it, he might well have believed that Vespucci had traveled eastward to India, as well as westward to America (newly named by Martin Waldseemüller and the St. Dié cosmographers, as discussed in Chapter 2). More's character Hythloday circumnavigated the globe several years before Magellan's fleet, by traveling to Africa, America, Ceylon, India, and finally to the faraway island of Utopia.[25]

In addition to the range of travel literature available in Antwerp, a second, more immediate factor that could have piqued More's curiosity about New World exploration was the small but influential Portuguese community living in Antwerp at that time.[26] Portuguese travel and trade, not only as it was described in print but also as it existed in Antwerp in 1515, provides a crucial context for understanding More's *Utopia*. Portugal had selected Antwerp as its principal distribution center for trade with the rest of Europe. From as

---

[24] The full title, translated, is *The Voyage from Lisbon to sail unto the island of Nagore which lieth in Great India, beyond Calicut and Cochin, wherein is the staple of the spices. Wondrous things befell us therein, and we beheld much, as hereinafter is described. This said voyage was undertaken by the will and command of Emanuel, the most serene King of Portugal.* "Nagore" could refer to a town in the kingdom of Tanjore on the southern mouth of the estuary of the Cauvery, on the east coast of India, in the Madras presidency. See C. J. Coote, ed. and trans., *The Voyage from Lisbon to India*, 2 and 51. Coote believed (or hoped) that this letter was, in fact, a genuine Vespucci. Current scholarship has determined otherwise. The actual author was most likely Balthasar Sprenger.

[25] Hythloday's circumnavigation of the globe, as well as More's skeptical view of Vespucci's *Quattro viaggi*, has been discussed by Dominic Baker-Smith, who argues that More understood that Vespucci's purported first voyage in 1497–1498 was a hoax. See *More's* Utopia, 91–92.

[26] J. A. Goris contends that there were approximately twenty Portuguese merchants based in Antwerp during the first quarter of the sixteenth century. Presumably many other Portuguese and colonials passed through Antwerp on the merchant ships that were loaded and unloaded there. See *Étude sur les colonies marchandes méridionales (portugais, espagnols, italiens) à Anvers de 1488 à 1567*, 53.

"In the summer of 1515 not a few persons who had been in India and Ceylon, and even resided for years in those quarters, were available in Europe," writes J. Duncan M. Derrett. More could have met Portuguese traders in Antwerp, and even Indian and African natives. A Syrian Christian from Cranagore known as Joseph traveled with Cabral's crew from India back to Portugal. He gave an account of Christians and Hindus in India, which was translated into Italian and published in *Paesi novamente retrovati et Novo Mondo da Alberico Vesputio Florentino intitulato* (see Chapter 2, n. 37). According to Derrett, More might have seen the Latin translation of this work published in 1508.

It is not just the Portuguese but also their stories of India that are represented in More's *Utopia*, Derrett argues. "Some of the details that Hythloday gave More are so remarkably clearly representative of India, and particularly of the western coastal strip, that no doubt remains in the present writer's mind but that . . . genuine Indian ideas have found their way into that book." "Thomas More and Joseph the Indian," 19, 23. See, too, Derrett's essay "More's *Utopia* and Indians in Europe," 17–18, and Vallavanthara, ed., *India in 1500 A.D.: The Narratives of Joseph, the Indian*.

early as 1501, Portuguese merchants, sailors, and slaves had been unloading their ships from Africa and India there. In 1508, King Manuel I of Portugal had founded in Antwerp the *Feitoria de Flandres*, a new branch of the *Casa da Índia* in Lisbon.[27] The *feitoria*, or "factory," was a set of warehouses that the Portuguese used for storing and distributing a wide variety of luxury imports, such as spices, drugs, precious stones and metals, and many other exotic trade goods. The *feitoria* was only a short walk from English House, as Romuald Lakowski has noted, and it is not unlikely that in his capacity as town clerk, Peter Giles might have introduced More to the staff members of India House, where More would have seen or met men who were as well-traveled as his main character Hythloday.[28]

A third factor of probable influence on More's *Utopia* – one about which very little has been written and of which the second can be considered a subset – was the highly international population of the Netherlands, and of Antwerp in particular, which More would have observed during his months abroad. In the early sixteenth century, Antwerp boasted one of the most ethnically diverse populations of Europe – far more diverse than that of More's native London.[29] Numerous painters who were active in Antwerp during the early decades of the sixteenth century reflected the city's ethnic and cultural diversity in their artwork. As noted in the previous chapter, the subject of the Adoration of the Magi provided a popular painterly vehicle for depicting and contemplating such diversity during the early modern era. Many such images were produced in Antwerp during the sixteenth century, particularly from 1510 to 1520, where they had become a "studio speciality." In turn, these paintings were widely exported throughout Europe.[30]

One such painting (Figures 3.3 and 3.4), created in 1504 in Antwerp by the so-called Master of the Morrison Triptych, features an African Balthasar in a billowing golden robe, who looks intently at the Holy Family. A multiethnic

[27] Braudel, 149. The *Casa da Índia* was a Portuguese organization that managed overseas trade during the era of maritime expansion and colonialism.

[28] "Thomas More's *Utopia* and the East: Portugal, Alexander the Great and India."

[29] Kint, 31–32.

[30] For example, the *Adoration of the Magi*, painted by the Master of the Antwerp Adoration between 1500 and 1520 and now in Antwerp's Koninklijk Museum voor Schone Kunsten, and Quentin Matsys' *Adoration of the Magi* (ca. 1526), currently in the Metropolitan Museum of Art in New York.

One shop that produced many such images was run by Jan van Dornicke and later reopened by his son-in-law Pieter Coeck van Aelst. These paintings reflect "the convergence of a vogue of the black and a reawakening of interest in the East." See Devisse and Mollat, *The Image of the Black in Western Art*, II, 2: 183.

For an excellent introduction to this theme, see Kaplan, *The Rise of the Black Magus in Western Art*.

3.3. Master of the Morrison Triptych, *Adoration of the Magi* (1504), Oil on panel, 65 3/4 ×
42 3/4 inches (167 × 108.6 cm). Image courtesy of The John G. Johnson Collection,
Philadelphia Museum of Art. Such images had become a studio specialty of Antwerp at
the turn of the sixteenth century. (See color plate.)

3.4. Master of the Morrison Triptych, *Adoration of the Magi*, detail of the Magus Balthasar and other worshippers. Image courtesy of The John G. Johnson Collection, Philadelphia Museum of Art. These portraits are thought to have been modeled on persons residing in Antwerp at the beginning of the sixteenth century.

crowd of visitors appears behind him. These figures were in all likelihood modeled on persons living in or visiting the city at that time. In this image, representatives of the world's diverse nations, clustered on the left side of the painting, come to visit the infant Jesus and his mother. The group on the

right side of the painting, in contrast to that on the left, appears to be of
northern European descent. The two clusters are separated by a spatial divide
that reveals Antwerp and its harbor, which bridge the two groups. Like Grão
Vasco's *Adoration*, this painting can be considered an assimilationist fantasy,
in which the peoples of the world have been incorporated into the family of
European Christians, while also perhaps being held at a distance. Antwerp
was not the only city in early sixteenth-century Europe in which such
diversity of population existed, but it was among the most cosmopolitan.
This demographic context informing *Utopia's* frame narrative must also be
taken into consideration as one of the variables that likely influenced More's
conception of an ideal commonwealth on the other side of the equator and
of the world. Like the contemporary travel narratives available in Antwerp,
actual people would have conveyed information to More about groups and
group identity around the globe – as much or more than the book learning
for which More is rightly celebrated.

Thus More's choice of Antwerp as the setting for his frame narrative was
not random. As political theorist Karl Kautsky noted in his seminal study of
the *Utopia*, "Antwerp became in the sixteenth century what Constantinople
had been in the fourteenth century and what London was to become in the
eighteenth century: the center of world trade, the focus of the treasures of
the East, to which the Americas were now added, whence they were poured
out over the whole of Europe."[31] In Antwerp, More witnessed the economic
power of the new global economy of the early sixteenth century. Antwerp
was a nexus in the emerging world-system, a place where people, material
wealth, and information circulated and collected. Book II of More's *Utopia*
offered a *camera obscura* image of that city, its mercantilism, and its peoples –
upside down yet still recognizable.

Insulation

More's *Utopia* articulated many of the conflicting sentiments of Europeans
regarding the overseas contacts and empire-building then underway: excitement, optimism, curiosity, and a sense of possibility on the one hand, and
uncertainty, anxiety, fear, and hostility on the other. These contradictory
emotions underpinning the work account for some of the difficulties that
modern readers have in gauging More's intentions and opinions. These contradictions could attest to the author's ambivalence about the world in which
he would exercise progressively greater political and ideological authority on

---

[31] Kautsky, *Thomas More and His Utopia*, 165.

behalf of his sovereign, King Henry VIII of England, and about the larger
social, religious, and economic power struggles into which he would be
drawn. More's projection of a model state neutralizes potential conflicts
between persons and the group by bringing their interests into close alignment and by downplaying the role of a leader or sovereign. His projection
also envisions a way in which conflicts between groups could be managed
to promote ethical, social, and economic stability. For these reasons and
more, Utopia, a distant island deliberately cut off from the mainland, must
be considered a fantasy of insulation.

Insulate: "to make into an island by surrounding with water; to convert
into an island," from the Latin insŭlātus. Although the verb insŭlāre is not
recorded in late or medieval Latin, it may have emerged in the latter or in
Renaissance Italian.[32] In this context, the word enters the English language
in the early sixteenth century. A later figurative meaning takes hold in the
eighteenth century – namely, "to cause (a thing, person, etc.) to stand alone
from its surroundings; to separate or detach from its fellows or the rest; to
set or place apart; to isolate."[33]

As if anticipating the later developments of that word and concept, More
wrote, "The island of the Utopians is two hundred miles across in the middle
part, where it is widest, and nowhere much narrower than this except towards
the two ends, where it gradually tapers." Hythloday explains at the beginning
of Book II, "These ends, curved round as if completing a circle five hundred
miles in circumference, makes the island crescent shaped, like a new moon.
Between the horns of the crescent, which are about eleven miles apart, the
sea enters and spreads into a broad bay" (109). The bay is dangerous to enter,
because hidden reefs, rocks, and shallows pose a threat to unfamiliar sailors
attempting to penetrate it. "[H]ardly any strangers enter the bay without
one of their [the Utopians'] pilots," Hythloday reports.

The island of Utopia was not always an island, however; it was insulated –
literally and figuratively – by its conqueror Utopus. This king, "who brought its
rude, uncouth inhabitants to such a high level of culture and humanity that
they now surpass almost every other people, also changed its geography."
This he accomplished by cutting a channel fifteen miles wide that would
separate his new island from the mainland and allow the sea to flow around
it (111) – an extraordinary feat of geographic remodeling.

The unnamed illustrator of the first edition of *Utopia* visualized this somewhat contradictory description for the readership, including the long Anyder

---

[32] *Oxford English Dictionary*, 1: 1453.
[33] *Ibid.*, 1453.

river also mentioned by Hythloday (Figure 3.5). The island's architecture, like the boats entering the Utopian bay, looks distinctively European. The mainland looms protectively behind it.[34] Although the island's position near the mainland could suggest England in relation to Europe, it is arguably Europe itself, with England, that is insulated *in* and *as* Utopia: insulated, that is, from the rest of the world. At the beginning of Book I, More emphasizes that it is "civilized nations" (*populos . . . civiliter conviventes*) that interest him; this is the topic that he and Giles pursue with Hythloday in their conversation. "We made no inquiries, however, about monsters, for nothing is less new or strange than they are. There is no place where you will not find Scyllas, ravenous Celaenos, man-eating Laestrygonians and that sort of monstrosity, but well and wisely trained citizens you will hardly find anywhere" (48–49). The monsters – Scyllas, Celaenos, Laestrygonians – derive from classical sources such as the *Odyssey* and the *Aeneid*, rather than the "real-life" stories of other seafaring storytellers of that era. The effect of More's *Utopia* is thus an insulating one, not yet sufficiently recognized as an expression of and a response to collective anxieties and desires of the time, as populations once largely unknown to each other came into increasing contact. Arguably More managed those anxieties by imagining an insulated group body, a "fortunate island" of self-sufficient men and women who are neither anxious about nor desirous of much in particular.

Unlike the natives of Vespucci's tales but like their European counterparts, Utopians wear clothes. Their work clothes are made of leather or pelts, which last seven years. They wear undyed wool cloaks over their rough work clothes, and they also wear white linen (133). "Their clothing," Hythloday says, "which is, except for the distinction between the sexes and between married and unmarried persons, the same throughout the whole island and throughout one's lifetime, and which is by no means unattractive, does not hinder bodily movement and serves for warm as well as cold weather – this clothing, I say, each family makes for itself" (125). Their clothing design aims for practicality, simplicity, and relative uniformity. Hythloday explains, "In body they are nimble and vigorous, and stronger than you would expect from their stature, though they're by no means tiny" (179). Hythloday does not indicate any distinctive differences in body or dress between Utopians and Europeans, or among Utopians themselves (except, of course, in their unusual uses for gold, silver, and gemstones). In his refusal to foreground

---

[34] In the 1518 Basel edition of *Utopia*, Ambrosius Holbein, brother of Hans Holbein the Younger, provided a different map of the island, still more European in look. Gone is the large bay featured prominently in the earlier woodcut but added are three figures in the foreground, one of whom is Hythloday.

MAP OF UTOPIA

UTOPIAE INSULAE FIGURA

3.5. *Utopiae insulae figura.* Anonymous woodcut from the 1516 Louvain edition of *Utopia.* Image courtesy of Cambridge University Press.

phenotypic differences, varieties in clothing and fashion, or simply the bare body itself, More created a travel narrative strikingly different from all of the others that were published in his day.

Ethnically, More's Utopians are a hybrid people. The ancient occupants of the island, which was originally called Abraxa, were "rude" and "uncouth" (111). Utopus, who conquered the land 1760 years before Raphael's arrival there, brought laws and a high level of culture to the island (111, 121); then, twelve hundred years before Hythloday's arrival on the island, a group of shipwrecked Romans and Egyptians was cast ashore there. Subsequently the natives "learned every single useful art of the Roman empire either directly from their guests or by using the seeds of ideas to discover these arts for themselves" (107). Since that time, they have lived in isolation from the "Ultra-equatorials" – that is, people from the other side of the equator, such as Europeans, although slaves from nearby countries come to Utopia as prisoners of war or as willing servants eager to escape the poverty or penal codes of their own nations (185–187). Although it is a hybrid collective consisting of multiple ethnic or cultural groups, Utopian society nevertheless remains highly homogeneous in its cultural, political, and economic practices. Exchanging houses by lots every ten years (119), with few exceptions, Utopians are not defined or distinguished by their property, status, or, for the most part, social position (though some differentiation exists according to sex, age, education, and a few other variables).

Despite the diversity of belief represented within Utopian society, religious difference is also mitigated. Hythloday reports a variety of religious forms on the island, including sun, moon, and planet worship, and the worship of a "man of past ages," distinguished for his virtue or glory. "But the vast majority, and those by far the wiser ones, believe nothing of the kind: they believe in a single divinity, unknown, eternal, infinite, inexplicable, beyond the grasp of the human mind, and diffused throughout the universe, not physically, but in influence. Him they call their parent..." (219). This native deity, named "Mythra" in the language of the Utopians, resembles the deity of the ancient Persians.[35] More imagines a monotheistic religion for his Utopians, situated within a conceptual framework of known rather than unknown belief.

Unlike Vespucci's cannibals, who "have no temple and no religion,"[36] the denizens of Utopia cultivate strong and visible religious traditions. Moreover, they are highly receptive to the Christianity introduced by Hythloday

---

[35] See *Utopia*, 219, n. 114.
[36] *Mundus novus*, in *Letters from a New World*, edited by Formisano, 49.

and his fellow travelers. "[A]fter they heard from us the name of Christ, and learned of his teachings, his life, his miracles and the no less marvellous constancy of the many martyrs whose blood, freely shed, has drawn so many nations far and near into their religion, you would not believe how eagerly they assented to it, either through the secret inspiration of God or because Christianity seemed very like the sect that most prevails among them" (219–221). Like the non-Europeans depicted in the Master of the Morrison Triptych's *Adoration*, the Utopians eventually choose to be incorporated into the Christian large group, either because of divine guidance or because their largely monotheistic culture readily aligns with Christianity.

The Utopians, distinctive in their sheer lack of distinctiveness, contrast starkly with native groups featured in the travel narratives of More's day. Columbus, Vespucci, Peter Martyr, and other explorers invariably drew attention to differences in appearance, cultural practices, and religious beliefs, and frequently supplemented ethnographic observation with outright fantasy. Many visual illustrations of these works also demonstrate similar sensationalizing tendencies (e.g., as in Figures 2.4 and 2.7). It is essential to read *Utopia* in the context of these contemporary works, both verbal and visual, the ethos of which More would invert in his representation of the staid island civilized long ago by Utopus and then by errant Romans and Egyptians. In certain ways Utopians are more like Europeans than the Europeans themselves are; as J. H. Hexter argues, the Utopians, although pagans, are better Christians than their counterparts in Europe.[37]

More actively effaced ethnic and cultural difference by imagining an island on the other side of the world that was nevertheless 1) like Europe in many respects but perhaps more civilized, and also 2) more homogeneous, both culturally and socially. The natives of Utopia wear clothes and avoid unusual dietary and sexual practices (save for the prophylactic rite of scanning the bare body of the betrothed before marriage to rule out unexpected defects or diseases [189]). In contrast, popular European travel narratives of the day generally presented lurid and sensational views of recently encountered native populations.

The question that remains is why More chose to write a *faux* travel narrative that, unlike others of the time, did not foreground the differences in body and dress of "newly discovered" peoples – differences that consumed the imaginations of Europeans at that time and those of the groups with whom Europeans came in contact. One possible effect of such a fantasy – specifically, of a society in which everyone is alike, and in which corporeal

[37]Surtz and Hexter, *Utopia*, lxxvi.

differences, as well as other differences in wealth, status, and choice of work, have been minimized but not completely eliminated – might have been to defend against or deny the many forms of difference that preoccupied the minds of Europeans and that were sensationalized in virtually all other travel narratives of the era.

The European Prenaissance

In his analysis of the history and functions of utopian thought, Frank Manuel states: "If the ordinary dream often derives its content from a need denied or a wish repressed and transformed, the utopia may well be a sensitive indicator of where the sharpest anguish of an age lies."[38] He argues that the urge to imagine utopia, an impossible and ideal alternative reality, expresses a hidden wish, one often shared by the author and his readers. Connected to the wish is anxiety: the author's, as well as that of many of his contemporaries. Dreams of utopia speak to those collective but not fully understood sentiments and attempt to resolve them through fantasy or even through direct action, if a group manages to instantiate its utopian vision.

The French psychoanalyst and group theorist René Kaës offers a similar but more corporeal interpretation of this category of fantasy. Kaës also links such fantasies to eras of profound social and cultural transformation.[39] Utopias provide a highly stable, secure, and comfortable fantasy of escape during times of intense social upheaval. The spatial, social, and psychological organization of such fantasies provides an imaginary defense against the threat of an outside world in transition.

Kaës also observes that utopian fantasies tend to have certain constant features: namely, the separation of an inside from an outside world perceived to be problematic or dangerous; a lingering connection between the inside and the outside, because neither is fully cut off from the other; an internal organization aimed at stockpiling goods (e.g., nourishment or riches); and soldiers or guards who constantly protect those goods. "Everything there is regulated and obsessively codified in order to exert collective control over the interior of the utopian body."[40]

---

[38]"Toward a Psychological History of Utopias," *Utopias and Utopian Thought*, 69–98, p. 70.
[39]Examples of such periods of change include, according to Kaës, the Renaissance, the nineteenth century, the era of the Beat Generation, or May 1968. *L'appareil psychique groupal: constructions du groupe*, 74.
[40]*Ibid.*, 74 (my translation).

As discussed previously, groups imagine or create various kinds of "bodies" for themselves, although such fantasies need not enter the conscious awareness of group members; indeed, in becoming conscious, they could lose their effectiveness. A group also can imagine a relation to a particular type of body or even to a body part. In Kaës's psychoanalytic view, utopian fantasies represent a desire to return to a protective womb, which envelops the group and provides an escape from an unsettling outside world. For that reason, Kaës argues, utopias are often set in an isolated or enclosed space (e.g., a cloister, a garden, a space ship, a cave, or an island). Additionally, however, such fantasies contain an opposing defense against that impossible and (on some level) highly threatening return.[41]

The enclosed spaces of More's *Utopia* lend support to such interpretations, linking the group to regressive fantasies of the maternal body and infancy. The initial meeting of More, Hythloday, and Peter Giles takes place inside the Cathedral of Our Lady in Antwerp (Figure 3.2), or close by, and inside the walled city. Their discussion then moves to a private and protected garden adjacent to More's lodgings in that city.[42] Kaës, however, would argue that the most important image of the maternal body in this work of fiction is the actual island of Utopia. Hythloday's description of the island at the beginning of Book II, as well as the 1516 frontispiece (Figure 3.5) representing the island of Utopia, suggests a womblike interior space — the bay — protected by the land surrounding it and fed with an umbilical river.[43] Amaurot, the capital

---

[41] *Ibid.*, 74. In a related vein, literary historian David Bleich explains utopian fantasies as carryovers from earliest childhood. These fantasies, he writes, "appear as the adult symbolization of the infant's search for a 'basic trust' of his environment and his future. . . . " Bleich follows the theories of psychoanalyst Erik Erikson, outlined in *Childhood and Society* (1950). Bleich further explains, "As the Golden Age has in fact not arrived, the infantile search remains in adult life as a *wish*, the wish for the return of the Golden Age of satiation, felicity, and inner equilibrium." Bleich also notes a rebellious adolescent component of some utopian fantasies, e.g., that of Thomas More. Arguably the more infantile elements are present, as well. *Utopia: The Psychology of a Cultural Fantasy*, 14.

[42] The garden enclosed served as a symbol of the Virgin Mary throughout the Middle Ages. It should also be noted, however, that the crises of enclosure described in Book I offer a dystopian perspective on the "bad womb"/mother that was More's England. Kaës would see these as two sides of the same coin, because utopian fantasies easily shade into dystopian ones.

[43] This visual analogy has been discussed by Manuel, v. See also Ferns' discussion of Utopian womb imagery in *Narrating Utopia*, 41–42, et passim.

Hythloday's description of the river Anyder does not totally match the image of the river created by the artist. "The Anyder rises from a small spring eighty miles above Amaurot, but other streams flow into it, two of them being pretty big, so that as it runs by Amaurot the river has grown to a width of about five hundred yards. It continues to grow even larger until at last, sixty miles farther along, it is lost in the ocean. In all this stretch between the sea and the city, and also for some miles above the city, the river is tidal, ebbing and flowing every six hours with a swift current" (*Utopia*, 117).

city, is explicitly described as lying "at the navel of the land" (*in umbilico terrae* [112–113]).[44] Deliberately cut off from the mainland and carefully insulated from the malign influences of the outside world, Utopia can be construed as a fantasy of isolation, of escape to a mythical, womblike space.[45] The fact that the island of Utopia could stand for England, as well as Europe, lends support to a "prenascent" interpretation of the work, because it was his own society above all that More wanted to recreate.

Utopian fantasies are almost as old as writing itself. One of the earliest is Hesiod's description of the Golden Age in the *Works and Days* (ca. eighth century BCE), nearly 3000 years old.[46] Given their possible links to our earliest childhood wishes, dreams of safety, plenitude, and bliss may be a permanent fixture of the human psyche. It is nevertheless essential to recognize that such yearnings or aspirations are also marked in specific ways as products of the epochs in which they were produced. Although More's *Utopia* can be read as an imagined return to a well-regulated, protective, maternal space, it is also much more than that. To consider More's vision as *merely* an escape, reducing it to those regressive and simultaneously idealist elements common to other utopian dreams and systems, is to ignore the stamp of its time and place, as well as its pivotal role in the history of group fantasies. *Utopia* speaks to individual and collective sentiments emerging in the so-called age of discovery, an epoch marked, as the psychogeographer William Niederland has observed, by "a variety of myths, conscious and unconscious strivings, haunting anxieties, [and] superstitious beliefs."[47]

A century before Galileo and the scientific method that his work would help to introduce, More's *Utopia* would speak to a world very much in flux. By the early sixteenth century, knowledge of the world's geography was expanding at an exponential rate. Only 200 years earlier, Dante had envisioned the other side of the world as the Hemisphere of Water, empty save for the Mount of Purgatory at its center, and crowned by the Garden of Eden. Dante's Purgatory/Eden is one of many such mysterious islands imagined to exist just beyond the reaches of the known world. The trope of the *Fortunatae Insulae*, the Fortunate Isles (also known as the Isles of the

---

[44] More's intriguing image also calls to mind Freud's intriguing image of the "navel" of a dream, discussed in the Foreword to this book, xxxi–xxxiii.

[45] As Tom Conley writes in his psychoanalytic study of early modern cartography, "the *navel* is constructed to be a site where the relation of the unknown has its first noticeable, physical trace. It becomes the site of a ruptured attachment to the world. . . ." *The Self-Made Map*, 9.

[46] Bleich, 13.

[47] "River Symbolism, Part II," 50–75.

Blessed), appears in many medieval maps of the world. Niederland links these representations with dreams of the womb, birth, and bliss.[48]

By the early sixteenth century, however, European voyagers and cosmographers were rapidly charting and filling in this once-blank conceptual space.[49] Copernicus would situate that recently explored and connected globe within a new conceptual system – one with the sun at its center. More's *Utopia* was written on the cusp of those monumental and accelerating changes in the human understanding of the world. His response was to imagine a radical form of social reorganization, and a reimaging of the self–other divide through a renaissance of the group.

More's *Utopia*, one of the most potent and influential group fantasies of the Renaissance, captures one of the great transformations of human history – the inception of the modern world-system, at that time centered in Europe and in Antwerp itself, if we accept Braudel's analysis.[50] In reading *Utopia*, we come to understand how the fantasies of a single visionary person could be catalyzed by and in turn further catalyze the actions and organization of groups. Marshaling his prodigious learning, sensitivity to injustice, humor, and also resistance to change, More not only described the nascent modern world of European hegemony but also attempted to "reconceive" it, by envisioning, at least hypothetically, a society that miminized the gross inequalities and injustices of his world through the collectivization of wealth and property. In his *Utopia*, More also imagined a world in which many other differences between persons and groups – cultural, sexual, or somatic – could be deemphasized. In doing so, he recorded the anxiety and ambivalence of his age, which arguably he wanted to come to terms with and not necessarily escape.

Where on this filled-in map of the world did More imagine his "*no-place,*" and with it a group both known and unknown, alien yet familiar? More is deliberately vague about its geographic location and not simply because, in

---

[48] Such images appear, for example, on the thirteenth-century Hereford Map, drawn in the Cathedral of Hereford. On that map, this set of six islands appears on the site of the Canaries. The 1339 Dulcert Map, drawn by the Mallorcan Angelinus Dulcert, places the "Isles of the Blessed" near the site of the Madeira islands. A legend on the Dulcert Map also calls them the *Insulae San Brandani,* the legendary Isles of St. Brendan. There are numerous other phantom Islands of St. Brendan, long associated with Paradise, that appear on medieval maps. These islands in medieval and early Renaissance cartography, and their associations with the female body, are discussed by Niederland in his essay "River Symbolism, Part II," 56 ff.

See, too, T. J. Cachey's book *Le Isole Fortunate*, which studies the transformation of the Canary Islands (the Fortunate Islands) from mythic spaces on the western boundaries of the known world to launching pads for transatlantic conquest.

[49] On the "filling in" of the globe's blank spaces, see Conley, 1–23, *et passim.*

[50] See p. 133.

an increasingly known world, he had to be. The Utopian group is a liminal fantasy, poised on the threshold between selves and others. To find oneself on either side of that divide – to shift into the alterity of differentiation – was the non-desideratum of More's dream. The good place that is no-place exists only *between* the individual person and the group, between one's own and all the rest. Temporally liminal as well, More's *Utopia* stands poised between past and present, looking backward to classical and medieval dreams of the Fortunate Islands, ever elusive, and forward across the threshold of a new era, when the globe would be charted, mapped, and investigated, and its peoples and its resources increasingly regulated. More would respond with a regulatory fantasy of his own: namely, a group body that processes and reabsorbs its own waste – a fetal group body nourished and purified through an imagined maternal umbilicus.

The Birth of a Nation-State

The fantasy of prenascence subtending the *Utopia* is in no sense incompatible with More's more concrete speculations on the ideal commonwealth; in fact, it is quite the opposite. The human body and its functions are never far removed from group concepts and fantasies. Indeed, specific corporeal fantasies can give rise to new ways of thinking about old problems, such as the optimal distribution of a society's wealth and resources.

Although More avoided many of the somatically sensational features of Vespucci's accounts of the New World – nudity, free love, and cannibalism, to name the obvious ones – More gravitated toward another feature that he incorporated into his Utopia: namely, the Americans' purported lack of private property. Of the New World natives, Vespucci had written, "Nor have they private property, but own everything in common: they live together without a king and without authorities, each man his own master," and "There are no merchants among them, nor is there any commerce."[51] This report from the *Mundus novus*, although not fully accurate, appears to have struck More with considerable force – so much so, according to Arthur Slavin, that he "developed a theory to fit the new facts [of American communism]." This theory would serve as a critique of "the emerging order of European capitalism," the tools for which More found "not in his mind but in the less familiar territory of America."[52]

---

[51] Formisano, 49–50. A similar report was made by Peter Martyr d'Anghiera. See Arber, ed., *The First Three English Books on America*, 71.
[52] Slavin, "The American Principle from More to Locke," 1: 146.

As Karl Kautsky observed, "a thinker who takes his stand on the material conditions may be a whole epoch in advance of his time, if he perceives a newly evolving mode of production and its social consequences not only sooner than most of his contemporaries, but straining far into the future, also glimpses the more rational mode of production into which it will develop." As a lawyer and public official with long-standing connections to England's own merchant class, and as a profoundly philosophical and ethical humanist, More was the man for that season. Kautsky writes that he was "one of the few who have been capable of this bold intellectual leap," perceiving a possible solution to problems of the new economy "at a time when the capitalist mode of production was in its infancy."[53] According to Kautsky, that solution was to envision a comparatively egalitarian society that anticipated modern forms of socialism.

It was not socialism per se that More embraced in the *Utopia*, however, but a "cleaner," less wasteful version of the sixteenth-century state. The rise and consolidation of states and not the later concepts of individualism and free enterprise signaled the arrival of a new world-scale economic order, defined by a capitalist mode of production. The disjunction between the political and economic is another key feature of the modern world-system as described by Wallerstein, because political matters are essentially contained by and within each state, whereas economic matters extend beyond the state structure and are directed toward a larger world-system that exceeds any single state structure. To paraphrase Wallerstein, we might say that (early) modernity can be defined as the reformation of individuals and groups into states, the privileged containers of collective identity. These states also played a role within a larger system or network, however. This process did not occur in a homogeneous or uniform way; there were centers, peripheries, and even regions external to the emerging world-system in the sixteenth century. "[T]he capitalist world-economy," Wallerstein writes, "was built on a worldwide division of labor in which various zones of this economy [i.e., core, semiperiphery, and periphery] were assigned specific economic roles, developed different class structures, used consequently different modes of labor control, and profited unequally from the workings of the system."[54]

Sixteenth-century rulers of core states had at their disposal four major mechanisms that they used to manage and control their realms and extract wealth from their subjects and from the larger world economy: these were "bureaucratization, monopolization of force, creation of legitimacy, and

[53] *Thomas More and His Utopia*, 161.
[54] *Modern World-System*, I, 162.

homogenization of the subject population."[55] State bureaucracies emerged
in the sixteenth century with the power to tax and to borrow, using any
increased revenues to augment their coercive power (though the concept of
state was defined in many ways). National debts, or deficitary state budgets,
also emerged while More was writing his *Utopia*. Standing armies or mercenary forces at the service of the state also became standard at that time.[56]
The power of the new states and their rulers was consolidated through such
legitimizing ideologies as the divine right of kings, ideologies that in turn
enabled the formation of absolute monarchies.[57] Finally, statism in the sixteenth century depended on the degree to which the subject population
could be made into a culturally homogeneous group. Core states moved
toward greater ethnic homogeneity, Wallerstein argues, whereas peripheral
states became more heterogeneous.[58]

In his *Utopia*, Thomas More would theorize each of these four mechanisms governing the modern group container, the nation-state. This container was also a prenascent state – a group identity and mode of organization
and collectivization as yet in the process of becoming. Visionary that he was,
More not only described in great detail how these mechanisms contributed
to surplus appropriation that benefited only a few but also envisioned possible curtailments on the wealth-extraction powers of kings and the wealthy.
Moreover, More re-imagined the possible relation of states to the global
economy that was then taking shape, but he still maintained those four
distinguishing features of modern states in his fantasy of Utopia. More's
Utopia, very much a "statist" work, remains deeply inscribed in the political
and economic paradigms of his epoch, paradoxically retaining and recasting
the key features of early modern states, including colonialism, mercenary
warfare, and slavery.

To call Utopia a proto-socialist polity, as Kautsky did, is to ignore precisely
those features that mark it as a quintessentially European Renaissance state.
The Utopians practice a form of colonialism, as More imagined it, handling
increases in population by creating colonies on the mainland "wherever the

---

[55] *Ibid.*, I, 136.

[56] *Ibid.*, I, 138.

[57] *Ibid.*, I, 144.

[58] Wallerstein specifies that it was less the masses who were homogenized within the core states than
the cadres in the broadest sense: the king, his bureaucracy and courtiers, the rural landowners
(large and small), and the merchants. He offers as a case in point the Jews in the sixteenth century.
Largely absent from Western Europe, they immigrated to peripheral and semiperipheral regions –
parts of southern and eastern Europe, for example. *Ibid.*, I: 147–151.

On critiques and revisions of Wallerstein's model, see Introduction, n. 27.

See also Chapter 4 on the emigration of Spanish and Portuguese Jews to South Asia during the
sixteenth century.

natives have plenty of unoccupied and uncultivated land" (135, 137). If the natives choose to join the Utopians (thereby suggesting that the colonized land might not be entirely vacant), "the two peoples gradually and easily blend together, sharing the same way of life and customs, much to the advantage of both" (137). If, however, natives decline to live under the laws of the Utopians, they are then driven from the land. If they refuse to leave, the Utopians wage war against them, on the grounds that land should not lie idle when many might be supported by it (137).[59]

It is difficult to say whether More the author fully endorsed this position, because he does not claim the views of the Utopians as his own. It is possible, however, that More believed that the type of colonialism practiced by the Utopians was justified by its populism – similar, perhaps, to the populist impulses that appear in Book I of *Utopia*. There Hythloday offers a famous description of enclosure, the British practice of fencing off, or privatizing, lands that were formerly used or held in common. Wealthy landowners used England's newly enclosed lands for the grazing of sheep, exporting wool to the Netherlands for the production of cloth. In turn, this finished cloth was distributed and traded throughout the world. More understood this trade network well; his 1515 embassy to Flanders, the occasion for his travel abroad, had been devoted to negotiating better terms for the trading of English wool to the Dutch.

Concerning the wool trade and its effects on those displaced from English commons, Raphael recounts a conversation held earlier with Cardinal Morton, former Archbishop of Canterbury and Lord Chancellor of England:[60]

> Your sheep . . . that commonly are so meek and eat so little; now, as I hear, they have become so greedy and fierce that they devour human beings themselves. They devastate and depopulate fields, houses and towns. For in whatever parts of the land sheep yield the finest and thus the most expensive wool, there the nobility and gentry, yes, and even a good many abbots – holy men – are not content with the old rents that the land yielded to their predecessors. Living in idleness and luxury without doing society any good no longer satisfies them; they have to do positive harm. For they leave no land free for the plough: they enclose every acre for pasture; they destroy houses and abolish towns, keeping the churches – but only for sheep-barns. (63).

[59] As Dominic Baker-Smith has noted, "the entire proceeding has a painful similarity to the early settlement of the New World." Baker-Smith also mentions that More's brother-in-law John Rastell participated in a 1517 expedition to found a colony on Newfoundland. *More's Utopia*, 186.

[60] As a youth, More had served as a page in the household of Cardinal John Morton (1420–1500), whom he greatly admired.

It was the privatization of English common land and people's dispossession of their homes and livelihoods that drew the animus of Hythloday and presumably of More himself, inspiring the vision of man-eating sheep (a distant echo of the cannibalistic motifs in Vespucci's works, and of out-of-control consumption). In Hythloday's view, private property and social justice cannot be reconciled, because, in the words of Dominic Baker-Smith, the former subverts the "whole conception of community."[61]

This dichotomy raises a fundamental question about the boundaries of Utopia, a commonwealth separated – and thereby insulated – from the mainland, as well as other more distant polities, yet still reliant on a far-larger economy for certain resources such as iron, new land for colonial expansion, and slave labor. Utopians maintain an autonomous political life but nevertheless participate in a larger economic network that allows them to maintain large trade surpluses.[62] After stockpiling enough food and essentials to survive for two full years, Utopians sell their excess commodities to foreign governments. They accumulate in return immense quantities of gold and silver, as well as promissory notes for which they may or may not claim payment, because they do not wish to take advantage of the neediness or misfortune of other states. They maintain their well-stocked treasury "as a protection against extreme peril or sudden emergency," using it "above all to hire, at extravagant rates of pay, foreign mercenaries, whom they would much rather risk in battle than their own citizens" (147). They even buy off enemy soldiers when possible. Surplus gold and silver are converted into Utopian chamberpots, humble vessels, and the chains of slaves (149), rather than hoarded. The accumulation of these metals for their own sake is discouraged by this process.

As Richard Halpern has astutely argued, the transmutation of gold into base objects in Utopia is perhaps the most striking emblem of More's imag-ined counter-economy. These strange, devalued objects nevertheless retain "the logic of the commodity."[63] More's golden chamberpots conceal not only the origins and social content of gold but also suggest a forbidden desire for that precious metal. Similarly jewels, clothing, and other items are marked with a mysterious reverse status in *Utopia*. "The island itself,"

---

[61] Baker-Smith, 137.

[62] It is this separation of the political and the economic that for Wallerstein marks the modern world-system.

[63] "What the text has done," Halpern contends, "is to transform social value (gold as the congealed product of social labor: exploration, mining, refining, and so on) into a quality of the thing itself. This is the very process Marx immortalized as the fetishism of the commodity." "Rational Kernel, Mystical Shell: Reification and Desire in Thomas More's *Utopia*," in *The Poetics of Primitive Accumulation*, 136–175, p. 146.

Halpern writes, "is constructed as the repression of desires it cannot locate and of which it cannot take account."[64] Paradoxically, gold and silver become acceptable only through their debasement; lucre, made filthy in a unique way, become symbols of the "clean" capital of Utopia.

One could also argue, however, that gold and silver are not debased in Utopia, but that *waste* is effectively revalued in the second book of More's fantasy. The physical waste products of the citizens are symbolically transmuted into gold (the classic alchemical fantasy), as are the more figural forms of waste within the Utopian polity. Criminals wear gold rings, earrings, necklaces, and headbands; these items of jewelry can be read as markers not only of their transgressions but also of a recapturing process by which those transgressions are transmuted into what is socially valuable. Undesirable forms of labor within Utopia are thus performed by those who will be changed into better citizens through that process of servitude. Finally, slaves wear fetters of gold or silver (147–151), as if their enslavement, voluntary or involuntary, can be converted into something of great value as well – their freedom and full membership in the Utopian polity.

The Puzzle of Slavery in Utopia

One of the more perplexing features of *Utopia* for contemporary readers is the institution of slavery practiced by the citizens of that island. Critics have sought to understand why More chose to introduce slavery in Utopia when he was under no compunction to do so.[65] For modern readers, the concept of slavery does not mesh with the "utopian" goal of sharing the wealth – seemingly the visionary project of Book II of More's work. As Baker-Smith has noted, "Any discussion of this remarkable society and its relevance as a model for admiration, and even emulation, must take account of those

---

[64]Halpern, 149.

[65]See, for example, Surtz, *The Praise of Wisdom*, 258 ff. Surtz provides an interesting summary of debates concerning slavery in More's own time in response to the practices that were then developing, but he does not relate More's writings to his own probable exposure to the practice in Antwerp.

Elizabeth McCutcheon highlights the tone of the *De Servis* section, in her view ironic, and explores the word play in More's use of the term *servus*. "There is no private property in Utopia, one person cannot own another, and no one is born into servitude. So Utopia's *servi* are not slaves in our sense of the word, and the usual translations are misleading in this and other ways." "Puns, Paradoxes, and Heuristic Inquiry," 93.

Shlomo Avineri, in contrast, highlights the dystopian quality of More's imagined world in "War and Slavery in More's *Utopia*."

practices which from our point of view appear quite out of harmony with the enlightened idealism that animates their social relations."[66] In which sense might More's depiction of slavery have been intended by the author or construed by his contemporaries as a commentary on the institution of slavery as it was then practiced? How might *Utopia* have reflected the practices of slavery as More would have witnessed them during his travels to the Netherlands, and specifically to Antwerp, a city in which slave labor, although officially outlawed, was nevertheless clearly present and visible on the loading docks of the Scheldt River, on incoming ships from around the world, and in the homes of wealthy resident aliens and some natives of the region?

As noted previously, it is essential to read More's group fantasy in relation to the actual groups he encountered during his travels – not just those that he had read about or imagined in books such as Plato's *Republic* or Vespucci's letters from the New World. Although we cannot determine with certainty what More witnessed in Antwerp or how he felt about it, it is reasonable to assume that his lived experience and perceptions during his transformative trip to the Continent – the journey thought to have inspired the *Utopia* – would also have influenced the content of that work. It was probably not a coincidence that he chose to write about slavery and that the perspectives presented in both books of *Utopia* would be complicated and ambivalent ones.

Although the Dutch did not become active in the slave trade until later in the century,[67] Portuguese, Spanish, and northern European slaveholders resided in or visited Antwerp. For example, the Portuguese official João Brandão, who served as factor (chief agent) of the *Feitoria* in Antwerp from 1509 to 1514 and again from 1520 to 1526, held slaves. Brandão's commercial activities were considerable, and he received important concessions from the town of Antwerp.[68]

Some historians have argued that because Antwerp had close trade relations with Portugal, and because it was increasingly involved in the sugar industry, it had the greatest number of African inhabitants of any city in

---

[66] *More's* Utopia, 182.

[67] See Emmer, "The History of the Dutch Slave Trade," 728–747.

[68] Goris, *Étude sur les colonies marchandes méridionales*, 231. See also Goris's "Uit de Geschiedenis der vorming van het Antwerpsch Stadsrecht: Slavernij te Antwerpen in de XVI^{de} eeuw," 541–544.

  Another Antwerp merchant of German origin, Jacob Groenenborch, went to the island of Palma in 1515, set up a plantation, and later made a huge fortune. He called himself Heer van Canariën (Lord of the Canaries). He too was a slaveholder. J. Denucé, *L'Afrique au XVI siècle et le commerce anversois*, 24.

Europe after Lisbon.[69] Although historians disagree on the number of slaves in Antwerp at the time of More's visit,[70] More would have likely seen African, Moorish, South Asian, and possibly Native American and Central European slaves working on the docks and in the homes of some of the people whom he visited during his time abroad.

The *Stadsarchief van Antwerpen* holds many records concerning slaves brought to the city in the fifteenth and sixteenth centuries. These documents describe escapes, slaveholders' attempts at recovery, slaves' conversions to Christianity (resulting in manumission), slaveholders' deathbed releases of slaves, and the actual sale of slaves.[71] One such document, a city ordinance dated August 16, 1516 – one year after Thomas More's visit to the city – offered a reward to anyone who would return "twee Mooren nog niet kersten wesende" (two Moors who had not yet been baptized) to George de Sulco Lobo from Portugal. These slaves had been "ontleyd, ontvremd of onthouden" (stolen, purloined, or withheld) – a phrase that, J. A. Goris states, sheds light on the Antwerp judicial authorities' view that unbaptized slaves were considered objects or property.[72]

Another document of the period describes the case of a previously freed slave called "Balthasar the Moor," who joined with another merchant. This second merchant tried to sell him, claiming that the slave had, in fact, escaped from his previous master. Balthasar submitted a formal request for his freedom to the city magistracy, declaring himself "to have been born in the Portuguese Indies of Christian parents, as the whole country there is Christian, and the petitioner had thus undergone Holy Baptism immediately after birth, as is there and here the custom of the Holy Church."[73] Given that he had been baptized, Balthazar insisted that he should never have been

---

[69] *Ibid.*, 30–31. See also Goemaere, "Anvers et ses esclaves noires"; Debrunner, *Presence and Prestige: Africans in Europe*, 57; and Blakely, *Blacks in the Dutch World*, 226.

[70] Denucé's claim that Antwerp was second only to Portugal in the number of blacks there has been challenged by A. C. de C. M. Saunders in *A Social History of Black Slaves and Freedmen in Portugal, 1441–1555*, 188. Saunders, following Goris in "Uit de Geschiedenis der vorming van het Antwerpsch Stadsrecht," claims that there were only a few slaves there during this period. Saunders offers little evidence for his counter-claim, however. Clearly more work needs to be done in this field, which has been largely neglected for many decades.

  Whether there were many Africans in Antwerp at the time of More's visit or relatively few, I argue that their presence is refracted in More's *Utopia* in a complex and deracialized way.

[71] See especially Goris, "Uit de Geschiedenis der vorming van het Antwerpsch Stadsrecht."

[72] Stadsarchief van Antwerpen, Requestboeck, IV, 1563, folio 132 verso. *Ibid.*, 543. With thanks to Ria Vanderauwera for her translation of this article.

[73] "[G]eboren te zyn uyt de Indien van Portugael van cristen ouders gelyck het heel landt aldaer cristen is en alsoe de suppliant zynde ten heyligen doopsel gecomen zoe haest hy geboeren was gelyck aldaer en alhier de manieren vander heyligen kercke is." *Ibid.*, 543.

enslaved at all, for that was the law in Antwerp and theoretically throughout Christendom.[74]

During the sixteenth century, Antwerp was a city where slaveholding was officially outlawed but in practice was tolerated. Artists of the time documented the presence of slaves in Antwerp. For example, among the many images that he recorded during his visit to the city, Albrecht Dürer left a silverpoint portrait of "a Moorish maid" (1521). The young woman, known as Katharina (Figure 3.6), was the slave of the Portuguese factor Brandão mentioned earlier.[75] This sharply melancholic portrait presents a domestic image of chattel slavery in Antwerp at this time; the reality was in all likelihood grimmer still. During the sixteenth century, the Antwerp city magistracy regularly offered rewards for runaway slaves,[76] a practice that suggests not only the undesirable circumstances of their captivity but also the increasing collaboration of the city in enforcing the distinction between free persons and slaves in Europe.

Perhaps commenting on what he had observed directly or heard about, More reimagines the institution of slavery in the chapter entitled *De servis* ("On Slaves") in Book II of the *Utopia*. Hythloday explains,

> The only prisoners of war the Utopians keep as slaves (*pro servis*) are those captured in wars they fight themselves. The children of slaves are not born into slavery, nor are any slaves obtained from foreign countries. They are either their own citizens, enslaved for some heinous offense, or else foreigners who had been condemned to death in their own cities; the latter sort predominate. Sometimes the Utopians buy them at a low price; more often they ask for them, get them for nothing, and bring them home in considerable numbers. These kinds of slaves are not only kept constantly at work, but are always fettered. The Utopians, however, deal more harshly with their own people than with the others, feeling that they are worse and deserve stricter punishment because they had an excellent education and the best of moral training, yet still couldn't be restrained from wrongdoing. A third class of slaves consists of hard-working penniless drudges from other nations who voluntarily choose slavery in Utopia. Such people are treated

---

[74] A third case dating from 1532 demonstrates the ambivalent view of the city of Antwerp and other cities in the Netherlands toward slavery and slaveholding. In March of that year, the slave of the Portuguese factor in Antwerp fled his master. The factor appealed to Mary of Hapsburg to have the slave arrested and returned. The face of the slave had been branded with the letters P and M. The Queen in turn submitted the request to the Council of Malines, which rejected the plea of the Portuguese agent, on the grounds that slavery was unknown in the Netherlands. Algemeen Rijksarchief. Mémoriaux du Grand Conseil de Malines, III, folio 376. *Ibid.*, 544.

[75] Voet, 46, n. 75.

[76] *Ibid.*, 46.

3.6. Albrecht Dürer, *Katharina* (1521), drawing, 19.6 × 13.4 cm. Gabinetto dei Disegni de della Stampe degli Uffizi, Florence. Photo credit: Scala/Ministero per i Beni e le Attività Culturali / Art Resource, New York. Katharina was the slave of official João Brandão, the Portuguese factor in Antwerp.

with respect, almost as kindly as citizens, expect that they are assigned a little extra work, on the score that they're used to it. If one of them wants to leave, which seldom happens, no obstacles are put in his way, nor is he sent off empty-handed (184–187).

In this passage, More uses the classical Latin word *servus* to describe the slaves of Utopia. As Edward Surtz notes, that word contained two possible meanings that were not yet clearly differentiated in that time period: that is, *slave* and *servant*.[77] This word captures the dual aspect of servitude in Utopia, because in some cases, such as punishment for serious crimes, servitude is a form of involuntary punishment. In other cases, servitude may be voluntary, as in the case of those who prefer to be *servi* in Utopia rather than downtrodden poor people in their own countries. The ambiguity of the word *servi*, with its lack of distinction between voluntary and involuntary forms of servitude, may have served More's purposes as he explored possible justifications for and uses of slavery, without directly endorsing them.

In analyzing possible precedents for the model of slavery put forward in *Utopia*, Edward Surtz argues that More may have been following classical authors such as Plato, who incorporated slavery in his *Republic*, as well as later political theorists such as Duns Scotus, who held that there were three legitimate justifications for slavery: 1) voluntary submission, 2) punishment for extreme transgression, and 3) the enslavement of prisoners of war as a fate preferable to execution.[78] These are also the three conditions for enslavement in Utopia, as Hythloday describes them. Surtz holds that although it is not possible to ascertain More's intentions fully, More most likely agreed that "theoretically, at least among non-Christians, voluntary submission, criminal activity, and capture in war were just causes of enslavement." Surtz concludes that slavery in Utopia is "mild, humane, permissive of manumission, and not very extensive – but still slavery in the strict sense of the word."[79]

Clearly More was conversant with the political, philosophical, and theological discourses around the institution of slavery, an ancient institution that was in the process of being redefined at the time of his writing. More engaged

---

[77] In the *City of God*, Augustine hypothesized that the Latin word *servi*, meaning *slaves*, was based on the fact that captives were preserved (*servabantur*) and made servants (*servi*). Surtz, *Praise of Wisdom*, 260, 262–263.

More also uses the word *famuli* (bondsman) to describe those who slaughter animals in Utopia (138, 139n.), although elsewhere he refers to *servi*.

On the evolution of the word *slave*, see Verlinden, "L'origine de 'sclavus'-esclave," *Archivum latinitatis medii aevi*, XVII (1943): 97–128, and "Encore sure les origines de *sclave* – *esclave* et à propos de la chronologie des debut de la traite italienne en mer noire," 599–609.

[78] Surtz, *The Praise of Wisdom*, 263.

[79] *Ibid.*, 269.

that tradition, reflecting on the possible uses of slavery as a punishment for "crimes" such as adultery (191–193). In Utopia, slavery thus serves as an extreme punishment for modes of transgression that often went unpunished in More's own society. Protection or safeguarding of the institution of marriage and family life seems to have been one possible intention behind the Utopian insistence on monogamy, fidelity, and heterosexuality.[80] Hythloday discusses Utopian views on marriage at length, with their interdictions on premarital sex and adultery. No other transgressions are mentioned specifically (except the unpunishable crime of unsanctioned suicide), although Hythloday notes that in general, "the gravest crimes are punished with slavery, for they think this deters offenders just as much as getting rid of them by immediate capital punishment, and convict labour is more beneficial to the commonwealth" (193). In this thought experiment, the reader is asked to consider the possible value of slavery as a means of killing two birds with one stone: slavery serves as a mode of criminal deterrence less severe and more effective than the death penalty, and as a means of extracting certain kinds of labor from citizens deemed unworthy, as well as would-be citizens, for the benefit of the commonwealth. In Utopia, crime is recycled as labor, and social waste is made economically and morally productive through that recycling process.[81]

These intragroup measures of social regulation have their counterpart in various extragroup strategies of labor extraction, modes of incorporation both voluntary and involuntary. As noted above, foreign prisoners of war – enemies of the state – can become slaves in Utopia, as can a certain number of those assigned the death penalty in other countries – persons who are rescued from death and reclaimed for Utopian use. Poor people who volunteer to be slaves in Utopia to escape the debased conditions of life in their countries of origin provide yet another source of recycled labor in the ideal commonwealth.

The Sweetness of Utopia: Sugar Production and Slavery

In the chapter entitled "The Travels of the Utopians," Hythloday reports on the efficient surplus production of the islanders:

After they have accumulated enough for themselves – and this they consider to be a full two-years' store, because next year's crop is always

---

[80] Same-sex relationships are not discussed in *Utopia*, but heterosexual marriage is certainly the norm within the culture.

[81] Also suggested by McCutcheon in "Puns, Paradoxes, and Heuristic Inquiry," 96.

uncertain – then they export their surpluses to other countries: great quantities of grain, honey, wool, flax, timber, scarlet and purple dyestuffs, hides, wax, tallow and leather, as well as livestock.... In exchange they receive not only such goods as they lack at home (in fact, about the only important thing they lack is iron) but immense quantities of silver and gold (147).

This largely utilitarian list of products grown or produced in Utopia, which they exchange for metals and other goods not available in their own country, includes honey. With the possible exception of "scarlet and purple dyestuffs," for which the pragmatic Utopians would seem to have little use, these goods seem both fundamental and necessary to the natives and to their trading partners. Although items on the list are not ranked in order of importance, honey seems to occupy a place of honor between the basic components for bread and clothing. Is Utopian honey a luxury item or a necessity? Why do Utopians produce honey rather than sugar? Why do they sell honey to other nations? As it turns out, these questions are central to understanding the puzzle of slavery in More's imaginary commonwealth.

The rise of the slave trade at the end of the Middle Ages was closely bound up with sugar production, an industry that grew exponentially during the colonial era to meet the ever-increasing demand for sugar in Europe and in other parts of the world. As in many other areas of commerce, Antwerp was increasingly at the forefront of the sugar trade in the early sixteenth century; there More could have observed directly or indirectly the economic, social, and cultural links between sugar, slavery, and the creation of wealth.

At the time that More was writing the *Utopia*, sugar was a luxury product that was available on a limited basis in Europe to those who could afford to pay comparatively large amounts for it. Sugar, rather than honey, epitomized gastronomic pleasure for the affluent, as well as power for those who controlled its means of production.

By the beginning of the sixteenth century, the sugar industry on the Atlantic islands was strongly linked not only to Portugal and Spain but also to Flemish, Italian, and English capital, and to western European commercial centers, especially Antwerp, where sugar was refined and sold.[82] The

---

[82] Mintz, *Sweetness and Power*, 31. See also Denucé's *Afrika in de XVIde eeuw en de Handel van Antwerpen*, still in many ways unsurpassed; Greenfield, "Plantations, Sugar Cane and Slavery"; Thijs, "De Geschiedenis van de Suikernijverheid te Antwerpen (16de – 19de eeuw)"; Everaert, "The Flemish Sugar Connection"; and Harreld, "Atlantic Sugar and Antwerp's Trade with Germany."

growing economic significance of this trade probably would have been evident to More during his visit to Flanders and the Brabant, as would its many links to the slave trade.

To understand the state of global sugar production circa 1515, it is useful to trace its earlier history. Native to South Asia, the sugar cane plant (*Saccharum officinarum*) was cultivated in India in ancient times.[83] Sugar production continued to develop and expand in the Islamic world, gradually spreading to Persia and the Mediterranean region. In the late thirteenth century, Christian Crusaders may have brought sugar canes from the Middle East to Cyprus, where sugar would soon become a principal crop of that island.[84] In the fifteenth century, the Portuguese began cultivating sugar on the Atlantic islands of Madeira, the Canaries, and São Tomé (Figures 3.7, 3.8 and 3.9).[85] Sugar cane was carried to Hispaniola on the second voyage of Columbus in 1493.[86] By 1515, gold supplies on the island were nearly exhausted, and sugar would take its place as the premier export.[87] Sugar cultivation was also introduced to numerous other regions of the New World, including Brazil, ultimately eclipsing production on the Atlantic Islands.

From the late Middle Ages on, slavery was increasingly linked to the cultivation and refining of cane sugar. Slave labor was used to a limited extent on the Portuguese-controlled island of Madeira, as it had been in the Mediterranean sugar trade in earlier centuries, but was modest in comparison to later sugar colonies of the Atlantic.[88] By contrast, sugar cultivation on several of the Canary Islands, including Tenerife, Grand Canary, La Palma, and Gomera, had by the late fifteenth and early sixteenth centuries developed into a highly organized and hierarchical system of land use, an essential component of which was the slave labor of the Guanches, the native inhabitants of the islands; Berbers; black Africans; and contract laborers from Spain, Portugual, and Madeira, whose labor was used in the fields and especially in the processing mills.[89]

---

[83] Sugar cane may have been domesticated in New Guinea as early as 8000 BCE. It seems to have been brought from that location to the Philippines, India, and Indonesia sometime thereafter. The Hindu scripture *Buddhagoṣa* (ca. 500 CE) is the first text to describe sugar production: the boiling of sugar juice and reduction to molasses and the rolling of balls of sugar. Mintz, *Sweetness and Power*, 199–23.

[84] Toussaint-Samat, *A History of Food*, 553. See also Galloway, *The Sugar Cane Industry*, 42.

[85] Galloway, 48–61; Mintz, 24.

[86] Mintz, 32.

[87] Galloway, 64.

[88] *Ibid.*, 53–54. For a somewhat different view of slavery's prevalence on Madeira, see Disney, 2: 88–89.

[89] *Ibid.*, 57. Fernández-Armesto, *The Canary Islands after the Conquest*, 20–21.

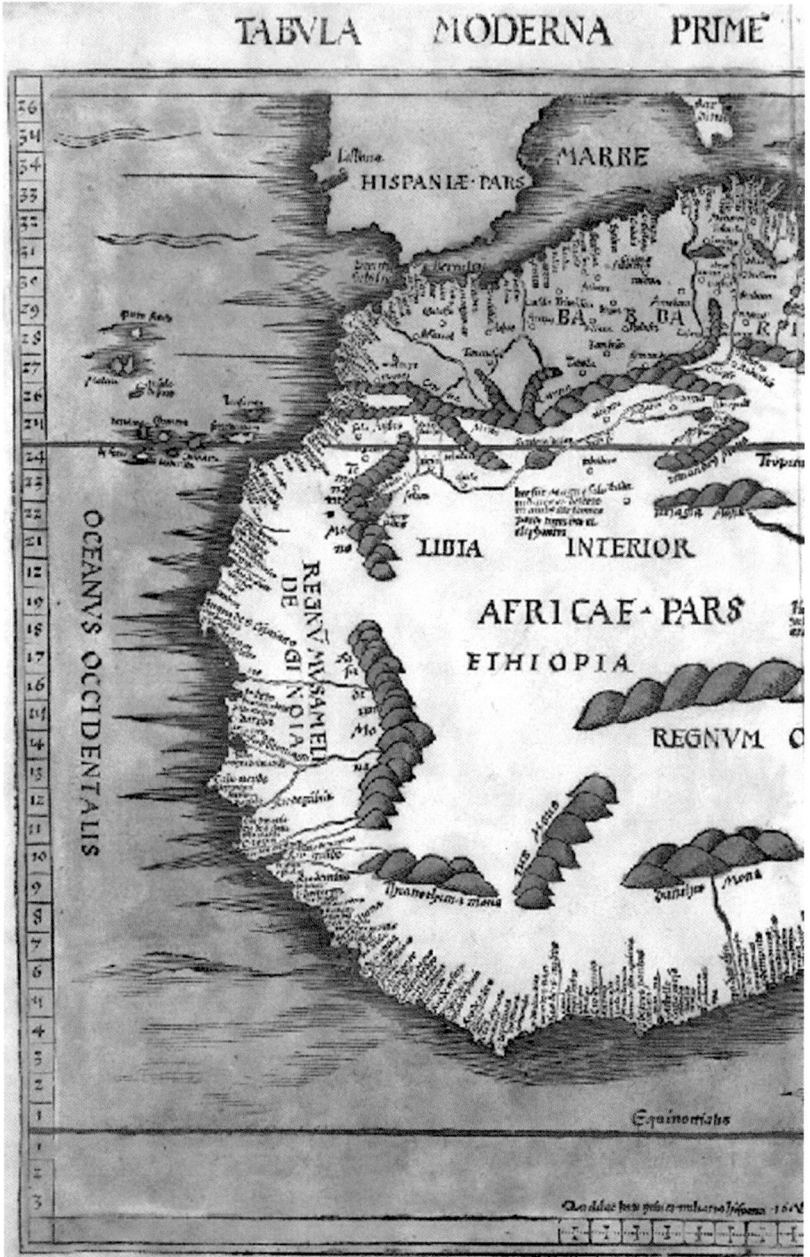

3.7. *Tabula moderna prime partis Aphricae*, from Waldseemüller's *Ptolemy* Atlas. Strasbourg (1513), 41 cm. × 57 cm. Stanford University Libraries Digital Collections and Department of Special Collections. The African interior was largely unknown to Europeans at the time this map was made.

3.7

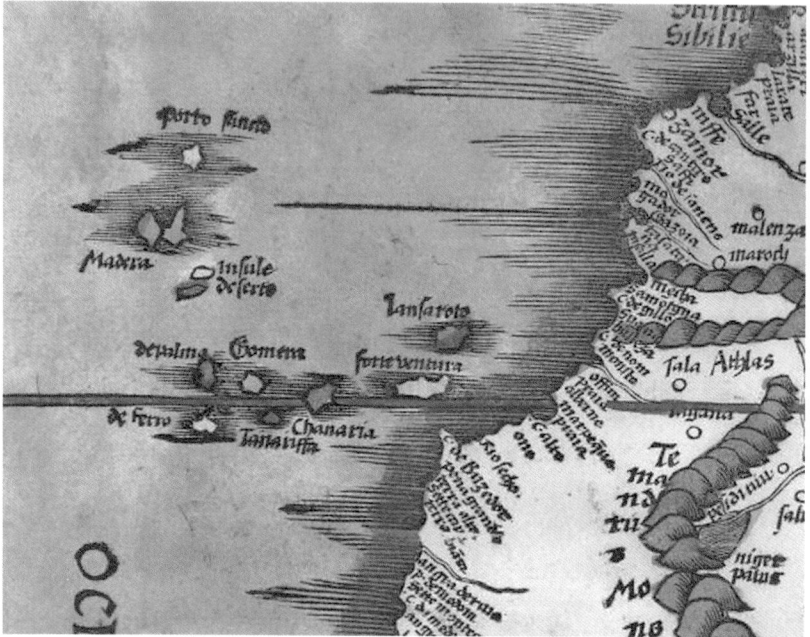

3.8. *Tabula moderna prima partis Aphricae*, detail of Madeira and the Canaries. Stanford University Libraries Digital Collections and Department of Special Collections. These were important sugar-producing islands in the early sixteenth century.

São Tomé, an uninhabited Atlantic island near equatorial Africa that was discovered in 1470, would also play a key role in the sugar industry and in the Portuguese overseas empire and its slave trade. The island's strategic importance in the Gulf of Guinea led to its settlement in the 1480s and 1490s, partly through a decree by King João II requiring that it be populated with condemned Portuguese prisoners and with 2000 children of enslaved Castilian Jews, separated from their parents and sent to their tragic fate.[90] African slaves were soon brought to the island to serve as the labor force for the European settlers. The sugar industry gradually developed on São Tomé, although cultivation there was still limited in 1515.

Meanwhile, this island would also become a hub for the Portuguese slave trade in the Gulf of Guinea, starting in 1500 and peaking between

---

[90]Greenfield, 115. See also Soyer, "King João II of Portugal 'O Príncipe Perfeito' and the Jews (1481–1495)," 79; Garfield, "Public Christians, Secret Jews: Religion and Political Conflict on Sao Tome Island in the Sixteenth and Seventeenth Centuries"; and Blackburn, *The Making of New World Slavery from the Baroque to the Modern*, 108–123.

3.9. *Tabula moderna prima partis Aphricae*, detail of São Tomé, Principis, and the Gulf of Guinea. Stanford University Libraries Digital Collections and Department of Special Collections. São Tomé (St. Thomas) became a hub of the Portuguese slave trade in the sixteenth century.

1520 and 1530. Slaves were brought to the island from the Niger Delta and the Kingdom of Benin, as well as nations to the east, and subsequently traded to African agents near São Jorge da Mina, a Portuguese enclave further to the west, primarily for gold.[91] The Portuguese exchanged a large variety of goods, including cloth from North Africa, Europe, and India; beads and semiprecious stones; glass and ceramics; spices, exotic foods, and drugs; metal containers such as basins, pots, and pans; and unworked or semiprocessed metals (e.g., iron, copper, brass, lead, gold, and silver),[92] which were fashioned by Africans into tools, personal objects, or art (Figures 3.10 and 3.11).

On Hispaniola, the native American population, which had initially provided most of the island's slave labor for mining and sugar cultivation and which by 1520 had declined by 90 percent, would be replaced by

[91] Vogt, "The Early Sao Tome-Principe Slave Trade with Mina, 1500–1540," 453–467. See also Disney, 2: 56–65.

[92] Alpern lists many other kinds of trade goods in addition to those listed. "What Africans Got for Their Slaves," 5–43.

3.10: Waist Pendant with Oba and Two Attendants (Benin, Edo State, Nigeria; mid-sixteenth to early seventeenth century), copper alloy, 8 × 6 1/4 × 2 1/4 in (20.3 × 15.9 × 5.7 cm). Brooklyn Museum, Brooklyn, New York. 1998.38. Gift of Beatrice Riese. The central figure on this pendant represents Ohen, the fifteenth-century *oba* or king of Benin, flanked by important court officials, the *edaiken* (crown prince) and the *egonio* (war chief). The pendant was made for a later king who wore it on a belt around his waist at state events.

Africans.[93] In 1514, the Dominican priest Bartolomé de las Casas would give up his *encomienda*, or plantation, and free his own slaves after a crisis of conscience. In 1515, he sailed to Europe to inform the dying King Ferdinand of Spain of the desperate situation of the natives and attempt to reverse it; he would make the same case to the regents of the young Charles V in

[93] Galloway, 64.

3.11: Plaque of a Portuguese Explorer (Benin, Edo State, Nigeria; sixteenth or seventeenth century), copper alloy, 19 13/16 × 15 9/16 × 2 1/2 inches (50.3 × 39.5 × 6.4 cm). Brooklyn Museum, Brooklyn, New York. Brooklyn Museum, Brooklyn, New York. 56.6.74. Gift of Arturo and Paul Peralta-Ramos. This portrait provides an intriguing view of a Portuguese trader from an African artist's perspective.

the following year. In his 1516 *Memorial de remedios par las Indias*, Las Casas advocated the reliance on black and other slave labor in the Indies rather than that of American Indians – a recommendation that he would later regret.[94]

[94]See Remedio 11 in Baptiste, ed., *Bartolomé de las Casas and Thomas More's* Utopia: *Connections and Similarities*, 22–25.

It is possible that More learned of Las Casas' mission on behalf of the
Caribbean Indians before the publication of the *Utopia* in that same year,
and of the Dominican's rationales for the enslavement of other groups.[95] In
any case, these questions were highly topical at the time, and More himself
participated in those debates through his *Utopia*.

On the surface, honey as the Utopians' sweetener of choice might seem
like a minor detail of the narrative, but what it tells us is important. Although
slave labor was an essential component of the Utopian economy, More
purposefully avoided a sugar plantation or mining economy relying on slave
labor in the manner that was common in his own day, at least in this instance,
even though the Utopians practice a form of colonialism. *Utopia* is full of
such contradictions.

It is essential to recognize that More's *Utopia* reflects the institution of
slavery as the author had witnessed it in Antwerp and perhaps elsewhere
(even in England) in 1515, and as he understood it operating in the world
around him at that time. Through Hythloday, More makes it clear that the
citizens of Utopia do not consider it a good thing to dragoon foreigners into
slavery. Those who end up as slaves must first earn their fate through some
form of transgression or choose that role. Moreover, in Utopia children of
slaves are free from birth – a practice that was generally not a feature of
European chattel slavery in the early sixteenth century.[96]

Although perhaps he did not completely identify with the values of
Utopia, it is likely that More sought to rethink, modify, and improve the
institution of slavery rather than abolish it (as indeed Las Casas was attempting at exactly the same moment). Despite his interest in social justice and
the ideal commonwealth, More could not imagine a world in which the
worst work was genuinely socialized – or in any case he chose not to write
about such a world. In *Utopia* he preserved the idea of maintaining a powerful class distinction based on moral purity and impurity, rather than some
other marker of identity – namely, the religious, ethnic, and somatic markers then in effect. For better and for worse, More's meritocratic, "clean"
model of slavery denied and decontextualized the actual slaving practices

---

[95] This intriguing possibility has been suggested by Baptiste, although the evidence of an Erasmian
role in the conveyance of such information remains conjectural. *Ibid.*, 1–10.

[96] In the 1530s, Nicolas Cleynaerts, a Flemish tutor to Dom Henrique, the brother of King João
III, wrote, "Richer households have slaves of both sexes, and there are individuals who derive
substantial profits from the sale of the offspring of their household slaves. In my view they raise
them much in the same way as one would raise pigeons for sale in the marketplace." Russell-
Wood, "Iberian Expansion," 22. See also Fonseca, "Black Africans in Portugal during Cleynaerts's
visit (1533–1538)."

of his day.[97] It is likely that More found such practices disturbing and inhumane.[98]

Ironically, however, More's use of the practice of slavery in the Utopian commonwealth might have helped to habituate Europeans to this practice despite his probable desire to do otherwise, perhaps because he did not take a stronger stand.[99] Because of, or more likely despite More's model of

[97] In *Capitalism and Slavery*, Eric Williams made the famous argument that racism arose from the practice of slavery and not the other way around (7). In "The Iberian Roots of American Racist Thought," James Sweet elaborates on Williams' theory but traces racist ideology about black Africans back to Muslims, who arrived in Spain in 711 CE and who held slaves throughout the Middle Ages. These views were absorbed and consolidated by the Christian population of Iberia, particularly when they became actively involved in slaving. "By the time of the Columbian encounter, race had evolved into an independent and deeply etched element of the Iberian consciousness, not simply a manifestation of more fundamental social and cultural relationships" (166).

More recently, Michael Guasco has offered a different argument: "Racial slavery, or the subjugation of one particular group of people because of their perceived phenotypical and biological characteristics, was not common in the early modern Atlantic World." Religion – or rather religious difference – was the most frequently employed excuse for enslavement in the medieval and early modern worlds. "From Servitude to Slavery," 83.

For a broader survey, see Eliav-Feldon, Isaac, and Ziegler, eds., *The Origins of Racism in the West*.

On the evolution of race and racism in the context of European slavery, see also Davis, "Constructing Race: A Reflection," *The William and Mary Quarterly*, 3rd Ser., 54, No. 1. (1997): 7–18.

[98] More's effacement of race as a basis of European slavery in the early sixteenth century (perhaps second to religion in 1516) might have been based on his own partial identification with Moors – that is, with Africans. More was a humanist intensely fond of puns and wordplay, and he was keenly aware of the range of available puns on his own name. His family coat of arms, granted to his father during the reign of Edward IV, featured three sable "moorfowl," a type of grouse found in the moors of England. The head of a "blackamoor" served as a crest atop the escutcheon. More would use this device in his seal when he served as undertreasurer of England a few years later.

The English word *Moor* was rendered in Latin as *Maurus* or its variant *Morus*. In an essay on More's coat of arms, Germain Marc'hadour clarifies that Maurus was also a synonym of Niger or Aethiops (544), noting that Erasmus referred to More as "Niger" in a coded letter written to Vives in 1528, as the divorce crisis loomed: "Nigro commiseram epistolam" (I have entrusted the Moor with my letter to Queen Catherine). "A Name for All Seasons," 544.

On some level More identified – and was identified with – Africans. This is not to say, however, that he was completely sympathetic or attuned to the predicament of actual slaves, African or otherwise, or he probably would not have defended the institution of slavery in *Utopia*. The psychology of More's identifications merits further study.

[99] Robin Blackburn has suggested that More's *Utopia* may have helped to inspire England's Vagrancy Act of 1547, with its provision of slavery for those vagrants who refused the opportunity of gainful employment. Blackburn also discusses the influence of this book on the English colonial enterprise, noting that *Utopia* was translated into English in 1551 and went through many editions. He argues that More's equivocal views on slavery most likely helped to justify England's involvement in the slave trade, claiming that "More challenges some features of Tudor social relations while endorsing others, displaying an experimental approach to social arrangements in which servitude or colonialism would be perfectly justifiable if they promoted the more intensive use of natural and human resources." *The Making of New World Slavery*, 57–59.

See also Pagden, *Lords of All the World*, 76–77.

meritocratic slavery – a slavery not based on religious or racial difference – England would soon become an active participant in the African slave trade, along with many other nations of Europe.

The Dissemination of a Dream

As with any imaginative work, it is impossible to know exactly how an author's personal history, perceptions, and fantasies shape his or her creation – although inevitably a complex genealogy links a work of art and its creator. This chapter has explored the possible significance of Antwerp as the setting for More's *Utopia*. One of the centers of the early sixteenth-century global economy, Antwerp afforded More a view of the larger world and a glimpse of the future. Reflecting on both, More responded with a fantasy of retreat and insulation that I have called "prenascent." Although the *Utopia* might be called escapist, it represented, paradoxically, an escape *into* reality – a way of understanding the changes in the world by envisioning their opposites. *Utopia* represents not so much a program or template for change as a set of reflections on a possible and impossible present.

More's *Utopia* affords modern group theorists a vantage from which to view the circulation of fantasies between individuals and collectives – in this case, an individual writer and his groups – More's family and friends; his English countrymen; the men and women of Antwerp, Africa, and the Americas; freemen and slaves; Christians and non-Christians; and many other groups past and present, real and imagined. More's fantasy was shaped by all of those groups and undoubtedly many more. In turn, his fantasy expanded the available range of group metaphors from his own time up to the present. Among the most influential group fantasies of the European Renaissance, *Utopia* exerted that influence – and continues to do so – by providing a powerful new word and concept that gradually became part of the languages of the world. That paradoxical word/concept would eventually go global.

In his 1532 satire *Pantagruel*, Rabelais would playfully introduce the word/concept *Utopie* to the French lexicon.[100] That was only the beginning, however. The word *Utopia* would later precipitate into English, Catalan, Croatian, Czech, Danish, Dutch, Finnish, German, Greek, Indonesian, Italian, Latvian, Norwegian, Polish, Portuguese, Romanian, Slovak, Slovenian, Spanish, and Swedish. The term would be transliterated into Russian,

---

[100] *Pantagruel roy des Dipsodes*, Chapter 23ff., in *Oeuvres Complètes*, 308 ff.

Bulgarian, Serbian, Ukrainian; it would be adopted into Arabic, Hebrew, Chinese, Japanese, and Korean, as well.

In each of these languages, *utopia* as word and concept functions as a nameable ideal that nevertheless remains out of reach, despite many social and political experiments aiming to instantiate some goal of collective perfection. The ongoing project of utopianism suggests that it is in the nature of groups to reinvent themselves, to reflect on and return to their origins, their very conditions of being, in order to give birth to themselves anew. Individuals can sometimes voice those fantasies of renaissance for the group. Those who do so successfully may be called visionaries or saints. They may even change the language, incrementally altering the very terms in which groups think and operate in the world. This was perhaps More's greatest contribution: to imagine the world in a prenascent state, and to give it an ambiguous, lasting name.

4

THE BUDDHA'S TOOTH RELIC:
THE GROUP MYSTERY
JAFFNA, 1560

Thereafter, by the power of the gods, fire was kindled in the pile; there was neither soot nor ashes of the body of the Teacher when burnt.

By the will of the Buddha there remained relics of the colour of pearls and of the lustre of gold scattered in various ways.

– The *Dāṭhāvaṃsa*

And these days shall be remembered and celebrated throughout every generation, in every family, every province, and every city, and these days of Purim shall not be revoked from amidst the Jews, and their memory shall not cease from their seed.

Book of Esther 9:31

He looked in stature and appearance exactly as we had formerly known him, lying there in his priestly robes complete and fresh as if he had been buried only an hour ago.

Manuel Teixeira, *Life of St. Francis Xavier*

The Capture of the Relic

THIS CHAPTER MOVES FROM THE IMAGINARY ISLAND OF UTOPIA TO A SET of islands and coastal regions in South Asia – specifically Ceylon, Goa, and Cochin – in which religious and other large-group differences were managed quite differently than they were in More's fictional polity. In 1560, Portuguese Goan forces, led by the Viceroy Dom Constantino de Bragança, attacked the coastal town of Jaffna in northeastern Ceylon (modern-day Sri Lanka) and its natives. While plundering the area, they discovered a reliquary containing a sacred artifact. Although they did not understand its meaning, the Portuguese carried the relic back to Goa, capital of Portuguese India, along with persons and objects that they had seized in Jaffna. There they debated what to do with the mysterious object, which they had heard was considered extremely valuable by the Ceylonese and by other kingdoms of the region.

For more than 2000 years, the Buddhists of Ceylon had venerated a tooth relic known as the दळदा, or *daḷadā*, the sacred left canine tooth of Gautama Buddha.[1] One of several corporeal relics said to have been collected from his funeral pyre in 543 BCE,[2] the *daḷadā* was considered one of the most precious objects of veneration throughout Buddhist South Asia. Its history is described in the *Dāṭhāvaṃsa*, or "Chronicle of the Tooth," an ancient Ceylonese Buddhist scripture chronicling the relic's history. Based on a chronicle written in the Elu language circa 310 CE and translated into Pali in the twelfth century, the chronicle recounts the transport of the relic to the Indian city of Dantapura (literally "tooth-city," and possibly modern Rajamahendri).[3] There it was venerated for eight centuries, and many miracles and conversions were said to have been performed under its auspices.

According to this chronicle, the *daḷadā* was removed from India to Ceylon in the fourth century CE by the princess Hēmamālā, who concealed the relic in her long hair during her arduous journey to Anurādhapura, which was then the capital city of the island (Figure 4.1). She did so to preserve the priceless object from capture by Hindu chieftains hostile to Buddhism and to convey it to King Mahāsena of Ceylon, who had contracted to purchase it.[4]

---

[1] The Sinhalese word *daḷadā* refers specifically to the tooth relic of the Buddha. It derives from earlier root words meaning "(canine) tooth" and "relic." Geiger, *An Etymological Glossary of the Sinhalese Language*, 74.

[2] The exact date of the Buddha's death remains disputed.

[3] Concerning the recovery of the relics from the funeral pyre of the Buddha, the *Dāṭhāvaṃsa* reads,

> 46. Thereafter, by the power of the gods, fire was kindled in the pile; there was neither soot nor ashes of the body of the Teacher when burnt.
> 47. By the will of the Buddha there remained relics of the colour of pearls and of the lustre of gold scattered in various ways.
> 48. These seven relics, the bone of the forehead, the two collar-bones, (and) the four tooth-relics of Buddha, were not dispersed.
> 49. Streams of water descending from the skies, and rising from the earth on all sides, extinguished the fire of the pile.
> 52. The sage called Khema, possessed of kindness, (and) freed from Saññójana, took then the left tooth-relic from the funeral pile.
> 57. Then Khema gave the tooth-relic taken by him to Brahmadatta, king of Kaliṅga, in Dantapura.

> *The Dathávansa*, trans. Mutu Coomára Swámy, 36–38. Quoted in Gerson da Cunha, *Memoir on the History of the Tooth-Relic of Ceylon*, 27–28.
> On the dating of the *Dāṭhāvaṃsa* I follow Herath, *The Tooth Relic and the Crown*, 9.

[4] Mahāsena died before Hēmamālā reached Ceylon. Herath, 34.

The history of the *daḷadā* is also recounted in the *Mahāvaṃsa*, the renowned
Ceylonese Buddhist chronicle recording the lives of the island's kings, and
in the *Cūḷavaṃsa*, the continuation of the earlier *Mahāvaṃsa*. According to
the *Cūḷavaṃsa*, the relic was ensconced in Anurādhapura, then transferred
to other shrines on the island, and finally moved to the Māligāwa temple
at Kandy in 1268 CE.[5] By that time, the *daḷadā* had become an important
symbol of the political and spiritual legitimacy of each successive ruler.[6]
More than a symbol, however, the *daḷadā* served for centuries as a national
palladium, a sacred object thought to protect the integrity of the state and
its social institutions. Defending the island from drought, warfare, and other
calamities, the *daḷadā* was considered by many to be the single most valuable
object in Sinhalese Buddhist Ceylon.[7]

The Portuguese knew nothing about this relic and its long history when
they arrived in Jaffna in 1560. The phenomenal market value of the sacred
object soon became apparent, however, as rumors of the plundering spread
across Buddhist southeast Asia. Later Portuguese historical sources related
that Bayinnaung, the King of Pegu (in what is today Myanmar), sought to
ransom the tooth from its captors, offering an immense sum for its recovery.
Bayinnaung dispatched his ambassadors to Goa, who were authorized to
negotiate a trade. In exchange for the sacred relic, he offered the equivalent of
at least 300,000 *cruzados*, plus his perpetual friendship and an unlimited supply
of rice for the Portuguese settlement at Malacca. Extensive deliberations over
the fate of the *daḷadā* took place in Goa in the spring of 1561. Secular and
religious authorities in Goa squared off against one another, offering various
reasons either to sell the tooth or to destroy it. Because the amount of money
promised was astronomical, the Viceroy considered the King of Pegu's offer
carefully. The religious authorities of Goa prevailed in the debates, however,
and the relic was destroyed in a flamboyant public ritual – an execution
of sorts. First the tooth was ground up in a mortar in the presence of the
Goan townspeople, and then the pieces were dumped into a brazier and
reduced to ashes. Finally those ashes were thrown into the Mandovi River
nearby.[8]

---

[5] The account of the transport to Ceylon appears in the *Dāṭhāvaṃsa*, and its reception there is
recounted in the *Cūḷavaṃsa* (37: 92–98), trans. Geiger and Rickmers, 1: 7–8. See also Gerson da
Cunha, 37–38, and Geiger, *Culture of Ceylon in Medieval Times*, 213–214.

[6] Seneviratne, *Rituals of the Kandyan State*, 17.

[7] According to the seventh-century Chinese account, Sir Lankans believed that if the tooth relic
were ever lost, the country would be devoured by demons. Strong, *Relics of the Buddha*, 196–199.

[8] Pearson, 121; Couto, *Da Ásia de João de Barros e Diogo de Couto*, 429.

4.1. Solias Mendis, *Danta and Hēmamālā Transporting the Sacred Tooth Relic to Sri Lanka*, (20th century), mural. Kelaniya Temple, Kelaniya, Sri Lanka. World Religions Photo Library / The Bridgeman Art Library. The tooth concealed in Hēmamālā's hair is indicated by the halo it projects.

In the account of one Portuguese historian, however, not one but two *daḷadās* surfaced in Ceylon in 1566 – one in Colombo and the other in Kandy. Authenticity was claimed for each artifact, whereas the object captured in Jaffna and destroyed in Goa was denounced as a fake. The relic that appeared in Kandy in 1566 is in all probability the same one that is today enshrined at the Māligāwa temple in Kandy, Sri Lanka (Figure 4.2). It is not clear if the Portuguese destroyed the authentic *daḷadā*, a replica thereof, or another ritual object. What is clear, however, is that they did not succeed in destroying the cult of the relic or the beliefs and culture of the people whom they sought to conquer. The history of the *daḷadā* before, during, and after its capture by the Portuguese provides an object lesson regarding group conflicts (e.g., religious, ethnic, and cultural) during the Renaissance. Chapter 2 traced the destruction, absorption, and hybridization of groups and group identities in the colonial Brazilian context; in contrast, this chapter explores the durability and resilience of group identity despite conditions of extreme duress, warfare, or persecution, and analyzes the defenses and survival mechanisms of groups. In psychoanalytic terms, a *defense* is any mental operation that aims to reduce or eliminate whichever changes threaten a person's psychic stability.[9] Groups have psychological defenses as well, aimed at preserving their sense of collective integrity and security, and at protecting the "group body," its projected boundaries and its internal organization.

In numerous ways, relics such as the *daḷadā*, as well as other sacred objects and rituals, help to solidify and to maintain group identity and belief and to ensure the survival of the collective by enabling certain shared defenses. Shared belief, which can be conscious, unconscious, or both, sometimes crystallizes around an actual body or body part deemed sacred, such as a relic. The sacred object stands synecdochically for the group itself and for the imagined body of the collective. The protection and veneration of the sacred object thus represent the group's sanctity, integrity, and survival. Violations of the object or destructive acts in relation to it are experienced as and constitute, in effect, attacks on the group body. In sum, the future of the group – its conception of a collective destiny – is bound up in its relation to its sacred objects and to the idea of the sacred in general. A group that holds nothing sacred is not in fact a group with a strong identity.[10] The

---

[9] Laplanche and Pontalis, *The Language of Psychoanalysis*, 105 ff.

[10] This is not to say that groups must have a shared religious or spiritual identity but that they must have values and beliefs that they hold sacred. Notions of the sacred, whether strict or loose, religious or secular, bind members of the group to each other and also bind the group to its imagined body.

4.2. The Māligāwa temple complex in Kandy today. The actual temple is situated under a copper roof in an interior courtyard. Photo credit: Don Stadner.

link between the sacred object that stands for the whole and the sense of collective well-being deriving from its preservation is what I call the "group mystery."

The long and complicated history of the *daḷadā* also can be read as a record of a collective defense, because the relic was viewed as perpetuating Buddhism in Ceylon, protecting the kingdom, and further consolidating Sinhalese group identity on that island. The captivity of the relic during the sixteenth century also allows us to understand the methods that groups employ to destroy or to assimilate rival collectives, not only through the usual means of conquest or killing, but also through the destruction of the particular beliefs and identities of the rival group that are made concrete by the group mystery. The "torture" and destruction of the *daḷadā* in 1561 provide one noteworthy example of such an attempt at collective subjugation by means of an attack on a sacred object. By examining the recorded histories and other narratives of these events, we can also recognize how one group's mystery can be extraordinarily threatening to those outside the group or to a rival collective. Finally, we can perceive in these accounts the resilience of the group mystery and its resistance to destruction.

It is not a coincidence that the burning of the relic captured in Jaffna took place in 1561, because the Portuguese Inquisition had arrived in Goa during the previous winter. Two inquisitors, Aleixo Dias Falcão and Francisco Marques Botelho, had sailed to India from Portugal with Dom Gaspar de Leão, the new archbishop.[11] The Goa Tribunal of the Portuguese Holy Office was officially established on March 2, 1560; it was housed in the Sabaio Palace, which until that point had been the residence of the Viceroys. Autos-da-fé would usually be held in the Great Hall of that palace or sometimes in churches, whereas executions and burnings would take place on the Campo São Lázaro, facing the sea.[12]

The arrival of the Inquisition in Goa was a major event – one terrifying to many people, some of whom had fled Europe to escape its reach, and others who were familiar with its reputation. To understand the significance of the tooth-burning episode, it is important to place it in the wider context of surveillance and persecution then gearing up in Portugal, Goa, Cochin, and other Portuguese colonial bases in Asia as a means of controlling populations that were viewed as heterodox in their religious and cultural beliefs. Indeed, the burning of the tooth must be considered a precursor to the thousands of autos-da-fé that would be conducted in Goa over the next two and a half centuries.

Which factors drove the Portuguese to establish the Inquisition in Goa? Why was an inaugural act of the Inquisition dedicated to the debate over the tooth? What were the stakes in the relic controversy for all of the persons and groups involved? What was the outcome, and how did that outcome set the stage for later group conflicts in Portuguese India – particularly those orchestrated by the Goan Inquisition, a brutal institution that was not finally abolished until 1812? As we shall see, the tooth controversy presents a microcosm of extreme group conflict and violence in a colonial setting – and of group conflict in general. That controversy also sheds additional light on what Walter Mignolo has in a different context called the darker side of the Renaissance.[13]

Arguably it was not simply the fear of rival religions that motivated the actions of the Portuguese and the Catholic Church. Because the tooth is a body part, to value or devalue the tooth assumes a certain relation to another imagined body part: the mouth. As discussed in Chapter 2, oral fantasies play a powerful and constitutive role in the unconscious lives of groups, both past and present. In the words of Didier Anzieu, the group

---

[11]In his brief discussion of the founding of the Goan Inquistion, Couto describes them as "dous Letrados leigos, canonistas." *Da Ásia* VII; 17: 335. See also Priolkar, *The Goa Inquisition*, 25.

[12]Saraiva, *The Marrano Factory*, 350.

[13]*The Darker Side of the Renaissance.*

is a mouth.[14] The imagined functions of that mouth vary considerably, depending on the state of the group, its degree of arousal or regression, and the shared sense of fear or well-being among its members.

The primary groups involved in the controversy over the tooth – the Buddhists of Ceylon and Pegu and the Portuguese Catholics – had very different perceptions of this virtual mouth and body – one arguably the opposite of the other. Other religious, ethnic, and cultural groups, such as the Hindu Tamils of Jaffna, the Hindu and Muslim populations living in the environs of Goa, and the Portuguese Jews and "New Christians" of Cochin and Goa, would also play significant roles in the tooth controversy. Protestant and Catholic readers back in Europe who learned of the incident were also drawn into the conflict, although more remotely; the tale of the tooth would help to intensify national, ethnic, and religious rivalries that were being acted out on a global stage.

A fragment from a fifteenth-century Ceylonese poem provides one evocative view of the *daḷadā*, or tooth relic, which was said to enjoy "the touch of the body of doctrine which originated in the Sage's mind."[15] This powerful metaphor suggests the point of contact between the physical, the "touch" of the tooth, and the spiritual, the "body" of doctrine coming from the Buddha's mind – presumably through the mouth. The touch of this body consists of nourishing words or ideas.[16]

The *Mahāvaṃsa* also sheds light on the importance of the tooth and other relics of the Buddha within Sinhalese tradition. The chronicle recounts that during the rule of Dēvānaṃpiyatissa (ca. 252–212 BCE), a *thēra*, or senior monk, begged the king to bring relics of the Buddha to Lanka. "Ruler of men," he said, "it is a very long time since we have seen our teacher, the Buddha. We live a life of deprivation. There is nothing for us to worship here." The King replied, "Venerable Sir, have you not told me that the Buddha had passed into Nibbana?" The *thēra* responded, "When relics are seen, the conqueror is seen."[17] These verses suggest that the corporeal

[14] *Group and the Unconscious*, 160.

[15] From the *Sāḷalihiṇi sandēśa*, v. 16: "The tooth relic 'that enjoyed the touch of the body of doctrine which originated in the Sage's mind' was placed in caskets of gold and jewels." Quoted in Herath, 20.

[16] Teeth have other resonances as well. John S. Strong writes, "In Buddhist literature, one of their meanings centers around the fact that teeth are the only bones of the living body that are commonly visible while a person is still alive. They thus provide a glimpse of what the body is and will become, and so serve as reminders of impermanence that help to bridge the divide between life and death." *Relics of the Buddha*, 180.

[17] Mahānāma *The Mahāvaṃsa*, trans. Guruge, 111. The alms bowl and collarbone of the Buddha arrived in Ceylon at this time, and a segment of the Boddhi tree, as well. The tooth relic, as noted earlier, arrived some centuries later.

relics of the Buddha and the objects he used in life bring the devout into contact with his presence – intriguingly, that of a conqueror. The image of Buddha as conqueror suggests possible phallic connotations attaching to the relic, as well as oral ones. The alms bowl of the Buddha, which was brought to Ceylon in the third century BCE, was one such object infused with the Buddha's continuing presence, as was the collarbone, brought at the same time. The bodhi tree was another. This was the tree in India under which Buddha achieved enlightenment during his six years of continuous meditation; King Aśoka sent a cutting of that tree to Ceylon in the third century BCE that was planted in Anurādhapura. The footprints of the Buddha, said to have been imprinted on Adam's Peak, were still another. According to Buddhist legend, these were imprinted when he magically flew to Ceylon during his lifetime to disseminate his teachings there. These relics, especially the tooth, were once in contact with the physical body of the Buddha or were actual parts of his body. Later they brought the devout into imagined contact with the body of the historical Buddha, as well as his timeless metaphysical being. The relics fostered a shared belief in the Buddha's transcendence of the visible, material world, in which his presence is nevertheless rendered partly tangible.[18] As suggested previously, sacred objects such as these give rise to the group mystery, the shared fantasy that the group, through its imagined, sustained contact with the mystical body of its figurehead, will remain intact, defended, and safe from destruction forever.

For the Buddhists of Ceylon, relics such as the *daḷadā* presented – and continue to present – an exceedingly complex aspect of Buddhist tradition, connected to esoteric beliefs regarding the Buddha's body. Buddhist relics are not considered remnants or leftovers of bodies (i.e., a connotation of the Latin *relinquere* that carries over into the English word *relic*). They are considered instead to be the essence extracted from a dead or living body. (The Sanskrit and Pali word *dhātu* means "constituent element or essential ingredient."[19])

Moreover, Buddhist relics are considered miraculous objects that are not subject to the rules of nature. They proliferate mysteriously, appear

[18]As Jacob Kinnard has suggested, it is not that the Buddha is so much made present by the relic but rather that the believing viewer is made past, that is, transported into the era of the historical Buddha and his deeds. "The Field of the Buddha's Presence," 134.

[19]See Strong, xvi, following Gombrich, *Precept and Practice: Traditional Buddhism in the Rural Highlands of Ceylon*, 105–106, and especially Obeyesekere, "Anthropological Studies in Theravada Buddhism," 8.

On the subject of relic worship within Buddhist tradition, also see Germano and Trainor, eds., *Embodying the Dharma*, and Trainor, *Relics, Ritual, and Representation in Buddhism.*

miraculously, and sometimes have lives of their own.[20] They are thought to be remarkably resistant to destruction, as the histories and legends surrounding the *daḷadā* suggest.

For centuries, the *daḷadā* played a central role in the group organization of the Buddhists of Ceylon, conferring legitimacy on the kings of the island. For many Christians of the Portuguese Indies, the relic aroused a frightening range of somatic fantasies, including that of a demonic mouth that aimed to rip them apart and devour them. The corporeal imagery that chroniclers attached to the tooth in their accounts of the capture, trial, and "execution" of the tooth reveals a great deal about the psychology of a highly aggressive group that nevertheless felt threatened. These texts make explicit the fear of group fragmentation, imagined or real, which the Portuguese projected onto a symbolic object, the mysterious and uncanny tooth relic captured in Jaffna.

Budão and *Bugio*: Diogo do Couto's *Da Ásia*

The story of the tooth became the stuff of legend, chronicled by numerous European travelers and historians, who perceived the incident as a highly dramatic and significant moment in Portuguese colonial history. The earliest published accounts of these incidents appear in Portuguese and other European histories of the late sixteenth and seventeenth centuries, many decades after the original incidents supposedly took place. In these accounts, the Christian authors report the relic to be one of several things: the tooth of a demon, the tooth of a holy man, or, in most European accounts, an ape's or monkey's tooth. The fabulous tooth, either subhuman or superhuman in various tellings, embodied for the Portuguese and for other European visitors to the region the beliefs and practices of their rivals in south India. The tooth tale appears in these colonial writings as an image of extreme alterity, a recurring dream − or nightmare − of the alien body in Portuguese colonial psychic life.

In 1602 or shortly before, Diogo do Couto penned one of the first authorized accounts of the tooth story, and also one of the most detailed.[21]

---

[20] Strong, xiv.

[21] The publication history of Couto's work is extremely complicated. As George David Winius writes, "Probably no historian before or since has seen more writing stolen, misplaced, or destroyed." *The Black Legend of Portuguese India*, 6.

Couto made two or three manuscript versions of *Década* VII. The first was sent back to Portugal in 1602 but never arrived. Dutch pirates captured the *Santiago*, the Portuguese ship that was carrying the manuscript. Couto rewrote this document the next year, although it was licensed for publication ten years later and published three years after that in 1616. A third version, partly in Couto's own hand, was recovered in the twentieth century; some speculate that this version is

Couto arrived in India in 1559 and remained there until his death in 1616, serving first as a soldier and later as the principal archivist in Goa. Using archival resources, he would write one of the most important official histories of Portuguese colonial India. In his chronicle *Da Ásia*, also known as the *Décadas* (Decades), Couto continued the chronicles of João de Barros, which were begun earlier in the sixteenth century and which he took over after Barros' death.[22]

In Decade VII, Couto refers to the artifact as the *dente do Bugio*, or "the monkey's tooth," as well as the tooth of "Budão," the Buddha. Of the conquest of Jaffna, Couto wrote,

> And out of their principal temple they brought to the Viceroy a tooth mounted in gold, which was commonly called that of a monkey, but which these Heathens held as the most sacred of all objects of worship. The Viceroy was promptly informed that it was the greatest treasure of all, and they confirmed it by offering a great sum of gold to recover it.
>
> The Heathens believed it to be the tooth of their great saint Buddha [Budão]. . . . This Buddha, according to their legend, went to Pegu after he left Ceylon, converting the heathens and performing miracles across these realms. And when he got ready to die, he wrenched the said tooth from his mouth and sent it to Ceylon as a great relic. And so it was venerated by them, and by the Heathens of Pegu, so much so that they valued it above all other things.[23]

Why did Couto, who knew something about the life of the Buddha, a famous "saint" of the Ceylonese, call the relic a "monkey's tooth" in the same paragraph? Was this simply Portuguese slander, as one nineteenth-century

Couto's revised original, which contains material never included in the published versions. C. R. Boxer, *Three Historians of Portuguese Asia*, 15.

[22] Couto, keeper of the Goa archives, continued the chronicles begun by João de Barros begun earlier in the sixteenth century. Couto brought the *Decades* up to the year 1600. He could not publish the later parts of his work during his lifetime because they were too controversial. *Ibid.*, 15.

[23]   E de um seu principal Pagode leváram ao Viso-Rey hum dente encastoado, a que commummente chamavam de bugio, que era havido antre aquelles Gentios todos pela mais religiosa cousa de todas as de sua adoração; do que o Viso-Rey foi logo avisado, e lhe affirmáram que era o mór thesouro que podia haver, porque lhe haviam de dar por elle grande somma de ouro.

   Haviam aquelles Gentios que aquelle dente era do seu Budão, (que he aquelle seu grande Santo. . . .) Este Budão tem elles em sua lenda, que depois que se foi de Ceilão andou pelas partes de Pegú, e por todos aquelles Reynos, convertendo Gentios, e fazendo milagres; e que quando quiz morrer, arrancou da boca aquelle dente, e o mandou a Ceilão por mui grande reliquia sua. E assim era havida por tão grande antre elles, e antre toda a gentilidade dos Reynos de Pegú, qu não havia cousa, que sobre todas mais estimassem. . . .
Da Ásia, Dec. VII, liv. 9, cap. ii; 17: 316–317.

   Translations of Couto are my own, with refinements by Miguel Santos-Neves.

historian suggests?[24] Was it intended as a humiliating and possibly racialized insult to Buddhist Ceylon?[25] Was the substitution perhaps based on some phonetic slippage — that whichever word or pronunciation used by the Ceylonese to designate the Buddha sounded to the Portuguese like *bugio*?[26] Perhaps the Portuguese had confused contiguous worship systems in South India: because *Budão* sounds something like *bugio*, the word for monkey, perhaps the slippage between Buddhism and the worship of the Hindu god Hanuman makes more sense.[27] There could have been another reason for such confusion, however; the Hindu Tamils of Jaffna, who emigrated from South India, held the monkey god Hanuman in great devotion. A certain syncretism between Buddhism and Hinduism, particularly in Jaffna, could be indicated by this overlapping. Finally, to the Portuguese who captured the relic, the tooth might have appeared nonhuman — that is, of animal origin. If so, then perhaps the relic was venerated by Hindus as part of the worship of Hanuman.[28] These multiple possibilities have given rise to much controversy and discussion among later historians.

[24]Albert Gray, the editor and translator of Pyrard de Laval's narrative of his travels to India, wrote: "That the daladá was a monkey's tooth is of course only a Portuguese slander, in which Buddhism is confused with the Hindu worship of Hanuman." *The Voyage of François Pyrard of Laval*, 45.

Fr. Fernão de Queyroz, the seventeenth-century Deputy Inquisitor of Goa and the author of a remarkable history, *The Temporal and Spiritual Conquest of Ceylon*, describes the Portuguese discovery of the tooth among the spoils of Jafnapatão, "which our Historians said by a manifest error was that of a monkey, and which was one of the most sacred objects of worship in the heathendom of the South and of Tartary. . . . " 364.

[25]The *Dicionario Universal Lingua Portuguesa* (http://www.priberam.pt/DLPO/) defines *bugio* first as "de Bugia, cidade da Argélia, de onde vinham os macacos." *Bugio* also could have functioned as a racial slur against the natives of Ceylon, similar to the word *macaca* in English today.

The word developed other negative connotations as well. The phrase *macaco bogio* meant "lying monkey," for example; adjectively it denoted "lying" or deceptive." It also came to mean ugly. Meanwhile, *bugia*, the feminine form of the word, came to mean "prostitute" in Goan Portuguese. See Antônio Houaiss, Mauro de Salles Villar, and Francisco Manoel de Mello Franco, eds., *Dicionário Houaiss da língua portuguêsa*, (Rio de Janeiro: Editora Objetiva Ltda., 2001), 526; and Francisco da Silveira Bueno, *Grande dicionário etimológico-prosódico da língua portuguêsa*, Vol. 2 (São Paolo: Edição Saraiva, 1964), 556–557.

According to Anson C. Piper, however, the sixteenth-century meanings were not necessarily negative when applied to people. In the mid-sixteenth-century writings of Jorge Ferreira de Vasconcellos, for example, *bogio* functioned as a familiar term of endearment, as well as a mild insult. "Jorge Ferreira de Vasconcellos and the Spirit of Empire," 46.

[26]Both spellings appear in the facsimile edition of Couto's text, as well as a third in Decade VIII, where the author refers to the tooth as the "dente do Bogio, ou do seu Quiar," and later, "do seu idolo Quijay." *Da Ásia* 18: 76–77, 82.

[27]This confusion of Hanuman and Buddha was suggested by the nineteenth-century scholar of South Asia, James E. Tennant, in *Ceylon: An Account of the Island*, 201.

[28]This interpretation was suggested by Donald Obeyesekere, who states that the artifact was an actual ape's tooth worshipped by Hindu devotees of Hanuman (*Outlines of Ceylon History*, 226).

Without clarifying the matter, Couto provided additional information regarding the debate that took place between the various authorities of colonial Goa. The Archbishop Gaspar de Leão let it be known that the Viceroy "should not allow the tooth to be ransomed for any amount of money, because it was against the honor of our Lord God."[29] The Archbishop announced his views from the pulpit, and because the Viceroy Dom Constantino was *muito Catholico* ("very Catholic"), he decided to convene an assembly of secular and religious authorities of Goa to discuss the fate of the tooth relic. In all likelihood, the Viceroy feared excommunication or some worse form of reprisal from the newly arrived Inquisition, yet nevertheless he attempted to convince his council to accept the ransom. He presented to the assembly the state's financial need and explained how the ransom could solve many financial problems.[30] Church officials, however, insisted that to allow the tooth to be ransomed would be a serious sin and that no bargains should be struck with the King of Pegu.

Couto then describes the destruction of the tooth. In a theatrical public ceremony, the Archbishop reduced the relic to powder, burning the remains in a brazier, and throwing the ashes into the river before a large assembly of bystanders. Couto also describes the smoldering resentment of those who sought to profit from the sale of the tooth – those who realized that destroying the relic would not destroy the religion of their adversaries and who felt outmaneuvered by the Inquisition authorities who had moved into Goa. Meanwhile, Couto reports, a commemorative device was painted that featured the Viceroy, the Archbishop, and the other religious authorities around the burning brazier, along with the Peguan ambassadors carrying purses full of money. Above the scene the letter C was repeated five times, with the words *Constantinus, coeli, cupidine, cremavit, crumenas*. This motto Couto loosely translates as "Constantino, with his intentions on heaven, rejected the treasures of the earth."[31]

Despite these pious sentiments, however, it soon became clear that although the Portuguese might have succeeded in destroying a relic, they not only failed to destroy the relic cult but also possibly fortified it. In a later book of *Da Ásia*, Couto describes the resurgence of the tooth cult in Ceylon and in Pegu just a few years later. In 1566, Dhammapāla, King of Kōttē, one of the rival kingdoms in Ceylon, declared that he had the authentic relic in his keeping all along and that the Portuguese had captured

---

[29]"não podia resgatar aquelle dente por nenhum thesouro do mundo, porque era contra a honra de Deos nosso Senhor..." *Da Ásia*, Dec. VII, 17: 430.

[30]"apresentou as grandes necessidades, em que o Estado estava, que todas se podiam remediar com aquelle resgate." *Ibid.*, 17: 430.

[31]"Constantino com os intentos no Ceo, engeitou os thesouros da terra." *Ibid.*, 17: 432–433.

4.3. The Mahazedi Pagoda; Bago (Pegu), Myanmar. Construction of the Mahazedi was begun by Bayinnaung in 1559, and eventually housed the tooth relic received from Dhammapāla, King of Kōttē, as well as the alms bowl of the Buddha. Damaged by earthquakes in the twentieth century, the temple was rebuilt in the 1950s. Shutterstock Photos. (See color plate.)

only a replica of the *daḷadā*. According to Couto, this tooth was presented to Brahma [Bayinnaung], King of Pegu, as part of the dowry of the princess whom the King of Kōṭṭē presented as his daughter. The relic was enshrined in the Mahazedi Temple (Figure 4.3), begun by the king in 1559.[32] Meanwhile, a second tooth relic appeared that same year in Kandy, whose king attempted to discredit the claims of Dhammapāla to have the true relic in his possession.[33]

Couto presents Dhammapāla, whom he refers to as Dom João (a name he had assumed sometime after his conversion to Christianity in 1557),[34] as a trickster who sought to deceive both the King of Pegu and the Portuguese. An astrological prophecy made in Pegu at Brahma's birth predicted that he would marry the daughter of the King of Ceylon. To fulfill this prophecy, Brahma petitioned João for the hand of his daughter. Brahma offered one million in gold for the *daḷadā*, as well as the princess.[35] Lacking a daughter of his own, João offered the daughter of his chamberlain, claiming her as his own child. According to Couto, he also fabricated a new *daḷadā* out of a stag's horn, encasing it in gold and jewels. João conducted these negotiations secretly, without the knowledge or consent of the Portuguese, who sought to control him, or of the Peguans. The transaction went through despite discrediting rumors, and the princess and the relic were received by the Peguan king with great pomp.

[32] See Couto, *Da Ásia*, Dec. VIII, Cap. xii–xiii. 18: 74–88.

In 1559, Bayinnaung began building the Mahazedi Pagoda in Pegu. Relics received from Sri Lanka – a tooth-relic and the alms bowl of the Buddha – are enshrined therein. Stadtner, *Sacred Sites of Burma*, 129.

The Myanmar historian Tun Aung Chain offers different dates for these events, stating that the Sri Lankan princess arrived in Pegu in 1573, whereas the tooth relic arrived in 1576. This chronology raises questions about the accuracy of Couto's account, which, as we shall see, is also problematic in other ways. See "The Portuguese Trade in the Kingdom of Hanthawaddy," *Selected Writings of Tun Aung Chain*, 80.

[33] Couto, *Da Ásia*, Dec. VIII, Cap. xii–xiii. 18: 86–88.

[34] Dhammapāla, who had been educated by Franciscan missionaries, officially converted to Catholicism in 1557 at the age of 18. At that time, he confiscated temple lands and gave them to the Franciscans. These included the Temple of the Tooth in Kōṭṭē. This action had a devastating effect. In the city of Kōṭṭē, a group of Buddhist monks incited the people to riot. In retaliation, thirty Buddhist monks were seized and put to death. Mounting internal and external pressures forced the Portuguese to abandon Kōṭṭē in 1565 and to retire to their fortress in Colombo. Dhammapāla went with them. Because Dhammapāla was almost completely powerless at that point, Couto's story of the young king's subversive actions against the King of Pegu and the Portuguese is almost certainly erroneous.

On the exceedingly complicated history of internal and external Sri Lankan conflicts in the middle of the sixteenth century, see Chandra Richard de Silva, *Sri Lanka: A History*, 122–123; K. M. de Silva, ed., *History of Sri Lanka*, 2: 61–104; and especially Weerasooria, *Ceylon and Her People*, 1: 253–275.

[35] Couto, *Da Ásia*, Dec. VIII, Cap. xii–xiii. 18: 77.

Meanwhile, Couto reports, a second *daḷadā* appeared that same year in Kandy, whose king attempted to discredit the claims of João. When the King of Kandy found out about the exchange of the *daḷadā* and the princess by his Ceylonese rival, he attempted to thwart the double bargain by exposing both the relic and the daughter as fakes. The Kandian ruler then offered his own daughter and informed Brahma that the authentic *daḷadā* remained in his control and that he could prove it. According to Couto, Brahma sought to acquire the second relic as well, without openly revealing the possibility that he had been deceived. He sent two ships laden with gifts for the kings of Kōttē and Kandy. The ship that anchored in Kandy ran ashore, however, and the ambassadors and the gifts were lost. Couto described this shipwreck as a plot emanating from the court of Kōttē.[36]

Although Couto himself makes it clear that he did not believe in the authenticity of either of the two relics that surfaced in 1566 in Ceylon, he praises Brahma, the King of Pegu, for his devotion to the relic. Subversively, he assails Christian piety by pointing out that the Christians were not willing to ransom relics of equivalent value from the Turks.[37] About the loss of 300,000 or 400,000 *cruzados* he says little, nor could he, although his discussion subtly casts the Portuguese authorities in an unfavorable light. Any critiques of the colonial administration had to be handled very carefully for reasons to be explored in more detail later.

A Protestant Account: Linschoten's *Itinerario*

Another great chronicler of sixteenth-century Portuguese India, Jan Huyghen van Linschoten, would describe the reappearance of the *daḷadā*.[38] In 1583, the twenty-year-old Dutchman had sailed to India with the Portuguese flotilla. He would remain abroad for the next nine years, serving for most of that time in the household of Vincente da Fonseca, Archbishop of Goa. When he returned home from the east, settling in Enkhuizen, Linschoten soon converted to Protestantism.[39]

Subsequent to that conversion, he published a book damning the Portuguese on numerous counts. In several ways, Linschoten's book greatly facilitated Dutch and English colonial expansion to India and other regions

[36] *Ibid.*, 18: 86–88.

[37] Decade VIII, chapter XII, in *Da Ásia*, 18: 82. Couto suggests that Christian piety also does not stand up to that of the Buddhists of Pegu.

[38] Linschoten provides the earliest published account of the capture of the relic, although it is full of factual errors (as Couto's could be as well).

[39] Linschoten joined the Dutch Reformed Church on his return to the Netherlands. Parr, *Jan van Linschoten*, 188.

4.4. Joannes à Doetechum, The Leilaõ of the City of Goa, from *Iohn Hvighen van Linschoten. His Discours of Voyages into ye Easte & West Indies* (London, 1598). Harry Ransom Humanities Research Center. University of Texas at Austin. This fold-out illustration, based on Linschoten's sketches, depicts the principal town square of Goa. Two female slaves stand in the left center foreground.

of South Asia. His travels, which initially were published in Dutch under the title *Itinerario* in 1596, were quickly translated into English and German (1598), Latin (1599), and French (1610). The original Dutch edition included thirty-six vivid etchings, drawn by the author and engraved by Joannes and Baptista à Doetechum, which were carefully hand colored in some copies (Figures 4.4 and 4.5).[40] As his biographer Charles McKew Parr writes, "One of the great shifts of world power in all history [the decline of the Spanish

[40]The Huntington Library in San Marino, California, owns an exquisite hand-colored copy of the original 1596 Dutch edition. The English editions that I have viewed at the Huntington and at the Harry Ransom Humanities Research Center at the University of Texas feature the same illustrations, but they are not aquarelled. In addition, six large foldout maps made by Arnoldus and Henricus Florentii à Langren were also incorporated. Jan Huyghen van Linschoten, *Voyage . . . to the East Indies*, 1: xxxi.

A Mifericordia

que portat et Indus
in Oceano.
'Ploogerb.

Fori Goenfis tabernarum mercium et mercatorum illud frequentantium aperta ex-
plicatio per N.Linschoten.

Claere opdoeninge vande merckt van Goa
met haer winckelen warrn en daegelickse
Coophuyden. door I·H·V· Linschoten——

Joannes a Doetechum fecit.

56.&57

4.4

global empire and the rise of English and Dutch colonialism] got under way
during Jan Huyghen van Linschoten's lifetime, and it is not too much to
say that he was one of its major instruments."[41] Linschoten revealed to his
readership the Portuguese sea routes to the Orient – highly specific nautical information that for more than a century had been a well-kept secret.[42]
Moreover, he helped to give currency to the Black Legend against the Spanish and Portuguese, penning what was among other things an extremely
inflammatory and influential piece of propaganda.[43]

[41] Parr, xxv.
[42] Linschoten's data were quickly snapped up by the Dutch, English, and French, and its dissemination
proved devastating to Portuguese and Spanish interests. Linschoten not only connected the dots
for his European readers (explaining exactly how to sail to the Orient) but also painted unflattering
and at times merciless portraits of the Portuguese and Spaniards with whom he had spent most
of the previous decade. Thus he not only told the rivals of these Iberian nations how to move in
on their overseas empires but also suggested that it was feasible to do so, because he depicted the
Portuguese and Spanish as indolent, corrupt, and potentially domitable.
[43] Winius, *The Black Legend of Portuguese India*, 29ff.

Linschoten, whose account of the relic has a decidedly Protestant cast, tells the story of the tooth as follows:

> In the Iland of Seylon, whereof I have [alreadie] spoken, there is a high Hill called Pico d'Adam, or Adams [Hill], upon the top whereof standeth a [great] house, as big as a Cloyster: wherein standeth a Pagode of great account. In this place in time past there was a Toothe of an Ape [*een tant van een Aep oft Simme*], shrined in gold and precious stones, and therein was kept this Toothe, which for costlynes and worthynes was esteemed the holyest thing in all India, and had the greatest resort unto it from all the countries round about it: so that it passed both S. James in Galisia, and S. Michaels Mount in France, by reason of the great indulgences [and pardons] that were there [daylie] to be had: for which cause it was sought unto with great devotion by all the Indians within 4. or 500. miles round about in great multitudes.[44]

The historical Buddha does not figure into Linschoten's version of the story, which is considered the earliest. Moreover, the polysemy of the relic, evident in Couto's account, does not appear in the Dutchman's abbreviated treatment. Linschoten, newly converted to Protestantism, makes a connection that the Portuguese historians do not, however: that the tooth relic and the temple that housed it were in some sense like the renowned pilgrimage sites of Europe – Santiago in Spain, and Mont St. Michel in France. Linschoten's account implies a Protestant critique of relic veneration and of the concept of "indulgences," but his erstwhile Catholic sensibilities and upbringing are also manifest. The phrase "Toothe of an Ape" conveys his skepticism not only about the supposed power of the Asian relic but also perhaps about Catholic ones in Europe.

Linschoten generally conveys great cynicism about the Portuguese colonial enterprise in Asia, emphasizing in his version the greed of Dom Constantino rather than his good sense, as Couto highlights. In so doing he adds one more flourish to his hostile report on the Portuguese in Goa. Linschoten also expresses hostility toward the natives of South Asia. He describes the reappearance of the tooth after its supposed destruction:

> Not long after there was a Beniane (as [the Benianes] are full of subtiltie), that had gotten an other Apes tooth, and made the Indians and Heathens believe, that hee had miraculously found the same [Apes tooth that the Viceroye had], and that it was revealed unto him by a Pagode in a vision, that [assured him] it was the same, which [hee said] the Portingales thought

[44]Linschoten, 1. 292; *Journael*, 67.

4.5. Baptista à Doetechum, Indian Pagodas and Mosques, from *Iohn Hvighen van Lin-schoten. His Discours of Voyages into ye Easte & West Indies* (London, 1598). Harry Ransom Humanities Research Center. University of Texas at Austin. A "pagoda," or temple, appears on the left; a mosque on the right.

they had burned, but that he had beene there invisible [and taken it away], laying an other in the place.[45]

Linschoten, like Couto and many of the Europeans of the time, conflates Hindus and Buddhists or is unaware of the difference. He claims that a "Benian" produces a new ape's tooth – the term Benian designating a Hindu or Jain of the merchant caste.[46] In Linschoten's telling, the greed of the Portuguese or at least of Dom Constantino, the Viceroy, is surpassed by the cunning of the Hindu adversaries. Indeed, the Portuguese are outdone by them. Linschoten also states that the false relic was later purchased by the

---

[45] *Ibid.*, 1, 294.
[46] The *vanias* were part of the *vaiśya* caste, one of four traditional castes of India, yet consisting of forty-one internal divisions, further dividing into Hindu and Jain segments. Pearson, *Merchants and Rulers in Gujarat*, 26.

King of Bisnagar (Vijaynagar). In this way, Linschoten further confuses and conflates the religious groups of the region, because Vijaynagar was a Hindu kingdom, not a Buddhist one.[47] For Europeans, the distinctions between religious groups in India and Asia, between ethnic groups sharing the same or related religions, and between castes were a constant source of confusion. The desire to separate Christians and Christianity from these groups and to prevent forms of syncretism or hybridization was also a constant preoccupation – indeed, an obsession – for some religious authorities.

The Devil and His Dentist: Faria e Sousa's *Asia Portuguesa*

The story of the tooth and its capture, destruction, and reappearance would be told again and again by seventeenth-century Portuguese chroniclers and by European visitors to Portuguese Goa. Pedro Teixeira, François Pyrard de Laval, Nicholau Pimenta and many others related the tale of the tooth, which became a recurring topos in Goan and Portuguese history.[48] One particularly interesting and developed version of the story appeared in the first volume of Manuel de Faria e Sousa's *Asia portuguesa* (Portuguese Asia), published posthumously in Lisbon in 1666. Faria e Sousa was Portuguese, but he wrote his compendious history in Spanish. According to his sources, the tooth came from a white monkey (*mono blanco*), which, like white elephants in Siam, was worshipped for its unusual color, as well as its exceptional deeds: "There was a king among the ancients of India, whose wife, whom he loved very much, ran away from him."[49] No one could find the wife, so the king dispatched the said monkey to track her down, which the monkey did. In gratitude, the king rewarded the monkey while alive, and after its death he idolized it.

The story that Faria e Sousa recounts, at the expense of both Hindu and Buddhist traditions, is a garbled version of the great Hindu epic, the *Rāmāyana*. In that poem, Queen Sītā, wife of Rāma, is captured by his evil adversary Rāvaṇa, and is rescued through the intervention of Hanumāna (Hanuman). In his account, the historian confuses Hindus and Buddhists

---

[47] As noted previously, however, the relic captured in Jaffna might not have been a Buddhist one. See n. 28.

[48] Pimenta, *Indian Observations* in *Purchas His Pilgrims*, 9: 208–209; Teixeira, *The History of Persia*, 251–252; Pyrard de Laval, *Voyage*, 45.

[49] "Huvo un Rey entre los antiguos de la India, a quien se le huyò la muger, que él mucho amava." Faria e Sousa, *Asia portuguesa*, 2: 351. Translations are my own, with refinements from Marcella Rossman and Paul Harford.

and also distorts the essential points of this episode from the *Rāmāyana* in a way that reflects badly on "Gentile" marriages and masculinity.

Faria e Sousa soon reverses himself, however: "Other sources indicate that it was a man's tooth, rather than a monkey's."[50] Still other sources assert that it was the tooth of *un Hombre santo*, "a holy man," "and if that were the case, then the Heathens did not err too much in worshipping the tooth, except in the way that they did it."[51] Here Faria e Sousa injects something new into the story – a hint of cultural relativism – even though he ultimately writes a very nationalistic account of the event.

Faria e Sousa reports that during the deliberations over the fate of the relic, a captain present declared that even though "the devil can devour many souls with this tooth," the Portuguese could build enough Catholic altars to offset the damage caused by its release.[52] Still others who supported the sale of the tooth contended that "the mouth of Idolatry will not stop chewing up the souls of barbarians just because it finds itself short of a tooth."[53]

Ultimately, the chronicler gives the last word – several pages of them – to the vocal theologian at the meeting, who denounced any and all depraved persons who would dare to sell the artifact. After listing various Old Testament prooftexts justifying the destruction of pagan idols, the theologian closed his arguments with more striking imagery of the mouth: "A mighty torment we will deal [the infernal dragon] if today we crush this tooth in his own mouth."[54]

When the tooth particles were finally consigned to the flames, there resulted "a smoke so extremely foul," Faria e Sousa writes, "that it greatly exceeded that which would normally come from a mere burning bone."[55] It was, the author stated dramatically, "a losenge from Hell" (*pastilla del*

---

[50]"Otras relaciones dizen, que era de un hombre, y no de Mono el diente." *Ibid.*, 2: 351.

[51]"y siendo assi no erravan los Gentiles en venerarle mucho, si no en el modo con que lo hazian." *Ibid.*, 2: 351.

[52]"Concedo, sin alguna dificultad, que si el Demonio con este diente ha de morder muchas Almas, quando este Rey nos le saque de las manos con tal dadiva, para colocarle adonde los Gentiles de uno y otro Reyno le busquen; Nosotros con ella podemos levanter en muchas Provincias, muchas Aras Catolicas, adonde exceda el fruto dellas al daño de esse idolo." *Ibid.*, 2: 354.

[53]"No dexará, por cierto, de mazcar Almas barbaras la boca de la Idolatria por hallarse con un diente menos." *Ibid.*, 2: 355.

[54]"Cumplase aqui de algun modo la divina Escritura, quando assegura que ha de ser conculcado el Dragon infernal; y arda segunda vez en otro fuego: y este, ninguno puede ser mayor para quemarse más que el de la Fé Portuguesa, que de muchos años le abrasa tanto como el propio de su abismo. Insigne tormento (con esto concluyo) le daremos oy, si oy le quebramos este su diente en su misma boca." *Ibid.*, 2: 363.

[55]"a humo de que resultò un olor con tal excesso malo, que excedia del que naturalmente pudo esperarse de un huesso quando se quema." *Ibid.*, 2: 364.

Infierno). Despite his earlier humor and irony, Faria e Sousa chooses to end on this patriotic, devotional, and sensational note. He mentions that two replacement teeth appeared on the scene shortly after the destruction of the captured one – a fact upsetting to those who argued for the sale of the tooth in the first place. The detail of the foulness of the smoke from the burning tooth suggests that Faria e Sousa chose to frame the relic as a "live" artifact. In his heavily embroidered retelling, the tooth is a genuine Satanic source of evil that had to be destroyed, unlike the replacement relics that appeared later.[56]

For Faria e Sousa, there is a moral of the story:

> It is certain that even though the Devil substituted two teeth for one, he could do less mischief with them, since ultimately they were fakes. Moreover, he had to remain in perpetual pain for having seen his mouth caught in the pliers of the Portuguese faith, which most masterfully plays the Devil's dentist when yanking out his teeth.[57]

Thus the armchair historian closes his story with a joke that evokes pain and fear even today, and even more so in preanesthesia days: that of a sadistic dentist – in this case, the dentist of Christendom torturing the devil.

By comparing these three quite different versions of the story by Couto, Linschoten, and Faria e Sousa, the modern reader can recognize how the Portuguese colonials defined themselves against the foreign body represented metonymically by the tooth,[58] as did some other European groups, such as Protestant audiences in the Netherlands and England (who also defined themselves against the Portuguese and the Papacy in general). It was a memorable story, destined for legend, because it crystallized so perfectly the paranoid relations of the Goan leadership or certain factions within it with those whom they construed as their adversaries. Whereas the *daḷadā* embodied for the Buddhist populations of South Asia not only their beliefs but also their collective identities, for the Portuguese the tooth relic enabled, at least temporarily, the fantasy of destroying those whose very existence seemed dangerous. The symbolic act of violence was imagined by the historian as a

---

[56] On the preoccupation with Satan and the European perception of native peoples as demonic, cp. Cañizares-Esguerra, *Puritan Conquistadors*, discussed in Chapter 2, 104.

[57] "Peró lo cierto es que por màs que el Demonio por un diente natural sustituyó dòs, siempre obraria menos con ellos, pues alfin eran postizos, y le ha de quedar perpetuo dolor de aver visto su boca en las tenazas de la Fé Portuguesa, que màs diestramente es sacamuelas del Demonio, quando más fieramente se las saca." *Ibid.*, 2: 364.

[58] For Freud, this type of imagery would evoke the perennial phobia of the "vagina dentata," here racialized as well as gendered.

ritual killing of the enemy compacted into a highly compressed form – the "lozenge of Hell." Faria e Sousa's fantasy of the devil's dentist – the punishing figure who tortures the dangerous mouth of the adversary to "defang" it, to render it harmless, and to keep from devouring the faithful – clearly demonstrates the oral element that recurs in colonial fantasies of the epoch, suggesting several parallels to those discussed in Chapter 2.[59] The adversarial group – the *other* group – is a mouth that threatens to eat, dismember, destroy, digest, and implicitly, excrete all those who stand in its way. The prevalence of the fantasy in its many variations during the sixteenth century is noteworthy, with the violent responses, imagined or real, that it elicited from groups that believed themselves to be in danger of being devoured. Once again, the persistent fear of cannibalism – here in a symbolic form – proved to be a defining element of the colonial psyche around the globe, often provoking extreme backlashes against native groups and paradoxically against some of the colonials as well.

Couto, Linschoten, and Faria e Sousa provide important clues to the particular sense of embattlement and vulnerability of many of the colonial Portuguese, especially the clergy. All of these chroniclers focus on the semiotics of the tooth; among them, Faria e Sousa is particularly creative in his depiction of the devouring mouth of pagan Asia. Clearly the fantasy of bodily fragmentation was not simply his personal fantasy, but a collective one that circulated widely.

Fragmentation Anxiety in the Paranoid Group

The psychoanalysts René Kaës and Didier Anzieu have argued that human collectives have a tendency to somatize their experience of the group. In other words, people tend to imagine, either consciously or unconsciously, that the group has a body. This imagined envelope or container is a crucial part of what holds its members together. By imagining a shared body, groups constitute themselves as a group. Anzieu offers a profoundly interesting insight about human interaction, one that also serves as a tool for understanding more about the past and the present.

The three chroniclers discussed previously expressed that embattlement through somatic images and metaphors. Each one of them – Faria e Sousa in particular – focuses on the tooth or the mouth. Clearly the fantasy of bodily fragmentation was not just his fantasy but also a collective one

---

[59] Despite the orality of Faria e Sousa's discussion of the devil's dentist, his account of the destruction of the relic can also be read as a castration fantasy.

being destroyed in a particular way – chewed up, masticated, and implicitly digested by the alien culture around them.[60] There were many factors that contributed to this anxiety, not least of which was the internal fragmentation of Goan society, arranged in rigid castes,[61] divided between New and Old Christians, and subject to constant and extreme internal violence (a conflict to which I shall return later). This fragmentation anxiety was also provoked by the violence of their military conflicts with numerous groups across Africa, Asia, and the South Seas. In fantasy, the violence was provoked by attacks on them.

Aspects of Hindu and Buddhist culture and belief were in fact quite intimidating to many Christian colonizers, as vastly different belief systems often are to those who do not share them. The quite different somatic conceptions of divinity among Hindus, their concept of reincarnation, their respect in certain cases for animal bodies, the practice of cremation – all of these factors and many more posed tremendous psychic challenges for the Portuguese, whose immediate response was to raze the Hindu temples and statuary within their purview. I shall return to this implicit concept of bodily diffusion, individual and collective, in Chapter 6.

As the previously quoted chronicles suggest, the distinction between Hindus and Buddhists was unclear to most Europeans in the sixteenth century, although the Jesuits in particular made an effort to understand the religions of those whom they sought to convert. One Jesuit, Francisco de Sousa, was born in Brazil and emigrated to Goa as a young seminarian. Sousa wrote an important history called *Oriente conquistado*, published in 1710. He too lingers on the story of the tooth, but writing from the vantage of greater temporal distance, he expatiates on the Buddha as well. Sousa's thoughts on Buddhist culture reveal his fascination with and fear of that religion. His understanding of Buddhism is far more detailed and complex than that of the previously discussed chroniclers writing a century or more before him, however. In the *Oriente conquistado*, Sousa states,

[60] Regarding the group fear of being devoured by enemies, I am strongly indebted to Geraldine Heng's innovative study of European cannibalism fantasies and the genre of romance during and after the Crusades. See *The Empire of Magic*.

[61] The basic subdivisions of Goan society were as follows: at the top of the social hierarchy were the *reinois*, aristocratic Portuguese nationals who came to India to occupy high positions. The *casados*, unlike the *reinois*, were Portuguese who married local women and settled in Goa. *Castiços* were offspring of the *casados*, whose parents were of Portuguese extraction. *Mestiços* were those of Portuguese and Indian parentage, and *mulattos* were persons of Portuguese and African descent. Last there were the *naturais*, the natives, who were further subdivided into Christians and non-Christians. Xavier, *Goa: A Social History*, 29ff.

Buddha was a renowned philosopher and the son of the king of Delhi in Hindustan, who flourished a thousand years before the coming of Christ. He endeavored to travel throughout the interior of India and went along the Ganges, teaching his sect, and working many miracles, according to the Sinhalese chronicles. But it is certain that he was a great magician, as one can clearly infer from the false doctrine that he left behind in his writings.[62]

Sousa explains this doctrine as follows:

He claims to prove in the greater part of his writings that there is nothing else in this world but making and unmaking, being born and dying, because all things proceed from nothing and must return to nothing. And he confirms this false doctrine with 25,000 examples of sublunar species that have a beginning and an end.

This idea of the noncontinuity of the body is antithetical to Christian beliefs about the resurrection of the body, discussed in great detail in Augustine's *City of God* and with renewed enthusiasm in the high Middle Ages.[63] That noncontinuity of the individual as body and as soul, expressed in some forms of Buddhism,[64] to the extent that Europeans understood it, was at odds with their quite different conceptions of somatic identity and integrity. The Buddhist concept of the impermanence of individual identity was understood only gradually by Europeans, but it would serve as one of many factors contributing to the fragmentation anxiety expressed by members of the colonizing group.

There are several possible defenses against the fear of group fragmentation, which is at root a primal fear of corporeal dismemberment. For example, one can imagine one's group as an island body, cut off from civilization and

---

[62] *Oriente conquistado*, I, Div, II. No. 82. 188–189.

[63] On medieval theories of resurrection, see, for example, Bynum, *Fragmentation and Redemption*.

[64] The philosophical ideas, in the time of Buddha were dominated by the Vedic and post Vedic theory of the existence of soul i.e. the existence of Ātma as a link between one (Eh-Loka) and another life (Par-Loka) according to Karmas. According to Upanishads, the individual soul (Ātma) is not different from the great soul and is the Ātma (self) of the Phenomenal world. (Ahm-Tatmo-asi). It has, thus a permanent identity.

Buddha, however, rejected this idea of permanence of soul. In Parinibbana – Sutta (S.B.E. XI. 63, p. 59) he declares " – whatever is born, brought into being, and organized, contains within itself the inherent necessity of dissolution . . . how can then this be possible that such a being should not be dissolved? No such condition can exist: the constituents of a being cannot be identified with permanent self. They are all subject to decay and dissolutions."

Khosla, *The Historical Evolution of the Buddha Legend*, 117.

On the concept of *anatman* (literally "non-self"), Buddhism's rejection of "an intrinsic, unchanging entity at the core of a person," see Trainor, ed., *Buddhism*, 58 *et passim*.

self-sufficient. This was the fantasy of More's *Utopia*, begun in Antwerp just six years after the Portuguese conquest of Goa.[65] It is more common, however, for a group to defend itself against the fear of somatic fragmentation with real or fantasized violence. Consider the frontispiece of de Sousa's *Oriente conquistado* (Figure 4.6). Sousa's history has more of a religious than a secular focus, and so the image depicts Jesuit clerics, including perhaps St. Francis Xavier, slaying the lions of Asian heresy.

When aroused to a highly defensive state, groups frequently take on a paranoid-schizoid personality. On the subject of collective paranoia, Anzieu writes,

> If the group is in a paranoid-schizoid position, if it projects its bad con-
> science on to the outside world, if it is in overt or latent conflict with the
> portion of society in which it finds itself, if it finds its cohesion in the
> struggle against an enemy, this is because it is diffusely overwhelmed by
> the 'spy' image. The intrusion of the 'out-group' is seen as destructive; it
> is, for the group, the equivalent of that invasion of the body by the bad
> object that Melanie Klein regards as a child's basic phantasy. This intru-
> sion is greeted with suspicion and fear of persecution; it immobilizes group
> aggressivity and crystallizes it around the foreign body, encysts it and expels
> it violently.[66]

When Anzieu speaks of the expulsion of the bad object, he is specifically referring to the tendency of groups to scapegoat. The *bad object*, a term adapted from Melanie Klein's thought, can be someone or something, real or imagined, either inside or outside the group. Anzieu refers to this mechanism as negative transference, a shared psychic state in which the group ego splits off its hostility and aggression onto a person, object, or group.

The fantasy of expulsion as a means of restoring health and wholeness can be imagined in any number of ways. In the case of the tooth relic, crushing, burning, and drowning of the imaginary foreign body was not enough, particularly because the tooth was resurrected from the dead, so to speak, and invested with mysterious power. Images of torture, presented with attempted comedy in Faria e Sousa's account, betray a profound anxiety, a desire to transfer the threat of dismemberment, of consumption by a giant terrifying mouth, onto the relic. The object itself, the notorious "lozenge of Hell," therefore had to be fragmented, consumed, and engulfed – first in a real-life ritual and then in commemorative retellings.

[65]It is possible that the island of Goa was one of the key inspirations for More's geo-somatic fantasy, as described in Chapter 3.
[66]*Group and the Unconscious*, 114.

4.6. Francisco de Sousa, S.J., Frontispiece, *Oriente conquistado* (Lisbon, 1710). Newberry Library, Chicago. This allegorical image shows Catholic clerics attacking the "lion" of heresy.

Buddhist Accounts of the Migrations of the *Daḷadā*

Francisco de Sousa, the previously mentioned seventeenth-century Jesuit historian, writes tersely about the Peguan emissaries' response to the tooth burning: "The Gentiles wept at the loss of the most prized relic of the Orient."[67] He also states that the Ceylonese

> claim that the tooth of the Buddha slipped out through the bottom of the mortar, when Dom Constantino wanted to destroy it, and went to Kandy upon a beautiful rose and so they dedicated a famous temple to it called the Dalidagis, which means "the house of the sacred tooth." They made up this story to convince the Peguans that the tooth was still in Ceylon.[68]

It is not clear which sources Sousa used, if any, to verify the viewpoint of the Peguans and Ceylonese, although the destruction of the *daḷadā* would indeed have been devastating to the Buddhists of South Asia. According to the Portuguese sources, the royalty of Kōṭṭē and of Kandy fabricated two new teeth to replace the old ones and to reconsolidate their power. According to early modern Ceylonese sources written in Pali, however, the *daḷadā* never left the region where it had always been – namely, around the Kandyan kingdom of the central highlands of the island. It is not clear that the relic was ever taken to Tamil Jaffna, an ethnically and religiously distinct region of the island even today. Jaffna would have been an unlikely place for the Buddhist relic to surface in 1561, and the Portuguese might have destroyed a different relic.[69]

The *Cūḷavaṃsa* says a great deal about the locations of the *daḷadā*, both before and after the sixteenth century. For several centuries, the relic was moved from city to city across the island, as rival rulers took possession of the relic or as royal residences changed. By the late fourteenth century, the royal

---

[67] *Oriente conquistado*, I. II. 79, 187.

[68] *Ibid.*, 189.

 I have not succeeded in locating any early modern Buddhist accounts of the destruction of the relic. As we shall see, it is far from clear what really happened.

[69] The only possible explanation that I have found for this mysterious migration of the relic from Sinhalese Buddhist territory in the central highlands of Ceylon to Tamil Hindu territory in the north appears in Fernão de Queyroz's seventeenth-century history, *The Temporal and Spiritual Conquest of Ceylon*, which was unpublished and more or less unknown until this century. Queyroz claims that Tribule, the father of the youthful king of Kōṭṭē, was imprisoned by the Portuguese but escaped to Jaffna, carrying the relic with him for protection. There he was murdered, and the relic came into the possession of the King of Jaffna immediately before the Portuguese conquest. Queyroz placed the relic in Jaffna, but he could not prove that Tribule was in possession of the *daḷadā*. See 1: 314, 333, 364–5.

 Others have argued that the Portuguese destroyed a replica of the *daḷadā* or another altogether different relic. See, for example, Hocart, *The Temple of the Tooth in Kandy*, 3–4.

residence was at Kōttē, and King Parakkamabāhu VI (ca. 1412–1467) built a shrine and reliquaries for the *daḷadā*, which is described in the *Cūḷavaṃsa* as follows:

> Then at a later time, in the year one thousand nine hundred and fifty-three after the final Nirvana of the holy Enlightened One, came King Parakkamabāhu, an abode of wisdom and manly virtue, a scion of the race of the Sun, in the charming town named Jayavaḍḍhana [Kōttē] to the incomparable, sublime fortune of the royal dignity and with faith in the three (sacred) jewels, he set about the holding of a festival. For the tooth of the Prince of the wise the Ruler built a three-storeyed, splendid pāsāda which offered a superb sight. Then he fashioned a golden casket, fair, beautifully set with the nine precious stones, and another casket in the form of a shell, gleaming in manifold splendour and set with the most exquisite jewels and which held the first casket; and yet another golden casket into which he also put the second. Finally the King who strove after salvation in the present as in future existences, made a (fourth) large, incomparably magnificent casket which he covered with gold of the finest lustre, and in these four superb caskets he placed the tooth.[70]

The creation of multiple nesting reliquaries made of precious materials attested to the importance and value of the *daḷadā* in medieval Ceylon, as well as the legitimacy and sacred status that possession of the relic conferred on the ruler. It played an organizational function in Sinhalese Buddhist culture, because yearly religious festivals were structured around it.

The *Cūḷavaṃsa* is somewhat cryptic about the migrations of the tooth in the sixteenth century, after the arrival of the Portuguese. In the 1540s, it places the tooth in Kandy, under the guardianship of King Vīravikkama.[71] In this portion of the history, the relic remains safely ensconced in Kandy. The author, writing his continuation of the chronicle in the 1700s,[72] states nothing about the Portuguese wreaking havoc in sixteenth-century Ceylon.

---

[70] *Cūḷavaṃsa*, 91.15–19. (2: 215–216).

[71] Vīravikkama "gladdened his subjects by the four heart-winning qualities and undertook in his faith meritorious works. The fair relic of the Prince of the wise he brought to a piece of land charmingly situated not far from his royal palace." *Cūḷavaṃsa* 92: 8–10 (2: 220). Geiger notes that Vīravikkama ruled a separate kingdom in Kandy, different from the dynasties of Kōttē and Sītāvaka.

[72] The *Cūḷavaṃsa* spans twelve centuries. The first part (37–79) covers eight centuries, from the reign of Siri Mēghavaṇṇa to the end of Parākkamabāhu I, and was written by a *thēra* named Dhammakitti. The second part, of unknown authorship, picks up with chapter 80 and continues through verse 102 or 104 of chapter 90. The third and final section, which continues chapter 90 and ends at chapter 100, was written by the *thēra* Tibboṭuvāvē Buddarakkhita. This section, which touches on the sixteenth century, was composed during the reign of Kitti Siri Rājasiṃha (1747–1782). Herath, 3–4 (following Geiger's dating).

The relic is mentioned two chapters later in the history of King Vimala-dhammasūriya, ruler of Kandy from 1591 to 1604. About him the *Cūḷavaṃsa* offers many praises:

> The Ruler of men reflected where the tooth of the Enlightened One could be, and when he heard it was in the Labujagāma-vihāra, he rejoiced greatly. He had the Tooth Relic which had been brought to Labujagāma in the province of Saparagamu fetched (thence) and in order to venerate it day by day in his own fair town and to dedicate a ritual to it, the wise (prince) had a two-storeyed, superb relic temple erected on an exquisitely beautiful piece of ground in the neighbourhood of the royal palace. Here he placed the tooth and in lasting devotion brought offerings to it.[73]

The relic enshrined in Kandy today is believed to be the same one brought there in the late 1500s.[74] Several more recent histories of the tooth relic written by Sri Lankans end at 1500 or begin at 1600, leaving out the turbulent and confusing period in question. The subject of the relic's possible desecration or destruction in the sixteenth century remains a highly sensitive subject for many Sinhalese Buddhists today.[75]

Anti-Semitism and the Rise of the Goan Inquisition

Lest we conclude that the conflict over the tooth relic was exclusively or even primarily a struggle between Portuguese Catholics and Sinhalese

---

[73] *Cūḷavaṃsa* 94: 11–14 (2: 228).

[74] Geiger, following the *Cūḷavaṃsa*, supports the argument that the tooth was hidden during the decades of Portuguese attacks on Ceylon: "The royal residence at the end of the fourteenth century was Jayavaddhana (Kōṭṭē) where Parākkamabāhu VI (r. 1467–1412) built a Pāsāda for the Tooth relic (91.17). Vīravikkama, in the sixteenth century, was the first who erected a temple for it in Senkhaṇḍa-Sirivaḍḍhana, namely Kandy (92.9), and from this time onward Kandy remained the shelter of the *daḷadā*, with short interruptions. When the Hindu king Rājasīha, in the sixteenth century, persecuted the Buddhist community, it was temporarily kept hidden in Labujagāma (Delgamuva, north of Ratnapura) and brought back to Kandy by Vimalahammasūriya I (1592–1604) who again built a temple for it near his palace (94.11 sq.). [Numbers refer to verses in the *Cūḷavaṃsa*.] Geiger, *Culture of Ceylon in Mediaeval Times*, 215.

[75] The *daḷadā* is still venerated in Sri Lanka today; hence attacks against it arouse strong feelings. In 1998, when Tamil insurgents attempted to blow up the Daḷadā Māligāwa, the Temple of the Tooth in Kandy, the specter of corporeal fragmentation was raised again.

Mabubhashini Ratnayake wrote an essay for the *Times* in Colombo about the attempted destruction of the *daḷadā*:

> What was it that sent shockwaves more powerful than any bomb could have made across the country last Sunday, when it was known that terrorists had exploded a bomb at the Temple of the Sacred Tooth in Kandy? Perhaps it was the knowledge that what was hit was the heart of the Sinhala Buddhist identity and pride, for the Tooth Relic of the Buddha is perhaps the most valuable possession we have in this country. Even for a non-Sinhala, non-Buddhist the act could not have been without horror, for an object such as this is the heritage of all humanity.

Sunday Times Mirror, Feb. 1998. www.lacnet.org.

Buddhists for ascendancy, it is essential to consider the network of group affiliations and conflicts associated with the symbolic act of destroying the tooth relic. The destruction of the relic in 1561 coincided with the arrival of the Portuguese Inquisition in Goa, as well as the persecutions of New Christians that immediately preceded that incident. In this context, we might wonder whether the Viceroy capitulated not so much to the purportedly superior arguments of the Archbishop and his camp, as to the superior force of the Inquisition that was then establishing its rule by intimidation. Perhaps the Viceroy stood to profit in other ways by collaborating with the Inquisition. In any case, the images of the torture of the tooth, which occur in all versions of the story but most pronouncedly in Faria e Sousa's telling, must be read against the subtext of the Inquisition's actual practice of torture and intimidation, which in the first thirty years of its existence were primarily, although not exclusively, directed at so-called lapsed Christians, who were defined by the Inquisition as Jewish or "Judaizing," and later at Hindus, Muslims, and converts from both groups. The torture of the tooth thus was not an isolated incident of symbolic and psychological violence but part of a larger program to enforce intragroup conformity, promoted by both ecclesiastical and secular authorities in Goa. The Goan Inquisition, authorized in 1560, played a significant role in enforcing such religious and cultural conformity and in promoting a regime of intimidation and terror for many colonials or natives accused of nonconformity.

The buildup took many decades, however. In the first decades of Portuguese colonial rule, the boundary between Christian and non-Christian was porous. In Goa itself there was at first an unprecedented degree of contact and exchange between Christians and Hindus, Muslims, Buddhists, Jews, and members of other religious groups. Official policies concerning the status of non-Christians in the Portuguese colonies were benign only in comparison to the increasingly repressive measures imposed by the State from the 1540s onward.

On May 16, 1546, Francis Xavier, Jesuit missionary to the Indies, wrote to King João III of Portugal, requesting the creation of an Inquisition in India. The reason for this, he said, was the fact that "there are many here who live according to the Mosaic law and the Moorish sect without any fear of God or shame of the world. And since there are many of these, and they are spread throughout all the fortresses, there is need of the Holy Inquisition and of many preachers. May Your Highness provide your faithful and devoted vassals in India with such necessary things!"[76] It was Muslims and especially Jews, the perceived internal adversaries "spread throughout

[76]Schurhammer, *Francis Xavier*, 3: 139. Xavier wrote from Amboina, on the Malay Archipelago.

all the fortresses," who aroused the outrage of Xavier, rather than the other religious groups of Asia. Xavier was not the only person involved in bringing the Inquisition to India, for others shared that agenda.

Dom Constantino de Bragança, who served as Viceroy from 1558 to 1561, reversed the more tolerant policies of his immediate predecessor. In March of 1559, the Portuguese crown decreed that on the islands of Goa, all "pagodas" and idols, public or secret, should be burned and destroyed, a policy implemented by Bragança.[77] The making of "idols" was to be punished with slavery in the galleys. No "gentile" (Hindu) festivals were to be celebrated in any households on the islands, and Brahmins were exiled from the area and their property confiscated.[78] In November of that year, the Viceroy also condemned to death several persons declared sodomites, while branding others and exiling them to Brazil.[79] In 1560, widow-burning (*satī*) was officially outlawed in Goa.[80] In that same year, a royal decree formally established an Inquisition in Goa. The Hindu population began to flee the Goan territories in large numbers, leaving behind their land and property.[81] The primary target of that newly established branch of the Inquisition was not Hindus, but Portuguese New Christians accused of Judaizing – that is, of covertly or openly practicing the Jewish faith.[82] Enraged by fraternizing between the Portuguese New Christian émigrés[83] and the ancient Jewish community of Cochin, religious authorities of Cochin and Goa had conducted trials against twenty New Christians in 1557–1559, just a few years prior to the arrival of the Inquisition. These trials were the immediate impetus for its creation.[84]

---

[77] This was not a new policy, however, because 159 Goan temples were destroyed by Vicar General Miguel Vas after his return from Portugal in 1546. Later, in 1567, 280 temples in Rachol would be razed, and 300 temples in Bardez. The historian P. P. Shirodkar writes, "The destruction of the temples en masse created an unimaginable impact on the Hindu populace making a terrible dent on their psyche from which they never recovered even after the abolition of the Inquisition in 1812." "Socio-Cultural Life in Goa during the 16th and 17th Centuries," *Researches in Indo-Portuguese History*, 2: 40–41. Approximately 36,000 Indians were baptized in Goa alone during Bragança's rule. Disney, 2: 165.

[78] Cunha, *A Inquisição no Estado da Índia*, 112.

[79] *Ibid.*, 93, 113.

[80] In contrast to the other interdictions, most people today would consider this a positive action. See n. 95 for a discussion of Europe's forms of widow-burning in the same era.

[81] Shirodkar, 41.

[82] Baião, *A Inquisição de Goa*, 1, 30–35; Saraiva, 350.

[83] New Christians were Portuguese or Spanish Christians of full or partial Jewish ancestry. Large numbers of Iberian Jews were forced to convert to Christianity by the Christian monarchs of those two countries at various times during the late fifteenth and early sixteenth centuries. They remained a suspect and persecuted group even after conversion.

[84] Saraiva, 348–350. See also the sixteenth-century account provided by Alessandro Valignano, S. J., *Historia del principio y progresso de la Compañía de Jesús en las indias orientales*, 2: 342–43, and by de Sousa, *Oriente conquistado*, Conquista I, Div. ii, 29–31, pp. 134–137.

In 1507 – about the time that Grão Vasco had finished his great altarpiece at Viseu and the recovered *Laocoön* was making an impact on the cultural world of Italy – King Manuel of Portugal abolished the distinction between Old and New Christians, passing a law that enabled the previously stigmatized group to travel to any part of the Christian world and declaring that the latter group "be considered, favored and treated like the Old Christians and not distinct and separated from them in any matter."[85] In 1519, however, Manuel reversed his earlier policy and ramped up anti-Semitic measures in the Indies, prohibiting the naming of New Christians to influential positions, such as judge, town counselor, or municipal registrar in Goa. He stipulated, however, that New Christians already appointed to those positions not be dismissed. This edict suggests that emigration of Portuguese and Spanish New Christians to the Indies had been under way for some time. Emigration would increase significantly thereafter, especially when Portugal created a national branch of the Inquisition in 1531 and criminalized New Christian emigration in 1532, making it a capital offense. Terrified New Christians began to escape to Flanders, Italy, the Ottoman Empire, Portuguese India, and North Africa, and by the middle of the sixteenth century, to England, France, the Spanish Americas, and Brazil, hoping to evade the climate of persecution in Portugal. Cochin and Goa seem to have been chosen by many New Christians as places of possible refuge from 1530 to 1560.[86]

The literary historian António José Saraiva has described the complex communities of colonial Cochin, south of Goa, at this time. Cochin consisted of a lower town, which contained the Portuguese colony, and an upper town, which remained under native control. The upper town contained large Hindu, Muslim, and Jewish populations. Jews of Spanish, Syrian, Ottoman, and other origins were classified as "white," whereas the long-established population of native (Malabar) Jews was classified as "black."[87] Several synagogues existed in the area (see Figures 4.7 and 4.8), and many New Christians of the lower town resumed the practice of their former religion and culture. Periodically during the decades leading up to the establishment of the Inquisition, the Portuguese authorities punished or killed persons accused of Judaizing. Nevertheless, in those middle decades of the mid-sixteenth

[85] Saraiva, 347.

[86] Cunha, 17–75; Saraiva, 347. See also Augusto da Silva Carvalho's excellent monograph *Garcia d'Orta*, which describes the flight of Portuguese and Spanish Jews to the Indies during the early sixteenth century, and particularly the persecution of the Orta family, also discussed here.

[87] Saraiva, 348. On the color line among Cochin Jewry, the religious debates surrounding the divisions between Jews, and their similarity to Hindu concepts of caste, see Katz and Goldberg, *The Last Jews of Cochin*, 126–167.

4.7. Tablet from the Cochangadi Synagogue, built in 1345 and rebuilt in 1539 CE. Now in the courtyard of the Paradesi Synagogue, built in 1568. Photo credit: P. N. Subramanian. The inscription gives the year 5105 (Hebrew calendar) as the date of the Cochangadi Temple's completion.

century, the two Portuguese colonies housed highly diverse, interactive, and fairly tolerant mixed communities, in which religious and ethnic groups mixed freely and frequently.[88]

Leonor Caldeira, Widow of Cochin

That climate of quasi-tolerance would ultimately give way to a completely different reality. The precipitating incident, or set of incidents, revolved around the persecution of a woman named Leonor Caldeira, more than 70 years old. Caldeira had been born in Spain to Jewish parents. After the expulsion of Spanish Jewry in 1492 and the family's emigration to Portugal, she was one of approximately 20,000 Jews who were compelled to engage in

---

[88] Saraiva, 348; Da Silva Carvalho, 37.

4.8. Paradesi Synagogue; Cochin, India. In 1568, the Jews of Kerala built the Paradesi Synagogue next to the Mattancherry Palace, Cochin. The previous synagogue in Cochin had been destroyed by the Portuguese a few years earlier. Shutterstock Photos.

the notorious 1497 mass baptism in Lisbon.[89] Having immigrated to Cochin in 1533 with her husband Afonso Nunes and residing in the lower town, Caldeira seems to have freely practiced the faith of her parents and ancestors there.

In 1557, the unfortunate and ultimately vulnerable Caldeira, along with nineteen other New Christians from Cochin and Goa, would be brought before ecclesiastical tribunals on charges of Judaizing. Charges against Caldeira included visiting synagogues in the upper town, drinking *ada-fina*, or kosher wine, and eating unleavened bread. Significantly, she was also accused of a practice associated with the celebration of the Jewish feast of Purim in Cochin, a festive holiday that in India coincided with Holī, a Hindu festival of social reversals and carousing.[90] This practice was the burning of effigies of Haman, as well as of his ten sons. According to testimony against her, Caldeira, together with other Jews of Cochin, burned dolls individually called *filho de Hamam* (Son of Haman), taken by Christian authorities as a parody of *filho de homem* (Son of Man). Caldeira and some of the others were accused of burning effigies of Jesus.[91] In the terms of the present argument, Caldeira and the others became scapegoats for a perceived attack on the Christian group mystery, the collective conscious and unconscious relation of that colonial group to the body of Christ. The reprisals against them would be devastating. Caldeira's fate, like so many other episodes in the long and savage history of anti-Semitism, predictably revolved around the peren-nial Christian fantasy of "Christ-killing" – and a possibly retributive and liberatory Jewish fantasy, as well. As Ana da Cunha has suggested, the burn-ing in effigy of Haman and his parodic identification with Christ might have represented an attempt to exorcise the collective fear of further persecutions for Jews, especially for those New Christians forced to practice their reli-gion in secrecy and peril, an attempt to exorcise the collective fear of further persecutions.[92]

Caldeira, with the nineteen other accused New Christians from Cochin and Goa, was imprisoned, while testimonies against them were gathered, mainly from servants, slaves, personal enemies, and persons of lower social

---

[89] Saraiva, 349. See also 12ff. on the 1497 mass conversion in Lisbon.

[90] Holī commemorates the defeat of the demoness Holikā, while also celebrating Krishna's dalliances with his female companions in the forest of Vṛindāvana. During Holī, the lowest may attack the highest with impunity. Katz and Goldberg, 195.

[91] This and other practices relating to the holiday are described in detail by Cunha, 182 ff.

[92] *Ibid.*, 183.

    In more recent times, the name *Hitler* or *Nasser* was substituted for that of Haman, traditional enemy of the Jewish people, during the reading of the *Megillah Esther* during the festival of Purim in Cochin. Katz and Goldberg, 196–197.

status than those accused.[93] Further denunciations against them revolved around questions regarding the dietary habits of the accused (Did they eat pork? Did they pretend to eat pork around Old Christians?); the observance of Catholic rites (Did they observe Lenten and other fasts, go to confession, receive Communion, go to Mass on Sundays and holy days, say prayers, and display crucifixes and images of saints in their homes?); and whether they Judaized (Did they observe Jewish holidays, bury the dead according to Jewish custom, observe the Sabbath rite? Did they give alms to Jews of the upper town? Did they contribute money for the construction of a new synagogue?).[94] These and other questions were intended to determine whether the accused really belonged to the Christian group or merely pretended to belong while practicing Judaism in secret. The modern reader can note in these questions the interrogators' attempts to police the boundaries of the group. Persons close to the edges, so to speak, would be condemned, expelled from the group, dispossessed of their property, and imprisoned, tortured, or killed. Such actions were intended to have an effect not only on the scapegoats but also on all members of the group, by enforcing conformity through terrifying punishments.

Caldeira and the other people accused of Judaizing were ultimately sent to Lisbon and tried by the Portuguese Inquisition. Of those twenty people, Caldeira was the only one sentenced to death.[95] From the denunciations against her and from her sentence, Ana da Cunha suggests, Caldeira must be viewed as the bearer and transmitter of a certain collective memory of Jewish practices and habits, carried from Europe to India. These autos-da-fé occurred in March and July of 1561, the very year when the Buddha's tooth relic was burned in Goa, half a world away. The trials contributed to the establishment of the Goan Inquisition in that same year. They also indicate a sea change in the nature and degree of ecclesiastical repression in the Portuguese Indies.[96]

[93] Cunha, 171 ff.

[94] Ibid., 175 ff.

[95] She died on March 16, 1561, having been excommunicated, dispossessed of her goods, and subjected to one of Europe's own forms of widow-burning. Ibid., 213; Saraiva, 349–350. See also Banerjee, *Burning Women: Witches, Widows, and Early Modern Travel Writers in India.*

[96] Ines G. Županov describes the collective perception of Goan decadence and decline that had begun to set in by the second half of the sixteenth century, and that was reflected in different ways in the writings produced there – specifically the botanist Garcia de Orta's *Colóquios* and the Archbishop Dom Gaspar de Leão's *Desengano de perdidos*, both published in 1563. "The Wheel of Torments," 24-25. See also Županov's excellent book *Missionary Tropics*, as well as Subrahmanyam, *The Portuguese Empire in Asia*, 80–106, for a more systemic view of the mid-century crisis.

So began the roughly 250-year reign of terror of that organization.[97] Between 1560 and 1774, more than 16,000 cases were tried.[98] The individual records of these trials are presumed to have been destroyed in 1812, when the Goan Inquisition was finally shut down. Nevertheless, a 1623 inventory of 3,800 cases tried between 1561 and that date provides the names, ages, offenses, and punishments of those who were tried.[99] This inventory also provides important demographic information about which groups were targeted. From 1561 to 1590, the Goan Inquisition tried 321 people for crypto-Judaism; from 1591 to 1623, 21 people. This information suggests that the New Christian population of the Portuguese Indies was effectively destroyed, silenced, assimilated, or driven into exile during the first thirty years of the Goan Inquisition's existence. Although many more people were tried for crypto-Hinduism or occasionally crypto-Islam, the severity of punishment for New Christians brought up before the Inquisition was in general far more extreme.[100]

From this data we may also conclude, apropos of the present study of group conflict, that persons perceived as inhabiting the border region between groups were also viewed as highly threatening to those who were – or who wanted to be – at the center of the dominant group. Leonor Caldeira had moved freely across the boundary between the two Cochins and between two group identities – New Christian and Jewish – for several decades before

---

[97] The Jews of Cochin were protected by the maharajas of Cochin and the Royal House even after the founding of the Inquisition; without that protection they would not have survived. After the Portuguese conquest of Cochin in 1500, the maharaja had become a vassal of the Portuguese. Jewish immigrants from Cranganore, Spain, Portugal, and elsewhere nevertheless were granted cultural and religious autonomy by the local Hindu rulers. Velayudhan et al., eds., *Cochin Synagogue Quatercentenary Celebrations*, 19–22. See also Katz and Goldberg, 86–87.

[98] Pearson states that between 1560 and 1774 no fewer than 16,172 cases were tried by the Goan Inquisition (120). See also Saraiva's estimates in *The Marrano Factory*, 345–347. All the complete and incomplete trial records were burned in the early 1800s at the behest of the Portuguese Viceroy of India, the Count of Sarzedas, who found the history of the Inquisition entirely too incriminating for his comfort. Two thousand other documents from the Goan Inquisition were culled for preservation by Friar Tomás de Noronha at that time and sent to Rio de Janeiro. These were identified and classified in 1987. Saraiva, 345–346.

 Despite the destruction of these records, the infamy of the Inquisition was publicized by certain of its victims, especially the Frenchman Gabriel Dellon, who wrote a horrifying exposé based on his prison experiences. See *History of the Inquisition as It Is Exercised at Goa*.

[99] This inventory, called in English the "General Repertory of 3800 trial records dispatched in Goa and elsewhere in India, 1561–1623," was written by the Inquisitor João Delgado Figueira, who assumed his position in 1625. Saraiva, 346.

[100] Saraiva reports that New Christians, although only 9 percent of the total number of those convicted by the Inquisition during its first 62 years, suffered the death penalty in disproportionately high numbers: 69 percent. This figure includes sixty-eight executions and thirty-five burnings in effigy – that is, executions of those who had already died (346–347).

her trial and execution. In the case of the Cochin Ecclesiastical tribunal's pursuit of Leonor Caldeira, and of the Goan Inquisition's persecution of at least 20,000 other victims after her, the violent and paranoid impulses of the colonial leadership were directed at real persons. By shaming, confining, or torturing their bodies, by dispossessing them of their goods and power, by exiling them from the community and sometimes by killing them, and by terrorizing other border-inhabiters of the colonial group, the Inquisition maintained the paranoia of the group and the fear of its own permeable borders.

What marked these interventions as modern – that is, as new developments in the history of group consciousness – was not the policing of borders per se but a technology of surveillance, interrogation, and documentation that had gone global, at least to a certain extent, linking Lisbon, Antwerp, and Rome to colonial outposts in India, Africa, Brazil, and other parts of the world. Interdictions against certain ambiguous forms of subjecthood deemed dangerous to the state – New Christian identity, most prominently – would be enforced with greater efficacy and intrusion into the private lives and psyches of all those who found themselves within a machine aimed at identifying and eliminating ideological and cultural differences within the collective. This was not the first time in history that such intrusions assumed prominence, nor would it be the last. It differed from what had gone before in the metastasizing scope of its reach, both geographically and psychically. What had been since the thirteenth century a European institution had become by the middle of the sixteenth century a far more global one. The Inquisition was, in its turn, merely a glimmer of the systematic intrusions and modes of coercion that would arise in what was then a far-distant future.[101]

The next chapter explores the metaphor of the group as machine. I shall return in my final chapter to address the group mystery and the survival of collective identity against all odds, although its contours can be perceived here in the endurance of Sinhalese Buddhism against the onslaught of the Portuguese, and later the Dutch and British. That mystery also can be seen in the survival of the Jewish people, despite the protracted and genocidal history of anti-Semitism. It can be seen in the survival of Christianity, structured around the mystery of the Resurrection, a metaphor of its own resilience

---

[101] My account owes much to the thinking of Michel Foucault, who locates one origin of such surveillance mechanisms, which he calls *panopticism*, in the quarantining of plague victims in the seventeenth century. Certainly there are multiple origins for this shift in group consciousness during the early modern age, as cities and states exercised increasing power to gather information and control individual as well as group behavior. See *Discipline and Punish*, 195ff.

and hopefulness. Indeed, wherever there is religion, one can find a group mystery that unifies the members of a collective around its shared beliefs.

When the boundaries of collective identity become blurred – as, for example, in colonial Goa and Cochin during the early decades of the sixteenth century – the threatened loss of identity within the dominant group or sectors thereof can catalyze extremes of violence against its subcultures. This behavior can occur as the dominant group attempts to assert the primacy of its mystery over those of other groups contained within its borders or poised just beyond them. The ongoing consolidation of religious ideology and state power in the Renaissance made the practice of dissident collective identity riskier than ever before, precisely because such performances would be increasingly regulated by mechanisms of policing and technologies of enforcement, such as censorship, dispossession of property, imprisonment, torture, and execution. These mechanisms were not new to the Renaissance, although they would be applied in more systematic ways during that era.

Saint Francis Xavier and the Catholic Group Mystery in Goa

As discussed before, a coherent group identity arises from the cultivation of a group mystery, which often although not necessarily revolves around a miraculous body or body part that stands for the integrity and endurance of the group. The *daḷadā* performs this function for Sinhalese Buddhists up to the present day. The incorrupt body of St. Francis Xavier performed a similar function for Catholics of the Counter-Reformation world and to a certain extent continues to do so, especially for Catholics of South Asia. Because the Goan Catholic group mystery formed at approximately the same time as the trials of the New Christians of Cochin and the tooth relic debate, it is important to consider the three events in relation to each other.

When the Jesuit missionary Francis Xavier arrived in Goa in 1542, he was struck less by the intense beauty of the region than by the fact that here was "a city wholly Christian, with a populous Franciscan friary, a cathedral of much distinction and many canons, as well as numerous other churches."[102] Xavier began his ministry in India by visiting the hospital, the terrible colonial prisons, and the leper colony. He also began teaching the catechism to the children of Goa. Five months later he was sent out of that region to proselytize the natives of the Cormorin coast, 800 miles to the south. He would return to Goa only sporadically during his ten-year career in the Indies, never anticipating that after his death his body would be

---

[102] Brodrick, *Saint Francis Xavier*, 114. Valignano, *Monumenta Xavieriana*, 1: 252.

inextricably bound up with the colony where he began his mission to the Indies.

When the forty-six-year-old Jesuit, exhausted by ten years of hard living in the Orient, died on December 3, 1552, on Sancian island off the coast of China, he had been ill for more than a week with a high fever and dysentery. A member of his entourage suggested that his body be covered with quick-lime before burial so that the flesh would be consumed quickly; later, if they needed to, they could more readily transport the missionary's bones back to India for reburial. Ten weeks after Xavier's death, the Portuguese crew exhumed his coffin. To their great surprise, the body had not decomposed but remained intact and fresh.

On March 22, 1553, the ship arrived in Malacca, at that time a Portuguese enclave on the Malay Peninsula. There Francis was buried for the second time in the church of Our Lady of the Mount. When Xavier's friends and supporters in India learned of his death, they arranged with a few supporters in Malacca to deliver the body to Goa. Those who exhumed the body five months after its second interment were stunned to discover that the body appeared lifelike and well preserved. Xavier's body was taken to the house of Diogo Pereira in Malacca, where it was placed in a coffin lined with Chinese damask and covered with brocade.

The body was returned to Goa on Friday, March 16, 1554. A large crowd of about 6,000 people gathered on the roads of the town and on the banks of the Mandovi river to participate in the spectacle. The Viceroy and key figures in the Portuguese colonial administration waited on the banks of the river for the arrival of the body. When the sloop arrived, the body was carried in procession to the Jesuit College of St. Paul's nearby. Xavier's first biographer Manuel Teixeira wrote of that occasion:

> He looked in stature and appearance exactly as we had formerly known him, lying there in his priestly robes complete and fresh as if he had been buried only an hour ago. Under the vestments next to the skin the body was clothed in a rich garment which the Father had taken with him from Goa to wear at his interview with the Emperor of China. Though it had been more than a year under the earth, it was so clean and intact that Father Nunes [the Jesuit vice-provincial] claimed it for his own to put on when later he paid visits to the kings of Japan.[103]

---

[103] *Vida del bienaventurado Padre Francisco Xavier*, in *Monumenta Xaveriana*, 2: 910. Trans. by Brodrick, 531.

On the return of Xavier's body to Goa in 1554, and its impact on the city and ultimately the larger world, see Gupta, *The Relic State*, especially 104–124; and Županov, "The Sacred Body: Francis Xavier, the Apostle, the Pilgrim, the Relic," in *Missionary Tropics*, 35–86.

The devout began to pour into St. Paul's to venerate the body. For four days after Xavier's arrival in Goa, people crowded into the church to view the miracle and to kiss the missionary's feet. Father Melchior Nunes Barreto declared,

> I have never seen anything comparable to the devotion, to the enthusiasm of these people. They wept, they beat their breasts, they asked of God pardon for their sins. They made violent efforts to make their rosaries and other articles touch the body of the blessed father. They could never have enough of kissing of his feet. If we had not been present, I believe that each would have taken away a piece of the body as a relic.[104]

Another eyewitness, Fernão Mendes Pinto, described the Goans' reactions in similar terms: "because of the enormous crowds that came, there was a great deal of shouting and disorder on the part of both women and children who were in danger of being suffocated."[105] Pinto also stated that many conversions took place on the spot.

In 1559, the body of Xavier was removed from its resting place in the Church of St. Paul's when that building was demolished. It was kept in the rector's room for a time, and later removed to several other locations over the next few years. In time, Francis Xavier's body came to be identified with the state of Goa as well as its people. The cult of the saint ultimately consolidated Goan Christian identity, becoming in a sense interchangeable with it.

In 1614, Claudio Aquaviva, Superior General of the Society of Jesus, asked for a relic that would be sent to Rome, thereby proving the incorrupt state of the body. In the middle of the night and in secrecy, the body was exhumed yet again, and the lower portion of the right arm was removed surgically and sent back to the Church of the Gesù in Rome. According to legend, silver flasks caught the blood that flowed from the Saint's body on that occasion.[106]

In 1619, the rest of the arm was removed and distributed to Jesuit colleges in Malacca, Cochin, and Macau. Francis was beatified that year by Pope Paul V. A year later the intestines and internal organs were removed and disseminated all over the world as relics, and in 1622, Xavier was officially canonized a saint. In 1659, Xavier's body was enshrined in a magnificent silver reliquary and housed in a chapel of the Bom Jesus, now a minor

---

[104] Letter to Ignatius Loyola dated May, 1554. Wicki, *Documenta Indica* III (1553–1557), 77. Translation from Correia Afonso, *The Spirit of Xavier*, 132.

[105] *The Travels of Mendes Pinto*, 502.

[106] Figueiredo, *S. Francisco Xavier*, 107.

basilica. The baroque mausoleum was provided by the Grand Duke Cosimo III of Florence in 1698.

The miracle of Xavier's incorrupt body was commemorated in a variety of ways and not just in Goa. In 1716, Dr. Manuel Porras, His Majesty's surgeon at the Royal Court Hospital, published in Lisbon a medical compendium called *Anatomia galenico-moderno*. In his book, Porras provided an image of the surgical removal of Xavier's arm, which had taken place a century earlier. Porras dedicated the anatomy to St. Francis, thanking him for his many consolations.[107] This medical textbook demonstrates that even in the eighteenth century, it was possible to reconcile a scientific understanding of anatomy with a belief in the miraculous potential of certain bodies to defy the laws of nature.

It is probably significant that the return of Xavier's body to Goa, the stepped-up persecution of New Christians in Cochin and Goa, and the capture, trial, and destruction of the tooth relic happened within the same seven-year period. The emergence of a new group mystery specific to the Goan and South Asian Catholic community could have intensified, at least in some people, the desire to attack other groups whose mysteries provided incomprehensible reflections of their own.

The Tooth Relic as Legend and Hallucination

This chapter reconstructs an episode of symbolic violence – the capture, trial, and "execution" of a relic purported to be the tooth of the historical Buddha. The destruction of the relic was not merely symbolic but must also be considered a form of psychological violence against the group mystery of South Asian Buddhists – that is, the expression of a wish to eradicate the religious beliefs of a rival collective. The tooth-burning episode was, moreover, coextensive with actual violence against persons deemed to be enemies of the colonial state – victims of the ecclesiastical tribunals, such as Leonor Caldeira, as well as the Ceylonese and Peguans, and the Hindus of Goa.

One question remains to be answered. Why did the tooth-burning story become topical – or publishable – only at the end of the sixteenth century? Linschoten released his version of the story in the Dutch edition of 1596. We do not know for certain when Couto first wrote Decade VII of the *Da Ásia*, which contained his account of the events in Ceylon and Goa from 1560 to 1561; we know only that one manuscript was lost at sea in 1602 after having been dispatched to Portugal for publication. These two chroniclers

<hr>

[107] *Ibid.*, 106.

recounted their stories at roughly the same time, perhaps having shared the story sometime previously or having heard the story through intermediate sources. The means of transmission are not clear.

There are, however, reasons to question the accuracy or even the reality of the tooth-burning episode that supposedly occurred in Goa in 1561. The *Dāṭhāvaṃsa*, or "Chronicle of the Tooth," mentioned at the beginning of this chapter, describes an ancient trial of the tooth relic in the fourth century CE. In that legend, Paṇḍu, the Hindu king of Pāṭalīputra (Patna, capital of Bihar), was appalled that his tributary king Guhasiṃha, ruler of Dantapura (the "Tooth-city"), was worshipping a "bone of the dead" (*cavaṭṭhi* in Pali). Paṇḍu sent an army to bring the relic, along with Guhasiṃha, to him. The army and their leader converted to Buddhism along the way, thanks to the power of the relic.

Nevertheless, Guhasiṃha and the relic were escorted back to Pāṭalīputra, whereupon King Paṇḍu subjected the tooth to a series of trials. First he cast the relic into a pit of glowing charcoal. A lotus flower the size of a chariot wheel appeared over the flames, and the sacred tooth mysteriously alighted on top of it. Next Paṇḍu attempted to destroy the relic by throwing it into a ditch. The filthy water therein immediately grew clear, and lotus flowers began to blossom in it. On one of those flowers, the tooth rested. Subsequently the frustrated Paṇḍu had elephants stomp on the relic, attempting to crush it and bury it in the ground. Once again, however, the tooth appeared at the center of a golden lotus flower that sprouted from the earth. Finally, Paṇḍu attempted to smash the tooth on an anvil with a sledgehammer, but the indestructible tooth became embedded in the anvil. When all else failed, Paṇḍu converted to Buddhism and built a great temple for the tooth relic.[108]

The pronounced similarities between these two narratives – that of the ancient trials of the tooth recounted in the *Dāṭhāvaṃsa* and the Goan trial recounted by Couto and others – raise questions about what actually happened in 1561. Indeed, it is impossible to know what happened or to which extent the Portuguese "execution" of the tooth, recounted many decades after the incidents in Ceylon and Goa had supposedly occurred, might have been conflated with a story from an ancient Buddhist scripture, in which the relic was subjected to similar trials only to survive them.

[108] *Dāṭhāvaṃsa*, pp. 46ff. Also recounted in Gerson da Cunha, *Memoir on the History of the Tooth-Relic of Ceylon*, 35–37, and in Herath, 27–28.

Nell identifies the *niganthas* (v. 73) as Jains, adversaries of the Buddhists who urge Paṇḍu to destroy the tooth (*The Annals of the Tooth-Relic*, 6). Law, editor and translator of another edition of the *Dāṭhāvaṃsa*, concurs (24). Coomára Swámy, however, states that the *niganthas* were a sect of Sivites (93), as does Gerson da Cunha (35).

We do know that Diogo do Couto, the official historian of the Portuguese colonial enterprise in India, took his job seriously enough to name his sources – at least some of them. Couto claims to have found a document in the *Torre do Pombo*, or record office at Goa, a document signed by the Goan Archbishop, the Inquisitors, the Viceroy, and many other leaders involved in the deliberations over the fate of the tooth.[109] Concerning the double reappearance of the relic in Kōttē and Kandy five years later, Couto cites one Antonio Toscano, stationed at Pegu, as a source.[110] It is likely therefore that Couto told what he thought was the story of the tooth, although his account could be shot through with urban legend, as well as subtle (or not-so-subtle) biases against the Ceylonese, Peguans, and Portuguese. The strange resemblance of Couto's account of the trial of the tooth to the *Dāṭhāvaṃsa* raises more questions than it answers.

Still another interpretation is possible, however, which is that Couto told the story of the Inquisition's persecutions in Goa in the only way that he could do so safely. Couto had learned to navigate within the boundaries of his group very carefully lest his historical representations highlight too fully the contingencies of colonial group identity and the rampant abuses of power. Having sailed to India at age fifteen in 1559, a pivotal year in the histories recounted in this chapter, Couto would serve as a soldier there for nine years (although not, it seems, in the battles against the Ceylonese).[111] In February of 1569, he would sail back to Portugal only to return in 1571, remaining there until his death in 1616. Gifted in mathematics and geography and fluent in Latin and Italian, Couto was admired as a humanist and man of letters.[112]

It was only after the accession of the Spanish King Philip II to the Portuguese throne in 1580, however, that Couto would consider completing the history of the Portuguese Indies, *Da Ásia*, the work of his predecessor João do Barros. On December 4th of that same year, the Inquisition conducted a trial and *auto-da-fé* of Garcia de Orta, the great Goan botanist who had died in 1568 – a fact possibly significant to Couto's project. Orta's remains were exhumed and burned with his effigy; his crime was Judaizing.[113]

---

[109] *Da Ásia*, Dec. VII, ix., cap. xvii (17: 431).

[110] *Ibid.*, Dec. VIII, cap xiii (18, 78).

[111] Bell, *Diogo do Couto*, 6ff.; Boxer, 13.

[112] In his *Discursos varios politicos* (1624), Couto's early biographer Manuel Severim de Faria wrote that Couto "soube bem a lingua Latina e italiana nas quais compôs alguns versos." A. Farinha de Carvalho, *Diogo do Couto*, 25. Couto was also a longtime friend of Luís de Camões, epic poet of the Portuguese Indies.

[113] In October of 1568, Catarina de Orta was arrested after the death of her brother. She was executed in the Goan *auto-da-fé* of October 25, 1569. On the basis of her denunciations against

Given that Couto lived in India for more than forty years and served in later life as the chief archivist of the *Estado da Índia* during the time of bizarre and turbulent events such as Orta's posthumous condemnation, it is not surprising that the historian never talks about the Inquisition in any detail. In Decade VII, Couto mentions the arrival of Dom Gaspar de Leão, the new Archbishop, as well as Falcão and Botelho, who had come to India with Papal orders to found the Inquisition. Couto also mentions that there had been *muitos Cristãos novos, que judaizavam, e tinham synagogas separadas* ("many New Christians who were Judaizing and who had separate synagogues"), also stating that some had been sent back to Portugal for sentencing in the years immediately prior to the arrival of the Inquisition in Goa. In his brief description, Couto seems to support the arrival of the Inquisition in Goa, noting that the three officials had been "sent by so Catholic a king, so zealous for the honor of our Lord God, and in the time of so Christian and so God-fearing a Viceroy" (*"mandados por hum Rey tão Catholico, e tão zeloso da honra de Deos nosso Senhor, e em tempo de hum Viso-Rey tão bom Christao, e tão temente a Deos"*).[114] Of the several thousand Inquisition trials that took place between the time of their arrival and the time of his writing, Couto says nothing. The repetition of the word *tão* ("so") in his account (*tão Catholico, tão zeloso, tão bom Christao, tão temente*) could be taken to suggest the author's cynicism and also could represent a form of "speaking between the lines" of his own official history of the Portuguese Indies.

Some have argued that Couto not only exercised extreme caution in his treatments of the Holy Office but also that he was afraid of falling afoul of the Inquisition.[115] Couto was not lacking in moral courage, however. For example, in Decade IV, which was sent back to Portugal in 1597 and later published in 1602, Couto spoke positively of Garcia de Orta, an act that probably entailed personal risk for the historian.[116] As the historian Charles Boxer attested, "All the more credit therefore is due to Diogo do Couto for defying the prevailing bigotry, by his laudatory mention of Orta, an attitude which contrasts favorably with the shamefaced silence of most of his countrymen and contemporaries."[117]

---

her dead brother, which she later revoked during her trial, Garcia de Orta would be punished postmortem in 1580. Saraiva, 346–347; Da Silva Carvalho, 72–79.

[114] *Da Ásia*, Dec. VII, IX, v (17: 335–336).

[115] So argued by Baião, 35; and Farinha de Carvalho, 46. Baião suggests that Couto had New Christian ancestors, but this point is debated today.

[116] *Da Ásia*, Dec. IV, III, xi (7: 321), and IV, VI, xix, (8: 132). Admittedly Couto reappraised Garcia de Orta and his work eighteen years after his *auto-da-fé* and thirty years after his death.

[117] Boxer, 19.

In a letter to King Philip III, dated November 6, 1603, and dispatched with the rewritten version of Decade VII – the first having been lost at sea – Couto wrote: "I myself marvel: because I know not what spirit led me to gather and discover things that were so forgotten, and of which there was almost no remembrance."[118] Couto could not tell the full history of things forgotten without risking his reputation and even his life, however; he could not tell the stories of Leonor Caldeira and others, nor could he relate the history of the Inquisition. While he mentioned Francis Xavier's life and works from time to time, he did not discuss the disposition of his body after death. Couto did tell other stories, however, among them the trial of the tooth relic of the entity identified as both *Budão*, the "great saint," and *bugio*, the monkey. It is possible that Couto planted in this enigmatic tale of paranoia, fear, and greed a commentary on the founding of the Goan Inquisition, one hidden in plain sight. One of the many senses of the Portuguese word *bugio* is "lie," "deception," "trick," as well as "threat" or "joke."[119] Moreover, in sixteenth-century Italian, a language in which Couto was fluent enough to write verses, *una bugia* meant – and still means– "a lie" or, more temperately, "a *story*."[120] Through the ironic potential of Couto's narrative and through his wordplay, which nimbly elides languages, religions, and cultures, we come to imagine life at the borders of a distant empire and on the edges of the group.

[118] Ferguson, 8.

[119] Houaiss et al., eds., *Dicionário Houaiss da língua portuguêsa*, 526. See also n. 25.

[120] Both the Portuguese *bogio/bugio* and the Italian *bugia* entered their languages from a common root: the classical Arabic Budjâya or later Arabic Budjìa – the name of a city on the shores of North Africa (present-day Bejaia, in Algeria), which exported candles to Europe, and possibly macaques as well. See Bueno, *Grande dicionário etimológico-prosódico da língua portuguêsa*, 556–557; Houaiss, et al., *Dicionário Houaiss da língua portuguêsa*, 526; and Pianigiani, ed., *Il vocabolario etimologico della lingua italiana* (online edition).

5

HAMLET'S MACHINE:
THE INORGANIC GROUP
LONDON, 1600

When they divided the Man, into how many parts did they apportion him?

What do they call his mouth, his two arms and thighs and feet?

His mouth became the Brahmin; his arms were made into the Warrior.

His thighs became the People, and from his feet the Servants were born.

– Rg-Veda

[T]he laws are the nerves and ligaments that keep the machine of the state standing.

– Alessandro Campiglia, Delle turbulenze della Francia in vita del re Enrico il grande

We are much less Greeks than we believe. We are neither in the amphitheatre, nor on the stage, but in the panoptic machine, invested by its effects of power, which we bring to ourselves since we are part of its mechanism.

– Michel Foucault, Discipline and Punish

Reconfigurations of the Group Body

FOR MORE THAN TWO MILLENNIA, SOCIAL POLITIES AROUND THE WORLD relied on the metaphor of the body politic to justify and explain their structures. The hierarchical organization of the group was likened to that of a human body, with the king or ruler serving as the head. Philosophers, historians, and political writers have long used the metaphor of the body politic to describe human collectives as organic and unified entities.[1] The

---

[1] Analogies between the social collective and the human body, with its imagined anatomies, its inventories of parts, and its healthy and diseased states, can be traced far back into antiquity. The metaphor of the body politic and its numerous variants can be found in manifold literary and visual representations, in theological, philosophical, and political treatises, and in histories and *res gestae* of cultures around the globe; it seems to have been a virtually omnipresent trope in premodern thought. Versions of the metaphor can be located, for example, in the Hindu *Rg-Veda*

implications of that metaphor underwent significant modifications over the centuries, as David George Hale has argued, but what remained constant was a shared view of reality that took for granted a system of correspondences between the individual, the state, the church, the world, and the cosmos. The human body was perceived as a microcosm, a "small world," that corresponded analogically to larger structures, or macrocosms.[2] The body politic metaphor would reach its apogee in Renaissance thought, whereafter it would gradually be supplanted by different metaphors for the state or social order. Hale attributes this conceptual transformation to various "challenges to the anthropomorphic view of the universe, challenges which eventually wrought a profound change on man's understanding of himself and his environment."[3]

This chapter explores one of the most important new group concepts to emerge during the Renaissance and its aftermath. This new metaphor, the group as machine, would ultimately take the place of the metaphor of the body politic as the primary descriptor and explanatory principle of the political collective. The body as a set of reference points for groups and their functions would gradually be eclipsed within European political discourse by that new group concept, one seemingly rational, systematic, and stable, and free of the messy organicism of the body-politic metaphor.

This shift in the dominant political metaphor did not happen quickly; rather, it occurred through a gradual process of imaginative, cultural, and social transformation that unfolded over several centuries (arguably millennia) and that extends forward into our own time, although the Enlightenment era represented a turning point in the conceptualization of the group and its body. This paradigm shift would have profound consequences for how people would come to understand their relation to other individuals and to society at large. Indeed, the group as machine can be regarded as the fundamental organizing fantasy of modernity, a conceptual stage in the later history of colonialism, and in the development of capitalism, industrialism,

---

and the *Mahābhārata*; in the astrological traditions of East and West; in the recurring topos of the microcosm/macrocosm; in the writings of Plato, Aristotle, Cicero, and Livy; in Augustine and the early Church fathers; in the *Encyclopedia* of the Arabic Brotherhood of Sincerity; in the Jewish mystical texts called the *Kabbalah*; in the medieval devotional classic *Ayenbite of Inwyt*; and in the classic dramas of William Shakespeare. These are but a few of hundreds, if not thousands, of instances of the body politic metaphor, many of which are discussed in David George Hale's study *The Body Politic*.

[2] Hale, *The Body Politic*, 13. See also Tillyard, *The Elizabethan World Picture*, 95; Conger, *Theories of Macrocosms and Microcosms*; and C. A. Patrides, "The Microcosm of Man," (1960): 54–56, and (1963): 282–286.

[3] Hale, 47.

and the modern world.[4] For the group to be rendered inorganic, mechanical, and above all predictable and controllable, the human body itself had to be reconceived as a machine, as did the world itself.[5] The technological advances of the Renaissance and the development of modern science, with the mechanistic philosophies of the Enlightenment, would give rise to startlingly new conceptions of the individual body, gradually incorporating fantasies of systematicity, invulnerability, perfectibility, power, and lack of affect. Over time, the body-machine concept would migrate to the collective and often would be accompanied by compensatory fantasies of durability, invulnerability, and invincibility.

This radical transformation of the group concept occurred for particular reasons during the pivotal centuries that we must in this context refer to as the early modern age rather than the Renaissance, because the rise of the machine group anticipated an unknown and mysterious future rather than signaling the rebirth of a remote and glorious past. As we shall see, the increasing mechanization of tangible and concrete areas of daily life in early modern Europe, accompanied by a philosophy and science responding to that mechanization, had much to do with this process of individual and group transformation. New technologies would generate a different set of approaches for viewing the world and humankind along with it. These new views of humans and their place within the world would in turn precipitate the further development and elaboration of novel social technologies, which in the Foucaultian sense established the control and discipline of social organizations as small as the family or as large as the nation-state, the colonial empire, or the world-system.

The mechanization of the social metaphor must also be regarded as an extension of what sociologist Norbert Elias called the "civilizing process" – the collective repression of the body and its drives that began to take place at an accelerating rate toward the end of the European Middle Ages. Elias linked this increase in individual affect control to the rise of the nation-state and to the concentration of physical power over individuals within the apparatus of the state or central governing authority.[6] The emergence of the metaphor of the group machine would project a vision of social collectives free of organicism, and also conveniently of destabilizing individual or group affect.

---

[4] On the role of technology and its metaphors in western colonialism, see, for example, Adas, *Machines as the Measure of Men*.

[5] On the conceptualization of the body as a machine in the early modern era, see Rosenfield, *From Beast-Machine to Man-Machine* (1968); Judovitz, *The Culture of the Body* (2001); Wolfe, *Humanism, Machinery, and Renaissance Literature* (2004); and especially Sawday, *Engines of the Imagination* (2007).

[6] Elias, *The Civilizing Process*.

Machines do not have emotions or humors (at least not yet). The fantasy of the group as machine must itself be understood as a form of technology implemented at a given point in history, serving as a means of regulating the functions of the social collective and its components for better or for worse – that is, the machine bodies of humans.

When Did the Body Become a Machine?

Hamlet, Act II, Scene ii: The courtier Polonius reads to the King and Queen of Denmark a private letter turned over to him by his daughter Ophelia. It is, we soon learn, a love letter written to her by her ardent suitor. It reads,

> "Doubt thou the stars are fire,
>   Doubt that the sun doth move,
> Doubt truth to be a liar,
>   But never doubt I love.
> O dear Ophelia, I am ill at these numbers. I have not
> art to reckon my groans. But that I love thee best, O
> most best, believe it. Adieu.
>   Thine evermore, most dear lady, whilst this
>   machine is to him, Hamlet." (116–124)[7]

A self-confessed bad poet, Hamlet is made "ill" by – i.e., disenchanted with– his own attempts at poetry ("numbers"). What he lacks in art, however, he claims to make up for in sincerity, of which his groans serve as testament. He states that his body articulates what he himself cannot easily put into words. Hamlet's passions, his sufferings, defy representation in language – love and pain, the pain of love, or the pain of expressing complex emotions in verse. The hackneyed rhymes of the young prince (fire/liar, move/love), far from undermining his expression of feeling, mark the unrepresentable nature of the lover's passions ("But that I love thee best, O most best, believe it").

Attempting to interpret what has not been fully revealed by Hamlet's letter, Polonius asks of the King and Queen:

> [W]hat might you think,
>   When I had seen this hot love on the wing–
>   As I perceived it, I must tell you that,
>   Before my daughter told me–what might you,
>   Or my dear Majesty your queen here, think,
>   If I had played the desk or table book,
>   Or given my heart a winking, mute and dumb,

---

[7] *The Complete Works*, ed. Bevington, 1112.

> Or looked upon this love with idle sight?
> What might you think? (131–139)

Observed and manipulated by others, the "hot love on the wing" points expressively to the body and its passions, which the elders of the play seek to control or suppress in the next generation.

Hamlet's love letter ends on a strange and jarring note – one seemingly removed from Polonius's description of the relationship: "Thine evermore, most dear lady, whilst this machine is to him, Hamlet." His closing turns on the ambiguous word *machine*. Possibly for the first time in the history of the English language, Shakespeare appears to use the word *machine* to describe the human body or perhaps a body part – hand, penis, or other member.[8] The *Oxford English Dictionary* cites this passage from *Hamlet* as the first occurrence of the noun *machine* "applied to the human and animal frame as a combination of several parts."[9] This seemingly new use of the word represents a significant development in the history of an idea.

Most modern editions of the play gloss the word "machine" in *Hamlet* simply as "body."[10] Occasionally, an editor's note is slightly more interpretive; in the Signet edition, Sylvan Barnet defines the unusual word as "a complex device (here, his body)."[11] Modern editors assume that Hamlet is in some way referring to his own body with the word *machine*; however, they do not explain the unusual metaphor or note that in all likelihood it makes its English debut in Shakespeare's play.

Machine is not a common word in the Shakespearean corpus: it appears only twice in his plays – in *Hamlet* and in the late play *Two Noble Kinsmen*.[12] Even if we assume that *machine* refers to Hamlet's body, it is not fully clear what the word means in this context. How, the reader must ask, is Hamlet's body like a mechanical device? What might that odd and, for

---

[8] Shakespeare, a master of erotic wordplay, might well have invested Hamlet's "machine" with sexual undertones.

[9] *Oxford English Dictionary*, 1: 1687.

[10] For example, Bevington, 1112; *The Norton Shakespeare* (New York: Norton, 1997), 1693; *The Riverside Shakespeare* (New York: Houghton Mifflin, 1974), 1154; and *The Complete Pelican Shakespeare* (New York: Penguin, 1969), 944. For the "body" gloss, see also Shewmaker, *Shakespeare's Language*, and Onions, *A Shakespeare Glossary*.

Michael R. Martin and Richard Harrier, in *The Concise Encyclopedic Guide to Shakespeare* (New York: Horizon Press, 1971), note more helpfully that "machine" in the sense of "body" is not used prior to Shakespeare and "is considered an affected use of the word."

[11] Sylvan Barnet, ed., *Hamlet* (New York: Signet, 1998), 44.

[12] In *Two Noble Kinsmen*, "machine" apparently connotes the entertainment being presented: "And I that am the rectifier of all,/ . . . Do here present this machine, or this frame" (*TNK* III.v.112, 116).

the early seventeenth century, uncommon word in English be taken to
mean?

The appearance of the word *machine* in *Hamlet* raises another question
crucial to this exploration: when in history did it become possible to imagine the body as a machine? Moreover, when did the machine evolve into
an available metaphor for the individual person *and* for the group body
or envelope? Which implications does the imagined "machine body" of
the individual person – or the group – have for other bodies, organic or
inorganic, with which it comes in contact?

A Loaded Word

Like *gruppo*, discussed in Chapter 1, the word *machine* and its variants in
the Indo-European languages have a long and interesting history, evolving
considerably over millennia. In classical Latin, the term *māchĭna* could refer
to a siege engine, such as a device for breaking down walls or hurling
missiles. It could also refer to a mechanical device or contrivance, as well as
a stratagem or artifice.[13] Less common usages included a platform on which
slaves were displayed or sold, or a cage or pen for confining animals such
as cattle, or human beings, sometimes for the purpose of torture.[14] More
abstractly – and more positively – *machina* could refer to a fabric or structure,
as of the universe or cosmos.[15] In *De rerum natura* Lucretius would describe
the cosmos as the *machina mundi*, the "machine of the world."[16]

The Latin word *māchĭna* derives from the Greek *mēkhanē* (μηχανή),
which could also signify a contrivance or wiles, as well as an engine of war, a
theatrical apparatus for raising gods above the stage, a crane for lifting things,
an oil-press, or an irrigation device, among other things.[17] By extension,
mēkhanē could refer to "any artificial means or contrivance for doing a
thing."[18] In the *Symposium*, Plato describes the *mēkhanē*, or device, of Zeus,
who takes pity on recently halved humankind by moving their privy parts

---

[13] The *Grand Larousse de la langue française* explains the etymology of the French word *machine* as
follows: n. f. (lat. *machina*, ouvrage composé avec art, engin, expédient, artifice, du gr. dorien
makhana, gr. attique *mékhané*, invention ingénieuse, machine de guerre ou de théâtre, moyen,
expédient, artifice" . . .). (Paris: Librairie Larousse, 1971–), 4: 3147.

[14] P. G. W. Glare, ed., *Oxford Latin Dictionary* (Oxford: Clarendon Press, 2003), 1057.

[15] *Ibid.*, 1057.

[16] *De rerum natura* 5: 96, p. x, discussed by Wey Gómez in *The Tropics of Empire*, 93.

[17] Liddell and Scott, *A Greek-English Lexicon* (Oxford: Clarendon Press, 1996), 1131.

  On the history of the concept of the machine in classical antiquity, see Micheli, *Le origini del
concetto di macchina*.

[18] Liddell and Scott, 1131.

from back to front, thereby helping each being to reconnect with its missing half.[19] Thucidides speaks of the *mēkhanai*, the military engines that the Peloponnesians brought up against the city of Plateia.[20] In his well-known treatise, *ta mēkhanika*, Aristotle wrote on the science of mechanics. *Mēkhanē* and numerous Greek derivatives can be traced back to the Indo-European root *magh-*, meaning "to have power," and in another sense, "to fight."[21] The words *magus* and *magic* in their ancient and modern variants derive from that same root, by means of the Old Persian *maguš*, a member of the priestly caste. The word *Amazon*, the woman warrior, is also etymologically related, having passed from the Old Iranian *ha-maz-an* (the warrior) through Greek into later languages.[22] The *machine* is thus linked to a wide array of words and concepts having to do with power, conflict, and action, as well as the supernatural, the superhuman, and also the extraordinary. *Machine* is a loaded word.

The Latin word and concept *machina* also has a long history within classical, medieval, and Renaissance cosmology, as Nicolás Wey Gómez has recently shown.[23] In his thirteenth-century treatise *De sphaera*, John Sacrobosco describes the *universalis machina mundi* as consisting of both the incorruptible celestial region and the mutable region of the elements. Only God could disrupt his own machine by miraculous interventions. In European geographical works of the sixteenth and seventeenth centuries, the *machina mundi* would refer to a specifically Christian cosmos in which heavenly bodies, the intermediaries of God, governed motion and change in the sublunar world.[24]

In his 1552 *Historia de las Indias*, Bartolomé de Las Casas would invoke that same divinely organized view of the *máquina mundial*, while investing it with novel political significance. In his Prologue to that work, he states his intention "to offer readers of many ancient things clarity and certainty concerning the principles upon which this world-machine was discovered." By "world machine" (*máquina mundial*), Las Casas refers to the western hemisphere, a newfound part of the earth. In so doing, he underscores the fact that the New World is part of a larger whole and governed by the same natural order, as Wey Gómez explains.[25] Las Casas' use of the *máquina*

---

[19] *Lysis, Symposium, Gorgias*, 136.

[20] *History*, 2.76.4, 2: 398.

[21] *American Heritage Dictionary*, 1527. See also Julius Pokorny, *Indogermanisches etymologisches Wörterbuch*, 2: 695–696.

[22] *American Heritage Dictionary*, 1527.

[23] *Tropics of Empire*, 94.

[24] *Ibid.*, 95.

[25] *Ibid.*, 95. de Las Casas, *Historia de las Indias*, in *Obras completas*, 3: 346. Translation by Wey Gómez.

mundial metaphor represents a further development in the history of this word/concept, for it draws the New World into the framework of the Old in a very concrete way. Although not yet a group concept in Las Casas' writings, the *máquina mundial* anticipates the extension of the machine metaphor to human groups – whether in one or both hemispheres of the world.

About this time the noun *machine* entered the English language, passing from Latin through French into English only in the sixteenth century. By 1549 the word designated "a structure of any kind, material or immaterial; a fabric, an erection."[26] In the sixteenth and seventeenth centuries, the world itself was frequently described as a machine, as in the 1672 English translation of the Jesuit Famiano Strada's *De bello belgico* ("On the Wars in the Low Countries"), a work that describes the notorious 1585 siege of Antwerp by Spanish forces and the use of what some consider the first weapon of mass destruction (Figure 5.1). Under the instruction of an Italian military engineer, Federico Giambelli, the inhabitants of Antwerp sent an exploding fireship down the Scheldt River toward the Spanish blockade that had cut off the city's food and supplies. Detonating on contact with the bridge, the bomb killed more than 800 troops with an enormous explosion that temporarily drove the river from its banks. The consequences were devastating, although they did not end the siege. In the words of Strada's English translator:

> [O]n a sudden the fatall ship burst, with such a horrid crash, as if the very Skies had rent asunder, heaven and earth had charged one another, and the whole Machine of the Earth it selfe had quaked. For the storm of stones, chaines, and bullets, being cast out with Thunder and lightning, there followed such a slaughter, as no man, but that actually it happened, could have imagined.[27]

In 1585, the Antwerp that Thomas More had visited became a distant memory, as the city and environs were torn apart by warfare. In Strada's account, the word *machine* describes the earth itself, violently shaken by the cataclysmic explosion that sent munitions, nails, chains, gravestones, and other shrapnel flying a mile in all directions.[28] Strada's usage condenses two Latin meanings of the word, as the fabric of the earth came in contact with a powerful weapon of war and was fantastically disrupted by it.

---

[26] *Oxford English Dictionary*, 1687.

[27] *An account of the famous siege of Antvverp by Alexander prince of Parma*, 86.

[28] Strada's Latin original reads differently: "ferale navigium horrendo usque adeo fragore concrepuit, ut ruere coelum, misceri superis infera, ipsa quati terrarum moles videretur." *De bello belgico, Decas secunda*, 339. Strada describes the fireship as a *machinamentum*, translated as "engine," but the word also suggests a strategem or machination, as well.

Pontis Antuerp

A . *Pons.* B . *Flottæ ante pontem* . C . *Arx S. Mariæ.*

D . *Naues septendecim Antuerpia in pontem immisſæ* .

E . *Quatuor ex his maiores ignem foris, intus cuniculos portantes* .

F . *Vna ex maioribus, extincto aquis igniario, in fumum abit* .

G . *Altera, et tertia, ad ripam uento impulſæ, ruinam euomunt* .

5.1. Carl Decker, *Destruction of the bridge of Farnèse* (second half of the seventeenth century), etching, 270 mm. × 348 mm. Museum Plantin-Moretus/Prentenkabinet, Antwerp – UNESCO World Heritage. Photo credit: Peter Maes. This engraving depicts the destruction of the pontoon bridge and blockade over the Scheldt River with an exploding fireship – what some consider the first weapon of mass destruction.

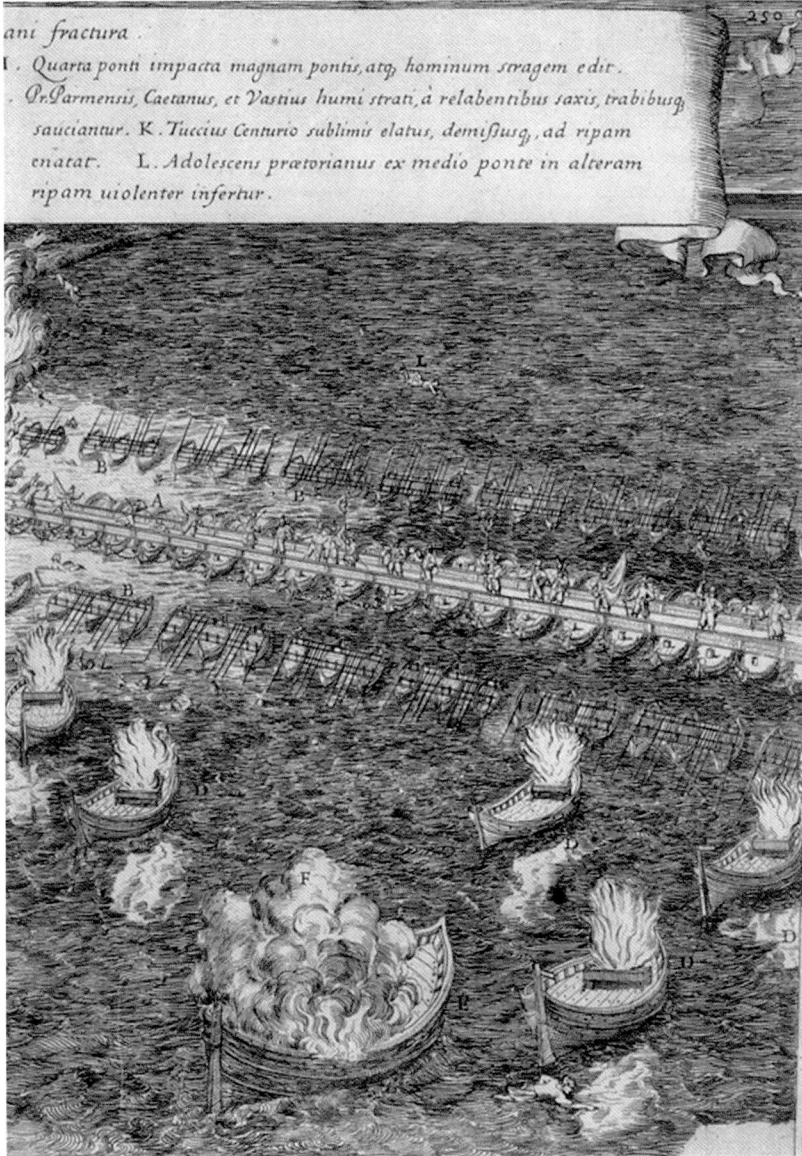

ani fractura .

I . Quarta ponti impacta magnam pontis, atq, hominum stragem edit .
. Qr.Parmensis, Caetanus, et Vastius humi strati, à relabentibus saxis, trabibusq,
sauciantur. K . Tuccius Centurio sublimis elatus, demissusq,, ad ripam
enatat . L . Adolescens prætorianus ex medio ponte in alteram
ripam uiolenter infertur .

5.1

In the seventeenth century, the English word *machine* also came to signify the military engine or the mechanical device for doing work – meanings that had long been present in the Italian. Ships, coaches, and other vehicles; siege towers, theatrical appliances, and devices for drawing water – all are possible significations of the noun *machine* by the mid- to latter half of the seventeenth century. By 1692, the word had acquired a meaning familiar to us today: "a combination of parts moving mechanically, as *contrasted with* a being having life, consciousness and will."[29] Machine would also become increasingly linked not only to human bodies but also to social collectives.

Continental Innovations

Shakespeare's use of the word machine in his play *Hamlet* remains enigmatic, because it appears to have no precedents in the English language. Hamlet's *machine* may in fact be an Italian import, because Shakespeare's use of the word resonates with developments in the Italian word/concept that were current during the late fifteenth and sixteenth centuries. He or others in his circle might have been familiar with the Italian metaphor of the body as machine, which was already in wide circulation by the time that Shakespeare wrote his great tragedy.

In the late fifteenth and early sixteenth centuries, Leonardo da Vinci frequently referred to body parts and to the body itself, human or animal, as a machine (*macchina*). More than a century before the composition of *Hamlet*, da Vinci would write the following lines in one of his notebooks:

> O observer of this machine of ours (*questa nostra macchina*) let it not distress you that you give knowledge of it through another's death, but rejoice that our Author has established the intellect in such an excellent instrument.[30]

Throughout his anatomical studies, da Vinci assiduously sought to identify the parts of the body and their functions and to theorize the various systemic operations of the body. The artist approached the body mechanistically, conveying in his drawings of the tissues and bones of the human body a method of analysis similar to that of his studies of machines.[31] In both cases, da Vinci explored the relation of component parts to the whole, puzzling over how one part of a system could cause another to move or act. As Paolo Galluzzi has noted, by the beginning of the sixteenth century, da

---

[29] *Oxford English Dictionary*, 1: 1687.

[30] "O speculatore di questa nostra macchina, non ti contristare perchè coll'altrui morte tu ne dia notizia, ma rallegrati che il nostro autore abbia fermo lo intelletto a tale eccellenzia di strumento." An. C II 5 v CA 182 vc. In *Scritti scelti*, 515.

This manuscript consists of 32 leaves. It contained a treatise, now lost, entitled "On shadow and light." Quoted from Keele, *Leonardo da Vinci's Elements of the Science of Man*, 288.

[31] On da Vinci's mechanistic approach to the body, see *ibid.*, especially Chapter 13, "Muscles, the Forces of 'This Machine of Ours,'" 267–288.

Vinci had begun to look for the constant mechanical laws and models that applied to all things – organic or inorganic, animate or inanimate. This unity based on motion that he sought to theorize encompassed machines, buildings, the Earth, animals, and man.[32] Galluzzi also notes that da Vinci's anatomical studies followed chronologically the mechanical studies of his earlier years; hence, his analyses of the body and its workings made use of the general principles of his mechanical models, as well as vocabulary, graphic techniques, and expressive analogies.[33]

In several sketches of the human rib cage, spine, and neck, for example, da Vinci analyzes the musculature and bones involved in the process of breathing. In one sketch (Figure 5.2), he compares the muscles and ribs that connect to the spinal column to the shrouds that hold a ship's mast in place. This analogy he explains through drawings and also the accompanying text: "But such a convergence of muscles on the spine holds it erect just as the ropes of a ship support its mast and the same ropes, tied to the mast, also support in part the framework of the ships to which they are attached."[34]

In another drawing of the rib cage and spine (Figure 5.3), da Vinci attempts to analyze the action of voluntary respiration (breathing and sighing). The analogy between man and machine is clearly indicated by his side-by-side comparison of the muscles of breathing, which lift the ribs, to a pulley lifting a rod by means of a counterweight.[35] Similar diagrams that analogize the organic systems of the body to an inorganic mechanism or device may be found throughout Leonardo's anatomical drawings and accompanying notes.

Analogies between machines and the human or animal body had their limitations, however, as da Vinci recognized. In one notebook he commented, "Although human ingenuity in various inventions with different instruments yields the same end, it will never devise an invention either more beautiful, easier, or more rapidly than does Nature, because in her inventions nothing is lacking and nothing is superfluous, and she *does not use counterweights* but places there the soul, the composer of the body. . . ."[36] As Galluzzi argues, da Vinci's recognition of a key difference between the human body, with its obscure and hidden source of motion, and the machine

---

[32] Galluzzi, *Renaissance Engineers from Brunelleschi to Leonardo da Vinci*, 78; originally published as "Leonardo da Vinci: From the 'elementi macchinali' to the man-machine," 235–265.

[33] Galluzzi, *Renaissance Engineers*, 78.

[34] This page, K/P 149v, is dated ca. 1510. Translation by O'Malley and Saunders, *Leonardo da Vinci on the Human Body*, 74.

[35] K/P 154v. This and the preceding figure have been discussed by Galluzzi, 230–232. See also O'Malley and Saunders, 94.

[36] Galluzzi, *Renaissance Engineers*, 80; K/P 114v.

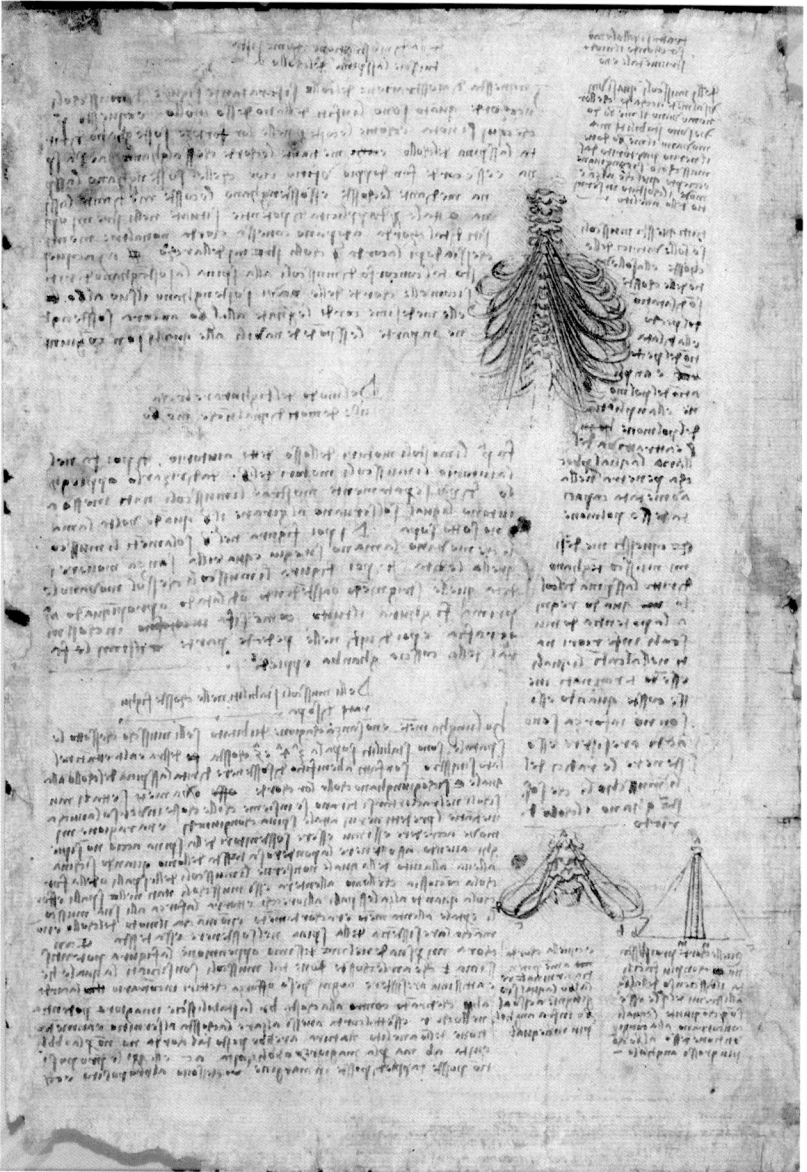

5.2. Leonardo da Vinci, anatomical drawings and notes on the mechanisms of breathing, 19015v; K/P 149v; ca. 1510 (detail). The Royal Collection © 2010 Her Majesty Queen Elizabeth II. In one sketch (lower right), Leonardo compares the muscles and tendons to the ropes connecting sails to a ship's mast.

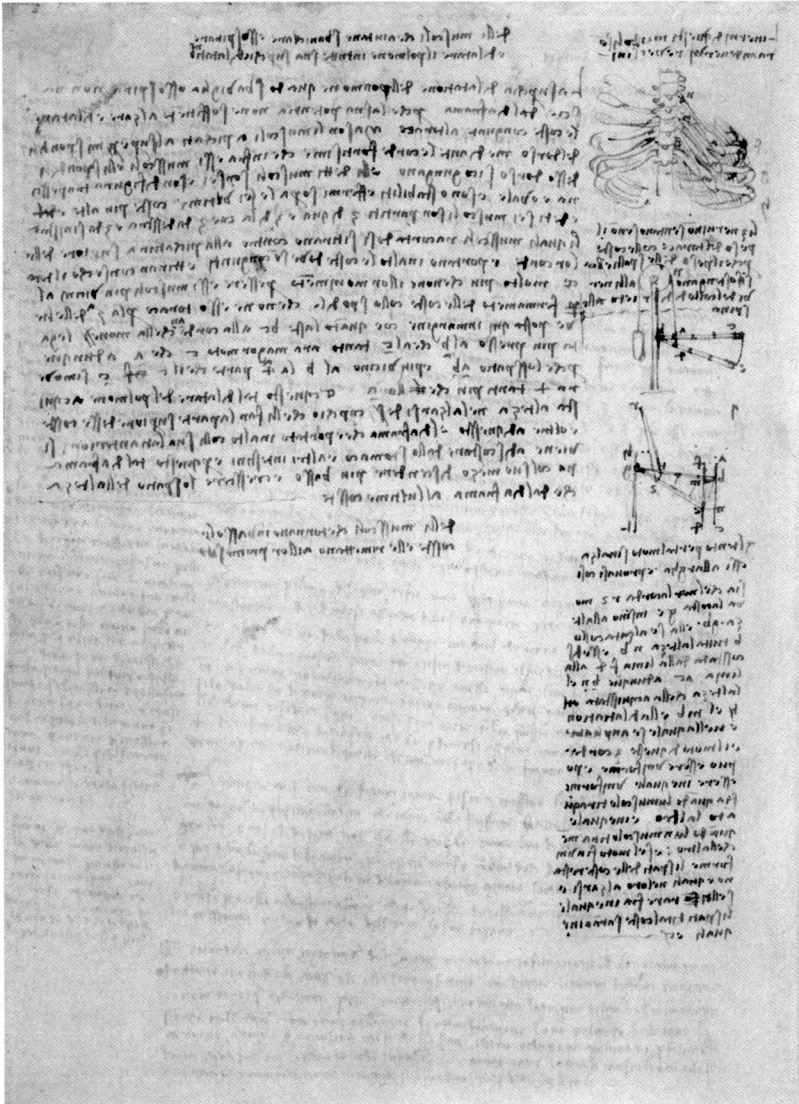

5.3. Leonardo da Vinci, anatomical drawings and notes on the mechanisms of breathing, 19061v; K/P 154v; ca. 1510 (detail). The Royal Collection © 2010 Her Majesty Queen Elizabeth II. Leonardo compares the muscles of breathing to a pulley lifting a rod by means of a counterweight.

"seemed to shake the very foundation of [da Vinci's] tenaciously pursued plan of unification," although this recognition did not cause him to abandon his quest to explain the body in mechanistic terms.[37]

Da Vinci's comparisons of the human body to the machine may not have been exclusively a matter of speculation. In 1495 or thereabouts, he designed and may have constructed a humanoid robot, inspired by the descriptions of automata that appear in ancient sources with which he appears to have been familiar.[38] He documented his conception across a series of drawings, as Mark Rosheim has persuasively argued.[39] This robot was an armed knight capable of sitting up, waving its arms, moving its head, and opening and closing its jaw. In the drawings for this robot, we observe that the robot's armor followed the late fifteenth-century conventions of German and Italian design. Its inner workings consisted of leather and metal parts operated by cables.

Although we do not know whether da Vinci actually constructed his humanoid robot, he was reported to have built another automaton in 1517. This was a mechanized lion created for the court entertainment of Francis I at the Château d'Argenton and funded by the Medici. This mechanical lion, led into the gathering by a hermit, was reported to have caused the ladies present to draw back in terror. When Francis touched the automaton three times with a magic wand that was handed to him by the attendant hermit, the lion's mouth opened and spilled out an impressively large quantity of fleurs-de-lis, to the delight of the assembled crowd.[40]

Leonardo da Vinci was not alone in envisioning the body as a machine, because the metaphor circulated widely in sixteenth-century Italy and beyond.[41] In his 1543 *De humani corporis fabrica*, the physician and anatomist

---

[37] *Ibid.*, 80–81.

[38] Ctesibus, an engineer working in Alexandria, produced the first organ and water clocks with moving components in the third c. BCE. His accomplishments are known only through the writings of Vitruvius in his *De architectura* (9.8). In his *Pneumatics*, Hero of Alexandria described automata that were used for theatrical and religious purposes in the 1st c. CE Galluzzi, "Leonardo da Vinci," 254. See also Hill, *A History of Engineering in Classical and Medieval Times*, 199ff.

[39] Rosheim, *Leonardo's Lost Robots*, 69ff. Rosheim, following a suggestion by Carlo Pedretti, reconstructed da Vinci's robot. See also Pedretti, ed., *Fragments at Windsor Castle from the* Codex Atlanticus, 39–40.

[40] The story was reported by da Vinci's friend and disciple Francesco Melzi. Gille, *The Renaissance Engineers*, 134. See also Rosheim, 21. In his chapter on da Vinci's programmable automata and lion, Rosheim cites Michelangelo Buonarroti, nephew of the artist, who dates the appearance of the mechanical lion to 1515, on the occasion of Francis I's triumphal entry into Lyon. This was also, interestingly, the date of More's trip to the Netherlands.

[41] For additional examples, see Battaglia, *Grande dizionario della lingua italiana*, 9: 359.

Vesalius made frequent recourse to machine analogies to describe body parts and their functions. In describing the anatomy of the human hip, for example, he offered the following comparison: "And do not overlook a depression in the posterior or inner region of the coxendix beneath the aforesaid grooves, around which, thanks to Nature's extraordinary ingenuity, the tenth muscle moving the thigh bends as around the sheave of a pulley."[42] Although less attuned to the world of engineering, mechanics, and weaponry, Vesalius often explained the body's interior systems by means of analogies to machines or to mechanical parts, as Leonardo had.

In his *Dix livres de chirurgie*, published in 1564, the French army physician Ambroise Paré presented his ideas for a mechanical foot and leg, hand, and arm, intended as prostheses for amputees and victims of war.[43] The illustration of the hand accompanying the text shows a cutaway that reveals its internal mechanism of gears, springs, and triggers that open and close the artificial limb (Figure 5.4). Similarly, his image of a prosthetic arm depicts a mechanical elbow that springs open at the touch of a lever. Without using the word *machine*, Paré envisioned a mechanized supplement to the human body.[44]

It was not only the anatomic explorations of da Vinci, Vesalius, Paré, and others that contributed to the rise of the body-as-machine metaphor, but also the technological breakthroughs of engineers who reconfigured the human–machine interface through their innovations. Jonathan Sawday has argued that this conceptual shift toward the mechanized body, which would become a central trope of Enlightenment philosophy, was well under way during the sixteenth century.[45] In philosophy, this fusion of man and machine was incipient, as it was in other discourses of the time. As Sawday writes, "The two nascent 'sciences' . . . – the science of technology and the science of anatomy – found themselves conspiring together to offer a complete 'mechanical' image of the world and the creatures which inhabited that world."[46]

Evidence of this shift can be found in the many how-to manuals in the sixteenth century for the design and construction of large machinery. Noteworthy among these manuals is *Le diverse et artificiose machine* of Agostino

---

[42] Andreas Vesalius, *On the Fabric of the Human Body*, 1: 308–309.

[43] This example from Paré's work is discussed by Mazlish in *The Fourth Discontinuity*, 17–18.

[44] *Dix livres de la chirurgie, avec Le Magasin des Instrumens necessaires à icelle*, VII, 121r–123r.

[45] "The Renaissance Cyborg," 171–195. See also Sawday's *Engines of the Imagination*, esp. 70–124.

[46] "The Renaissance Cyborg," 181.

Ramelli, published in 1588.[47] Born in Italy in 1531, Ramelli served as an engineer to the French kings Henry II and Henry III, participating in military campaigns against Huguenot forces during the Wars of Religion. Under the patronage of Henry III, he later published a collection of his projects and ideas in a lavishly illustrated engineering handbook published in a bilingual French and Italian edition. Ramelli's handbook included descriptions and images of water pumps, fountains, mills, cranes, drainage devices, bridges, and weaponry for breaking down enemy defenses and for launching cannon balls and other projectiles, as well as other types of devices and inventions. Following in da Vinci's footsteps, Ramelli and other sixteenth-century engineers explored the mechanical world, elaborating or updating versions of older machines and offering innovative laborsaving technologies. Not only did Ramelli instruct others on how to build extraordinary machines, but he and engineers like him continued to reconceptualize the world in mechanical terms.

Ramelli's machines offered tremendous power to their users. Plate 20 (Figure 5.5), for example, depicts a man drawing water from a well by turning a large wheel with a crank. The water flows from the breasts of a female/animal hybrid before pouring into a basin and channel below.[48] This machine-body calls to mind the Edenic breast fantasies of New World explorers. Here, however, the fantasy (indeed, a type of coupling) incorporates a complex pumping system that connects the man turning the crank to the mechanized and simultaneously bestialized woman. Plate 146 (Figure 5.6), also powered by humans, shows a portable bridge designed to span a moat encircling a fortification.[49] One notes that the wall of the fortress or city has already been partly demolished by artillery fire. In this illustration, only two soldiers are needed to extend the bridge across the moat by means of a large screw. This mechanical bridge evokes the military connotations of the word *machina*, like many of Ramelli's imagined engines. Finally, in Plate 182 (Figure 5.7), Ramelli introduces a large device for hauling extremely heavy loads.[50] Although Ramelli's machines do not necessarily depart from the usual understandings of that word/concept, his detailed and aesthetically pleasing representations of the human–machine interface, and of the

---

[47] The full title of the 1588 edition is *Le Diverse et artificiose machine del capitano Agostino Ramelli dal Ponte della Tresia Ingegniero del Christianissimo Re di Francia et di pollonia, Nelle quali si contengono varii et industriosi Movimenti, degni di grandissima Speculatione, per cavarne beneficio infinito in ogni sorte d'operatione* (spelling partly modernized).

[48] *Ibid.*, 30v.

[49] *Ibid.*, 239v.

[50] *Ibid.*, 299v–300r.

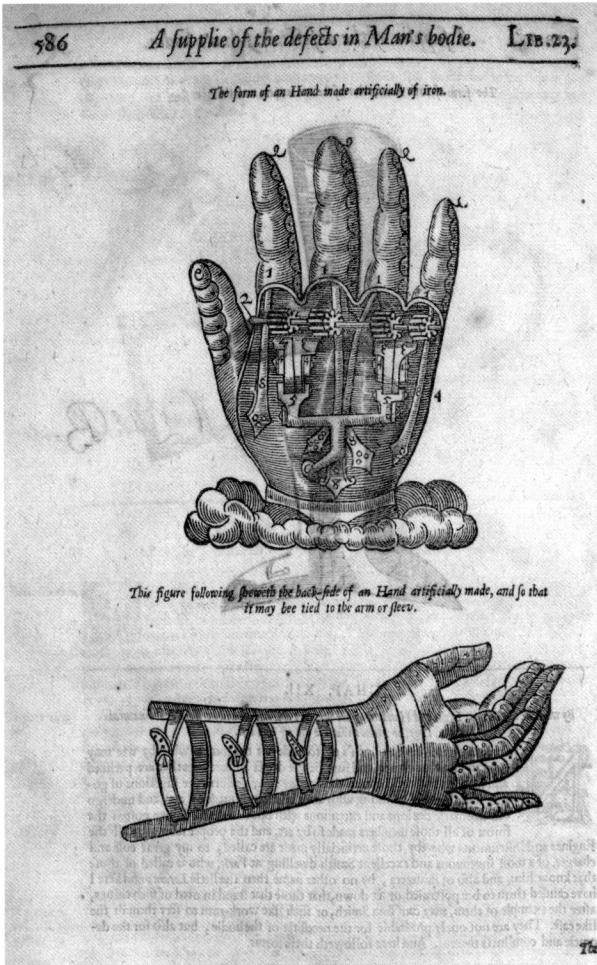

5.4. Ambroise Paré, design for a prosthetic hand. From *The Workes of that famous chirur-gion Ambrose Parey* (London, 1649). Harry Ransom Humanities Research Center. The University of Texas at Austin. Paré, an army surgeon, envisioned artificial limbs for amputees.

group interface *through* the machine, functioned as a stage in the eventual conceptualization of the group as a machine – like da Vinci's before him.

Handbooks for the creation of machines, military weapons, and fortifica-tions circulated widely during this period. In 1607, Vittorio Zonca published in Padua his *Novo teatro di machine et edificii per varie et sicure operationi*, a treatise that featured many machines similar to those represented by Ramelli two decades earlier, as well as commercial machines for the manufacture of paper,

5.5. Agostino Ramelli, Design for machine to draw water from a well. From *Le diverse et artificiose machine del capitano Agostino Ramelli* (Paris, 1588). Harry Ransom Humanities Research Center. The University of Texas at Austin. A labor-saving approach to what might otherwise be a chore.

5.6. Agostino Ramelli, Portable bridge design. *Le diverse et artificiose machine del capitano Agostino Ramelli* (Paris, 1588). Harry Ransom Humanities Research Center. The University of Texas at Austin. A system of pulleys makes it easy for soldiers to cross a moat with this extendable bridge, which can be put into place with the labor of only two men.

5.7. Agostino Ramelli, Machine for pulling very heavy loads. *Le diverse et artificiose machine del capitano Agostino Ramelli* (Paris, 1588). Harry Ransom Humanities Research Center. The University of Texas at Austin. While one man readily turns a set of gears with a crank, others facilitate the movement of the load by moving the beams on which it will roll.

5·7

cloth, wine, prints, and other items. One of his chapters describes a water-powered *filatoio*, a jenny or threadmaker, with which silk and other fibers could be spun into thread and then collected on numerous spools for easier use.[51] As the handbooks of Ramelli and Zonca suggest, the industrialization of Europe was already well under way by the seventeenth century and well before – possibly starting in the medieval period.[52] Large machines such as the *filatoio* were perceived as substitutes for groups of people because they did their work more efficiently. It was only a matter of time before groups of people would be conceptualized as machines.

In general, handbooks of machines focused less on civil engineering and more on the description and dissemination of the latest military technologies, which were widely sought out by princes and potentates throughout Europe for both offensive and defensive purposes. Such manuals hearken back to the Greek and Latin etymology of the word *machine* in its connotation of arms or weaponry. One such manual was the *Recueil de plusieurs machines militaires, et feux artificiels pour la guerre & recreation* (Compendium of several military machines and artificial fires for war and recreation), published by Jean Appier Hanzelet and François Thybourel in 1620. The *Recueil* offered detailed instructions on how to deploy cannons, mines and other explosive devices, and military machines to break down fortifications and gates, to damage one's adversaries in battle, or to defend one's city or troops. In their "Preface Apologetique," the authors self-consciously address the problem of disseminating potentially dangerous information. Aware that the use of machines, either for war or entertainment (the fifth treatise is devoted to fireworks), could raise ethical questions, the two authors acknowledge that they are writing in defense of those who could accuse them of "lacking charity and of having taught various means of ruining the Microcosm, and masterpiece of the all powerful Architect."[53]

Defending the value and moral worth of such machines, they argue that God himself often authorized war, commanding Saul to destroy the Amalekites, without sparing women, children, horses, cows, camels, sheep, or any living soul. Moreover, they note that the Books of Kings and Genesis

<hr>

[51] *Novo teatro di machine et edificii*, 68–75.
[52] On the technological revolution of the Middle Ages, see, for example, White, *Medieval Technology and Social Change* (1962); Gimpel, *The Medieval Machine* (1976); and Pacey, *Technology in World Civilization* (1990).
[53] "Lesquels nous supplions de nous excuser de la prolixité de ceste preface, d'autant que nous avons estré contraincts de la faire en forme d'Apologie & deffence, contre ceux qui nous pourroient arguer de peu de Charité, & d'avoir enseigné divers moyens de ruyner le Microcosme, & chef-d'oeuvre du tout-puissant Architecte." *Recueil de plusieurs machines militaires*, 15. With thanks to Karen Pagani for refinements to my translation.

are full of warfare. Christ himself combatively chased the merchants from the Temple.[54] As these lines from the *Recueil* demonstrate, designers of military machines were aware of their destructive potential – indeed, destruction was their main selling point – as well as the sense of greater security, strength, and power that these machines provided to those who owned or deployed them against their adversaries.

The conceptual link between machines and collective aggression, fortified during the sixteenth and seventeenth centuries, gave rise to a range of corporeal fantasies, both individual and collective, that fastened on the imagined invulnerability of the machine in contrast with the fragility of the human body. As its technological supplement and prosthesis, the machine increasingly fortified and defended the body, as its power merged with flesh and bone, either literally (as in the case of weaponry or of prostheses) or figuratively. Artillery and guns, explosive devices, and other weaponry – machines capable of reducing the human body to pulp – would simultaneously be revered for their power to fortify the body and reduce its vulnerability, while damaging or destroying individuals or groups without them.

The Renaissance machine had both highly positive and highly negative connotations, as indeed machines do in our own era. On the one hand, the machine was frequently envisioned as a "vital" supplement to the body's defenses. On the other, the machine was viewed as the means of the body's destruction, an aspect featured in sixteenth- and seventeenth-century military manuals. The dual capacity of the machine – what we might think of as its essential reversibility – to render the human body less vulnerable or to exploit its vulnerabilities – brings us back to the enigma of Hamlet's machine.

The Soft Machine

Hamlet's "machine" appears in a love letter to Ophelia, read by Polonius, Gertrude, and Claudius. What does this machine signify in its multiple contexts? Is Hamlet's machine a metaphor of the body as an inorganic structure, like an engine of war, or scaffolding? Does Hamlet's machine signify a stratagem or a device? Both of these possible connotations seem possible but out of place in the context of a love letter, although the missive itself strikes Polonius as a device intended to deceive, or as an engine of war with the potential to harm his young daughter. Moreover, its information will be used in a stratagem to snare Hamlet.

---

[54] *Ibid.*, 10.

Hamlet's machine, however, seems to refer to his body rather than to the letter itself. Hamlet's machine is that from which he, Hamlet, ultimately will be parted. "While this machine is to him," Hamlet closes, suggesting that "as long as I am alive, as long as I have this body, my love for you – this embodied love–will remain constant." The love letter hinges on an oddly mechanical metaphor, suggesting an aching sense of mortality, of physical and emotional vulnerability. Hamlet's epistolary closing foreshadows his own death by naming the body as the thing that he will leave, or the thing that will leave him – similar to Ophelia, perhaps, who abandons Hamlet at her father's behest. The closing phrase of the letter foreshadows the premature deaths of both lovers.

Hamlet's machine possesses dual and contradictory implications. On the one hand, its possibly inorganic resonances suggest relative indestructibility, durability, and power. In this sense, Hamlet's machine implies a defended or fortified body. On the other hand, the fact that the machine one day will be separated from Hamlet suggests his defenselessness or lack of control. Whatever it is, Hamlet's machine will not run without Hamlet inside of it. Ironically, Hamlet's machine simultaneously conveys the vulnerability and the invulnerability of the lover's body.

To understand the appearance of Hamlet's machine – on the theatrical stage and on the stage of history – it is essential to remember that *Hamlet* is a play about vulnerability. As John Hunt explains, "More than simply painting a bloody backdrop for his tragedy of revenge, in the manner of Webster, Shakespeare seems to be methodically deconstructing the body."[55] A highly corporeal play, *Hamlet* makes constant references to body parts, bodily functions, and unnatural growths on the body. Shakespeare highlights the body's organic qualities of impermanence: decay, disease, and death.

The ghost of Hamlet's father narrates the pivotal tale of bodily vulnerability in Act I, Scene 5, of the play. The ghost does not offer a realistic image of his own poisoning and death but an extraordinary fantasy of instantaneous corporeal decay:

> Sleeping within my orchard,
> My custom always of the afternoon,
> Upon my secure hour thy uncle stole
> With juice of cursèd hebona in a vial,
> And in the porches of my ears did pour
> The leprous distillment, whose effect
> Holds such an enmity with blood of man

[55] Hunt, "A Thing of Nothing," 30.

> That swift as quicksilver it courses through
> The natural gates and alleys of the body,
> And with a sudden vigor it doth posset
> And curd, like eager droppings into milk,
> The thin and wholesome blood. So did it mine,
> And a most instant tetter barked about,
> Most lazar-like with vile and loathsome crust
> All my smooth body.
> Thus was I, sleeping, by a brother's hand
> Of life, of crown, of queen at once dispatched. . . . (I. v. 59–75)

The king's "smooth body"– his healthy, whole, and intact body – neverthe-less remained vulnerable to insidious attack. In an evocative reading of the play, Eric Mallin locates in this scene a veiled description of the Black Death. Plague serves as a metaphor for the unexpected, contagion-like effect that Hamlet's words have on whomever they come in contact with; throughout, the characters of the play serve as "simulacra for epidemic disease."[56]

Another epidemic figures heavily as a corporeal theme within this drama: syphilis, the scourge of the sixteenth century. In the ghost's speech, there are several allusions to the disease, which was not a curable ailment at that time but a devastating and body-wasting illness. Gordon Williams glosses the syphilitic resonance of "tetter" in this speech, explaining that this referred to the pox in Shakespeare's England, as well as to leprosy – yet another assault on real and virtual bodies in the early modern era.[57] Johannes Fabricius has suggested an intriguing interpretation of the word hebona. This ambiguous word, confusing to many editors, might refer to ebony wood, which was sometimes confused with guaiac, the alternative to mercury therapy as a treatment for syphilis.[58] Finally, the phrase "swift as quicksilver" hints at the often crippling effects of the mercury cure for syphilis, described in poignant detail by the unfortunate Ulrich von Hutten, as well as numerous others who documented how many of the treatments were far worse than the disease.[59]

---

[56] Mallin, *Inscribing the Time*, 156.

[57] Williams, *A Glossary of Shakespeare's Sexual Language*, 304–305.

[58] It is not clear why ebony would have been viewed as poisonous by Shakespeare, even if confused with guaiac, and so Johannes Fabricius suggests he might have had a related plant in mind. *Syphilis in Shakespeare's England*, 38, 42–43.

[59] The humanist Ulrich von Hutten's firsthand experience of the disease, recorded in his 1519 *De guaiaci medicina et morbo gallico* (immediately translated into German and French, and in 1533 into English), offers perhaps the most astonishing account of not only the progressive stages of syphilis but also of the horrific treatments then available to the afflicted. Frequently abandoned by doctors, syphilitics often relied on nonproficient surgeons and mercenary quacks for mercury treatments. This foul and life-destroying "cure" specified the application of ointments and frictions of mercury

For the original audiences, the ghost's speech would have called to mind the dreaded effects of syphilis, plague, leprosy, and other blights on health and well-being.[60] The ghost's speech raises the specter of disease, injury, violation, and myriad other forms of bodily vulnerability almost too numerous to catalogue.

How might the original viewers of this play have responded to the ghost's overpowering tale of abject bodily suffering, and of a burning that continues beyond the grave? This scene, in fact the play as a whole, evokes a wide variety of phobias specific to early modern viewers; it speaks to their shared conception of the body as highly vulnerable and also susceptible to multiple modes of violation. The play served as a vehicle for those viewers to explore their corporeal fears, to experience the "thousand natural shocks that flesh is heir to." The ghost's speech demonstrates Shakespeare's grasp of that body, and his uncanny ability to represent the terrifying vulnerability of the body as English theatergoers imagined it in the early seventeenth century. Furthermore, the violation and destruction of the senior Hamlet's body stands for the corruption of the entire body politic: "Something is rotten in the state of Denmark," Marcellus announces upon seeing the ghost (I. iv. 90). In this play, the body politic, like the body itself, is envisioned as putrifying organic matter.

Hamlet's machine, a word/concept that appears only once early in the play, offers the audience little in the way of a defense against progressively more extreme images of corporeal decay, dissolution, and death that assault the viewer's ears and eyes as the play progresses. A futuristic metaphor of a defended, mechanized body not susceptible to the thousand shocks that flesh is heir to, Hamlet's machine imagines what the rest of the play refuses to deliver. We can detect in this metaphor and perhaps in others like it the contours of a shared early modern fantasy – a psychic defense against the extreme physical and emotional violations to which the body – individual and social – was prone. Machines could break down or fail, but they could not contract plague, syphilis, or leprosy. Machines could be disassembled but not maimed or killed. They could be destroyed, but they could not die in childbirth. Some machines could inflict pain but could not feel it. They

---

to the body of the sufferer, and sometimes fumigations. As Hutten attests, the mercury treatments tended to cause one's teeth to fall out, the palate to become ulcerated, large amounts of extremely foul-smelling saliva to drool from the mouth, and a fetid odor to emanate from the body. Other symptoms of severe mercury poisoning included neurological damage, visible in symptoms such as shaking and paralysis. Clearly, if the disease did not kill the patient, the cure was likely to do so.

[60] Williams, 305. It was not only disease, however, that would have been evoked by the ghost's tale, but also fratricide, incest, lèse-majesté, sudden death with no chance for repentance, and sodomitical rape.

could do violence but not suffer from the effects of warfare and other forms of social upheaval or chaos.

In the early modern age, new technologies began to grant whoever possessed them a greater sense of power and control over the body and its processes, which would gradually migrate to concepts of the state itself. Machines could provide some comfort against the mortifications of the flesh – an illusory comfort in an age of extraordinary physical and psychological fragility. The machines of the roiling civil, international, and colonial wars of early modernity were the same devices that tore bodies apart and that simultaneously gave rise to collective fantasies of wholeness and invincibility. It is this last explanation that captures the paradox of Hamlet's machine, its implied and contradictory fantasies of violence and vulnerability, of lasting import for the group and the individual person.

From Hamlet to Descartes

The body-as-machine metaphor (analogue to the machine group) would continue to evolve over the course of the seventeenth century, finding new expression within the mechanistic philosophies of Descartes, Hobbes, La Mettrie, Newton, and other Enlightenment thinkers. In his early *Traité de l'homme* (*Treatise of Man*), Descartes famously separated mind from body, conceptualizing the latter as a "machine." This treatise, composed during the years 1629 to 1633, was part of a two-part work entitled *Le monde* (*The World*), which also included the *Traité de la lumière* (*Treatise on Light*). As the historian of science I. Bernard Cohen explained, "*Le monde* conveys to the reader the author's intention to develop a system of cosmology founded on a physics so universal that it could apply to animal functions and to man himself, as well as to inanimate objects – to the world as a whole and all it contains."[61] This unified theory incorporated elements of Copernicanism and atomistic philosophy, while rejecting the precepts of Aristotelian physics and introducing Descartes' own "corpuscular" theory of matter and motion. Descartes held the work back from publication when he learned of Galileo's condemnation and house arrest by the Roman Inquisition, recognizing that his own views would likely be perceived as highly subversive. The two parts of *Le monde* were not published until more than a decade after Descartes' death in 1650.[62]

[61] Cohen, preface to *Treatise of Man: René Descartes*, trans. Hall, xv–xvi.
[62] The *Treatise of Man* first appeared in the Latin translation of Florentius Schuyl (Leiden: 1662). Two years later, the two parts of *The World* were published separately in French. *Ibid.*, xxiv.

Less well known today than the *Discours de la méthode* (*Discourse on Method* [1637]) or the *Meditationes* (*Meditations* [1641]), Descartes' *Treatise of Man* presents a mechanized conceptual model of the body. The philosopher begins by positing certain hypothetical beings:

> These men will be composed, as we are, of a soul and a body; and I must first separately describe for you the body; then, also separately, the soul; and finally I must show you how these two natures would have to be joined and united to constitute men resembling us.

> I assume their body to be but a statue, an earthen machine (*machine de terre*) formed intentionally by God to be as much as possible like us. Thus not only does He give it externally the shapes and colors of all the parts of our bodies; He also places inside it all the pieces required to make it walk, eat, breathe, and imitate whichever of our own functions can be imagined to proceed from mere matter and to depend entirely on the arrangement of our organs.

> We see clocks, artificial fountains, mills, and similar machines which, though made entirely by man, lack not the power to move, of themselves, in various ways. And I think you will agree that the present machine could have even more sorts of movements than I have imagined and more ingenuity than I have assigned, or our supposition is that it was created by God.[63]

As Dalia Judovitz has noted, here Descartes alludes to the story of creation recounted in the Book of Genesis, where God forms Adam from the earth and then breathes life into him (Gen. 2:7). In his recasting of the creation myth, Descartes desacralizes the breath of life. Formerly conceived of as *pneuma* (soul), breathing becomes in Descartes' conception a purely mechanical function.[64] Here and elsewhere in the *Treatise*, the philosopher compares his hypothetical man, the "earthen machine," to other mechanized devices such as clocks, mills, and the hydraulically powered automata of royal gardens and grottoes, such as those installed at Saint-Germain-en-Laye by Salomon de Caus, engineer and landscape architect for Louis XIII of France (Figure 5.8).[65]

---

[63] *Treatise of Man*, 1–4 and facsimile pages 1–2. Hall's translation begins, "I assume their body," to highlight the hypothetical nature of Descartes' project in the *Treatise on Man*.
[64] *The Culture of the Body*, 74.
In their edition of this work, John Cottingham, Robert Stoothoff, and Dugald Murdoch offer a different gloss on "earthen," noting that the term refers to the third of Descartes' three basic elements, which Descartes had discussed in his treatise *The World*. *The Philosophical Writings of Descartes*, 3: 99.
[65] *Les Raisons des forces mouvantes*.

5.8. Salomon de Caus, Fountain with automata, *Les Raisons des forces mouvantes* (Paris[?], 1624). DeGolyer Library. Southern Methodist University. Dallas, Texas. Vault Folio TJ144.C4 1624. Salomon de Caus, image of machine with automata of Neptune, Diana, and others spouting water as they turn. Caus's descriptions and images of automata helped to inspire Descartes' "earthen machine" in his *Treatise of Man.*

Later Descartes describes the flow of ultra-fine particles of matter within the body (animal spirits) that circulate from the center of the brain, where the rational soul is housed, outward through the nerves of the body, initiating its various movements. Again comparing humans to automata, he writes,

And truly one can well compare the nerves of the machine that I am describing to the tubes of the mechanisms of these fountains, its muscles and tendons to divers other engines and springs which serve to move these mechanisms, its animal spirits to the water which drives them, of which the heart is the source and the brain's cavities the water main. (22)

The body is set into motion not only by its own internal mechanisms, here likened to a hydraulic system, but also by the force of objects or conditions in the outside world that have what might be described as an atomic impact on the body's sensory mechanisms.

Expanding his garden analogy, Descartes explains,

> External objects which merely by their presence act on the organs of sense and by the means force them to move in several different ways, depending on how the parts of the brain are arranged, are like strangers who, entering some of the grottoes of these fountains, unwittingly cause the movements that then occur, since they cannot enter without stepping on certain tiles so arranged that, for example, if they approach a Diana bathing they will cause her to hide in the reeds; and if they pass farther to pursue her they will cause a Neptune to advance and menace them with his trident; or if they go in another direction they will make a marine monster come out and spew water into their faces, or other such things according to the whims of the engineers who made them. (22)

Judovitz has noted that in this description Descartes again recasts biblical imagery – here, the Garden of Eden – by comparing the human body to the artificial gardens and grottoes populated with hydraulic automata. We might also note that Descartes *collectivizes* the body machine in two ways. First, by atomistically breaking the body down into its component parts, he imagines the body as a group of moving and colliding particles. Humans thus contain within their bodies a type of group machine. Second, by analogizing the body to the artificial garden, a mechanical site in which human figures (e.g., Diana hiding or Neptune threatening with his trident) play an interactive role to produce an effect within a larger system, Descartes mechanizes not only the body's interior spaces but also its interactions with the world exterior to it – a world that contains other people. One machine interacts with or acts on another, inciting a sensory-motor response; each body is part of a larger mechanized group.[66]

Descartes' presentation of these hypothetical bodies in *The Treatise of Man* borders on a purely materialist explanation of the human body, despite the fact that the philosopher sought to demonstrate the presence of an immaterial, immortal, and rational soul that distinguished man from animals and that was housed in the pineal gland deep within the brain.[67] In the *Discourse on Method* (published anonymously in 1637), Descartes again returned to the man-as-machine analogy, carefully distinguishing the human machine, made by God, from any machines or automata made by mankind, and also from animals, which he considered to be machines of a different sort. In Part Five, Descartes declared that animals, lacking in speech and rational

---

[66]On Descartes' corpuscular theory of matter, see Hall, *Treatise of Man*, xxix, *et passim*. See also Chapter 6 of this book.

[67]How the immaterial soul could act on the material particles of the body was perhaps the most significant conundrum raised by Descartes' model and its accompanying mind/body split.

capacity, are categorically different from humans, who are distinguished by their possession of an immortal, rational soul.[68] "For after the error of those who deny God, which I believe I have already adequately refuted, there is none that leads weak minds further from the straight path of virtue than that of imagining that the souls of the beasts are of the same nature as ours, and hence that after this present life we have nothing to fear or to hope for, any more than flies and ants."[69] By separating humankind from animal machines, Descartes sought to fend off imputations of materialism – a potentially heretical stance at that time and hence a dangerous one for whoever espoused it.[70]

Many would challenge Descartes' attempt to theorize bodies mechanically while simultaneously drawing a categorical distinction between humans and animals. Traditionalists like Pierre Gassendi challenged Descartes by arguing that animals were not soulless, unthinking machines and by imagining both animals and humans as capable of thought. In contrast, radical materialists like the eighteenth-century philosopher Julien de la Mettrie extended Descartes' mechanistic view of animals to humans – offering in his *L'homme machine* (1748) a purely materialistic description of the human body that eliminated the distinction of the soul in humans.[71]

The Renaissance reconceptualization of the human body as a machine and of the natural world as a mechanical system would have a profound impact on the political thinking of that time and of the future. Descartes had already suggested such a continuum between the human particulate machine and the outside world acting on it. This notion made it possible to conceptualize the human body systemically – that is, as possessing an internal system of moving, interactive parts and as participating in an external system in which it was itself a moving part. The social theorists of the Enlightenment and eighteenth century would soon incorporate these new metaphors of mechanicity into their descriptions of human political and cultural life.

The Evolution of the Group Machine

To understand the seventeenth-century metaphor of the group as machine, it is useful to explore antecedent versions of that concept, which can be traced back to antiquity. In his *Myth of the Machine* (1967–1970), the historian Lewis

---

[68] Here Descartes followed Aquinas, who in the *Summa* had compared animals to machines, lacking free will of their own, and also likening them to clocks.

[69] *The Philosophical Writings of Descartes*, 1: 141.

[70] On this point, see, for example, Rosenfield, 22.

[71] This range of responses to Descartes has been discussed by Mazlish, 25.

Mumford argued that the "megamachine" – that is, a human organizational system – existed in ancient Egypt and Mesopotamia, and then in India, China, Persia, and the Andean and Mayan civilizations. The human machines of these civilizations were able to accomplish in a generation tasks that might otherwise have taken centuries – for example, the building of the pyramids and other monumental structures. "Now to call these collective entities machines is no idle play on words," Mumford wrote,

> If a machine be defined more or less in accord with the classic definition of Reuleaux, as a combination of resistant parts, each specialized in func-tion, operating under human control, to transmit motion and to perform work, then the labor machine was a real machine: all the more because its component parts, though composed of human bone, nerve, and muscle, were reduced to their bare mechanical elements and rigidly restricted to the performance of their limited tasks.[72]

Megamachines, Mumford argued, have been a feature of human societies for more than five millennia. These works-building human machines of antiquity could not be operated by their overlords without the coercive force of armies; indeed, work armies and military armies were often scarcely distinguishable from each other.[73]

If groups have operated in systematic ways throughout recorded history, when did they begin to conceptualize themselves in terms of their technolo-gies? When did groups begin to think of themselves as machines – especially as fighting machines? Again, the concept appears to be an ancient one. The Trojan horse, described by the priest Laocoon in Virgil's *Aeneid*, is presented as a machine by the poet: "Or 't is an engine (*machina*) rais'd above the town," he cries (II, 54–62).[74] Weapon of war, scheme, fabricated construc-tion – the Trojan horse is a machine in all these senses. The Achaean device

---

[72] *The Myth of the Machine*, 1: 191.

[73] *Ibid.*, 193.

[74]
> Primus ibi ante omnis magna comitante caterva
> Laocoon ardens summa decurrit ab arce,
> et procul: 'o miseri, quae tanta insania, cives?
> creditis avectos hostis? aut ulla putatis
> dona carere dolis Danaum? sic notus Vlixes?
> aut hoc inclusi ligno occultantur Achivi,
> aut haec in nostros fabricata est machina muros,
> inspectura domos venturaque desuper urbi,
> aut aliquis latet error; equo ne credite, Teucri.
> quidquid id est, timeo Danaos et dona ferentis.' (II: 40–50)

Virgil, *Eclogues, Georgics, Aeneid I–VI*, 318.

See also Chapter 1, 38.

is also pregnant, we might say, with several of its future meanings: namely, the group as weapon, the group as scheme, the group as construction. These concepts of the group, already implicit in Virgil's great epic, would become more common as machine technologies continued to develop and evolve over the centuries.

In medieval Europe, Mumford further argued, the Christian Church would contribute to the development of the group machine through the organizational mechanisms of monastic life. "[I]n its organization as a self-governing economic and religious society, the Benedictine monastery laid down a basis of order as strict as that which held together the earlier mega-machines: the difference lay in its modest size, its voluntary constitution, and in the fact that its sternest discipline was self-imposed."[75] The organizing and marking of units of time within monastic life was a key feature of mechanistic group organization that would carry over into the modern world, laying the groundwork for capitalist organization and further mechanization.[76] Technological breakthroughs between the twelfth and the sixteenth centuries – many or perhaps most of which were elaborations of earlier technologies developed by the Chinese, Islamic, and other civilizations – also helped boost the reorganization of groups in the modern age and the rise of modern megamachines.[77] These inventions, or reinventions, included the watermill, the windmill, the magnifying glass, the mechanical clock,[78] paper,[79] and above all, the printing press.[80]

Throughout the Middle Ages, men and women relied ever more heavily on machines, which they used for a wide variety of purposes.[81] The visual

---

[75] *The Myth of the Machine*, 1: 264.

[76] *Ibid.*, 1: 266.

[77] On the debt of western technology to earlier cultures, primarily those of the East, see for example McClellan and Dorn, *Science and Technology in World Civilization* (1999); Rahman, ed., *History of Indian Science, Technology and Culture AD 1000–1800* (1998); Pacey, *Technology in World Civilization* (1990); and especially Hobson, *The Eastern Origins of Western Civilization* (2004).

[78] On the relation of clocks and authoritarianism from medieval times forward, see Mayr, *Authority, Liberty & Automatic Machinery in Early Modern Europe*.

[79] Lienhard, *How Invention Begins*, 151–153.

[80] Of these, Mumford writes, "The enrichment of the collective human mind, through the printing and circulation of books, is comparable only to that linking together of individual brains and experiences through the invention of discursive language." *The Myth of the Machine*, 1: 285. "In more ways than one," Sawday writes, "the Renaissance machine was the invention of print culture." *Engines of the Imagination*, 78. Here Sawday follows Elizabeth Eisenstein, *The Printing Press as an Agent of Change*, 81. See, too, Lienhard's discussion of Gutenberg in *How Invention Begins*, 137–193.

[81] We must not assume that it was only in the West that the development of machine technology began to accelerate during the early modern era. According to John M. Hobson, the technologic and economic superiority of China vis-à-vis the West until approximately 1800 has rarely been

and verbal metaphor of the body as machine would come into prominence during the late fifteenth and sixteenth centuries, later becoming the central trope of Enlightenment philosophy. The metaphor of the group as machine would emerge alongside it, as machine technology became more elaborate and as the modern worldview came to be conceptualized, at least within scientific and philosophical discourse, in mechanistic terms.[82] Mumford highlights continuities in the five-millenium-long development of an idea; however, one can also locate discreet moments of change along that developmental trajectory. The most significant of these was the seventeenth-century expansion of the machine metaphor to encompass the entire world and its workings, which also coincided with a revival of atomistic philosophy. The relation of one individual to another, of individual people to the group, and of groups or collectives to each other would increasingly be described with mechanical metaphors after that time.

We can observe in da Vinci's notebooks not only the body analogized to a variety of mechanical devices but also, at least visually, the group analogized to a machine. For example, on one leaf of the *Codex Atlanticus*, Leonardo draws a proto-machine gun (Figure 5.9).[83] This is not simply a weapon: inside a treadwheel an archer is suspended; he keeps the arrows shooting or firing rapidly out of the machine. Meanwhile comrades of the archer, who are defended from attack by a planked shield, use their foot power to turn the wheel. In this drawing and elsewhere, Leonardo not only conceptualizes new machines but also visualized the group–machine interface – that is, ways that human bodies can interact with a machine and with each other *inside* a machine. One of the principal connotations of the word *mekhane* in Greek or *machina* in Latin is a weapon. In Leonardo's image, the group machine *is* a weapon – more effective at doing damage to an adversarial army than a single armed person.

Alhough the concept of the group as weapon predates da Vinci's conceptions thereof by many millennia, its prominence during the fifteenth and sixteenth centuries increased significantly with advances in military

---

acknowledged by Eurocentric historians. Hobson argues that China was *primus inter pares* from the fifteenth to the end of the seventeenth centuries and that the distribution of economic power in the world under oriental globalization was polycentric, including China, India, the Middle East, Northern Africa, Southeast Asia, and Japan as major players (61). Further studies could reveal the mechanization of the body or the group in other parts of the world during the Renaissance. *The Eastern Origins of Western Civilization*, 50–73.

[82] On the rise of mechanistic philosophy, see, for example, Dijksterhuis, *The Mechanization of the World Picture*.

[83] *Codex Atlanticus* XII, 1070 recto [9] 387 *recto*-a, pen and ink and wash with traces of metal point, c. 1485–1487.

technology. The handbooks of Ramelli and other military engineers offer similar perspectives on the group-as-machine concept. The rise of new, more destructive military technologies in the Renaissance, coupled with the increasing prevalence of the body-as-machine metaphor, slowly began to reconfigure conceptions of the social order, moving away from more organic understandings to mechanical accounts. These would emerge in conjunction with the overall mechanization of the world picture, characteristic of the philosophy and science of the European Enlightenment.

The increasingly elaborate and destructive weaponry developed in the Renaissance was one factor influencing military engineers, historians, and others to conceptualize groups as machines or weapons and to link metonymically the new technologies with their users. In the 1641 second volume of *L'istoria delle gverre civili d'Inghilterra tra le due case di Lancastro, e Iorc* (*An history of the civill vvares of England betweene the two Houses of Lancaster and Yorke*), the diplomat and writer Giovanni Francesco Biondi would compare the 18,000-man army of Charles VI of France to *una machina* – in the English translation of the Earl of Monmouth, "a marching *Machin*, conducted by gallant and experienced Commanders."[84] Although not a common metaphor for armies and military actions in the sixteenth and seventeenth centuries, the word *machine* was sometimes used to describe the systematic and usually destructive actions undertaken by one human group against another.

It was not only armies but also religious groups that would be conceptualized as machines (anticipating perhaps Freud's unfavorable comparison of the two in *Group Psychology and the Analysis of the Ego*).[85] More specifically, it was rival religious groups that were likely to be described throughout the sixteenth and seventeenth centuries as "machines" – a descriptive trend observable in many English sermons and disquisitions on spiritual matters. For example, in *The religion of protestants a safe way to salvation* (1638), the English churchman William Chillingworth compared the Catholic religion and specifically its priesthood to "a machine composed of an innumerable multitude of pieces, of which it is strangely unlikely but some will be out of order; and yet if any one be so, the whole fabrick of necessity falls to

[84] *L'istoria delle gverre civili d'Inghilterra tra le due case di Lancastro, e Iorc*, II: "Or di queste forçe, aggiunteui le proprie, ne fece un corpo di diciotto mila guerrieri; non computati gli sparsi per le prouinçie; da seruirsene come d'una machina andante sotto la condotta di braui, ed esperimentati Capitani" (39).

In 1641, the first two volumes were translated into English by Henry, the Earl of Monmouth, as *An history of the civill vvares of England betweene the two Houses of Lancaster and Yorke*, cited here. In the Italian, *machina* is a simile; in the English, a metaphor.

[85] See the Foreword to this book, xxxiii, n. 9.

5.9. Leonardo da Vinci, Treadmill-powered multiple crossbow, *Codex Atlanticus*, fol. 1070r recto. (1485–1487). Biblioteca Ambrosiana, Milan. Photo credit: Art Resource, New York. In this design for a proto-machine gun, da Vinci conceptualizes the group-machine interface.

5.9

the ground."[86] Similarly, Thomas Sheppey, the author of a 1679 pamphlet attacking Catholicism, declared,

[86] *The religion of protestants a safe vvay to salvation. Or An ansvver to a booke entitled Mercy and truth, or, charity maintain'd by Catholiques, which pretends to prove the contrary. By William Chillingworth Master of Arts of the University of Oxford* (1638).

We shall now take a View of that *Grand Machine* of the Pope's power over Temporal Princes, and make it most evident, that it is an Article and Doctrine of the *Roman* Church; and being so, that this alone were a sufficient Motive to forsake her Communion, since She Teaches Justifies and strictly Commands (even under the penalty of being accounted no Christians) Treason and Rebellion.[87]

Sheppey condenses multiple meanings of machine into his description of the Papacy, including the treasonous stratagem, the ideological weapon, and of course the army of dangerous religious fanatics.

Catholics and Catholicism were not infrequently likened to machines by Protestant authors, but other religious groups also were described mechanistically. For example, the English dissenter Henry Hickman would write in 1674 (paraphrasing the views of his opponent): "*Universal redemption by the death of Christ overthrows the whole* Machine *of the* Calvinian *predestination and the points thereon depending.*"[88] When applied to religious collectives or their belief systems in seventeenth-century discourse, the metaphor of the machine was rarely positive or neutral.[89] It generally betokened the capacity of such groups and their ways of thinking to cause harm or damage – similar to that caused by armies.

If the group-as-machine metaphor often signaled the *lethalization* of the collective – that is, its technological or ideological capacity to do harm – it could in other contexts represent the *neutralization* of lethal instincts that might otherwise be directed outward, toward other persons or groups, or inward toward its own members. Thomas Hobbes' *Leviathan*, published in 1651, offers a celebrated example of the group-as-machine metaphor describing the inhibitory function of properly governed groups on the otherwise chaotic lives of individual people. Hobbes, in dialogue with Descartes, Gassendi, Mersenne, and other mechanistic philosophers of the day, would apply the emergent atomistic paradigm of the natural world to politics, reconceptualizing human psychology in the process.[90]

In the *Leviathan*, we can observe how the ancient organic metaphor of the body politic had begun to fall out of conceptual fashion, as David

---

[87]The screed was entitled *Several weighty considerations humbly recommended to the serious perusal of all, but more especially to the Roman Catholicks of England to which is prefix'd* (1679). (Spelling partly modernized.)

[88]In his *Historia quinq-uarticularis exarticulata, or, Animadversions on Doctor Heylin's quintquarticular history*, Hickman was actually defending Calvinism against the mechanizing attacks of his adversary Heylin, whom he paraphrases here (1674).

[89]Sawday cites the poet Thomas Traherne as one writer who used the machine metaphor in a highly positive way to describe God's mystical power over the world. *Engines of the Imagination*, 243–245.

[90]Spragens, *Politics of Motion*, 163–202. See also Sarasohn, *Gassendi's Ethics*, 119–123.

Hale has compellingly shown.[91] In that work, Hobbes provided a new framework for the organization of the state: namely, social contract theory. In his Introduction to the *Leviathan*, Hobbes would write,

> NATURE (the Art whereby God hath made and governes the World) is by the *Art* of man, as in many other things, so in this also imitated, that it can make an Artificial Animal. For seeing life is but a motion of Limbs, the begining whereof is in some principall part within; why may we not say, that all *Automata* (Engines that move themselves by springs and wheeles as doth a watch) have an artificiall life? For what is the *Heart*, but a *Spring*; and the *Nerves*, but so many *Strings*: and the *Joynts*, but so many *Wheeles*, giving motion to the whole Body, such as was intended by the Artificer? *Art* goes yet further, imitating that Rationall and most excellent worke of Nature, *Man*. For by Art is created that great LEVIATHAN called a COMMON-WEALTH, or STATE, (in latine CIVITAS) which is but an Artificiall Man; though of greater stature and strength than the Naturall, for whose protection and defence it was intended; and in which, the *Soveraignty* is an Artificiall *Soul*, as giving life and motion to the whole body. . . .[92]

Here Hobbes finds himself on the cusp of a new metaphor, opening his monumental work of political philosophy with a description of an automaton, a machine body created in imitation of nature. It is not man's own body that he analogizes to a machine, as in Descartes' *Treatise of Man* (as yet unpublished in 1651), however, but rather the state itself, or commonwealth, which Hobbes likens to "an Artificiall Man." The polity still has a body, but that body has been automated, transformed into a machine.[93]

As did More in Book I of the *Utopia*, Hobbes confronted the worst tendencies of mankind while proposing his own version of a more rational approach to government. Hobbes' solution was not to redistribute property, however, and thereby create a greater degree of social equality in his ideal commonwealth, as More seemed to suggest, but instead to enable an absolute king or ruler to lead the group through their collective acceptance of the social contract.

According to Hobbes, men are equal in one important respect: namely, in their ability to kill each other, regardless of their differences in strength or

---

[91] *The Body Politic*, 127.

[92] *Leviathan*, 9.

[93] The mechanicity of Hobbes' "Artificial man" metaphor is not apparent in the famous illustrations of Leviathan accompanying the various editions of the book, in which the ruler is depicted as resembling either Charles I in the first edition or Cromwell in the later ones. That image is more suggestive of the traditional body-politic metaphor. Hale, 129.

intelligence, because "the weakest has strength enough to kill the strongest, either by secret machination, or by confederacy with others, that are in the same danger with himself."[94] Expressing deep cynicism about human motivations and behavior, Hobbes famously stated that in times of war, the life of man is "solitary, poore, nasty, brutish, and short."[95] These bleak sentiments had been conditioned by the English Civil War and the catastrophic Wars of Religion after the Reformation. Hobbes argued that good government would enable human life to become more tolerable, and therefore literally and figurally more livable. Men's fear of death and their capacity to reason could enable the creation of such governments by means of the social contract. It is the group – and specifically, the *artificial* group, the group as machine, governed and controlled by the absolute sovereign[96] – that contains or tempers the natural destructive passions of the individual (the desire for power and the "secret machination" against one's fellow human beings). We can also observe in Hobbes' descriptions the bifurcating meanings of the machine metaphor, trending toward either the rational and predictable (the ideal state) or the irrational and destructive (the "machinating" person or group, not controlled by the sovereign's power).

The Individual in the Machine

Hobbes' "Artificiall Man" is but one example among many seventeenth-century descriptions of the state as a mechanical device.[97] An earlier instance appears in Alessandro Campiglia's 1617 work *Delle turbulenze della Francia in vita del re Enrico il grande* (Concerning the French conflicts during the life of King Henry the Great). "The laws are the nerves and ligaments that keep the machine of the state (*machina dello stato*) standing," he would write.[98] Similar to Hobbes' metaphor of the Artificial Man, Campiglia's mixed metaphor

---

[94] *Leviathan*, 87.

[95] *Ibid.*, 89.

[96] Leo Strauss argues that during his earlier humanist phase, Hobbes seems to have been open to democracy as the ideal form of artificial state, although later he would reject democracy in favor of absolute monarchy. *The Political Philosophy of Hobbes*, 64.

[97] The complex links between concepts of mechanicity, machination or deception, and courtly or political organization have been extensively traced by Jessica Wolfe in *Humanism, Machinery, and Renaissance Literature*. Wolfe explains, "As metaphors in political and literary texts, machines redefine the moral and epistemological ramifications of instrumentality – the use of human, mechanical or intellectual instruments to achieve a particular end. Not only do machines materially transform the mediatory capacity of our sensual faculties, but they also participate in refashioning relationships between human beings and their instruments, from readers and their texts to rulers and servants" (5).

[98] *Delle turbulenze della Francia in vita del re Enrico il grande* (1617), 340. Cited in Battaglia, 9, 359.

of the state, containing both organic and inorganic elements, appears at the very historical moment that the machine begins to emerge as a metaphor of the group, and to replace the older organic concept of the body politic.

So it was that the group machine, already gestating on the island of More's Utopia, would reemerge at the end of the Renaissance, a counterpart to the other great invention of that age: the individual. As the European scientific understanding progressively decomposed the human body into its component parts and "component-partness," the concept of the individual – the undivided or indivisible – came into being. The complex evolution of this word/concept has been discussed by Raymond Williams, among others.[99] Williams notes that in medieval and early modern adjectival usages of the term, "the ground of human nature is common; the 'individual' is often a vain or eccentric departure from this."[100] By the late seventeenth century, the noun *individual* would emerge with a more positive set of connotations, almost invariably with reference to the group of which it formed a part and in which it constituted the smallest component. Williams connects the conceptual development of the individual to the new philosophy, as well as related mathematical developments such as calculus:

> The emergence of notions of **individuality,** in the modern sense, can be related to the break-up of the medieval social, economic and religious order. In the general movement against feudalism there was a new stress on a man's personal existence over and above his place or function in a rigid hierarchical society. There was a related stress, in Protestantism, on a man's direct and individual relation to God, as opposed to this relation MEDIATED (q.v.) by the Church. But it was not until lC17 and C18 that a new mode of analysis, in logic and mathematics, postulated the individual as the substantial entity (cf. Leibniz's 'monads'), from which other categories and especially collective categories were derived. The political thought of the Enlightenment mainly followed this model.[101]

The modern sense of the word *individual*, Williams further argues, is the result of a convergence of scientific and mathematical developments during the Enlightenment and of a range of political and economic discourses prominent from the seventeenth to the nineteenth centuries.

Thus, although Jacob Burckhardt held that "the individual" made its appearance at the end of the Middle Ages (as discussed in the Introduction to this book), it would be more accurate to regard the notion as a by-product

---

[99] On the evolution of this word/concept, see Raymond Williams' essay in *Keywords*, 161–165, and Lukes, *Individualism*. See also Introduction, 8, n. 16.

[100] Williams, 163.

[101] *Ibid.*, 163–164.

of the mechanistic paradigm that was already developing during the age of da Vinci and that would reach its fullest expression in the seventeenth century and thereafter. The concept of the individual arose differentially, in dynamic relation to the discourse of the group as machine, as well as the machine body.

Descartes' model of the particulate or atomized body, detailed in the *Treatise of Man*, withheld from publication by its author, and alluded to in the *Discourse on Method*, threatened to anatomize the human into invisibility, to dematerialize identity by fully materializing it. In so doing, it also threatened to redefine the human group by dissolving the barrier between humans and animals – a topic to be explored in the final chapter of this book. A version of that critique, however, had already appeared in *Hamlet*:

> What a piece of work
> is a man! How noble in reason, how infinite in faculties,
> in form and moving how express and admirable, in
> action how like an angel, in apprehension how like a
> god! The beauty of the world, the paragon of animals!
> And yet, to me, what is this quintessence of dust? (II, ii, 304–309)

Hamlet's depressive words anticipate Descartes' obsessive preoccupation and that of the European Enlightenment: how to demonstrate that the "paragon of animals" might be more than mere matter, animal or otherwise. As we shall see, the impetus for such questioning was not only the rise of a scientific mindset; the human identity crisis was also an effect of globalization.

Hamlet's critique of man could be taken on many levels – the individual body, the body politic, as well as the whole human community. The play is riddled with challenges to the older metaphor, as *Hamlet* moves toward its bloody conclusion. Commenting on the ripe body of Polonius, which he has hidden, and also on the esoteric doctrine of the King's two bodies – the natural body and that of the state – Hamlet declares, "The body is with the King, but the King is not with the body. The King is a thing –" "A thing, my lord?" the unfortunate Rosencrantz asks. "Of nothing," Hamlet replies enigmatically (IV.28–31). In *Hamlet*, the body-politic metaphor effectively collapses.

In the wake of that loss, political philosophers of the Enlightenment aimed to develop a more viable group concept, an endeavor most recognizable in Hobbes' philosophy. Yet the new mechanistic model of the state, as of the body, raised new difficulties and summoned forth new defenses. The seventeenth-century notion of the individual as an *undivided* or indivisible being, autonomous and self-directing, can be taken as a collective defense against the infinite regress posed by the Cartesian model of the body's machinery, its division into progressively smaller parts.

On a macroscopic level, however, the individual would be considered an entity regulated by and within progressively more elaborate organizational systems devised to extract loyalty, labor, reproduction, or other modes of participation in systemic group functions, especially warfare – a point elaborated by Freud in his 1915 essay *Zeitgemässes über Krieg und Tod* (*Thoughts for the Times on War and Death*). Describing the insanity of what would later be known as World War I, he wrote:

> The individual who is not himself a combatant–and so is a cog in the gigantic machine of war (*Kriegsmaschinerie*)–feels bewildered in his orientation, and inhibited in his powers and activities. I believe that he will welcome any indication, however slight, which will make it easier for him to find his bearings within himself at least. I propose to pick out two among the factors which are responsible for the mental distress felt by non-combatants, against which it is such a heavy task to struggle, and to treat of them here: the disillusionment which this war has evoked, and the altered attitude towards death which this – like every other war – forces upon us.[102]

In this extremely pessimistic text, to which we shall again turn in the conclusion, Freud applied the metaphor of the machine not to one group in particular, but to many groups at war with each other (the *Kriegsmaschinerie*). Individuals became cogs in this machine, whether they wanted to be or not.

Later Michel Foucault extended the group metaphor to the violence of everyday social life. Contending in *Discipline and Punish* that the classical age "discovered the body as object and target of power," Foucault expostulated,

> The great book of Man-the-Machine was written simultaneously on two registers: the anatomico-metaphysical register, of which Descartes wrote the first pages and which the physicians and philosophers continued, and the technico-political register, which was constituted by a whole set of regulations and by empirical and calculated methods relating to the army, the school and the hospital for controlling or correcting the operations of the body.[103]

Coercion, quiescence, and docility were, in Foucault's view, the ultimate outcome of the mechanistic tropes of the Enlightenment. Doubtless Foucault would agree that new chapters of the ongoing saga of the modern state and its disciplinary mechanisms are still being churned out in ways undreamt of by

---

[102] *Standard Edition*, 14: 273–302, 275; *Gesammelte Werke*, 10: 324–355, 325.
[103] *Discipline and Punish*, 136.

Descartes and Hobbes, thinkers who were, in balance, optimists concerning the machine and its human and social metaphors.

The group-as-machine concept is so commonplace today that it is difficult to imagine that it came into being at a comparatively recent point in history (or rather that it entered a new phase) during the periods of social reorganization and global upheaval optimistically called the Renaissance and the Enlightenment. Certain contemporary discourses of collective behavior and interaction – cybernetics, sociometry, or systems theory – can be said to hinge on metaphors of the mechanical, the measured, the inorganic, or the inanimate. These recent discourses for describing or predicting the behaviors of people owe much to the mechanistic turn of the late sixteenth- and early seventeenth centuries, when organic metaphors for the collective began to lose traction, only to be replaced by metaphors of the machine. Mechanical dreams of stability, inviolability, and immortality – for one's own group, if not for those of others – were the outgrowth of that schismatic age. Vulnerable, yet also durable and relentless, Hamlet's machine was an envoy for the world and the group that we imagine as modern.[104]

It is essential to recognize the fantasy element in the long history of the group-as-machine concept and its gradual exportation around the globe,[105] especially because of its familiarity and hence nontransparency. Because we have, at least in our collectively more secular moments, moved away from demonological or supernatural characterizations of nature and the social – particularly where other groups are concerned – it might also seem that we have moved toward a more rational and scientific understanding of groups and of ourselves. In many ways that is true, yet the irrational component of the group-as-machine concept lingers just below the surface. It expresses itself in the desire for the invulnerability of one's own group at the expense of some other, and the fantasy of weapon-like power to destroy with impunity and without pain or responsibility. Machines, weaponry, the earth and sky, power and magic, vulnerability and invulnerability – all of these have been woven together during the long evolution of that word and concept, and all of these are encompassed by and within the machine-group concept, which is a fantasy of our survival, of our everlasting place in the *machina mundi*.

---

[104] We may trace a genealogy from Hamlet's machine to the cyborg and the posthuman, celebrated by Donna Haraway in "The Cyborg Manifesto" and N. Katherine Hayles in *How We Became Posthuman*, to name but two influential conceptualizations of this interface.

[105] A more systematic study of this topic would explore the possibility of the synchronous development of the group-as-machine metaphor in other parts of the world.

6

THE ANIMAL HOSPITALS OF GUJARAT:
THE COLLECTIVE UNBOUND
CAMBAY, 1623

India, of all the Regions of the Earth, is the only publick Theatre of Justice and
Tenderness to Brutes, and all living Creatures; for not confining Murther to the
killing of a Man, they Religiously abstain from taking away the Life of the meanest
Animal, Mite, or Flea; any of which if they chance willfully to destroy, nothing less
than a very considerable Expiation must Atone for the Offence.

> – Thomas Ovington, *A Voyage to Suratt in the Year, 1689*

Hail to those who understand the mind's delusions.

> – Ganadharavālaya Yantra

The humanist discovery of man is the discovery that he lacks himself.

> – Giorgio Agamben, *The Open*

Pietro della Valle, Pilgrim to the East

ON JANUARY 19, 1623, THE ROMAN NOBLEMAN PIETRO DELLA VALLE
set sail for India from the port of Gombroon (Bandar Abbas) on the
Persian Gulf. Della Valle (Figure 6.1) had left his native Italy nine years earlier
to visit the Holy Land and to travel through Egypt and the Middle East.
A wanderer, as well as a seeker of Eastern wisdom, he had styled himself *Il
Pellegrino*, or "the Pilgrim."

A complicated personal history had incited the twenty-eight-year-old
nobleman to leave his own people and culture behind. Disappointed in
love, he had been encouraged by his friend Mario Schipano, a Neapolitan
doctor and man of letters, to travel abroad. In 1614, Della Valle sailed from
Venice to Constantinople, where he stayed for a year, studying the Turkish
and Arabic languages. During the next two years, he traveled to Alexandria
and Cairo and visited Jerusalem. After a brief stay in the Holy Land, he
journeyed to Damascus, then Aleppo. While abroad, della Valle sent long

Je cours toute la terre   Et parmy tant
Je trouue Mon pays   ou je me Crois l

6.1 Pietro della Valle, *Les fameux voyages de Pietro della Valle, gentil-homme romain, surnomme, l'illustre voyageur, avec un denombrement tres-exact des choses les plus curieuses, & les plus remarquables qu'il a veuës dans la Turquie, l'Egypte, la Palestine, las Perse, & les Indes Orientales,* Vol. 3 (Paris: 1664). Harry Ransom Humanities Research Center. The University of Texas at Austin.

descriptive letters back to Schipano in Italy, hoping one day to have them published.[1]

---

[1] In 1650, della Valle published his letters from Turkey. Between 1658 and 1663, the *Viaggi di Pietro della Valle,* a posthumous, multivolume edition of his letters, would appear in Rome. The author's letters from Persia were published as Part II of the set and consisted of two volumes (1658). The letters from Turkey were then republished as Part I (1662). Finally, the letters from India were published as Part III (1663).

6.2. Sitti Maani Gioerida. *Les famevx voyages de Pietro della Valle, gentil-homme romain, svrnomme, l'illvstre voyagevr, avec vn denombrement tres-exact des choses les plus curieuses, & les plus remarquables qu'il a veuës dans la Turquie, l'Egypte, la Palestine, las Perse, & les Indes Orientales*, Vol. 2 (Paris: 1664). Humanities Research Center. The University of Texas at Austin.

Arriving by caravan in Baghdad in 1616, della Valle soon fell passionately in love with Sitti Maani Gioerida, an eighteen-year-old Nestorian Christian of great intellect and beauty, whom he persuaded to marry him (Figure 6.2).

The first volume of Part II exists in a modern Italian critical edition, entitled *I viaggi di Pietro della Valle: Lettere dalla Persia*, Vol. I, ed. F Gaeta and L. Lockhart (Rome: 1972).

Part III, the letters from India, was translated by George Havers in 1664 and republished by the Hakluyt Society in 1892 as *The Travels of Pietro della Valle in India from the Old English Translation of 1664 by G. Havers.*, ed. E. Grey – hereafter referred to as *Travels*. An abridged version of the Hakluyt was produced by George Bull, entitled *The Pilgrim: The Travels of Pietro della Valle* (London: 1990).

As his descriptions reveal, Maani represented for the Pilgrim all the exoticism, seductiveness, and power of the East as imagined by the West. As Natalie Hester has argued, however, Maani also embodied for her husband various ideals of womanhood and of female heroism drawn from the Italian literary tradition – notably, that of Clorinda, the woman-warrior of Tasso's epic *Gerusalemme liberata*.[2] An avid hunter and horsewoman, Maani possessed a gold-handled dagger, and according to her husband, was "frequently well-armed, after the manner of an Amazon" (*armata bene spesso, a guisa di Amazone*).[3] She shared with her new husband a great sense of adventure and strong religious commitments.

Together the newlyweds left Baghdad the following year, to the great sorrow of her parents, and relocated to the Persian city of Isfahan under the patronage of the ruler Shah Abbas. There della Valle and Maani had hoped to help the Shah wage war against the Turks and to found an international community of Christian refugees in Persia; this wish, however, was not to be realized. After living in Isfahan until 1621, della Valle decided to return to Italy by way of India with his young wife.

Things did not go well on their journey. The couple and their entourage were unable to sail from the port of Ormuz because of a war between the Persians and the Portuguese. Maani, who was pregnant, became ill with a high fever at Minab, a village near the Gulf of Ormuz. There she miscarried and died some days later on December 30, 1621.[4]

In the published version of his letter to Schipano, della Valle grieved the loss of his wife as well as his son and heir, who he said would have assured the succession of his family line.[5] In his private logbook, however, he recorded those events quite differently. There he described the loss of twins, a son and a daughter – a strange omission from the public account. In the private journal, della Valle attempted to console himself by acknowledging that the fetuses died early in the course of their development. Thus "their souls were not lost" (*le anime lore non si perdessero*),

---

[2] *Literature and Identity in Italian Baroque Writing*, 75ff.

[3] *Viaggi di Pietro della Valle Il Pellegrino Descritti da lui medesimo in Lettere familiari All'erudito suo Amico Mario Schipano. La Persia Parte Prima* (Rome: 1658), 148. Hereafter referred to as *Viaggi* (my translations).

[4] In the published version of these events, della Valle speaks of the delivery of a stillborn son; however, in his private diary, he also discusses a second stillbirth, that of a daughter. This strange discrepancy has been discussed by Hester in her excellent study of della Valle's travels in *Literature and Identity in Italian Baroque Writing*, 89.

[5] *Viaggi di Pietro Della Valle Il Pellegrino Descritti da lui medesimo in Lettere familiari All'erudito suo Amico Mario Schipano. La Persia Parte Seconda* (Rome: 1658), 353.

because as yet they lacked a "rational soul" (*non havessero avuto ancora l'anima rationale*).[6]

Utterly bereft, della Valle determined that his wife's remains would be buried in his family chapel in the Church of Santa Maria in Aracoeli in Rome. This was no small undertaking. Della Valle had her body embalmed so that he could transport it back to Italy.[7] Although essential for long travel, the preparation process caused della Valle considerable distress. Especially troubling was the embalmers' recommendation that the internal organs be removed. Della Valle would write to Schipano in Rome shortly afterward:

> We believe according to our faith to have everything at the Resurrection, and it is clear that each of us is resurrected where our bodies are buried.[8]

But what would happen, the bereaved man wondered, when portions of the body are separated at death, either by chance or by necessity? He reflected,

> Some say that the dead will be resurrected wherever the head is buried; others, the heart.[9]

Deciding to err on the side of caution, della Valle requested that the dead woman's heart be embalmed separately and returned to the body, which he would keep with him at all times during his travels, so that he and all of her could be resurrected together after his death.[10]

Maani's body was sealed in a coffin, which he carried through India for the next four years before returning to Rome as he traveled with the couple's adopted daughter Maria, a Georgian orphan whom Maani had taken under her wing in Isfahan.[11] Maani's absent presence would provide

---

[6]Hester notes the striking discrepancy between the published story, which mentions a tiny, "perfectly formed" son, half the size of his palm, and the private logbook, which mentions the birth of a second stillborn child, a daughter. Hester suggests that one or both of the fetuses may have been malformed. Biblioteca Apostolica Vaticana, Codice Ottob. 3382, 1621, folio 160 verso, Dec. 22, 1621, and Hester, 86–87.

 On early modern discussions of fetal development, ensoulment, and rationality, see Erica Fudge's excellent chapter "Becoming Human," in *Brutal Reasoning*, 39–58.

[7]Della Valle's fascination with mummies and mummification and his quasi-necrophiliac urges have been discussed by Hester, 84ff., and by Antonio Invernizzi, *In viaggio per l'Oriente*, 99–127, among others.

[8]"Crediamo per fede, de hauer tutti a resorgere: e chiara cosa è, che ciascuno risorgerà, dove sarà sepellito il suo corpo." *Viaggi* II.ii, 353.

[9]"[a]lcuni dicono, che risorgeranno dove sarà la lor testa; altri doue sarà il cuore." *Ibid.*, 353.

[10]*Ibid.*, 353.

[11]In 1617, Maria Tinatin di Ziba, later to be known as Mariuccia, was about seven years old when she was placed in the care of della Valle and Maani Gioerida. Her father had been an army officer killed in a battle with the Persians. Orphaned, Maria was left by foster parents with Carmelites in Isfahan. Discussed in *Viaggi* II, xx.

an implied commentary on della Valle's travel letters to Schipano from India, posthumously published in 1663 in Rome as the last of his multivolume series of letters, entitled *Viaggi*, or "Travels."[12]

Although a devout Catholic, della Valle wrote letters from the Near East, Persia, and India that opened windows onto cultures that few Europeans of his day had attempted to view in any depth. An avid learner and ultimately an acclaimed Orientalist, della Valle was fascinated by what he saw and understood, but even more by what he did not. Compared with most European travelers of his day, he manifested an unusual degree of openness to people who thought and lived differently from himself, although there were definite limits to his tolerance as well.[13]

Della Valle's intriguing and detailed discussions of his travels through the Near East, Egypt, Persia, and finally India shed light on the history of East-West relations in the seventeenth century, specifically by revealing as well as facilitating the flow of information and ideas between East and West during the Renaissance and Enlightenment. The pilgrim's perspectives on group identities are also of special relevance to the present study, because they throw into relief the conceptual boundaries that define and separate one collective from another, as well as the conflicting emotions experienced by representatives of diverse groups (notably della Valle himself, as well as others with whom he came in contact). Della Valle's writings also show his struggle to understand ethical and metaphysical views not easily accommodated in his own belief systems and group definitions. Attitudes toward death and the afterlife occupied a space of particular prominence in the Italian traveler's letters from India. With an eye to those issues, della Valle explored the boundaries separating religious, ethnic, cultural, economic, and social groupings, as well as the boundaries of a still larger group – *uomini*, or "mankind" – in relation to groups of other living entities in the animal world.

As we saw in Chapter 5, the rise of the concept of the individual – the indivisible self – coincided with an increasingly mechanized view of the world and the social order. Della Valle's experiences, questions, and uncertainties throw into relief a clash of discourses about the individual in relation to the group; the human in relation to the animal; and the *anima*, or soul, in relation to the *corpo*, or mortal body. His internal conflicts can be taken as

---

[12] See n. 1.

[13] On this latter topic, see J. D. Gurney's essay, "Pietro Della Valle: The Limits of Perception," 103–116, which analyzes della Valle's letters from Persia. See also Joan-Pau Rubiés' more extensive treatment of della Valle's openness to other cultures in *Travel and Ethnology in the Renaissance*, especially 349–387.

symptomatic of a larger set of identity crises and confusion typifying an era of global encounters and exchanges regarding the subject of religion.

Mateless Birds

One of della Valle's principal destinations in India was the city of Cambay, among the "ancientest" of India, and reputedly one of the most interesting. At that time the most important port in Mughal India, Cambay was also a thriving center of trade and wealth;[14] however, della Valle had his own reasons for visiting the city: namely, to observe the *Gentili* ("Gentiles") there – that is, the non-Muslim peoples of India. He hoped to encounter in Cambay (today Khambhat), located in the modern state of Gujarat, a distilled form of eastern religious practice, whose "remarkable Curiosities" (*molte belle curiosità*) he sought to witness firsthand.[15]

Of the particular attractions of the place he would write,

> The people of Cambaia are most part Gentiles; and here, more than else-where, their vain superstitions are observed with rigor. Wherefore we, who came particularly to see these things, the same day of our arrival, after we had din'd and rested a while, caus'd ourselves to be conducted to see a famous Hospital of Birds of all sorts (*uno Spedale famoso, che vi è, di uccelli di ogni sorte*), which for being sick, lame, depriv'd of their mates, or otherwise needing food and care, are kept and tended there with diligence; as also the men who take care of them are maintain'd by the publick alms.[16]

It was the bird hospital of Cambay that della Valle and his company hastened to see on the first day of their visit, guided by their Dutch hosts in that city. Providing sanctuary for sick animals was a common practice among the Jains of Gujarat and some Hindus as well. Known as पांजरापाल or *panjrapol* in Gujarati,[17] these ancient institutions have been described as charitable asylums for domestic animals and birds.[18] Panjrapols existed throughout India

[14] Arasaratnam and Ray, *Masulipatnam and Cambay*, 124.

[15] *De' viaggi di Pietro Della Valle il Pellegrino descritti da lui medesimo in Lettere familiari All'Erudito Suo Amico Mario Schipano Parte Terza cioe L'india, co'l ritorno alla Patria* (Rome: 1663), 36 (hereafter referred to as *Viaggi* III); *Travels* I, 46.

[16] *Viaggi* III, 51; *Travels* I, 67–68.

[17] There are many variant spellings of the word in English, including *pinjrapol, pinjrapole*, and *pan-jarapor*. According to the Oxford English Dictionary, the first recorded use of the Gujarati word in English occurred in the early 19th century; the addition of an s to form the plural is an Anglicization.

[18] See Babu Suthar, *Gujarati-English Learner's Dictionary* (Philadelphia: Nirman Foundation and the University of Pennsylvania, n.d.), 123. http://ccat.sas.upenn.edu/plc/gujarati/guj-engdictionary.pdf.

but were especially widespread in Gujarat – as they still are today.[19] Their origins can be traced at least as far back as the reign of Aśoka (ca. 269–232 BCE). In all likelihood they began as Jain institutions.[20]

The evolution of the panjrapol in Gujarat owes much to the strong influence of Jainism in that region, as well as other influences. The patronage of medieval kings such as Mandalika of Saurāshtra (1059 CE–?), Siddharāja Jayasiṃha (1094–1125 CE), and Kumārapāla (1125–1159 CE), both of Gujarat, helped to foster the spread of Jainism in those areas. Under Kumārapāla, Jainism became the state religion. It is possible that panjrapols existed in Gujarat at this time, although the evidence is not yet conclusive.[21] These institutions probably took root there for several reasons: first, the comparatively large Jain presence in Gujarat; second, the copresence of other religious groups – notably Muslims and Hindus – who lived side by side with Jains and others in symbiotic communities; and third, surplus wealth generated by trade, which could be dedicated to such charitable institutions. Supported by donations from the prosperous, the panjrapols provided care and shelter not only for animals but also for the humans who worked there or who were occasionally housed there. A fourth reason, as suggested by Deryck O. Lodrick, is the climate of Gujarat, which is subject to variable precipitation and periodic shortages.[22] The panjrapol is historically and culturally related to, yet distinct from, the *goshala* (Sanskrit "bull" [go] or "cow" + [sála] "house"), a shelter primarily for sick or aged cows that is also common in India and that is more strongly associated with Hinduism.

---

[19]"The pinjrapole is clearly a Jain institution," Lodrick writes; however, these sanctuaries are also supported by the Vaishnava vania community in Gujarat. "The Hindu inhabitants of Gujarat... have been long exposed to the beliefs of Jainism and would have little difficulty in accepting concepts such as ahimsa common to both religions. With the cult of Krishna and its associated respect for the sanctity of the cow also well entrenched in Gujarat, and with prolonged contact between the Jain and Vaishnava vania communities in their mercantile activities, a certain overlapping of common interests would be natural." *Sacred Cows, Sacred Places*, 143.

Lodrick provides maps showing the concentration of panjrapols in Gujarat, as well as other northeastern states where larger Jain populations are located. *Vania* goshalas, in contrast, exist all over India but especially across the northern states (see Maps 1–4, 29–35).

[20]Aśoka adopted Buddhism as the state religion, and many scholars consider the official protection of animals under Aśoka to have its roots in Buddhist and also Jain thought. Although edicts from Aśoka's time make no specific mention of animal hospitals, several scholars believe that they must have existed at that time. Lodrick, 57–60.

[21]*Ibid.*, 63. See also Sheth, *Jainism in Gujarat*.

[22]Lodrick, 31.

The term panjrapol likely derives from the Sanskrit nouns *pañjara*, or "cage," and *pala*, meaning "protector."[23] *Pañjara* has other resonances, however. Deriving from the root *paj*, "to become stiff or rigid," its Sanskrit meanings include 1) a cage, aviary, dovecote, or net; 2) a skeleton; 3) the body; and 4) the *Kali Yuga*, the 432,000-year cycle that is considered one of four stages of the world's development.[24] A concept appearing in the *Mahābhārata*, the Kali Yuga is regarded as the Dark Age, a time of disease, fatigue, anger, hunger, fear, and despair. The first three definitions point to the outside or the container (cage, skeleton, body). The fourth, in related fashion, can be said to indicate temporal, as well as spiritual "outsideness," by virtue of its distance from the *Krita Yuga*, or Golden Age. In the Kali Yuga (the current epoch), righteousness is said to have been reduced to a quarter of its original substance.[25] Connotations of transition, as well as transitoriness and entrapment, reverberate through each of these meanings of the Sanskrit term *pañjara*.

The animal hospital and the panjrapol are two different imagined communities, for the Gujarati word and concept *panjrapol* possesses a range of semantic resonances not found in della Valle's designation of *spedale* (hospital). In contrast, the Latin noun *hospes*, root of *spedale* and its cognates in many European languages, signifies "guest," "host," or "stranger."[26] In the Middle Ages, the hospital was a hostel for strangers or pilgrims, as well as a charitable asylum for the destitute, aged, or infirm, later evolving into an institution dedicated to the care and healing of the sick (the current meaning of the word).[27] *Hospes*, in turn, derives from the Indo-European root *ghos-ti-*, meaning "stranger," "guest," "host," or "someone with whom one has reciprocal duties of hospitality." The word is related to the Old Norse *gestr*, or "guest," the English words *host* (as well as *hostile*), as well as the

---

[23] *Ibid.*, 123. The etymology of this term is disputed. P. A. Xavier asserts the link to *pala*, or "protector." "The Role of Pinjrapoles in the Animal Welfare Work of India," 35. In contrast, Henry Yule and A. C. Burnell argue that the word derives from the Gujarati *pinjra* ("cage") and *pola* (the sacred bull released in the name of Shiva). *Hobson-Jobson*, 713. Discussed by Lodrick, 13–14, and 237, n. 2.

[24] Additionally, a *pañjara* can mean the name of particular prayers and formularies, a purificatory ceremony performed on cows, or a type of bulbous plant. Monier Monier-Williams, with E. Leumann, C. Cappeller, et al., *A Sanskrit-English Dictionary: Etymologically and Philologically Arranged with Special Reference to Cognate Indo-European Languages* (New Delhi: Asian Educational Services, 2001), 575.

[25] Schuhmacher and Woerner, eds., *Encyclopedia of Eastern Philosophy and Religion*, 435.

[26] E. A. Andrews, *A Copious and Critical Latin-English Lexicon* (New York: Harper & Brothers, Publishers, 1860), 727.

[27] *Oxford English Dictionary*, 1: 406.

Russian господин, *gospodin*, meaning "sir" or "master."[28] We might say then that the group concept animating this root and its branches describes power differentials between persons, and more fundamentally, a notion of social obligation toward other humans, especially strangers. The words and concept *animal hospital* in the European languages captured a paradox for the European imagination during the early modern age: namely, showing *hospitality* to animals, or having obligations toward them. A quite different group concept subtends the Gujarati word/concept *panjrapol*.

In his letter to Schipano, della Valle explains the religious and moral purpose of the hospitals as he understands them:

> The Indian gentiles, who, with *Pythagoras* and the ancient *Aegyptians* (the first Authors of this opinion according to Herodotus) believe in the Transmigration of Souls, not onely from Man to Man, but also from Man to brute beast, conceiving it no less a work of Charity to do good to beasts then to Men (*non meno opera di carità far bene alle bestie, che à gli huomini*).[29]

Della Valle, an ardent Catholic and believer in the resurrection of the body, went out of his way – very far indeed – to investigate what was for him a conundrum: a belief system in which the death of the body, as well as human identity itself in relation to the natural and spirit worlds, was understood quite differently. The pilgrim was intrigued by those *opere di carità*, the hospitalers' acts of charity, that seemed to blur the usual Western distinctions between man, or *huomo*, and *animale bruto*, or brute animal.

In this passage, della Valle identifies different versions of the idea of transmigration developed by the Indian "gentiles" on the one hand and Pythagoras and the Egyptians on the other. The question of which culture or set of ideas came first would preoccupy della Valle during his visit to Cambay, revealing his desire to fit Indian spiritual traditions into the Western paradigms with which he was already familiar. The question of priority may also have indicated what social psychologists today call *cognitive dissonance*, the discomfort created by attempting to hold contradictory ideas simultaneously. The paradoxical concept of the animal hospital raised profound questions for the Italian pilgrim about the proper treatment of animals, as well as the difference between the animal and the human, and finally the fate of the human body and soul after death. The *spedale*, which della Valle traveled to Cambay explicitly to see and which he sought out a few hours after his arrival to the city, was the external manifestation – the

---

[28] *American Heritage Dictionary*, 1518.
[29] *Travels* I, 68. *Viaggi* III, 51.

objective correlative – of a radically different thought system that troubled him and that he sought to confront and explore, if not embrace. In
that alternative system he probably sought some answers or consolation,
however.

On entering the Cambay bird hospital, della Valle was struck by the wide
array of birdlife:

> The House of this Hospital is small, a little room sufficing for many Birds:
> yet I saw it full of Birds of all sorts which need tendance, as Cocks, Hens,
> Pigeons, Peacocks, Ducks and small Birds, which during their being lame,
> or sick or mateless (*scompagnati*), are kept here, but being recover'd and in
> good plight, if they be wild they are let go at liberty; if domestick they
> are given to some pious person who keeps them in his House. The most
> curious thing I saw in this place were certain little Mice, who being found
> Orphans without Sire or Dam to tend them, were put into this Hospital,
> and a venerable Old Man with a white Beard, keeping them in a box
> amongst Cotton, very diligently tended them with his spectacles on his
> nose, giving them milk to eat with a bird's feather because they were so
> little that as yet they could eat nothing else; and, as he told us, he intended
> when they were grown up to let them go free wither they pleas'd.[30]

The hospital epitomized for della Valle the gentility of the Gentiles. Tenderness toward orphaned rodents in particular would not have been a widely
shared sentiment back in Italy or in plague-ridden Europe. The pilgrim was
particularly struck by the bearded old man feeding baby mice droplets of
milk with a feather, whose portrait is drawn with a sentimentality that was
typical of many European discussions of the panjrapols of Gujarat but that
was inconsistent with native views of these institutions.

Twice in his unique description of the Cambay bird hospital, della Valle
included a detail not found in other descriptions from the period: namely,
the condition of *matelessness* as a category of bird disability requiring hospi-
talization. Whether consciously or unconsciously, the pilgrim twice evoked
the survivor's position in alluding to birds deprived of their mates (*scom-
pagnati*). While explicitly exploring a profound question – what happens
when one dies – della Valle implicitly raised a related and no less important
question: what happens when a loved one dies, when the survivor must
separate from the living body of the beloved, the physical manifestation of
that person's existence. In the lives of the mateless birds, della Valle may have
recognized aspects of his own predicament. In focusing on orphans, he may
also have thought of his ward Maria Tinatin di Ziba, the girl whom he and

[30] *Travels* I, 68.

Maani Sitti had adopted in Isfahan and to whom he refers in his letters as Mariuccia, or "little Mary." The mouse may even have reminded della Valle of himself, an orphan of his own culture in a sense. Finally, the paradox of the animal hospital could also have reminded della Valle of the liminal status of della Valle's stillborn children, who had died before their own ensoulment in his belief. For the Italian pilgrim, as for many other European visitors of his era, the animal hospitals served as mirrors, providing complex reflections on whichever questions or problems of identity that each foreign viewer carried with him.

The next day, della Valle visited other animal hospitals in Cambay: one primarily devoted to the shelter of goats, kids, sheep, and wethers, sick or lame, as well as birds and other animals. Men and women who cared for these animals were also lodged in rooms at that same hospital, he reported. Subsequently he was taken to the cow and calf hospital (what today is called a goshala), where he saw a variety of elderly or injured animals, "some whereof had broke Legs, others more infirm, very old, or lean, and therefore we kept here to be cur'd."[31] "Among the beasts," he noted,

> there was also a Mahometan Thief, who having been taken in Theft had both his hands cut off. The compassionate Gentiles, that he might not perish miserably now he was no longer able to get his living, took him into this place, and kept him among the poor beasts, not suffering him to want anything. Moreover, without one of the Gates of the City, we saw another great troop of Cows, Calves and Goats, which being cur'd and brought into better plight, or gather'd together from being dispers'd and without Masters, or being redeem'd with Money from the Mahometans who would have killed them to eat, (namely the Goats and other Animals, but not the Cows and Calves) were sent in to the field to feed by neat-herds, purposely maintain'd at the publick charge.... [32]

By describing a vulnerable human being "among the beasts," cared for in the cow and calf hospital of the city, della Valle implicitly raised several questions: what separates humans from animals, and which aspects of identity do they share? Moreover, how might the valuing of animal life by humans entail a different set of moral obligations toward humans, as well as animals? Which religious and cultural group has the best or most appropriate ethical system? The Mahometans punish the thief for his transgression; the Gentiles take him in because of his inability to care for himself; the Christian plays the role of a supposedly detached observer. Finally, della Valle's description

[31] *Ibid.*, I, 70.
[32] *Ibid.*, I, 70.

implicitly raised the question of what it means to be a human – or to be dehumanized. These concepts would undergo significant transformation in the early modern age. Della Valle continued to puzzle over these questions during his travels in India and long after.

Is the Individual a Group?

By the early seventeenth century, the panjrapols and goshalas, or animal hospitals, of India, as they were conceptualized by Europeans, had become legendary attractions to visitors. Cambay, along with other cities in Gujarat, was renowned for its many sanctuaries for birds, cows, and other creatures. European visitors to the region like Pietro della Valle found the concept of such hospitals distinctly foreign and compelling – an intriguing marker of cultural difference. These sanctuaries, which served the needs of animals, birds, and even insects such as maggots and lice, challenged several standard assumptions of European thought – for example, concepts of the human–animal divide, the fate of the individual soul after death, and the definition of a human being. If humans can become animals or other humans in successive reincarnations, would such transformations signify that each individual is in some sense a group? European travelers to the panjrapols seem poised on the horns of that very dilemma.[33] A veritable oxymoron to these visitors, panjrapols posed the psychological threat of de-individuation and also implicitly of a "collective unbound" – a virtually endless diffusion or distribution of human identity across multiple persons and species. In the emergent colonial world of the sixteenth century, in which notions of ethnic or racial purity, as well as masculine superiority, would be codified in new ways and would circulate with increasing insistence, the prospect of identity diffusion may have accounted in part for the European preoccupation with the animal hospitals of Gujarat.

The Dutchman Jan van Linschoten, who visited India in the 1580s and who traveled to Goa by way of Africa, the Near East, and Cambay, offered an elaborate description of the region and its peoples, especially the "Banians" – the merchant (*vania* or *vaiśya*) caste (Figure 6.3). Europeans in the early modern period were generally unaware that the Banians encompassed two distinct but related religious and cultural groups – namely, Hindus and

---

[33]Describing the frequent discussions of reincarnation in seventeenth- and eighteenth-century Britain, Chi-ming Yang writes, "The potential re-birth of one's soul into multiple beings calls into question the defining core of personhood, the conceptual links between identity and consumption, as well as the ordering of the natural world." "Gross Metempsychosis and Eastern Soul," 29.

Jains.[34] Noting that the Banians excelled in trade and accounting, Linschoten provided the following explanation of their religious and dietary practices:

> They eat not any thing that hath life or blood in it, neither would they kill it for all the goods in the world, how small or unnecessary soever it were, for that they steadfastly believe that every living thing hath a soul, and are next [after men to be accounted of,] according to Pythagoras['] law, and know it must die: and sometimes they do buy certain fowls or other beasts of the Christians or Portingals, which they meant to have killed and [when they have bought them], they let them flee and run away.[35]

Like most European commentators of the era, Linschoten explained the Indian concept of reincarnation by way of analogy to the philosophy of the Greek Pythagoras, thereby providing a Western frame for the otherwise unfamiliar concept of transmigration. Pythagoras's belief in transmigration, as well as his supposed recollections of past lives, was widely known in early modern Europe.[36] ("I was never so berhymed since Pythagoras' time, when I was an Irish rat" says Shakespeare's Rosalind, "and that I can hardly remember."[37])

Linschoten also notes the fraught dynamic between Europeans, who assumed their right to kill and eat animals, and the native Banians, who did not and who aimed to protect animal life from people such as himself. The Dutchman further explained,

> They have a custome in Cambaia, in the high ways, & woods, to set pots of water, and to cast corn & other grain upon the ground to feed birds and beasts withal: & throughout Cambaia they have hospitals to cure and heal all manner of beasts and birds therein whatsoever they ail, & receive

---

[34] The *vanias* were part of the *vaiśya* caste, one of four traditional castes of India consisting of forty-one internal divisions, further dividing into Hindu and Jain segments. "Inter-dining between Hindu and Jain sections was common, but marriage was severely restricted even within the forty-one divisions." Pearson, *Merchants and Rulers in Gujarat*, 26.

It was not until the eighteenth century that English Indologists "discovered" Jainism as a separate religion. Tobias, *Life Force: The World of Jainism*, 30.

[35] Linschoten, *Voyage . . . to the East Indies*, 1: 253.

[36] Comparisons between Indian views of transmigration and those of Pythagoras abound in early modern travel writings – a fact that attests to Europeans' familiarity with at least a set of stereotypes about the Greek philosopher. Although today we possess little information about Pythagoras that dates from his own lifetime (the sixth century BCE), many later philosophers, including Plato, Iamblicus, Porphyry, and Diogenes Laertius, reported on his life and views and those of his followers. On the life of Pythagoras and the history of his thought in the West, see, for example, Riedweg, *Pythagoras: His Life, Teaching, and Influence* (2005); Kahn, *Pythagoras and the Pythagoreans: A Brief History* (2001); and Fideler, ed., *The Pythagorean Sourcebook and Library* (1987).

[37] *As You Like It*, III.ii.172–174. Bevington, 308. Shakespeare introduces Pythagoras several times but only in comic contexts.

6.3. Joannes à Doetechum, Goan Merchants, Banians of Cambay, and Brahmans of India, from *Iohn Hvighen van Linschoten. His Discours of Voyages into ye Easte & West Indies* (London, 1598). Harry Ransom Center. University of Texas at Austin. From left to right: a merchant of Goan India, a "Banian" of Cambay (shown with pen and paper), and Brahmin "priests" of India.

them thither as if they were men, and when they are healed, they let them fly or run away whither they will, which among them is a work of great charity, saying, it is done to their even neighbors. And if they take a flea or a Louse, they will not kill it, but take or put it into some hole or corner in the wall, and so let it go, & you can do them no greater injury then to kill it in their presence, for they will never leave entreating and desiring withal courtesy not to kill it, and that man should not seem to commit so great a sin, as to take away the life of that, to whom God had given both soul and body: yea, and they will offer much money to a man to let it live, and go away. They eat no Radishes, Onions, Garlic, nor any kind of herb that hath any color of red in it, nor Eggs, for they think there is blood in them. They drink not any wine, nor use any vinegar, but only water.[38]

[38] *Voyage*, 253–254.

6.4. *Mahāvīra Enthroned in Heaven* (anonymous artist). A page from a manuscript of the Kalpasūtra: folio IV: Gujarat, Patan, 1416 (V.S. 1473). Opaque watercolor and ink on paper. Each folio: 3 1/2 in. × 11 1/4 in. 8.9 cm × 28.6 cm. Virginia Museum of Fine Arts, Richmond. Arthur and Margaret Glasgow Fund. Photo: Travis Fullerton. © Virginia Museum of Fine Arts. This Jain scripture, composed in the sixth century BCE, recounts the biographies of the twenty-four Tīrthaṅkaras.

Here Linschoten presents the animal hospitals of Gujarat as a concrete manifestation of the attitude and practice of nonviolence toward all life, even that of parasitical insects such as lice and fleas. Although he does not identify them as such, the protection of insect life and the dietary practices described by the Dutch traveler are most strongly associated with Jainism; ascetic Jains abstain from consuming the previously mentioned items to avoid the inadvertent killing of plants or even the smallest insects.[39]

An ancient and nontheistic religion of India, Jainism evolved alongside Hinduism, partly in reaction to certain Vedic restrictions of the older religion and the practice of animal sacrifice, later disavowed within Hinduism.[40] Some historians contend that Jainism first emerged in what is today Bijar, India, about 2,500 years ago, with the sage Mahāvīra, a contemporary of

[39] On Jain dietary rules, see Shah, *Jainism: The World of Conquerors*, 1: 246–254.
"It is no exaggeration to say that food is a potentially dangerous substance for the pious Jain. Strict and precisely defined vegetarianism, then, is the most tangible social expression of adherence to the doctrine of non-violence and the most significant marker of Jain identity," Paul Dundas writes in *The Jains*, 177.
[40] Sangave, *Le Jaïnisme*, 179–181.

6.5. Ganadharavālaya Yantra. India, Gujarat, possibly Cambay, 1600–1650. Opaque watercolor on cloth. 26″H × 26 1/8″W, 66 cm × 66.4 cm. Jain painting in the Western Indian Style. Virginia Museum of Fine Arts, Richmond. Nasli and Alice Heeramaneck Collection, Gift of Paul Mellon. Photo: Travis Katherine Wetzel. © Virginia Museum of Fine Arts. This *yantra* (mystical diagram) was intended for meditations by a Jain spiritual aspirant. The sixth concentric circle features the twenty-four Tīrthaṅkaras. The central figure is unidentified. (See color plate.)

Buddha, later spreading throughout India.[41] Others claim a more ancient origin for the tradition, according to which Mahāvīra is considered the last of a line of twenty-four sages, or *Tīrthaṅkaras*, on whose teachings Jainism is based (Figures 6.4 and 6.5). The protection of all living beings – human,

---

[41] Many historians of Jainism point out that although the religion was founded by Mahāvīra, a younger contemporary of Buddha, he was in fact reviving an earlier tradition.

animal, or plant – is a central practice of Jainism, which is based on the core principle of ahimsa, or nonviolence and a reverence for all life forms.[42] As Christopher Chapple explains, "According to Jainism, the best life pays attention to animals, not in a sentimental way, but in a way that gives them the freedom to pursue their own path, to fulfill their self-made destinies, and perhaps enter themselves into the path of virtue."[43]

Still known as animal hospitals in the West, panjrapols today represent one of many concrete expressions of ahimsa. Above a door or gateway in each panjrapol, one encounters the inscription *ahiṃsā parāmo dharma* (ahimsa is the greatest of religions).[44] These asylums have played an important role in Jain culture for many centuries and in Hinduism and Buddhism as well.

The principle of ahimsa is closely related to the doctrine of karma, the explanatory principle of reincarnation accepted by almost all systems of Indian philosophy. *Karma*, meaning "action" or "deed" in Sanskrit, has a uniquely material connotation within Jainism. In the Jain tradition, karma is thought to consist of inert, ultrafine particles of matter (*pudgala* in Sanskrit) that in effect clog, congest, weigh down, or otherwise envelope the immaterial soul.[45] According to the philosopher Vilas Sangave, Jains view every soul as endowed with the powers of perception and understanding and as the author of its own actions. The soul has no form or materiality, yet it occupies the body that encloses it. The soul has a natural tendency to elevate itself and is ultimately free in its state of perfection. Karma accrues or accumulates in the soul during a particular lifetime as a result of individual actions and also across multiple lifetimes. Particulate karma, which can take many forms (there are 8 large categories and 148 subcategories), ideally should be eliminated by means of the spiritual and ascetic practices of each person to liberate the soul from the cycle of births and deaths.[46]

---

[42] The three core tenets of Jainism, which have remained relatively constant over the centuries, are 1) *ahimsa*, or nonviolence and reverence for all life; 2) *aparigraha*, or nonattachment to worldly possessions, power, or position; and 3) *anekaantavaada*, relative pluralism, or multiplicity of views. Shah, *Jainism: The World of Conquerors*, 2: ix.

"Institutionalizing the belief in non-violence, the Jains created *panjaraa polas*, sanctuaries that serve the needs of animals, birds, and even insects. Part hospitals, part rest homes, these institutions continue to this day. In Gujarat in 1995, for example, a survey listed 80 such sanctuaries in existence." *Ibid.*, 2: 215.

[43] Chapple, "Inherent Value without Nostalgia: Animals and the Mina Tradition," 249.

[44] Lodrick, 16.

[45] In the Hindu and Buddhist traditions, by contrast, karma is not considered a material substance.

[46] For an overview of Jaina karmic theory, see for example, Sangave, *Le Jainisme: Philosophie et religion de l'Inde*, 47–54, and Shah, *Jainism: World of Conquerors* II, 64–77. For a mathematician's speculative account of the action of particle "karmons" on the soul, see K. V. Mardia's intriguing book, *The Scientific Foundations of Jainism*.

Jainism propounds a strongly works-centered, nontheistic philosophy in which acts of self-discipline, asceticism, and respect for all forms of life help to accomplish karmic purgation during the lifetime at hand.[47] There is no predestination within Jainism but rather a simple law of cause and effect; through their actions, human beings control their own destinies. By adhering to five principal vows, Jains work toward karmic liberation. These vows are 1) *ahiṃsā*, abstention from violence toward other living beings; 2) *satya*, the avoidance of lying; 3) *asteya*, the avoidance of theft; 4) *brahmacārya*, the avoidance of sexual impurity; and 5) *aparigraha*, lack of greed for earthly goods.[48] Jain ascetics observe still more vows, although the principle of respecting life in all of its multiple forms is fundamental for all practitioners.

Underpinning Jain philosophy is a notion of identity that is strikingly different from that of Western religions and philosophies. Although one may have lived many previous lives, one nevertheless experiences oneself as an individual, not as a group and not plural. As the philosopher C. R. Jain explains,

> The simplicity of the soul is proved by the fact that no one ever feels himself as many, which shows that the subject of knowledge, feeling, perception and memory is not a reality composed of many atoms or parts, but a simple individualist. Soul, then, is a reality which is not indebted to any other substance for its existence, and as such must be deemed to be eternal and uncreate. This amounts to saying that the line of existence of the very soul merges in infinity both in the past and the future, so that each and every living being has a history of his own, however much he might be ignorant of the events of his earlier lives in his present incarnation.[49]

The implication of this system of thought, made partly manifest to early modern Europeans in the concrete institutions of the panjrapols in Gujarat

---

[47] As Hira Lal Jain explains, "The accumulated Karma-matter constitutes the first body or casing of the soul, and it is called Karmana Sarira. This subtle material body is held together with the immaterial soul substance by another fine body called Taijasa Sarira, a sort of electric or magnetic body. The soul together with its Karmana and Taijasa Sarira forms the nucleus or primary germ of life. These two forms of bodies accompany the soul always in Samsara, even in its state of transmigration which is brought about by these two bodies. Death only severs the connection of a soul with its outermost gross body which in the case of worldly animals is called Audarika Sarira, in the case of heavenly and hellish beings is called Vaikriyaka, and in a special condition some-times occasioned in mighty sages is called Aharaka Sarira. Every organism of a Samsari Jiva is thus an organic unity of two distinct entities Jiva and Ajiva, soul and body. All mental states like Buddhi, Manas, Amhamkara are the affections or modifications of the conscious soul caused by the Karmic matter; and similar are the various sense perceptions. They are simply special manifestations of soul's consciousness." *Jaina Tradition in Indian Thought*, 321.

[48] Sangave, 79.

[49] Jain, *Fundamentals of Jainism*, 13–14.

and in other practices as well, is an apparent lack of attachment to the physical body. Perhaps it would be more accurate, however, to say that Jainism – as well as Hinduism and Buddhism, in related ways – posits a different concept of attachment to a particular body and existence. The soul's identity transcends that of its individual lives and of the sense of identity that emerges during each existence; moreover, the perfected soul, purged of its karmas, is a de-individuated one. Similar notions of the soul can be found in certain lines of Hindu and Buddhist.

The Cages of Perception

Because there were no strong analogues for Indian spiritual beliefs and practices in Western culture (save for those of the ancient Pythagoreans), many Europeans who visited India in the sixteenth and seventeenth centuries were struck by the profound differences between Eastern and Western thought systems. In their writings, they often fastened on the practice of nonviolence to animals, insects, and even plants. Within many of their narratives, the animal hospitals of Gujarat functioned as a topos of cultural difference, an outward signifier of worldviews that were otherwise difficult to grasp. Language barriers also contributed to the cartoonish explanations of Indian religious views and cultural practices provided by European travelers.

Such writers generally assumed a neutral or sympathetic tone in their discussions of animal hospitals, although not always. Manuel Pinheiro, a Jesuit who visited Cambay in 1595, described the city and its people in his letters to Nicolau Pimenta, the Provincial in Goa. Pinheiro and other Jesuits had traveled to the region in the hope of converting the great Mughal emperor Akbar to Christianity. In 1579, Akbar had sent two emissaries to Goa requesting that two priests visit his court and explain their religion to him.[50] These Jesuits participated in extensive debates held by Akbar in Fatehpur Sikri. These renowned debates at various times included representatives of other religious groups, including Muslims from multiple sects, Sikhs, Hindus, Parsees, Jews, and Cārvāka materialists[51] (Figures 6.6 and 6.7). Akbar's remarkable openness to interfaith dialogue intensified the missionizing efforts of these Jesuits, who hoped that eventually the Muslims and Gentiles of India would come to accept the Christian worldview. While Pinheiro and his colleagues awaited caravan transport to Lahore, where Akbar

---

[50] Lach, *The Century of Discovery*: 275.

[51] On these extraordinary debates, see Abu-l-Fazl, *The Akbar nāmā*, 364ff. See also du Jarric, *Akbar and the Jesuits* (1926); Maclagan, *The Jesuits and the Great Mogul* (1932); and Nizami, *Akbar and Religion* (1989).

On the Cārvāka school, see n. 81.

6.6. Narsingh, illustration from *The Akbar nāmā*: Akbar, Abu-l-Fazl, author of the *Akbar nāmā* (on his immediate right), Jesuit missionaries and other courtiers debate religious beliefs at Fatehpur Sikri (1605). Akbar's two young sons Murad and Daniyal stand to his left. © Trustees of the Chester Beatty Library, Dublin. Painting on paper (detail), folio size 43 × 26 cm. (See color plate.)

was based at that time, the Jesuit gathered and recorded information on the local culture of Cambay for the purpose of proselytizing.[52]

Like della Valle and Linschoten, Pinheiro records his visit to the bird hospital of Cambay, although he extracted a different moral lesson from it:

> Sometimes I would go to see the hospital that these people have for every type of bird, where they are cured when they are sick. There I saw some peacocks who could have been thrown out of the hospital because they were incurable. The problem was that a sparrow-hawk came into the hospital with a bad leg. After it got better, it jumped on top of the other birds and killed several of them. When the hospital worker saw this, he tossed it out for causing trouble. They have a hospital for birds, but they don't have one for humans, leaving the sick to suffer and to die abandoned. I don't want to bother your Reverence with these matters, but I will say that I will be able to go through the streets of Cambay preaching the Christian doctrine and raising the standard of the Cross without fear of either Moors or Gentiles. Many of them would accompany me, such is the respect and love that they show us.... Concerning our mission we are extremely hopeful, and even the natives say that Akbar has to finish this time – that is, he has to finish the business. May God in his mercy so will it.[53]

In his letter to his superior, Pinheiro ridiculed the Cambaian natives for their misguided attentions to birds and what he took to be their disregard for sick humans. In the eyes of the Jesuit, some birds are likely to be predators or prey, and the humans who cared for them were foolish to think otherwise. Himself a hunter in pursuit of the Mughal Emperor's soul, Pinheiro did not fully recognize that he too was the recipient of respect and compassion from both the "Gentiles" and the "Moors" of Cambay. To Pinheiro's frustration and that of many others, Akbar decided not to convert to Christianity, although he remained sympathetic to that religion and to the Jesuits throughout his life. While finding much of value in the Jesuits' Catholicism, Akbar objected that several of their beliefs and customs, such as the doctrine of the Trinity and the practice of monogamy, seemed untenable.[54] Certain Jesuits stayed in Akbar's entourage until his death in 1605, including Father Jerome Xavier, grandnephew of the Saint, who remained with the Emperor in Agra during the last decade of his life. Pinheiro also remained in Agra,

---

[52] On Pinheiro's mission to Akbar's court, and on his encounters with Jain and Hindu ascetics, also see Lach, *The Century of Discovery* I, 1: 458–467.

[53] Peruschi, *Informatione del regno, e stato del gran Rè di Mogor, della sua persona, qualita, e costumi, e delli buoni segni, e congietture della sua conuersione alla nostra santa fede* (1597), 50–51.

[54] *Ibid.*, 278.

6.7. Kesu Das, *Salim Album*: A Jesuit. Painting, 104 × 5.9 cm (ca. 1595–1600). © Trustees of the Chester Beatty Library, Dublin. The Jesuit, situated in a landscape of trees and rolling hills cut through by a large river, holds out a book.

a cultural center of the Mughal empire (Figure 6.8), leading a congregation there.[55]

Dreams of universal conversion would continue to lose traction in the seventeenth century (although never entirely dying away), whereas other modes of accommodating, denying, or suppressing large-group differences, especially religious ones, would be considered by European visitors to the East and also by other groups. Indeed, modernity can be defined as the oscillation on the part of individuals, as well as collectives, between limited toleration of religious and cultural differences on the one hand and the violent suppression thereof on the other – an oscillatory pattern that continues to this day.[56] Meanwhile, the fantasy of fully assimilating or incorporating other groups or belief systems into one's own (e.g., a fantasy expressed visually through the popular European Renaissance subject of the *Adoration of the Magi*) became increasingly difficult to sustain.

The topos of the animal hospital within European travel writings of the sixteenth and seventeenth centuries illuminates the psychic processes of coping with group difference, as further examples suggest. The German traveler Johan Albrecht de Mandelslo traveled to India in the late 1630s after serving as an attaché of the Duke of Holstein on a trade mission to Persia.[57] Commenting on the animal hospitals of Cambay, he would provide the following account of the concept of transmigration:

> They hold the immortality of the Soul, but believe with all, that, at its departure out of the first body, it transmigrates into that of some other Creature; and affirm, that the Soul of a good natur'd and docible person, is translated into the body of a Pidgeon, or Chicken; that of a cruel and wicked man, into that of a Crocodile, a Lyon, or a Tigre; that of a crafty man, into that of a Fox; that of a Glutton, into the body of a Swine; that of a Treacherous person, into that of a Serpent, &c. Before they are admitted to the enjoyment of a beatitude purely Spiritual. And this is the onely reason, why the Benjans abstain from the killing of living Creatures, even to the insects, how dangerous troublesome soever they may be. They also forbear keeping any fire, and lighting candles in the night time, out of a fear that the Flies, or Moths should burn themselves therein; Nay, they make some difficulty to pits of the Ground, for fear of drowning the Fleas and other Insects which might lye in the way. What is yet more superstitious,

---

[55] *Ibid.*, 277.

[56] On the limits of religious tolerance, the supposed outcome of Europe's Wars of Religion and the age of "Enlightenment," see Kaplan's *Divided by Faith*. Kaplan argues that the opposite was in fact the case.

[57] Lach and Van Kley, *A Century of Advance*, 3: 667.

This page from the illuminated memoirs of Babur, founder of the Mughal Empire and Akbar's grandfather, show an extraordinary sensitivity to animal life characteristic of Mughal painting. This manuscript was produced during the reign of Akbar and was the most popular book of that era. It exemplifies the importance of Agra as a center of manuscript production.

they do not onely redeem the Birds, which the Mahumetans had taken, but they also build Hospitals for Beasts that are hurt and wounded.[58]

Mandelslo held that the "onely reason" that the Benians chose not to kill animals was that they did not wish to kill their own kind under another species. Mandelslo imagined a quasi-allegorical (one might say Ovidian) correspondence between humans and the animals that they would become after death, as if a person's dominant affect or quality of temperament would be distilled in death, providing the template for a later bestial transformation.

As in other contemporary accounts, Mandelslo conflates Hindus and Jains under the title of "Benjan," while describing ascetic practices most strongly associated with Jainism – specifically, the avoidance of fires and candles at nighttime, which might inadvertently attract and consume flying insects.[59] The central concept of nonviolence within Jain and Hindu thought does not figure into Mandelslo's explanation. The German traveler instead construes the actions of the Indians solely as a means of ensuring more positive future lives.

As Tristam Stuart has recently argued, Europeans visitors to the animal hospitals tended to project onto Indians "the simplified Pythagorean idea that they abstained from killing animals for fear of hurting a reincarnated human soul. This implied that the Hindus were not valuing the life of the animal itself, but the soul of the human trapped within it."[60] Stuart also notes that the concept of nonviolence, a far more profound challenge to European morality of that time, was essentially lost on the visitors to India.

In 1673 the Scottish cosmographer John Ogilby compiled ethnographic and geographic information for the readers of his lavishly illustrated *Asia*. In his account of the animal hospitals of Gujarat, which had become *de rigueur* in travel narratives of the late seventeenth century, Ogilby incorporated the anecdote of a "pleasant Quarrel" between a Christian and a Benian:

> They often buy Birds, and other Creatures that are kept in Cages, with considerable Sums of Money; as also those that are taken by Huntsmen, whether Moors or Christians, for no other end but to preserve them from death, and give them liberty. From this Custom, which is very common amongst them, hapned once a pleasant Quarrel, viz. A Christian, clad after the Indian fashion, bought some Birds to eat of a Bird-Catcher, who by his Garb taking him to be an Indian, open'd his Cage, as soon as he had receiv'd his Money, and let them flie; whereupon the Christian contesting,

[58] Olearius, *The Voyages and Travels of the Ambassadors sent by Frederick Duke of Holstein . . . whereunto are added the Travels of John Albert de Mandelslo . . . into the East Indies* (1662), 68.
[59] Traditionally, Jain ascetics vowed not to eat after dark for these reasons.
[60] *The Bloodless Revolution*, 53.
    See also Spenser, *The Heretic's Feast.*

would have the birds deliver'd to him, or his Money; and in short, the Bird-catcher, though he lost his Birds, was forc'd to repay the Christian his Money in the presence of all the Spectators, to their no little laughter.

There is great deceit in this kind of dealing; for many poor People, of a contrary opinion, to make an advantage, take any live Bird, and bringing the same to sell amongst these Indians, cry like mad-men, I will kill it instantly, I will wring off its neck: Whereupon the innocent Indians immediately come running, and buy it above its worth, onely to release it from death.

To this purpose they have Cages in many places to keep lame or hurt Birds, and also for four-footed Beasts, which with great care are cured and fed at the Publick Charge.[61]

In Ogilby's rehashing of earlier treatments of this subject, Indian respect for animal life provides an opportunity for telling a joke at the natives' expense. His account of Banian interventions further reveals how Christians and others could use the Jain and Hindu commitment to nonviolence as a weapon against members of those groups – that is, as a means of controlling, manipulating, or gaining the upper hand in financial transactions with the very group that Linschoten had earlier characterized as master traders. Ogilby's anecdote reveals the European colonial mindset that had already begun to solidify in stories of "pleasant quarrels" such as this one – although such modes of extortion were by no means exclusive to the British.[62] In addition to serving as a source of income, threats of animal killing by non-Gentiles also could have represented a means of handling intellectual discomfort or anxiety resulting from the collision of incompatible belief systems. Psychological violence constituted one mechanism for dismissing a rival belief system otherwise difficult to assimilate.

An account published by Giovanni Gemelli Careri provides yet another seventeenth-century example of European criticism of the Gujarati people and their regard for animals. An Italian traveler and Hapsburg official, Careri traveled to India at the end of the seventeenth century. In his journal of a voyage to India in 1695, he recorded the following observations:

Thursday 20th, a young French Man conducted me to see an Hospital of the Gentils, where an abundance of irrational Creatures were kept. This

---

[61] *Asia, the First Part being An Accurate Description of Persia and the Several Provinces thereof,* 123.

[62] Barbosa, for example, describes animal hostage-taking as a practice of the "Moors," whereas Mocquet describes it as a Portuguese practice. See "Del regno di Guzzarat in India," *Libro di Odoardo Barbosa Portoghese,* in Ramusio, *Primo volume, & Seconda editione delle Navigationi et Viaggi in Molti Luoghi* (1554), 327v–328r; and Mocquet, *Voyages en Afrique, Asie, Indes Orientales & Occidentales* (1617), 245v.

they do because they believe the Transmigration of Souls, and therefore imagining those of the Forefathers may be in the vilest, and filthiest living Creatures they provide them with Food. Thus the wild Monkeys to eat what is provided for them. Besides the prodigious number of Birds and Beasts maintain'd there, particular care is taken of the Lame and Sick. But that which most amaz'd me, tho' I went thither to that purpose, was to see a poor Wretch naked bound Hands and Feet, to feed the bugs or Punaises, fetch'd out of their stinking Holes to that purpose. The best of it is that any Man should voluntarily expose himself to be so devour'd, for a small reward given him, according to the Hours he will continue under it.[63]

Careri's account, although highly unsympathetic, brings out an element that was otherwise uncommon in earlier European depictions of the "hospitals of the Gentils," including those for insects. His extreme revulsion at the thought of "the vilest, and filthiest living Creatures" carrying the souls of "the Forefathers" prefigures the outrage that would be heaped on Charles Darwin a century and a half later when the British biologist would introduce his theory of evolution. For Careri, as for many others to this day, human identity is predicated on the absolute divide between man and animal (or insect), a divide that licenses man's freedom to exercise his power over other life forms in whichever manner he should choose. The poor man's voluntary choice to be bound and fed to insects (as a means of earning income, as an act of asceticism, or both) complicated that hierarchy for the European observer, however, nor did he connect that act to forms of asceticism that were common in Europe.

The practice of the bodily feeding of insects would also be described by Thomas Ovington in his book *A Voyage to Suratt in the Year, 1689.* An English clergyman with a generally more open-minded perspective on the cultures of Gujarat, Ovington described a sanctuary for insects[64] that he visited at Surat:

Near this Hospital is another built for the preservation of Buggs, Fleas, and other Vermin, which suck the blood of Men; and therefore to maintain them with that choice Diet to which they are used, and to feed them with their proper Fare, a poor Man is hired now and then to rest all Night upon the Cot, or Bed, where the Vermin are put, and fasten'd upon it, lest the stinging of them might force him to take his flight before the Morning, and so they nourish themselves by sucking his Blood, and feedin[g] on his Carcass.[65]

[63] Gemelli Careri. *A Voyage Round the World* 4: 200–201.

[64] Some panjrapols of that era contained a *jīvat khān*, or insect room. Ovington's description suggests a separate sanctuary dedicated to vermin. Modern panjrapols can also contain such rooms. Lodrick, 19–22.

[65] Ovington, *A Voyage to Suratt in the Year, 1689,* 301.

Ovington's choice of the word *Carcass* in this description suggests a certain irony toward his subject matter. While highlighting the voluntary element of the feeding – the man hires out his body – he also notes that the volunteer must be bound to the cot lest the extreme discomfort of the procedure cause him to abandon his post.

In balance, however, Ovington's account is sympathetic to the culture that he describes. Noting the wide variety of animal hospitals that he visited, Ovington introduces a new concept within the ongoing discussion of these institutions: namely, the [European] maltreatment of animals as "inhuman":

> For within a Mile distance from Suratt is a large Hospital, supported by the Bannians in its maintenance of Cows, Horses, Goats, Dogs, and other Animals diseas'd, or lame, infirm or decay'd by Age; for when an Ox by many Years Toil grows feeble, and unfit for any farther Service; lest this should tempt a merciless Owner to take away his life, because he finds him an unprofitable Burthen, and his Flesh might be serviceable to him when he was dead; therefore the Bannian reprieves his Destiny, either by begging him from the Owner, or by buying of him at a certain Rate, and then places him in the Hospital, where he is rescued from any other Death, but what is due to Nature, and is there attended and fed, 'till he spins out the appointed customary term of life. This Charity which they extend to Beasts, is accounted by them an act of great Reputation and Virtue; nor can they be reconcil'd to that inhuman Cruelty, which destroys those Creatures which are the Nurses of our Lives, and by whose labour we live at Ease.[66]

If animals are the "Nurses of our Lives" – a metaphor that applies strongly but not exclusively to milk-producing animals such as cows and goats – then to kill them is a form of "inhuman cruelty." What, however, does "inhuman" mean, if not bestial? In Ovington's sentimental appraisal, animality is positively valued; hence, it can no longer serve as a synonym for "inhuman." Thus that adjective acquires a certain paradoxical quality in this context. Conversely, to be *human* is to nurture – that is, to act like an animal. Although clearly Ovington did not adopt the Hindu or Jain worldview – he remained a minister of the Anglican Church – he nevertheless attempted an accommodation of their views within his own thinking. He did so mainly by connecting the Indian protection of animals to the Christian notion of charity, as had many before him. Ovington also employed the standard strategy of reframing. Struggling to combine worldviews and group identities usually considered incompatible, he reminded his readers that in "our Nation," the

[66] *Ibid.*, 300–301.

ancient Druids abstained from the killing or eating of animals. This they did, he claimed, for reasons similar to those of the people of India, as well as those of the ancient Pythagoreans and others.[67]

Identity Crises of the Renaissance

The impact of Eastern thought on the West during the early modern era must not be underestimated – indeed, it should be explored more fully. The purported rise of individualism in the European Renaissance and Enlightenment may have been in part a defensive reaction to multiple strands of Eastern thought that were newly imported to the West. From Marco Polo's time forward, and indeed earlier throughout classical antiquity, knowledge of Eastern philosophies had circulated extensively in parts of the West. This dialogue intensified in the early modern age because of several factors, including the expansion of a global trading system,[68] the technologies of paper making and book publication, and the improvement of other systems that enabled the gathering, translating, and dissemination of information about large groups and their customs and beliefs. Over time, such large-group identities, with their similarities and differences to others, would come into progressively clearer focus.

Whereas della Valle, for example, did not grasp the nuances of Indian thought when he visited Gujarat and other regions, he did understand that "Gentile" thought systems posed a fundamental challenge to human identity as he understood it up until then – a challenge that had the power to provoke an identity crisis for other Europeans as well. We must not take the pilgrim's denunciations of Indian religious beliefs at face value, for even as della Valle dismisses transmigration and other Indian beliefs as the "vain superstitions" of idolaters, his curiosity and anxiety drive him to engage in dialogue with the very system that generates his intense confusion.

Della Valle struggled to preserve in his mind the very boundary between life and death as understood within the Christian tradition but that was challenged at every turn in Cambay. What happens to people when they die? Is there any more difficult question? The subtleties of this problem could not have been lost on della Valle, whose beloved Maani was on hand

---

[67] *Ibid.*, 284.

[68] Whereas Immanuel Wallerstein, following Braudel, argues that the modern world-system emerged in the sixteenth century, others such as Janet L. Abu-Lughod, Jack Goody, and John M. Hobson locate earlier world-systems centered in the East, and challenge the privileging of the former over the latter. See Abu-Lughod's *Before European Hegemony* (1989), Goody's *The East in the West* (1996), and Hobson's *The Eastern Origins of Western Civilization* (2004).

to remind him of the Christian mystery should he forget. This boundary and
the place of the physical body as the marker of that transition plays a crucial
role in the Christian doctrine of the resurrection (one, Carolyn Bynum has
explained, that evolved gradually to insist on the resurrection of the physical
body and not just the immaterial soul).[69] In the worldview of the pilgrim,
the body dies, the soul continues, and finally soul and body are reunited at
the end of time.

The body as a governing principle of identity, ultimately recoverable,
became central to the Christian notion of the resurrection during the Middle
Ages. "The idea of person, bequeathed by the Middles Ages to the modern
world, was not a concept of soul escaping body or soul using body; it was
a concept of self in which physicality was integrally bound to sensation,
emotion, reasoning, identity – and therefore finally to whatever one means
by salvation." As Bynum explains, "person was not person without body."[70]

The resurrected body is a perfected one, according to Aquinas, although
the meaning of "perfect" was subject to debate. Did resurrected bodies have
sex in Paradise? If so, did resurrected women have babies? Did resurrected
souls eat in heaven? If so, what if anything did they excrete? Aquinas had
asserted categorically that there was no sex or excrement in Paradise. He also
held that animal life and plant life had no place in heaven, because they are
and remain corruptible; they do not have souls.[71] In the words of the contemporary philosopher Giorgio Agamben, who writes on the paradoxical
views of Aquinas, "All flesh will not be saved, and in the physiology of the
blessed, the divine *oikonomia* of salvation leaves an unredeemable remnant."[72]

That remnant – of animal life, and of the animal parts of human life, both
loved and feared – continued to haunt the European cultural imaginary for
many centuries. The radical split between forms of life, of perfected and
imperfect modes of being, and of the stability and continuity of human
identity, was founded on a set of distinctions increasingly hard to maintain.
The medieval Christian solution would come under progressively greater
pressure to buttress itself while alternative views from the East and elsewhere
in the world began to circulate more widely in the fifteenth, sixteenth, and
seventeenth centuries, and when scientific debates began to challenge such
beliefs more directly, as discussed in the previous chapter.

Writing during an era of rapidly accelerating cultural transformation, della
Valle was perplexed and at times troubled by the Eastern cultural matrices

---

[69] Bynum, *The Resurrection of the Body*.
[70] *Ibid.*, 11.
[71] Aquinas, *Summa theologica*, Vol. 20, Part III (Supplement QQ. 69–86), 193.
[72] Agamben, *The Open*, 19.

that he resisted but that he had also deliberately sought out. As he already knew before he arrived in Gujarat, the Gentiles of India professed a different attachment to the physical body – whether living or dead. Those Gentiles, he observes, burn the bodies of the dead and have no sepulchers, unlike the Muslims of the same region.[73] Through his comparative ethnography, della Valle explored various religious and philosophical explanations of the soul, its relation to the body, and the role of both in determining identity. These were key questions in the philosophy of the European Renaissance, which was, from the fourteenth century onward, in dialogue not only with the recently recovered *fontes* of classical letters but also with various Eastern thought systems that inform the esoteric traditions above all.

Neoplatonist philosophers such as Pico and Ficino offered the topos of human variability: man is or can be *like* an animal or an angel. As Ficino would write in his 1482 *Theologia platonica de immortalitate animorum* (*Platonic Theology*):

> [The soul] lives the life of a plant insofar as it indulges the body by fattening it up; the life of the best insofar as it flatters the senses; the life of man insofar as it calls upon reason to handle human affairs; the life of the heroes insofar as it investigates things in nature; the life of the demons insofar as it contemplates mathematics; the life of the angels insofar as it inquires into the mysteries divine; and the life of God insofar as it does all things for God's sake.[74]

Ficino sought to defend the individuality of the human intellect and the immortality of the soul, as Charles Trinkaus has explained. When Ficino said, *Vitam siquidem agit plantae*, "the soul leads the life of a plant," or *vitam bruti*, it leads the "life of an animal," he was speaking figuratively: the soul (or man) can be *like* a plant, animal, demon, or god. The topos of upward and downward mobility construed similistically may have circulated more insistently at a time when accounts of alternative belief systems did the same in Renaissance Europe. This was a time when epistemes with upward and downward mobility were taken literally, and within which systems a different morality and a different set of ethical entailments toward other humans and toward the animal kingdom would require Europeans to examine their own, however glancingly. Other large groups did so, as well – the case of the Mughal Emperor Akbar's religious debates being a case in point.

Perhaps the greatest challenges to European philosophy and Christian theology were the deconstructed notion of boundary between human and

---

[73] *Travels* I, 69, *Viaggi* III, 53.

[74] *Platonic Theology*, trans. Allen, ed. Hankins, 4: 241. Also cited in Trinkaus, *In Our Image and Likeness*, 2: 489.

animal, and – at least to the European mind – the de-individuated notion of soul implicit in Hindu, Jain, and Buddhist philosophy. The Ficinian response was to metaphorize and thereby to stabilize the category of the self, potentially emptied out by its voluntary transformations into angel or beast. As Agamben provocatively writes, "The humanist discovery of man is the discovery that he lacks himself, the discovery of his irremediable lack of *dignitas*."[75]

Another response to the challenge, exemplified by Pomponazzi's Aristotelian *De immortalitate animae* (1516), was to reconnect the soul and the body, thereby calling into question the immortality of both. As Ernst Cassirer explains of Pomponazzi's unorthodox views:

> An individual soul can only be conceived of as such if it is thought of as the form of an individual *body*. In fact one can say that what we call the animation of a body consists in nothing other than in this its complete individuation. Through this, the body is distinguished from mere 'matter'; through this, it becomes an *organic* body which, in its individual determination, becomes the vehicle of a definite, concrete and individual *life*. The 'soul', therefore, is not added to the 'body' as an external principle of movement or animation; rather it is the very thing that forms the body in the first place.[76]

Was the soul or the body, for that matter, immortal in Pomponazzi's view? The philosopher did not really want to push the point, although Pomponazzi voiced his skepticism about immortality while simultaneously asserting his Christian orthodoxy.

The soul–body interface was, as discussed in the previous chapter, the key dilemma facing René Descartes as he attempted to develop a new science of man as machine and simultaneously a philosophy of man as possessor of a rational soul – a soul without material extension that nevertheless animated the matter of the human body, setting it above those of animals. In partly splitting off the soul/mind of man from the material body, Descartes paved the way for a monistic and purely material view of human life. Interestingly, he did so by introducing an atomic (corpuscular) theory of matter in his *Traité de l'homme* (*Treatise of Man*), which he withheld from publication throughout his lifetime because of its potentially subversive implications.[77] Galileo's trial had a dampening effect on free thought, especially free thought about the relation of souls and bodies.

[75] *The Open*, 30.
[76] Cassirer, *The Individual and the Cosmos in Renaissance Philosophy*, 136–137.
[77] See Chapter 5, n. 62.

In that work, Descartes not only drew categorical distinctions between soul and matter, both of which humans were said to possess, but also between humans and animals, which lacked the former. In his own time, scholars questioned whether Descartes believed that animals had no feelings and whether he genuinely believed that they were just "machines"; they continue to do so to this day.[78] Descartes practiced vivisection during the period when he wrote the *Treatise of Man*, believing that animals feel no pain. He was also a vegetarian, although supposedly for health rather than ethical reasons.

Despite his complicated views on animals, there is a marked resemblance between the atomistic view of matter expressed in Descartes' *Treatise of Man* and certain Indian forms of atomism. Perhaps that resemblance is not coincidental. At various times while he composed that work, Descartes resided in Amsterdam. Each day he walked through the center of town and saw ships laden with "the produce of the Indies and the most rare items from Europe."[79] Amsterdam was "one of the most active commercial and cultural centers in Europe," Desmond Clarke, Descartes' recent biographer, notes.[80] By the 1620s, and in fact long before, India had come to Europe. It is therefore possible that Descartes too was engaged in some sort of unacknowledged dialogue with Eastern thought in his revival of atomism, his denial of animal souls, and his preoccupations with mental illusions. Descartes' analysis of the soul–body interface bears a certain resemblance to the Jain notion of particulate karma accumulating in a nonmaterial soul, even more than with western forms of atomism.

We need not assume that the renaissance of atomistic thought in the West was purely the effect of a renewed awareness of the Greek and Roman scientific tradition. India too had its own ancient traditions of atomistic philosophy. These included the Jain theory of particulate karma, as well as the *Lokāyata* (later called the *Cārvāka*), a school of thought that represented a separate materialist tradition within Hindu thought. These were atomists who denied the existence of soul altogether, and who espoused a

[78] See, for example, Cottingham, "'A Brute to the Brutes?': Descartes' Treatment of Animals," 551–559; Peter Harrison, "Descartes on Animals," 219–227; Fudge, *Brutal Reasoning*, esp. 147–174; and Derrida, *The Animal That Therefore I Am*, 69–87.

[79] Descartes, *Oeuvres*, ed. Adam and Tannery. In a letter to Jean-Louis Guez de Balzac, dated May 5, 1631, Descartes writes of Amsterdam: "Que s'il y a du plaisir à voir croître les fruits en vos vergers, & à y estre dans l'abondance iusques aux yeux, pensez-vous qu'il n'y en ait pas bien autant, à voir venir icy des vaisseaux, qui nous aportent abondamment tout ce que produisent les Indes, & tout ce qu'il y a de rare en l'Europe. Quel autre lieu pouroit-on choisir au reste du monde, où toutes les commoditez de la vie, & toutes les curiositez qui peuuent estre souhaitées, soient si faciles à trouuer qu'en cettuy-cy? Quel autre pays où l'on puisse iouyr d'vne liberté si entiere, ou' l'on puisse dormir auec moins d'inquietude. . . ." (I: 204). Referenced by Clarke, *Descartes: A Biography*, 107.

[80] Ibid., 107.

purely material philosophy – one also strongly opposed to the Brahmanical caste privileges.[81] The essentials of Jainism and the heretical Cārvāka school could have been known to the Jesuits involved in the theological debates of Akbar's court and also the intensive study of Eastern languages.[82] Descartes could have encountered their thought either directly or through secondhand sources, although such connections remain as yet unproven.

Increasing contact between Asia, Africa, Europe, and the Americas contributed to Renaissance and seventeenth-century explorations of the always-perplexing questions of identity and selfhood in relation to the natural world and the conception of the transcendent. Such investigations must be recognized as occurring within a global framework, in which colliding epistemes gave rise to intense questioning, often followed by equally intense retreats and retrenchments. There is still much work to be done to uncover the history of identity, individual and collective, through its highly complex transmigrations during the early modern era – especially in non-European contexts. The stories of the animal hospitals of Gujarat offer one set of examples of the East–West encounter in an age of global group transformation.

Such encounters also had an impact on Indian group identities and cultures, as the later history of Indian goshalas suggests. As Lodrick has documented, many panjrapols and virtually all *vania* goshalas (as opposed to temple or court goshalas) that exist in India today were established within the last 150 years. He argues that this upsurge in protective institutions, especially for cows, could be attributed to several causes. These include economic factors, such as the need to protect cows during times of famine or drought (as in the case of the Bengal famine of 1891); the need to provide milk to schools, ashrams, and other institutions, or to aid in cattle development; and the increase in cattle populations, giving rise to a larger number of stray, sick, and aging animals.[83]

---

[81] On the history of the Lokāyata and Cārvāka schools of thought and their ongoing suppression, see, for example, Mittal, *Materialism in Indian Thought*; Roy, *Materialism: An Outline of the History of Scientific Thought*; Chattopadhyaya, with Gangopadhyaya, eds., *Carvaka/Lokayata: An Anthology of Source Materials and Some Recent Studies*; Krishna, *Studies in Hindu Materialism*; and Rao, *Charvaka Darshan: Ancient Indian Dalit Philosophy*. My thanks to Prashant Valanju for information about the Loyākata skeptical tradition.

[82] In "The Jain Knowledge Warehouses: Traditional Libraries in India," John E. Cort describes the rich resources of Jain libraries, particularly in Gujarat.

After visiting the Temple of Mahavir in Cambay, della Valle visited a library where he conversed with a learned 'Brachman' named Beca Azarg. This was probably a Jain library. The Italian nobleman attempted to discuss the relation of Pythagorean thought to Beca Azarg's own religion. The conversation was hampered by the language barrier, however, and inadequate translators. *Travels* I, 75–77.

[83] Lodrick, 69.

Lodrick also suggests an alternative explanation for the increase in animal shelters in India – namely, that these institutions functioned as potent symbols of Hindu culture in relation to that of the Mughals and later those of the West. The sanctity of animal life, especially that of cows, was one highly charged means of drawing a distinction between Hindus (and implicitly Jains) against the foreign groups visiting or occupying their country.[84] The violation of ahimsa by the imperial government of India, specifically with regard to cows, led to the founding of the Bombay and Poona panjrapols, among others, whereas the mistreatment of cows became the focus of anti-British sentiment among Hindus. "As in Moghul India," Lodrick writes, "the cow and attitudes toward the cow became associated with conflicting cultures, so much so that the traditional Hindu respect and reverence for the cow became a cause célèbre in the nationalist movement."[85] The cow remains a powerful marker of Hindu group identity as well as group trauma in India; as a signifier of "Indian-ness" and sometimes of Hindu nationalism, mobilized against Muslims and some other non-Hindu groups in India. Its force was intensified by the differential power of foreign occupation and visitation over the centuries, as well as internal ethnic and religious conflicts.

Concerning the sanctity of cows, the twentieth-century political and spiritual leader Mohandas Karamchand Gandhi would write,

> The central fact of Hinduism is cow protection. Cow protection to me is one of the most wonderful phenomen[a] in human evolution. It takes the human being beyond his species. The cow to me means the entire subhuman world. Man through the cow is enjoined to realize his identity with all that lives. . . . Cow protection is the gift of Hinduism to the world. And Hinduism will live as long as there are Hindus to protect the cow.[86]

Gandhi, who was born in Porbandar, a coastal town of Gujarat, was strongly influenced by both Hindu and Jain traditions; the concept of ahimsa would play a defining role in his conception of satyagraha, or nonviolent civil disobedience. For Gandhi, the imperative to nonviolence extended beyond the human sphere to the animal world, the community of all sentient beings. Gandhi would found several ashrams, including Sabarmati Ashram at

---

[84] *Ibid.*, 69–70.

[85] Lodrick continues, "Just as *khādi* and the Gandhi cap identified the wearer as a sympathizer with the nationalist cause, so veneration of the cow became the sine qua non for those who supported independence from the British. *Gomātā*, Mother Cow, became the emblem of "Indianness," and it is not surprising to find today that the symbol of the Congress Party, the successor to the Indian National Congress, is the cow and suckling calf." (70).

[86] From *Young India*, 11–11–1926, in *How to Serve the Cow*, ed. Bharatan Kumarappa, 3–4. Quoted in Lodrick, 25.

Ahmedabad, Uruli Kanchan near Poona, and Sevagram southwest of Nagpur. Each of these ashrams maintained a goshala, which served an important devotional function for those who stayed there. Many other Gandhian goshalas exist today, whether connected to ashrams or to rural educational institutions, such as the *gūrūkul*, or traditional Hindu school.[87] The goshala, or "place for cows," can be viewed both as cow or animal shelters within India and also as a synecdoche for Hindu India.

Gandhi would also chastise his fellow Hindus for their occasional mistreatment or neglect of cows, writing, "Our *pinjrapols*, though they are an answer to our instinct of mercy, are a clumsy demonstration of its execution. . . . Whilst addressing the religion of cow protection, we have enslaved the cow and her progeny, and have become slaves ourselves."[88] For Gandhi, cruelty toward "mother cow" was tantamount to violence against any and all more vulnerable beings, whether animal or human.[89] Such actions violate the fundamental mandate of ahimsa underpinning Hindu culture and amount to a debasement or loss of self – that is, a form of auto-enslavement.

Europeans who came to India in the sixteenth and seventeenth centuries understood that the cultures that they found there were not only different from their own in any number of ways but also that they posed important questions for how they would live their lives when they returned home. The effects of those encounters were not immediate but cumulative, and their impact is still being registered in the West and vice versa. Meanwhile, the meanings and values attributed to various forms of animal life remain powerful markers of group difference even today, as well as a source of cognitive dissonance and debate.

Della Valle's Return to His Group

The bizarre and compelling story of Pietro della Valle, Pilgrim to the East, offers a unique and valuable perspective on large-group identity formation at the end of the Renaissance. Confronted with a massive amount of

[87] Lodrick, 25–26.

[88] Gandhi stated, "I do not know that the condition of the cattle in any other part of the world is so bad as in unhappy India. We may not blame the Englishman for this. We may not plead poverty in our defense." Here he proposes that *pinjrapols* become model dairy farms, rather than "depots for receiving decrepit cattle." *Young India*, 6–10–1921, in *How to Serve the Cow*, 7.

Elsewhere Gandhi spoke of both goshalas and pinjrapols, using the terms more or less interchangeably. It is the protection of cows, rather than all animal life, about which he wrote frequently, however.

[89] "Mother cow," Gandhi wrote, "is in many ways better than the mother who gave us birth." *Hrijan*, 15–9–1940, in *How to Serve the Cow*, 4.

information about different religious, cultural, linguistic, ethnic, and caste groupings, della Valle sought to translate that information for himself and others, to categorize it, and to explain how these collectives were organized. Group differences, especially those pertaining to beliefs regarding the after-life, were of great interest and importance to him, resonating deeply with his own questions and personal difficulties. While he aimed to understand these differences, ultimately they did not shake or displace his basic religious beliefs, which remained strongly Catholic.

These beliefs would be confirmed when the pilgrim arrived in Goa in 1624 in time for the celebration of the still-recent canonization of Francis Xavier and of Ignatius Loyola, the founder of the Jesuits. The cel-ebration had been deferred for many months, della Valle explains, so that more time could be devoted to preparing for the momentous event. He describes the opening of the remarkable celebration, which bears quoting at length:

> On January the twenty-fifth the Jesuits of the Colledge of Saint Paul (this day being the feast of their Colledge) began to make part of their Solemnities, which where to be made for joy at the canonization of their Saints Ignatio and Sciavier. . . . They came forth with a Cavalcade of all their Collegians, divided into three Squadrons under three Banners, one of which represented the Asiaticks, one the Africans, and another the Europeans; those of each Squadron being clothed after the manner of their respective Countries. Before the Cavalcade went a Chariot of Clouds with Fame on the top, who, sounding her trumpet with the adjunction of Musick, published the news of the said Canonization. Two other Chariots accompanied the Cavalcade, the hindermost of which represented Faith, or the Church; the other in the middle was a Mount Parnassus, which Apollo and the Muses, representing the sciences professed in the said Colledge; both which Chariots were also full of very good music and many people. Moreover they remov'd from place to place amongst the Cavalcade five great Pyramids upon wheels, drawn by Men on foot, well cloth'd after the Indian fashion. Upon the first were painted all the Martyrs of the Order of Jesuits; upon another all the Doctors and Writers of Books; upon another figures of Men of all such Nations in their proper habits, where the said order hath foundations, to represent the Languages in which the Fathers of it preach. Another had abundance of Devices relating to all the Provinces of the said Religion; and lastly, another had all the Miracles both of Sant Ignatio and San Francesco Sciavier.[90]

---

[90] *Travels* II, 402–403. For an excellent analysis of these canonization festivies, see Gupta, *The Relic State*, 187–206.

This account of the Jesuit pageantry commemorating their two new saints is extraordinary for many reasons. Like the paintings of the *Adoration of the Magi* discussed earlier (Figures 2.1, 3.3, and 3.4), the parade stages the unification of the world's large groups, save for those of the New World, under the banner of Christianity – and, for that matter, under the banner of the Jesuits.

Also noteworthy in della Valle's description is the religious and cultural syncretism of the pageant. The Jesuits modeled the pyramid chariots on the juggernaut festivals of India, adapting them to different ends: conversion on the one hand and assimilation on the other. Curiously, Apollo and the nine Muses also had a place in the ceremony, since Greek and Roman mythology were not to be left out of the pageant but incorporated into it. An amalgam of group differences and group assimilation, the Jesuit pageant brought together the many paradoxes of the age and staged them in a now largely forgotten extravaganza.

Over several days in February, an outdoor play dramatizing the life of Francis Xavier was performed in the presence of the Viceroy and the people of Goa. Della Valle describes it as a tragedy that "comprehended not only the whole Life, but also the Death of San Francesco Sciavier, the transportation of his Body to Goa, his ascension into Heaven, and lastly his Canonization."[91] Finally, on February 19th, in the biggest parade of all, the body of Francis, encased in its silver reliquary-like coffin, was carried through the streets of the city. Della Valle further notes the resentment of the other religious orders of Goa, who apparently boycotted that procession on the grounds that the Jesuits had refused to attend their special events.[92] Della Valle, an avid participant in the canonization festivities, had begun the process of reentering his group.

After more than a decade of living in the East, della Valle returned to Rome, his birthplace. He arrived there with Mariuccia in April of 1626, after an arduous journey from India to Italy that lasted many months. On July 25th, he interred the body of Maani in the family vault at the Church of Santa Maria in Aracoeli. Of the burial of Maani in Rome, Pietro wrote in his letters – the last to be included in the *Viaggi*, or Voyages,

> This last remaining act of piety I paid to the mortal remains (*alle mortali spoglie*) of my sweet wife Sitti Maani – not, however, that it should be the last I pay to that other, better and immortal part of her, accompanying her with prayers for her repose; however, I have not abandoned those remains in the tomb, but have deposited them there in order to accompany them

[91] *Ibid.*, 411.
[92] *Ibid.*, 413–414.

once more with my own ashes (when it should please God) and rise again with her.[93]

In this, the conclusion to what would become his three-part opus, the *Viaggi*, della Valle reaffirmed his Catholic faith, his belief in the resurrection of the body, and his certainty that he and Maani would one day be joined again in the next life. Thus the woman whose name meant "wisdom" or "reason" in Arabic was memorialized by a husband who believed in the resurrection of the body at the end of time and who incorporated her Eastern wisdom, her distinctive cultural identity, and her narrative into his own.

For the memorial mass for Sitti Maani, held many months later on in that same church, della Valle built a catafalque in her honor (Figure 6.9). This elaborate and splendid monument, constructed of wood and painted to resemble marble, was supported by twelve bronze-hued statues of the Virtues, who upheld a golden crown. Atop the crown a swan sat, and on the swan, a cherub, representing the soul of Maani on its upward voyage to heaven. On the sides of the structure, twelve moral essays on Maani's life and virtues were artfully inscribed in the twelve languages that between them they knew.

At that memorial mass, della Valle delivered an eloquent elegy on Sitti Maani's behalf, comparing her excellence to that of the classical heroines Zenobia and Lucretia, as well as the orators Demosthenes and Cicero.[94]

---

[93] "Questo vltimo vfficio di pieta, che mi restaua, hò io pagato alle mortali spoglie Della mia dolce Consorte Sitti Maani; non però questo fia l'vltimo, ch'io spendo all'altra migliore, & immortale parte di lei, accompagnandola co' suffragij; se bene io non hò quelle abbandonate nella tomba, ma deposte per accompagnarle di nuouo con le mie ceneri (quando à Dio piaccia) e resorger con lei." Trans. from Blunt, *Pietro's Pilgrimage: A Journey to India and back at the beginning of the Seventeenth Century* (London: James Barrie, 1953), 302; *Viaggi* III, 506.

[94] Wilfred Blunt, della Valle's appropriately named English biographer, describes della Valle's final commemoration of Maani Gioerida in the Church of Santa Maria in Aracoeli, offering two conflicting accounts of that event:

When he came to speak of her beauty, Pietro, moved as much perhaps by his eloquence as by his grief, suddenly faltered, then collapsed in a flood of hysterical tears. And how, it may be asked, did the congregation react to this affecting scene? We shall never rightly know, for the two extant accounts of the incident are irreconcilable: according to one author, the whole band of mourners at once began to sob in unison with him; the other, however, relates that the tension found release in gust after gust of derisive laughter.

We do not know how della Valle himself reacted to these events, reported separately, because he does not record them in his letters. *Pietro's Pilgrimage*, 302–303. See also Girolamo Rocchi, *Funerale della Signora Maani Goerida della Valle* (Rome: Zanetti, 1627), discussed by Hester, *Literature and Identity in Italian Baroque Travel Writing*, 91.

6.9. Catafalque built by Pietro della Valle for Maani's memorial service in the Church of Santa Maria in Aracoeli in Rome, 1627. From *Les famevx voyages de Pietro della Valle, gentil-homme romain, svrnomme, l'illvstre voyagevr, avec vn denombrement tres-exact des choses les plus curieuses, & les plus remarquables qu'il a veuës dans la Turquie, l'Egypte, la Palestine, las Perse, & les Indes Orientales*, Vol. 3 (Paris: 1664). Humanities Research Center. The University of Texas at Austin.

Sometime after the memorial service, della Valle remarried. His bride was none other than Mariuccia, his adopted daughter and quondam Georgian refugee, whom Maani had rescued in Isfahan, and with whom della Valle had traveled throughout India. Together they had fourteen children.

Pietro Della Valle would live twenty-six more years. During that time, he continued his study of oriental languages, sharing with other interested parties the seventy-some manuscripts he had brought back from the East (now lodged in the Vatican Library). He delivered scholarly papers to the *Accademia degli Umoristi*, the learned society of which he had long been a member.[95] He composed music, and designed two new musical instruments: an enharmonic cembalo and a panharmonic bass viol.[96] In 1652, finally he too was laid to rest in the Church of Santa Maria in Aracoeli next to Sitti Maani. Meanwhile, Mariuccia lived another twenty-one years or more.[97] A Renaissance man, della Valle married two Eastern-born Renaissance women – the first, a would-be woman warrior who hoped to fight the Turks and save Christendom, and the second, the mother of their large brood, about whose life after her marriage regrettably little is known. Pietro della Valle fully embodied the contradictions of his age, the identity struggles, both individual and collective, and a profound curiosity begotten of global travel, exchange, and transformation. Sitti Maani Gioerida and Maria Tinatin, his two wives, were incorporated into his story; their lives, too, embodied many of the same contradictions of the age. In the animal hospitals of Gujarat, and in the mosques and temples of the East, della Valle traveled to the outer limits of his own group identity, crossing over its boundaries, however briefly. Those encounters would leave their traces on the Pilgrim, and on all the individuals and groups involved, the meanings and potentials of which continue to unfold today.

---

[95] Blunt, 9.

[96] On della Valle's musical interactions with members of the *Accademia dei Umoristi*, see Andrew dell'Antonio, *Listening as Spiritual Practice in Early Modern Italy*.

   Della Valle wrote an influential treatise on music theory entitled *Della musica dell'età nostra, che non è punto inferiore, anzi è migliore di quella dell'età passata; al sig. Lelio Guidiccioni* [16 January 1640]. In Angelo Solerti, ed., *Le origini del melodramma*, 148–179.

[97] *Ibid.*, 304–307.

POST-FREUDIAN CONCLUSIONS FOR THE
FUTURE HISTORY OF GROUPS

Metaphorical thought is the principal tool that makes philosophical insight possible and that constrains the forms that philosophy can take.

– George Lakoff and Mark Johnson, *Philosophy in the Flesh*

Syntheses

THIS BOOK BEGAN WITH A SET OF FRAMING IDEAS DERIVING FROM Freud's *Interpretation of Dreams*. Groups, I suggested, are somewhat like dreams; they are structured in ways that are obscure and frequently elusive. Also like dreams, groups can be organized around stories, although their narratives may be disjointed. They are, however, laden with metaphors, particularly of the body and its processes. Each of those metaphors around which real and imagined groups crystallize has a history. Each comes into being at a given point in time; it evolves and mutates until finally it becomes familiar – so much so that it is no longer recognizable as a metaphor.

Such is the case with the word *group* and its cognates, today our most familiar generic word for a collective. Its earlier meanings and its transformations during the Renaissance have been largely forgotten over the centuries. Once an aesthetic metaphor, the word *group* contains the distilled history of the era: musical, artistic, and theatrical arrangements that were described with a newly elaborated word, as well as a set of shared narratives about the beauty, vulnerability, death, and rebirth of the classical past. *Gruppo* may be the perfect metaphor for the European Renaissance and its creative accomplishments, at least in one familiar construction of that era.

Groups may or may not function as a "common veil" shrouding individuals in a shared mass identity, as Burckhardt argued in *The Civilization of the Renaissance in Italy*, and as Freud in his own way concurred. Arguably, however, it is our understanding of groups and their processes that has a

313

veiling effect. In our own time, for example, we often take the identities of groups for granted, making ready reference to religious, national, racial or ethnic groups, social classes, groups based on sex, gender, age, or some other classifications. These categories are invoked constantly, with the unspoken assumption that their meanings are fixed and also shared. As the preceding chapters have suggested, however, the identities of groups are harder to pin down; the beliefs, fantasies, and motivations of their members remain obscure and nonhomogeneous. Although group identities might appear relatively constant, they are constantly in flux. It is only by their insistent avowals of sameness ("we are *this*") and of difference from others ("we are not *that*") that individuals in groups create a compensatory illusion of stability on which collectives are founded.

A principal goal of this book has been to defamiliarize everyday assumptions about group identity through an archaeology of common metaphors such as *group, utopia,* and *machine* – words that came into being or that took on new connotations in the Renaissance, and that in multiple ways helped to define the epoch. Other chapters explored the appropriation or misappropriation of words and concepts – among them *caraíba/cannibal, Buddha/bugio, panjrapol/animal hospital* – to highlight the reorganizations of early modern group identities in the emergent world-system and the development or persistence of large-group conflicts and divisions that carry forward into our own era. Each chapter analyzed the myriad ways in which emergent group concepts came to define or to redefine collective identity. Although by no means the only such metaphors that could have been incorporated into such a study, they can be taken as paradigmatic examples of the types of transformations of collectives taking place in the global Renaissance.

The Renaissance (loosely defined here as the long sixteenth century) was a revolutionary phase in the history of group identity formation. Of course, making claims about any period of human history without simultaneously exploring other eras for comparison purposes is risky. Such a vast undertaking has been and will continue to be a group project and conversation. Still, within the limited framework of this book, I have held that the Renaissance was an era of unprecedented transformations of group identities. They were unprecedented because they took place on a truly global scale for the first time in human history and because they were the partial result of rapidly accelerating flows of information across a global network, information that accreted in the material residues of cultures and in the lived experiences of groups themselves. In this view, the Renaissance was a time when information about the world and its groups expanded at an exponential rate, reconfiguring individual and group identities in the process.

The transformations of group identities brought on by the forms of global networking discussed in this book (which must be taken as subsets of a far larger emergent system) can be linked to nonconcentric group schemas, as the sociologist Georg Simmel defined them. Simmel theorized a set of social changes during the Renaissance that enabled or fostered individuation in some parts of the world, while simultaneously fracturing both individual and group identities. This alteration of group schemas was undoubtedly more pronounced in some places than in others. This alteration also contributed to widespread crises of collective identity that were perhaps not new to the world – a world that has always been divided by wars, group migrations, and various forms of transculturation – but that nevertheless accelerated dramatically in the early modern age.

In this book, I have sought to convey the surprise of Renaissance encounters, the dreamlike pleasure or horror of one group brushing up against, embracing, or colliding with groups different from itself. The chapters of this book have thrown into relief the identity struggles and confusion, the loss of identity incumbent on such encounters, and the rise of new hybrid group identities. They have also highlighted the resilience of group identity (and the so-called group mystery) in the face of unusual internal and external challenges. Finally, they have analyzed the prominence of the body in descriptions of such encounters and in the group fantasies and metaphors that came from them.

Embodied Cognition and the History of Groups

The human body plays a central role in the formation of group metaphors and of narratives about groups. Individuals must organize themselves into a body before they become functional as a group; this envelope serves an essential defensive function for the group's members vis-à-vis outsiders and also each other.[1] The human body, its organs, members, and artificial supplements, and its real and imagined processes seem to be fundamental reference points in the psychic lives of groups. Gestation and birth; eating, digesting, and excreting; sex and reproduction; and aging and dying represent some of the bodily processes that can be mapped onto a group's fantasies about itself or about other groups. These fantasies can be unconscious or conscious in varying degrees – that is, present in the awareness of the individuals who participate in the group.

---

[1] See the Introduction, 19–24.

New models of embodied cognition may enable us to understand the "group body" phenomenon more clearly and to theorize it beyond the psychoanalytic accounts offered by Freud, Anzieu, and other psychoanalytic thinkers of the twentieth century. The rapidly evolving fields of cognitive neuroscience, linguistics, artificial intelligence and robotics, cognitive psychology, and philosophy of mind, among others, have generated fresh paradigms for understanding how humans think – namely, in and through our bodies.[2] The consensus that has emerged from these overlapping fields is that our thought patterns and perceptions are overwhelmingly determined by the fact of our embodiment.

Embodied cognition refers to not one phenomenon but to many that are still in the process of being explained. Two examples of recent discoveries include the following: bodily actions (e.g., smiling) generate related modes of cognition and emotional states, namely, the recovery of happy memories or a general feeling of well-being. Second, the ability to understand an observed action or event arises from neural reenactments within one's own brain – reenactments that are mirrored versions of what one has observed. Watching another person hit her fingers with a hammer causes a mirrored experience of pain in the observer; watching another person eat a candy bar induces a neural reenactment of tasting the candy bar oneself. These are not purely mental representations of pain or pleasure but actual (although partial) mirrored experiences of the physical and emotional states of others.[3]

Suffice it to say that the meta-discipline of embodied cognition, which is among the most exciting set of discoveries of our time, is as yet a largely

---

[2] Research by Andy Clark, Antonio Damasio, Shaun Gallagher, Vittorio Gallese, Elizabeth Grosz, Mark Johnson, George Lakoff, Humberto Maturana, Vilayanur Ramachandran, Giacomo Rizzolatti, Eleanor Rosch, Daniel J. Siegel, Evan Thompson, Mark Turner, and Francisco Varela – to name only a few of the luminaries within this meta-discipline – has revolutionized our collective understanding of the human mind-body relationship. See, e.g., Maturana and Varela, *Autopoiesis and Cognition* (1980); Maturana and Varela, *Tree of Knowledge* (1984); Lakoff and Turner, *More Than Cool Reason* (1989); Edelman, *The Remembered Present* (1989); Varela, Thompson, Rosch, *The Embodied Mind* (1991); Grosz, *Volatile Bodies* (1994); Damasio, *Descartes' Error* (1994); Clark, *Being There* (1997); Damasio, *The Feeling of What Happens* (1999); Lakoff and Johnson, *Philosophy in the Flesh* (1999); Turner, *Cognitive Dimensions of Social Science* (2001); Gallese, "The Shared Manifold Hypothesis" (2001); Turner and Fauconnier, *The Way We Think* (2002); Ramachandran, *The Emerging Mind* (2003); Gallese, "Embodied Simulation" (2005); Gallagher, *How the Body Shapes the Mind* (2006); Gallese, "Before and Below Theory of Mind" (2007); Siegel, *The Mindful Brain* (2007); Johnson, *The Meaning of the Body* (2007); Rizzolatti, *Mirrors in the Brain* (2008); Ramachandran, *The Tell-Tale Brain* (2011); and Clark, *Supersizing the Mind* (2011).

[3] See Bruce Bower's overview of embodied cognition, "Body in Mind," 24–28. See also Chapter 1, notes 65 and 76.

ahistorical discourse.[4] Theorists of embodied cognition, while sometimes focusing on the development of the individual mind from conception to death, have for the most part not explored the history of mind, except perhaps in broad evolutionary terms.

This need to historicize embodied cognition presents an excellent opportunity for the current generation of Renaissance scholars, for whom the history of the body and of subjectivity has been a primary topic of interest for more than two decades.[5] Only through the detailed study of particular contexts and events in a given time and place – that is, in history – will it be possible to understand the interplay between historical and transhistorical mental phenomena, whether of individual persons or of collectives. Only through the detailed study of metaphors and of their genesis and evolution over time will it be possible to grasp the history of psychic life and its possible futures.

For example, how might the study of the Renaissance be brought to bear on the current discourse of embodied cognition and vice versa? The Renaissance was an era in which collective bodily curiosity was extremely high and also unprecedented in its modes of exploration. Study of the body's exterior surfaces and its interior spaces and of bodily differences among individuals and groups became a central preoccupation of art, science and medicine, technology, and philosophy and religion, as well as many other fields.

This discovery of and fascination with the human body, and of nonhuman bodies, as well, had a profound impact on group concepts and identities, as the preceding chapters have argued. How did those shared perceptions feed into what we call modernity? We need only consider the *Laocoön*, recovered in 1506, and its profound impact on the perceptual and emotional systems of artists, poets, theologians, satirists, and many others in outward-expanding ripples of embodied experience to locate a multi-tiered example of shared embodied cognition unfolding over several centuries that helped to precipitate a brand-new group concept: the *gruppo*.

---

[4] Ellen Spolsky's 2007 book *Word vs. Image: Cognitive Hunger in Shakespeare's England* and Mary Thomas Crane's 2000 book *Shakespeare's Brain* are among the most innovative and important attempts within the field of Renaissance studies to historicize embodied cognition. See, too, Lisa Zunshine, ed., *Introduction to Cognitive Cultural Studies*, especially Part II, Cognitive Historicism, with essays by Alan Richardson, Spolsky, Crane, Zunshine, and Brian McConachie.

[5] The wave of Renaissance research in body studies represented the confluence of various psychoanalytic theories; Foucaultian social history and New Historicism; feminism, gender, and queer theory; ethnic and postcolonial studies; ecocriticism, studies of animality, and other theoretical movements that have reconfigured the humanities since the late 1960s.

It would require much more research to bring emerging theories of embodied cognition to bear on what I have called "group subjectivity," as well as group metaphors and the extraordinary narratives of groups everywhere. It must also be noted, however, that the models and intuitions of earlier psychoanalytic thinkers have pointed the way toward still more nuanced accounts of who we are as human beings and how we function socially.

It is possible that people's minds worked in the same ways throughout history; in the opinion of this author, it is more likely that they did not. Only by historicizing the study of embodied cognition will we be able to find out. Only by merging these humanistic and scientific fields will intellectual history and the history of mind take an embodied turn – a move that many in the fields of literary studies, art history, and history are now making.

If the past is truly different from the present, then perhaps the future might be too, particularly with respect to group behaviors. In his 1915 essay "Thoughts for the Time on War and Death," written shortly after the outbreak of World War I, Freud declared the following:

> It is, to be sure, a mystery why the collective individuals should in fact despise, hate and detest one another – every nation against every other – and even in times of peace. I cannot tell why that is so. It is just as though when it becomes a question of a number of people, not to say millions, all individual moral acquisitions are obliterated, and only the most primitive, the oldest, the crudest mental attitudes are left. It may be that only later stages in development will be able to make some change in this regrettable state of affairs. But a little more truthfulness and honesty on all sides – in the relations of men to one another and between them and their rulers – should smooth the way for this transformation.[6]

Freud's pessimism about groups was well founded, given the history of large-group conflicts during the centuries in which he lived, but the history of the mind might well be one of change and plasticity. Cautious optimism, although perhaps not fully justified, might induce shared hope and confidence in understanding more than we do at present and in accepting what we may never fully understand – the group mysteries of others.

---

[6] *Standard Edition*, 14: 273–302, p. 288. See also "Freudian Foreword," xxvii, n. 4.

BIBLIOGRAPHY

Abu-l-Fazl. *The Akbar nāmā*. Translated by H. Beveridge. 3 vols. Delhi: Ess Ess Publications, 1977.

Abu-Lughod, Janet. *Before European Hegemony*. New York: Oxford University Press, 1989.

Ackroyd, Peter. *The Life of Thomas More*. New York: Nan A. Talese/Doubleday, 1998.

Adas, Michael. *Machines as the Measure of Men: Science, Technology, and Ideologies of Western Dominance*. Ithaca, NY: Cornell University Press, 1989.

Afonso, Francisco Correia. *The Spirit of Xavier*. Bangalore: Good Shepherd Convent Press, 1922.

Agamben, Giorgio. *The Open: Man and Animal*. Translated by Kevin Attell. Stanford, CA: Stanford University Press, 2004.

Alighieri, Dante. *La divina commedia*. Edited by Siro A. Chimenz. Turin: UTET, 2003.

———. *The Divine Comedy*. Translated by Allen Mandelbaum. New York: Alfred A. Knopf, 1995.

Allport, Gordon W. "The Historical Background of Modern Social Psychology." In Vol. 1 of *The Handbook of Social Psychology*, edited by Gardner Lindzey and Elliott Aronson, 1–80. Reading, MA: Addison-Wesley Publishing Company, 1968.

Alpern, Stanley B. "What Africans Got for Their Slaves: A Master List of European Trade Goods." *History in Africa* **22** (1995): 5–43.

Anchieta, José de. *O Auto de São Lourenço*. Edited and translated by Walmir Ayala. Rio de Janeiro: Edições de Ouro, 1987.

———. *Cartas: informações, fragmentos históricos e sermões*. Vol. 3 of *Cartas jesuíticas*. Belo Horizonte: Editora Itatiaia Limitada/Editora da Universidade de São Paulo, 1988.

———. *Teatro de Anchieta*. Vol. 3 of *Obras completas*. Translated by Armando Cardoso, S. J. São Paulo: Edições Loyola, 1977.

Anderson, Benedict. *Imagined Communities: Reflections on the Origin and Spread of Nationalism*. London: Verso, 1983.

Anzieu, Didier. *The Group and the Unconscious*. Translated by Benjamin Kilborne. London: Routledge & Kegan Paul, 1984.

———. *Le Groupe et l'inconscient*. Paris: Dunod, 1975.

———. *The Skin Ego*. Translated by Chris Turner. New Haven, CT: Yale University Press, 1989.

————. *A Skin for Thought: Interviews with Gilbert Tarrab on Psychology and Psychoanalysis.* Translated by Daphne Nash Briggs. New York: Karnac Books, 1990.

————, Angélo Béjarano, René Kaës, and André Missenard. "Thèses du C.E.F.F.R.A.P. sur le travail psychanalytique dans les séminaires de formation" (October 1970). In *Groupes: Psychologie sociale clinique et psychanalyse,* unnumbered special issue of *Bulletin de Psychologie* (1974), 16–21.

Aquinas, Thomas. *Summa theologica.* 22 vols. Vol. 20, Part III. Supplement QQ. Translated by the Fathers of the English Dominican Province, 69–86. London: Burns Oates and Washbourne, 1912.

Arasaratnam, Sinnappah, and Aniruddha Ray. *Masulipatnam and Cambay: A History of Two Port Towns;* 1500–1800. Delhi: Munshiram Manoharlal Publishers, 1994.

Arber, Edward, ed. *The First Three English Books on America, (?1511–) 1555 A.D.: being chiefly translations, compilation, etc., by Richard Eden, from the writings, maps, etc., of Pietro Martire, of Anghiera, Sebastian Münster, and Sebastian Cabot.* Birmingham: Turnbull & Spears, Edinburgh, 1885.

Arens, W. *The Man-Eating Myth: Anthropology and Anthropophagy.* New York: Oxford University Press, 1979.

Aretino, Pietro. *Aretino's Dialogues.* Edited and translated by Raymond Rosenthal. New York: Ballantine Books, 1971.

Ariosto, Lodovico. *Orlando Furioso e Cinque Canti.* Edited by Remo Ceserani e Sergio Zatti. 2 vols. 1962; revised and enlarged, Turin: UTET, 1997.

Ascoli, Albert. *Dante and the Making of a Modern Author.* New York: Cambridge University Press, 2008.

Avineri, Shlomo. "War and Slavery in More's *Utopia.*" *International Review of Social History* 7 (1962): 260–290.

Bhabha, Homi K. *Location of Culture.* London: Routledge, 2004.

Baião, António. *A Inquisição de Goa: tentativa de história da sua origem, estabelecimento, evolução e extinção.* 2 vols. Lisbon: Academia das Ciências, 1945.

Baker-Smith, Dominic. *More's Utopia.* New York: HarperCollins Academic, 1991.

Balée, William. "Complexity and Causality in Tupinambá Warfare." In *Latin American Indigenous Warfare and Ritual Violence,* edited by Richard J. Chacon and Rubén G. Mendoza, 180–97. Tucson: University of Arizona Press, 2007.

Bandeira, Júlio. *Canibais no paraíso: A França Antártica e o imaginário europeu quinhentista.* Rio de Janeiro: Mar de Idéias Navegação Cultural, 2006.

Banerjee, Pompa. *Burning Women: Widows, Witches, and Early Modern European Travelers in India.* London: Palgrave Macmillan, 2002.

Baptiste, Victor N., ed. and trans. *Bartolomé de las Casas and Thomas More's* Utopia: *Connections and Similarities; A Translation and Study.* Culver City, CA: Labyrinthos, 1990.

Barbosa, Odoardo. *Libro di Odoardo Barbosa Portoghese.* In *Primo volume, & Seconda editione delle Navigationi et Viaggi in Molti Luoghi corretta, et ampliata, nella quale si contengono la Descrittione dell'Africa, & del paese del Prete Ianni, con varii viaggi, dalla città di Lisbona & dal mar Rosso à Calicut, & infin'all'isole Molucche, dove nascono le Spetierie, Et la Navigatione attorno il Mondo,* edited by Giovanni Battista Ramusio. Venice, 1554.

Barkan, Leonard. *Unearthing the Past: Archaeology and Aesthetics in the Making of Renaissance Culture.* New Haven, CT: Yale University Press, 1999.

Barker, Francis, Peter Hulme, and Margaret Iversen, eds. *Cannibalism and the Colonial World*. Cambridge: Cambridge University Press, 1998.

Baron, Hans. "The Limits of the Notion of 'Renaissance Individualism': Burckhardt after a Century." In Vol. 2 of *In Search of Florentine Civic Humanism*. Princeton, NJ: Princeton University Press, 1988.

Barrera-Osorio, Antonio. *Experiencing Nature: The Spanish American Empire and the Early Scientific Revolution*. Austin: University of Texas Press, 2006.

Bauer, Ralph. *The Cultural Geography of Colonial American Literatures: Empire, Travel, Modernity*. Cambridge: Cambridge University Press, 2003.

Bell, Aubrey F. G. *Diogo do Couto*. Oxford: Oxford University Press, 1924.

Bell, Daniel Orth. "New Identifications in Raphael's 'School of Athens.'" *Art Bulletin* **77**, no. 4 (1995): 638–646.

Benjamin, Walter. *Illuminations*. Edited by Hannah Arendt. Translated by Harry Zohn. New York: Schocken, 1969.

Bercht, Fatima, Estrellita Brodsky, John Alan Farmer, and Dicey Taylor, eds. *Taíno Pre-Columbian Art and Culture from the Caribbean*. New York: El Museo del Barrio/The Monacelli Press, 1997.

Bernstein, Eckhard. "Erasmus and Pieter Gillis: The Development of a Friendship." *Erasmus of Rotterdam Society Yearbook* **3** (1983): 130–145.

Bieber, Margaret. *Laocoön: The Influence of the Group since its Rediscovery*. New York: Columbia University Press, 1942.

Biondi, Giovanni Francesco. *An history of the civill vvares of England betweene the two Houses of Lancaster and Yorke*. Translated by Henry Carey, the Earl of Monmouth. London, 1641. Early English Books Online. ftp://eebo.chadwyck.com/home.

Blackburn, Robin. *The Making of New World Slavery: From the Baroque to the Modern; 1492–1800*. London: Verso, 1997.

Blakely, Alison. *Blacks in the Dutch World: The Evolution of Racial Imagery in a Modern Society*. Bloomington: Indiana University Press, 1993.

Bleich, David. *Utopia: The Psychology of a Cultural Fantasy*. Ann Arbor, MI: UMI Research Press, 1984.

Bleichmar, Daniela, Paula De Vos, Kristin Huffine, and Kevin Sheehan, eds. *Science in the Spanish and Portuguese Empires, 1500–1800*. Stanford, CA: Stanford University Press, 2009.

Blunt, Wilfred. *Pietro's Pilgrimage: A Journey to India and Back at the Beginning of the Seventeenth Century*. London: James Barrie, 1953.

Bober, Phyllis Pray, and Ruth Rubenstein. *Renaissance Artists and Antique Sculpture: A Handbook of Sources*. Oxford: Harvey Miller Publishers and Oxford University Press, 1986.

Boccaccio, Giovanni. *Il Decamerone*. Edited by Vittore Branca. 10 vols. Milan: Arnoldo Mondadori Editore, 1976.

———. *The Decameron*. Translated by Mark Musa and Peter E. Bondanella. New York: Norton, 1982.

Borges, Jorge Luis. "The Analytical Language of John Wilkins." In *Borges: Selected Non-Fictions*, translated by Eliot Weinberger, Esther Allen, and Suzanne Jill Levine. New York: Penguin, 2000.

Bottari, G. *Raccolta di lettere sulla pittura, scultura ed architettura scritte da' più celebri personaggi dei secoli XV, XVI e XVII*. 8 vols. Milan: Giovanni Silvestri, 1822.

Boucher, Philip P. *Cannibal Encounters: Europeans and Island Caribs: 1492–1763.* Baltimore: Johns Hopkins University Press, 1992.

Boxer, C. R. *Three Historians of Portuguese Asia (Barros, Couto and Bocarro).* Macau: Imprensa Nacional, 1948.

Braudel, Fernand. *The Perspective of the World.* Vol. 3 of *Civilization and Capitalism 15th–18th Century.* Translated by Siân Reynolds. Berkeley: University of California Press, 1992.

Bower, Bruce. "Body in Mind." *Science News* **174**, no. 9 (Oct. 25, 2008): 24–28.

Bray, Warwick. "European Impressions of the New World." In *The Meeting of Two Worlds: Europe and the Americas, 1492–1650,* edited by Warwick Bray, 289–326. Oxford: Oxford University Press, 1993.

Brilliant, Richard. *My Laocoön: Alternative Claims in the Interpretation of Artworks.* Berkeley: University of California Press, 2000.

Brodrick, James, S. J. *Saint Francis Xavier, 1506–1552.* London: Burns, Oates, 1952.

Brotton, Jerry. *The Renaissance Bazaar: From the Silk Road to Michelangelo.* Oxford: Oxford University Press, 2002.

Brown, Alison, ed. *Language and Images of Renaissance Italy.* Oxford: Clarendon Press, 1995.

Brucker, Gene. "The Italian Renaissance." In *A Companion to the Worlds of the Renaissance,* edited by Guido Ruggiero, 23–38. Oxford: Blackwell, 2002.

Brummer, Hans Henrik. *The Statue Court in the Vatican Belvedere.* Stockholm: Almquist & Wiksell, 1970.

Bucher, Bernadette. *Icon and Conquest: A Structural Analysis of de Bry's Great Voyages.* Translated by Basia Miller Gulati. Chicago: University of Chicago Press, 1981.

Buck, Carl Darling. *A Dictionary of Selected Synonyms in the Principal Indo-European Languages: A Contribution to the History of Ideas.* Chicago: University of Chicago Press, 1949.

Burckhardt, Jacob. *Briefe.* 10 vols. Basel: Benno Schwabe & Co. Verlag, 1961.

———. *The Civilization of the Renaissance in Italy.* Translated by S. G. C. Middlemore. 2 vols. New York: Harper, 1958.

———. *Die Cultur der Renaissance in Italien: ein Versuch.* 2 vols. Basel: Schweighauser, 1860. Google Books. ftp://books.google.com.

———. *The Letters of Jacob Burckhardt.* Edited by Alexander Dru. New York: Pantheon Books, 1955.

Burke, Peter. *The European Renaissance: Centers and Peripheries.* Oxford: Blackwell, 1998.

Bynum, Caroline Walker. *Fragmentation and Redemption: Essays on Gender and the Human Body in Medieval Religion.* New York: Zone Books, 1991.

———. *The Resurrection of the Body in Western Christianity, 200–1336.* New York: Columbia University Press, 1995.

Cachey, T. J. *Le Isole Fortunate: Appunti di storia letteraria italiana.* Rome: "L'Erma" di Bretschneider, 1995.

Caetano, Baptista, Capistrano de Abreu, and Rodolfo Garcia, eds. *Tratados da terra e gente do Brasil.* São Paulo, Brasil: Companhia Editora Nacional, 1978.

Cafezeiro, Edwaldo, and Carmem Gadelha. *História do teatro brasileiro: Um percurso de Anchieta a Nelson Rodrigues.* Rio de Janeiro: Editora UFRJ/EDUERJ/FUNARTE, 1996.

Calderón de Cuervo, Elena. "Las cartas de Amerigo Vespucci: hacia la conceptualizacion discursiva del Nuevo Mundo." *Cuadernos Americanos, Nueva Epoca* **33** (May–June 1992): 91–107.

Caminha, Pero Vaz de. "A Carta de Pero Vaz de Caminha." In *As Cartas do Brasil*, ed. Henrique Campos Simões, 47–139. Illhéus, Bahia, Brasil: Editus, 1999.

Campbell, Lyle. *American Indian Languages: The Historical Linguistics of Native America.* New York: Oxford University Press, 1997.

Campbell, Mary B. *The Witness and the Other World: Exotic European Travel Writing 400–1600.* Ithaca, NY: Cornell University Press, 1988.

Cañizares-Esguerra, Jorge. "Demons, Stars, and the Imagination: The Early Modern Body in the Tropics." In *The Origins of Racism in the West*, edited by Miriam Eliav-Feldon, Benjamin H. Isaac, and Joseph Ziegler, 313–325. Cambridge: Cambridge University Press, 2009.

———. "The Devil in the New World." In *The Atlantic in Global History: 1500–2000*, edited by Jorge Cañizares-Esguerra and Erik R. Seeman, 21–37. Upper Saddle River, NJ: Pearson Prentice Hall, 2007.

———. *Nature, Empire, and Nation: Explorations of the History of Science in the Iberian World.* Stanford, CA: Stanford University Press, 2006.

———. *Puritan Conquistadors: Iberianizing the Atlantic; 1550–1700.* Stanford, CA: Stanford University Press, 2006.

———. "Race, Theories of." In Vol. 5 of *Europe 1450 to 1789: Encyclopedia of the Early Modern World*, edited by Jonathan Dewald, 129–131. New York: Charles Scribner's Sons, 2004.

———, and Erik R. Seeman. *The Atlantic in Global History, 1500–2000.* Upper Saddle River, NJ: Pearson Prentice Hall, 2007.

———, and James Sidbury. "Mapping Ethnogenesis in the Early Modern Atlantic." *William and Mary Quarterly*, 3rd ser., 68, no. 2 (2011): 181–208.

Cardim, Fernão. "Do principio e origem dos indios do Brasil." In *Tratados da terra e gente do Brasil*, edited by Baptista Caetano, Capistrano de Abreu, and Rodolfo Garcia, 102–167. São Paulo, Brasil: Companhia Editora Nacional, 1978.

Carvalho, Augusto da Silva. *Garcia d'Orta:Comemoração do Quarto Centenário da sua partida para a India em 12 de março de 1534.* Coimbra: Imprensa da Universidade, 1934.

Cassirer, Ernst. *The Individual and the Cosmos in Renaissance Philosophy.* Translated by Mario Domandi. 1927. Philadelphia: University of Pennsylvania Press, 1963 (reprint).

Castelvetro, Lodovico. *Poetica d'Aristotele vulgarizzata e sposta.* Edited by Werther Romani. 2 vols. Rome: Laterza, 1978.

Caus, Salomon de. *Les Raisons des Forces Movvantes, Auec divers Machines tant utlies que plaisantes: Ausquelles sont adjoints pluusieurs desseins de Grotes & Fontaines.* Paris, 1624.

Certeau, Michel de. *Heterologies: Discourse on the Other.* Translated by Brian Massumi. Minneapolis: University of Minnesota Press, 1986.

———. *La fable mystique.* Paris: Gallimard, 1982.

Chain, Tun Aung. "The Portuguese Trade in the Kingdom of Hanthawaddy." In *Selected Writings of Tun Aung Chain*, 71–89. Yangon: Myanmar Historical Commission, 2004.

Chakrabarty, Dipesh. *Provincializing Europe: Postcolonial Thought and Historical Difference.* Princeton, NJ: Princeton University Press, 2000.

Chapple, Christopher. "Inherent Value without Nostalgia: Animals and the Mina Tradition." In *A Communion of Subjects: Animals in Religion, Science, and Ethics*, edited by

Paul Waldau and Kimberley Patton, 241–249. New York: Columbia University Press, 2006.

Chattopadhyaya, Debiprasad, with Mrinal Kanti Gangopadhyaya, eds. *Cārvāka/Lokāyata: An Anthology of Source Materials and Some Recent Studies.* Delhi: Indian Council of Philosophical Research, 1990.

Chiappelli, Fredi, with Michael J. B. Allen and Robert L. Benson, eds. *First Images of America: The Impact of the New World on the Old.* 2 vols. Berkeley: University of California Press, 1976.

Charry, Brinda S., and Gitanjali Shahani, eds. *Emissaries in Early Modern Literature and Culture: Mediation, Transmission, Traffic; 1550–1700.* Aldershot, Hants, England: Ashgate, 2009.

Chillingworth, William. *The religion of protestants a safe vvay to salvation. Or An ansvver to a booke entitled Mercy and truth, or, charity maintain'd by Catholiques, which pretends to prove the contrary. By William Chillingworth Master of Arts of the University of Oxford.* Oxford, 1638. Early English Books Online. ftp://eebo.chadwyck.com/home.

Christian, Kathleen Wren. *Empire Without End: Antiquities Collections in Renaissance Rome, c. 1350–1527.* New Haven, CT: Yale University Press, 2010.

Clark, Andy. *Being There: Putting Brain, Body, and World Together Again.* Cambridge, MA: MIT Press, 1997.

Clarke, Desmond. *Descartes: A Biography.* Cambridge: Cambridge University Press, 2006.

Clastres, Hélène. *The Land-Without-Evil: Tupí-Guaraní Prophetism.* Translated by Jacqueline Grenez Brovender. 1975. Urbana: University of Illinois Press, 1995.

Columbus, Christopher. *Accounts and Letters of the Second, Third, and Fourth Voyages.* Edited by Paolo Emilio Taviani and others, and translated by Luciano F. Farina and Marc A. Beckwith. *Nuova raccolta colombiana.* Rome: Istituto Poligrafico e Zecca dello Stato; Libreria dello Stato, 1994.

————. *Epistola de insulis nuper inventis.* Translated by Frank E. Robbins. March of America Facsimile Series, 1. Ann Arbor, MI: University Microfilms, Inc., 1966.

————. *Journal of the First Voyage, 1492.* Edited and translated by B. W. Ife. Warminster. England: Aris & Phillips Ltd, 1990.

Combès, Isabelle. *La tragédie cannibale chez les anciens Tupi-Guarani.* Paris: Presses Universitaires de France, 1992.

Conger, George P. *Theories of Macrocosms and Microcosms in the History of Philosophy.* New York: Columbia University Press, 1922.

Conley, Tom. *The Self-Made Map: Cartographic Writing in Early Modern France.* Minneapolis: University of Minnesota Press, 1996.

Cook, Harold J. "Ancient Wisdom, the Golden Age, and Atlantis: The New World in Sixteenth-Century Cosmography." *Terrae Incognitae* 10 (1978): 24–43.

Coote, C. J., ed. and trans. *The Voyage from Lisbon to India, 1505–1506.* London: Trafalgar Square, 1894.

Cort, John E. "The Jain Knowledge Warehouses: Traditional Libraries in India." *Journal of the American Oriental Society* 115, no. 1 (1995): 77–87.

Cottingham, John. "'A Brute to the Brutes?': Descartes' Treatment of Animals." *Philosophy* 53, no. 206 (1978): 551–559.

Couto, Diogo do. *Da Asia de João de Barros e Diogo de Couto: Dos feitos, que os Portuguezes fizeram na conquista, e descubrimento das terras, e mares do Oriente.* 24 vols. Lisbon: Edição da Libraria Sam Carlos, 1973.

Cūlavaṃsa, being the More Recent Part of the Mahāvaṃsa. Translated by Wilhelm Geiger from the Pāli, and from German to English by C. Mable Rickmers. 2 vols. 1930. Reprint, New Delhi: Asian Educational Services, 1992.

Cunha, Ana Cannas da. *A Inquisição no Estado da Índia: Origens (1539–1560)*. Lisbon: Estudos & Documentos, Arquivos Nacionais/Torre do Tombo, 1995.

Cunha, J. Gerson da. *Memoir on the History of the Tooth-Relic of Ceylon*. 1875. New Delhi: Asian Educational Services, 2001 (reprint).

Csikszentmihalyi, Mihaly. *Creativity: Flow and the Psychology of Discovery and Invention*. New York: HarperPerennial, 1996.

Dalzell, Alexander, Charles Fantazzi, and Richard J. Schoeck, eds. *Acta Conventus Neo-Latini Torontonensis: Proceedings of the Seventh International Congress of Neo-Latin Studies; Toronto, 8 August to 13 August 1988*. Binghamton, NY: Medieval & Renaissance Texts & Studies, 1991.

Damasio, Antonio R. *Descartes' Error: Emotion, Reason, and the Human Brain*. New York: Putnam, 1994.

———. *The Feeling of What Happens: Body and Emotion in the Making of Consciousness*. New York: Harcourt, Brace, 1999.

Damisch, Hubert. *The Origin of Perspective*. Translated by John Goodman. Cambridge, MA: MIT Press, 1994.

Darling, Linda. "The Renaissance and the Middle East." In *A Companion to the Worlds of the Renaissance*, ed. Guido Ruggiero, 55–69. Oxford: Blackwell Publishing, 2002.

Darwin, Charles. *The Expression of the Emotions in Man and Animals*. London: Julian Friedmann Publishers, 1979.

Dāṭhāvaṃsa. Edited and translated by Bimala Charan Law. Lahore: Mtoi Lal Banarsidas, 1925.

Dathávansa; or, the History of the Tooth-Relic of Gotama Buddha. Translated by Mutu Coomára Swámy. London, 1874. Google digital books.

Davis, David Brion. "Constructing Race: A Reflection." *The William and Mary Quarterly*, 3rd Ser., 54, no. 1 (1997): 7–18.

de Silva, Chandra Richard. *Sri Lanka: A History*. 1987. 2nd rev. ed., New Delhi: Vikas Publishing House Pvt. Ltd, 1997.

de Silva, K. M., ed. *History of Sri Lanka*. 3 vols. Nedimala-Dehiwala, Sri Lanka: University of Peradeniya, 1995.

Debrunner, Hans Werner. *Presence and Prestige: Africans in Europe; A History of Africans in Europe before 1918*. Basel: Basler Afrika Bibliographien, 1979.

Dell'Antonio, Andrew. *Listening as Spiritual Practice in Early Modern Italy*. Berkeley: University of California Press (forthcoming).

Della Valle, Pietro. *Della musica dell'età nostra, che non è punto inferiore, anzi è migliore di quella dell'età passata; al sig. Lelio Guidiccioni [16 January 1640]. In Le origini del melodramma: testimonianze dei contemporanei*, edited by Angelo Solerti, 148–179. Torino: Fratelli Bocca, 1903.

———. *The Travels of Pietro della Valle in India from the Old English Translation of 1664 by G. Havers*. Edited by E. Grey. 2 vols. Hakluyt Society, 84–85. 1892. B. Franklin, 1963 (reprint).

———. *I viaggi di Pietro della Valle: Lettere dalla Persia*. Edited by F. Gaeta and L. Lockhart. Vol. I. Rome, 1972.

———. *Viaggi di Pietro della Valle*. 4 vols. Rome, 1658–1663. Microfilm.

Dellon, Gabriel. *History of the Inquisition as It Is Exercised at Goa.* London, 1688. Early English Books Online. ftp://eebo.chadwyck.com/home.

Denucé, J. *Afrika in de XVIde eeuw en de handel van Antwerpen.* Antwerp: De Sikkel, 1937.

————. *L'Afrique au XVI siècle et le commerce anversois.* La Haye: Martinus Nijhoff, Editeur, 1937.

Derrett, J. Duncan M. "More's *Utopia* and Indians in Europe." *Moreana* **5** (1965): 17–18.

————. "Thomas More and Joseph the Indian." *Journal of the Royal Asiatic Society of Great Britain and Ireland.* Pts. **1** & **2** (1962): 18–34.

Derrida, Jacques. *The Animal that Therefore I Am.* Edited by Marie-Louise Mallet. Translated by David Wills. New York: Fordham University Press, 2008.

Descartes, René. *Oeuvres.* Edited by Charles Adam and Paul Tannery. 11 vols. Paris: J. Vrin, 1964.

————. *The Philosophical Writings of Descartes.* Edited by John Cottingham, Robert Stoothoff, and Dugald Murdoch. 3 vols. Cambridge: Cambridge University Press, 1985.

————. *Treatise of Man: René Descartes.* Edited and translated by Thomas Steele Hall. Introduction by I. Bernard Cohen. Cambridge, MA: Harvard University Press, 1972.

Devisse, Jean, and Michel Mollat. *The Image of the Black in Western Art.* Vol. 2, *From the Early Christian Era to the "Age of Discovery.* Part 2, *Africans in the Christian Ordinance of the World (Fourteenth to the Sixteenth Century).* Translated by William Granger Ryan. Cambridge, MA: Harvard University Press, 1979.

Dias, Eduardo Mayone. "Brazil's Birth Certificate: The Letter of Pero Vaz de Caminha." *Pacific Coast Philology* **27**, nos. 1–2 (1992): 10–15.

Dijksterhuis, E. J. *The Mechanization of the World Picture.* Translated by C. Dikshoorn. New York: Oxford University Press, 1961.

Disney, Anthony R. *A History of Portugal and the Portuguese Empire: From Beginnings to 1807.* 2 vols. Cambridge: Cambridge University Press, 2009.

Du Jarric, Pierre, S. J. *Akbar and the Jesuits: An Account of the Jesuit Missions to the Court of Akbar.* 1926. London: Routledge, 2004 (reprint).

Dundas, Paul. *The Jains.* 1992. London: Routledge, 2002 (reprint).

Dye, Joseph M., III. *The Arts of India: Virginia Museum of Fine Arts.* Richmond: Virginia Museum of Fine Arts/Philip Wilson Publishers, 2001.

Earle, T. F., and K. J. P. Lowe, eds. *Black Africans in Renaissance Europe.* Cambridge: Cambridge University Press, 2005.

Edelman, Gerald M. *The Remembered Present: A Biological Theory of Consciousness.* New York: Basic Books, 1989.

Eisenstein, Elizabeth. *The Printing Press as an Agent of Change: Communications and Cultural Transformations in Early Modern Europe.* 2 vols. Cambridge: Cambridge University Press, 1979.

Elias, Norbert. *The Civilizing Process: Sociogenetic and Psychogenetic Investigations.* Edited by Eric Dunning, Johan Goudsblom, and Stephen Mennell. Translated by Edmund Jephcott with some notes and corrections by the author. 1939. Revised edition. Oxford: Blackwell, 2000.

Emmer, Pieter C. "The History of the Dutch Slave Trade: A Bibliographical Survey." *Journal of Economic History* **32**, no. 3 (1972): 728–747.

Ettlinger, L. D. "*Exemplum Doloris*: Reflections on the Laocoön Group." In Vol. 2 of *De Artibus Opuscula XL – Essays in Honour of Erwin Panofsky*, edited by Millard Meiss. New York, 1961.

Everaert, J. G. "The Flemish Sugar Connection." *Bijdragen tot de Geschiedenis* **84** (2001): 257–264.

Fabricius, Johannes. *Syphilis in Shakepeare's England*. London: Jessica Kingsley Publishers, 1994.

Fara, Patricia. "Freudian Snaps." *Endeavor* **30**, no. 2 (2006): 48–49.

Faria, Miguel. "Brasil: visões europeias da América Lusitana." *Oceanos* **24** (October/December 1995): 70–100.

Faria e Sousa, Manuel. *Asia Portuguesa*. 3 vols. Lisbon, 1666–1674.

Ferguson, Donald, ed. and trans. *The History of Ceylon from the Earliest Times to 1600*. Colombo, 1909. New Delhi: Navrang, 1993 (reprint edition).

Fernandes, Florestan. *A função social da guerra na sociedade Tupinambá*. 1951. São Paulo: Editôra da Universidade de São Paulo, 1970.

Fernández, Oscar. "José de Anchieta and Early Theatre Activity in Brazil." *Luso-Brazilian Review* **15**, no. 1 (1978): 26–43.

Fernández-Armesto, Felípe. *1492: The Year the World Began*. New York: HarperOne, 2009.

———. *Amerigo: The Man Who Gave His Name to America*. New York: Random House, 2007.

———. *The Canary Islands after the Conquest: The Making of a Colonial Society in the Early Sixteenth Century*. Oxford: Clarendon Press, 1982.

———. "Empires in Their Global Context." In *The Atlantic in Global History, 1500–2000*, edited by Jorge Cañizares-Esguerra and Erik R. Seeman, 93–109. Upper Saddle River, NJ: Pearson Prentice Hall, 2007.

Ferns, Chris S. *Narrating Utopia: Ideology, Gender, Form in Utopian Literature*. Liverpool: Liverpool University Press, 1999.

Fideler, David R., ed. *The Pythagorean Sourcebook and Library: An Anthology of Ancient Writings Which Relate to Pythagoras and Pythagorean Philosophy*. Translated by Kenneth Sylvan Guthrie. Grand Rapids, MI: Phanes Press, 1987.

Figueiredo, João Manuel Pacheco de. *S. Francisco Xavier (Tentativa de um estudo médico-histórico)*. *Memórias da Academia das Ciências de Lisboa, Classe de Ciências*, Tomo XX. Lisbon, 1977. 93–122.

Fischer, Joseph, S. J., and Franz von Wieser, eds., with Charles George Herbermann. *The Cosmographiae Introductio of Martin Waldseemüller in Facsimile*. New York: United States Catholic Historical Society, 1907.

Fonseca, Jorge. "Black Africans in Portugal during Cleynaerts's visit (1533–1538)." In *Black Africans in Renaissance Europe*, edited by T. F. Earle and K. J. P. Lowe, 113–121. Cambridge: Cambridge University Press, 2005.

Formisano, Luciano, ed. *Letters from a New World: Amerigo Vespucci's Discovery of America*. Translated by David Jacobson. 1985. New York: Marsilio, 1992.

Foucault, Michel. *Discipline and Punish: The Birth of the Prison*. Translated by Alan Sheridan. 1975. New York: Vintage Books, 1977.

———. "What is an Author?" In *The Essential Foucault*, edited by Paul Rabinow and Nikolas Rose, 377–391. New York: The New Press, 2003.

Fox, Alistair. *Thomas More: History and Providence*. Oxford: Blackwell, 1982.

Freedberg, David, and Vittorio Gallese. "Motion, emotion and empathy in aesthetic experience." *Trends in Cognitive Sciences* **11** (2007): 197–203.

Freud, Sigmund. *Gesammelte Werke*. 16 vols. London: Imago Publishing, 1942.

———. *The Standard Edition of the Complete Psychological Works of Sigmund Freud*. Edited by James Strachey. 24 vols. London: The Hogarth Press, 1953.

Fudge, Erica. *Brutal Reasoning: Animals, Rationality, and Humanity in Early Modern England*. Ithaca, NY: Cornell University Press, 2006.

———, Ruth Gilbert, and Susan Wiseman, eds. *At the Borders of the Human: Beasts, Bodies and Natural Philosophy in the Early Modern Period*. Basingstoke, England: Palgrave, 2001.

Galeano, Eduardo. *Open Veins of Latin America*. Translated by Cedric Belfrage. New York: Monthly Review Press, 1973.

Gallese, Vittorio. "Before and Below 'Theory of Mind': Embodied Simulation and the Neural Correlates of Social Cognition." *Proceedings of the Royal Society B: Biological Sciences* **362** (2007): 659–669.

———. "Embodied simulation: From neurons to phenomenal experience." *Phenomenology and the Cognitive Sciences* **4** (2005): 23–48.

———. "The 'Shared Manifold' Hypothesis: From Mirror Neurons to Empathy." *Journal of Consciousness Studies* **8** (2001), 33–50.

Galloway, J. H. *The Sugar Cane Industry: An Historical Geography from its Origins to 1914*. Cambridge: Cambridge University Press, 1989.

Galluzzi, Paolo. "Leonardo da Vinci: From the 'elementi macchinali' to the man-machine." *History and Technology* **4**, nos. 1–4 (1987): 235–265.

———. *Renaissance Engineers from Brunelleschi to Leonardo da Vinci*. Florence: Istituto e Museo di Storia della Scienza, 1996.

Gandhi, Mohandas Karamchand. *Young India, 11-11-1926*. In *How to Serve the Cow*, edited by Bharatan Kumarappa. Ahmedabad: Navajivan Publishing House, 1959.

Garello, Edoardo Cesare, Vittorio Rossi, and Mario Salomone. *Raffaello: La Scuola di Atene: L'enigma del bozetto ritrovato e dei personaggi rivelati*. Cavallermaggiore: Gribaudo Editore, 1993.

Garfield, Robert. "Public Christians, Secret Jews: Religion and Political Conflict on Sao Tome Island in the Sixteenth and Seventeenth Centuries." *The Sixteenth Century Journal* **21**, no. 4 (1990): 645–654.

Geiger, Wilhelm. *Culture of Ceylon in Medieval Times*. Edited by Heinz Bechert. Wiesbaden: Otto Harrassowitz, 1960.

———. *An Etymological Glossary of the Sinhalese Language*. Colombo: Royal Asiatic Society, 1941.

Gemelli Careri, John Francis. *A Voyage Round the World*. . . . In *A Collection of Voyages and Travels, Some now first Printed from Original Manuscripts*. . . . 4 vols. London, 1704.

Gille, Bertrand. *The Renaissance Engineers*. London: Lund Humphries, 1966.

Gimpel, Jean. *The Medieval Machine: The Industrial Revolution of the Middle Ages*. New York: Penguin, 1976.

Goemaere, Pierre. "Anvers et ses esclaves noirs." *Revue mensuelle* (June 1963): 27–36.

Gombrich, Richard. *Precept and Practice: Traditional Buddhism in the Rural Highlands of Ceylon*. Oxford: Clarendon Press, 1971.

Goody, Jack. *The East in the West*. Cambridge: Cambridge University Press, 1996.

————. *Renaissances: The One or the Many?* Cambridge: Cambridge University Press, 2010.

Goris, J. A. *Étude sur les colonies marchandes méridionales (portugais, espagnols, italiens) à Anvers de 1488 à 1567: Contribution à l'histoire des débuts du capitalisme moderne.* Louvain: Librairie Universitaire, Uystpruyst, 1925.

————. "Uit de Geschiedenis der vorming van het Antwerpsch Stadsrecht: Slavernij te Antwerpen in de XVIde eeuw." *Bijdragen tot de Geschiedenis* **15** (1923): 541–544.

Gossman, Lionel. *Basel in the Age of Burckhardt: A Study in Unseasonable Ideas.* Chicago: University of Chicago Press, 2000.

Grafton, Anthony. *New Worlds Ancient Texts: The Power of Tradition and the Shock of Discovery.* Cambridge, MA: Harvard University Press, 1992.

Greenblatt, Stephen. *Learning to Curse: Essays in Early Modern Culture.* New York: Routledge, 1990.

————. *Marvelous Possessions: The Wonder of the New World.* Chicago: University of Chicago Press, 1991.

————, ed. *New World Encounters.* Berkeley: University of California Press, 1993.

————. *Renaissance Self-Fashioning: More to Shakespeare.* Chicago: University of Chicago, 1980.

————, et al. *Cultural Mobility: A Manifesto.* Cambridge: Cambridge University Press, 2010.

Greenfield, Sidney M. "Plantations, Sugar Cane and Slavery." *Historical Reflections* **6**, no. 1 (1979): 85–119.

Grosz, Elizabeth. *Volatile Bodies: Toward a Corporeal Feminism.* Bloomington: University of Indiana Press, 1994.

Guasco, Michael. "From Servitude to Slavery." In *The Atlantic World 1450–2000*, edited by Toyin Falola and Kevin D. Roberts, 69–95. Bloomington: Indiana University Press, 2008.

Guest, Kristen, ed. *Eating Their Words: Cannibalism and the Boundaries of Cultural Identity.* Albany: SUNY Press, 2001.

Gupta, Pamila. *The Relic State: St. Francis Xavier and the Politics of Ritual in Portuguese India.* Ph.D. dissertation. Columbia University, 2004.

Gurney, J. D. "Pietro Della Valle: The Limits of Perception." *Bulletin of the School of Oriental and African Studies, University of London* **49**, no. 1 (1986): 103–116.

Hale, David George. *The Body Politic: A Political Metaphor in Renaissance English Literature.* The Hague: Mouton, 1971.

Hale, John. *The Civilization of Europe in the Renaissance.* London: HarperCollins, 1993.

Hall, Marcia, ed. *Raphael's "School of Athens."* Cambridge: Cambridge University Press, 1997.

Halpern, Richard. *The Poetics of Primitive Accumulation: English Renaissance Culture and the Genealogy of Capital.* Ithaca, NY: Cornell University Press, 1991.

Hanzelet, Jean Appier, and François Thybourel. *Recueil de plusieurs machines militaires.* Pont-à-Mousson, 1620.

Harley, J. B. *Maps and the Columbian Encounter: An Interpretive Guide to the Travelling Exhibition.* Milwaukee: The Golda Meir Library, University of Wisconsin, 1990.

Haraway, Donna J. "A Cyborg Manifesto: Science, Technology, and Socialist-Feminism in the Late Twentieth Century." In *Simians, Cyborgs, and Women: The Reinvention of Nature*, 149–181. London: Routledge, 1990.

Harreld, Donald. "Atlantic Sugar and Antwerp's Trade with Germany in the Sixteenth Century." *Journal of Early Modern History* **7**, nos. 1–2 (2003): 148–163.

Harris, Elizabeth. "The Waldseemüller World Map: A Typographic Appraisal." *Imago Mundi* **37** (1985): 30–53.

Harris, Marvin. *The Sacred Cow and the Abominable Pig: Riddles of Food and Culture.* New York: Touchstone/Simon & Schuster, 1987.

Harrison, Peter. "Descartes on Animals." *The Philosophical Quarterly* **42**, no. 167 (1992): 219–227.

Haskell, Francis, and Nicholas Penny. *Taste and the Antique: The Lure of Classical Sculpture, 1500–1900.* New Haven, CT: Yale University Press, 1981.

Hay, Denys. "Historians and the Renaissance during the Last Twenty-Five Years." In *The Renaissance: Essays in Interpretation.* Edited by André Chastel. London: Methuen, 1982.

Hayles, N. Katherine. *How We Became Posthuman: Virtual Bodies in Cybernetics, Literature, and Informatics.* Chicago: University of Chicago Press, 1999.

Helminen, Juha Pekka. "¿Eran canibales los Caribes? Fray Bartolomé de Las Casas y el canibalismo." *Revista de historia de América (México)* **105** (1988): 147–158.

Helton, T., ed. *The Renaissance: A Reconsideration of the Theories and Interpretations of the Age.* Madison: University of Wisconsin Press, 1961.

Heng, Geraldine. *Empire of Magic: Medieval Romance and the Politics of Cultural Fantasy.* New York: Columbia University Press, 2003.

Herath, Dharmaratna. *The Tooth Relic and the Crown.* Colombo, 1994.

Hester, Natalie. *Literature and Identity in Italian Baroque Writing.* Aldershot: Ashgate, 2008.

Hexter, J. H. "More's Visit to Antwerp in 1515." In *Utopia,* vol. 4 of *The Complete Works of St. Thomas More,* Appendix A, edited by Edward Surtz, S. J., and J. H. Hexter, 573–576. New Haven, CT: Yale University Press, 1965.

Hickman, Henry. *Historia quinq-uarticularis exarticulata, or, Animadversions on Doctor Heylin's quintquarticular history.* 2nd ed. London, 1674. Early English Books Online. ftp://eebo.chadwyck.com/home.

Hill, Donald. *A History of Engineering in Classical and Medieval Times.* La Salle, IL: Open Court Publishing Company, 1984.

Hinde, John R. *Jacob Burckhardt and the Crisis of Modernity.* Montreal: McGill-Queen's University Press, 2000.

Hirsch, Rudolf. "Printed Reports on the Early Discoveries and Their Reception." In Vol. 2 of *First Images of America,* edited by Fredi Chiappelli et al., 537–562. Berkeley: University of California Press, 1976.

Hobbes, Thomas. *Leviathan.* Edited by Richard Tuck. Cambridge: Cambridge University Press, 1991.

Hobson, John. *The Eastern Origins of Western Civilisation.* Cambridge: Cambridge University Press, 2004.

Hocart, A. M. *The Temple of the Tooth in Kandy.* 1932. Facsimile edition. Rajagiriya, Sri Lanka: Trumpet Publishers, 1985.

Hulme, Peter. *Colonial Encounters: Europe and the Native Caribbean, 1492–1797.* London: Methuen, 1986.

———, and Neil L. Whitehead, eds. *Wild Majesty: Encounters with Caribs from Columbus to the Present Day: An Anthology.* Oxford: Clarendon Press, 1992.

Hunt, John. "A Thing of Nothing: The Catastrophic Body in *Hamlet.*" *Shakespeare Quarterly* **39**, no. 1 (1988): 27–44.

Hutten, Ulrich von. *De guaiaci medicina.* London, 1533.

Invernizzi, Antonio. *In viaggio per l'Oriente: le mummie, Babilonia, Persepoli/Pietro Della Valle.* Alessandria: Edizioni dell'Orso, 2001.

Israel, Jonathan I. *The Dutch Republic: Its Rise, Greatness, and Fall; 1477–1806.* Oxford: Clarendon Press, 1998.

Jain, C. R. *Fundamentals of Jainism.* 1916. Meerut, U. P., India: Phabhat Press, 1974 (reprint).

Jain, Hira Lal. *Jaina Tradition in Indian Thought.* Edited by D. C. Jain. Delhi: Sharada Publishing House, 2002.

Jantz, Harold. "Image of America in the German Renaissance." In Vol. 1 of *First Images of America,* edited by Fredi Chiappelli, 91–106. Berkeley: University of California Press, 1976.

Johnson, Christine R. *The German Discovery of the New World: Renaissance Encounters with the Strange and Marvelous.* Charlottesville: University of Virginia Press, 2008.

Johnson, Mark. *The Meaning of the Body: Aesthetics of Human Understanding.* Chicago: University of Chicago Press, 2007.

Johnston, Andrew G., and Jean-François Gilmont. "Printing and the Reformation in Antwerp." In *The Reformation and the Book,* edited by Jean-François Gilmont and translated by Karin Maag, 188–213. Aldershot, England: Ashgate, 1998.

Jones, E. *Essays in Applied Psychoanalysis* I. London: Hogarth Press, 1951.

Joost-Gaugier, Christiane L. *Raphael's Stanza della Segnatura: Meaning and Invention.* Cambridge: Cambridge University Press, 2002.

Jordan, William Chester. "'Europe' in the Middle Ages." In *The Idea of Europe: From Antiquity to the European Union,* edited by Anthony Pagden, 72–90. Cambridge: Cambridge University Press and the Woodrow Wilson Center Press, 2002.

Judovitz, Dalia. *The Culture of the Body: Genealogies of Modernity.* Ann Arbor: University of Michigan Press, 2001.

Kadir, Djelal. *Columbus and the Ends of the Earth: Europe's Prophetic Rhetoric as Conquering Ideology.* Berkeley: University of California Press, 1992.

Kaës, René. *L'appareil psychique groupal: constructions du groupe.* Paris: Dunod, 1976.

Kahn, Charles H. *Pythagoras and the Pythagoreans: A Brief History.* Indianapolis, IN: Hackett Publishing Company, 2001.

Kaplan, Benjamin J. *Divided by Faith: Religious Conflict and the Practice of Toleration in Early Modern Europe.* Cambridge, MA: Belknap Press/Harvard University Press, 2007.

Kaplan, Paul H. D. *The Rise of the Black Magus in Western Art.* Ann Arbor, MI: UMI Research Press, 1985.

Karrow, Robert W. *Mapmakers of the Sixteenth Century and Their Maps: Bio-Bibliographies of the Cartographers of Abraham Ortelius; 1570.* Chicago: Speculum Orbis Press/Newberry Library, 1993.

Katz, Nathan, and Ellen S. Goldberg. *The Last Jews of Cochin: Jewish Identity in Hindu India.* Columbia: University of South Carolina Press, 1993.

Kautsky, Karl. *Thomas More and His Utopia.* Translated by H. J. Stenning. New York: International Publishers, 1927.

Keele, Kenneth D. *Leonardo da Vinci's Elements of the Science of Man.* New York: Academic Press, 1983.

Kemp, Martin. *The Science of Art: Optical Themes in Western Art from Brunelleschi to Seurat.* New Haven, CT: Yale University Press, 1990.

Kernberg, Otto F. *Ideology, Conflict, and Leadership in Groups and Organizations.* New Haven, CT: Yale University Press, 1998.

Kerrigan, William, and Gorden Braden. *The Idea of the Renaissance.* Baltimore: Johns Hopkins University Press, 1989.

Khosla, Sarla. *The Historical Evolution of the Buddha Legend.* New Delhi: Intellectual Publishing House, 1989.

Kilgour, Maggie. *From Communion to Cannibalism: An Anatomy of Metaphors of Incorporation.* Princeton, NJ: Princeton University Press, 1990.

Kinnard, Jacob N. "The Field of the Buddha's Presence." In *Embodying the Dharma: Buddhist Relic Veneration in Asia,* ed. David Germano and Kevin Trainor, 117–143. Albany: SUNY Press, 2004.

Kint, An M. *The Community of Commerce: Social Relations in 16th-Century Antwerp.* Ph.D. dissertation. Columbia University, 1996.

Klein, Melanie. "Mourning and its Relation to Manic-Depressive States." In *The Selected Melanie Klein,* ed. Juliet Mitchell, 146–174. New York: Free Press, 1986.

Kohl, Karl-Heinz, ed. *Mythen der neuen Welt: zur Entdeckungsgeschichte Lateinamerikas.* Berlin: Frölich & Kaufmann, 1982.

Krishna, K. B. *Studies in Hindu Materialism.* Guntur: Milinda Publications, 1994.

Kristeller, Paul. "Changing Views of the Intellectual History of the Renaissance since Jacob Burckhardt." In *The Renaissance: A Reconsideration of the Theories and Interpretations of the Age,* edited by T. Helton Madison. Madison: University of Wisconsin Press, 1961.

Kubovy, Michael. *The Psychology of Perspective and Renaissance Art.* Cambridge: Cambridge University Press, 1986.

Kumarappa, Bharatan. *How to Serve the Cow.* Ahmedabad: Navajivan Publishing House, 1959.

Lacan, Jacques. *Jacques Lacan: Écrits.* Translated by Bruce Fink, with Héloïse Fink and Russell Grigg. New York: Norton, 2002, 2006.

Lach, Donald. *The Century of Discovery, Book 1.* Vol. 1 of *Asia in the Making of Europe.* Chicago: University of Chicago Press, 1965.

———, and Edwin J. Van Kley. *A Century of Advance, Book 3: South Asia.* Vol. 3 of *Asia in the Making of Europe.* Chicago: University of Chicago Press, 1998.

Lakoff, George, and Vittorio Gallese. "The Brain's Concepts: The Role of the Sensory-Motor System in Conceptual Knowledge." *Cognitive Neuropsychology* **22** (2005): 455–479.

———, and Mark Johnson. *Philosophy in the Flesh: The Embodied Mind and Its Challenge to Western Thought.* New York: Basic Books, 1999.

———, and Mark Turner. *More Than Cool Reason: A Field Guide to Poetic Metaphor.* Chicago: University of Chicago Press, 1989.

Lakowski, Romuald. "Thomas More's *Utopia* and the East: Portugal, Alexander the Great and India." Paper given at the Pacific Northwest Renaissance Conference, Bellingham, Washington; April 24, 1998.

Laplanche, J., and J.-B. Pontalis. *The Language of Psychoanalysis.* Translated by Donald Nicholson-Smith. Introduction by Daniel Lagache. New York: Norton, 1973.

Las Casas, Bartolomé de. *Historia de las Indias.* Vols. 3–5 of *Obras completas.* Edited by Paulino Castañeda Delgado. Madrid: Alianza Editorial, 1994.

_____. *History of the Indies*. Edited and translated by Andree Collard. New York: Harper and Row, 1971.

Laubenberger, Franz; trans. Steven Rowan. "The Naming of America." *Sixteenth Century Journal* **13**, no. 4 (1982): 91–113.

Leach, Linda York. *Mughal and Other Indian Paintings from the Chester Beatty Library*. 2 vols. London: Scorpion Cavendish, 1995.

Leonardo da Vinci. *Il codice atlantico: Edizione in facsimile dopo il restauro dell'originale conservato nella Biblioteca Ambrosiana di Milano*. 12 vols. Florence: Gaspero Barbèra. New York: Johnson Reprint Corp./Harcourt, Brace, Jovanovich, 1973–1975.

_____. *Fragments at Windsor Castle from the* Codex Atlanticus. Edited by Carlo Pedretti. London: Phaidon, 1957.

_____. *Leonardo da Vinci on the Human Body: The Anatomical, Physiological, and Embryological Drawings of Leonardo da Vinci*. Translated by Charles D. O'Malley and J. B. de C. M. Saunders. New York: Gramercy Books, 1982.

_____. *Scritti scelti di Leonardo da Vinci*. Edited by Anna Maria Brizio. Turin: UTET, 1966.

Léry, Jean de. *Histoire d'un voyage faict en la terre du Brésil*. Edited by Frank Lestringant. With an interview with Claude Levi-Strauss. Paris: Librairie Générale Française, 1994.

_____. *History of a Voyage to the Land of Brazil, Otherwise Called America*. Translated by Janel Whatley. Berkeley: University of California Press, 1990.

Lessing, Gotthold Ephraim. *Laocoön: An Essay on the Limits of Painting and Poetry*. Translated by Ellen Frothingham. New York: The Noonday Press, 1961.

Lestringant, Frank, ed. *Le Brésil d'André Thevet: Les Singularités de la France Antarctique*. Paris: Éditions Chandeigne, 1997.

_____. *Cannibals: The Discovery and Representation of the Cannibal from Columbus to Jules Verne*. Translated by Rosemary Morris. Berkeley: University of California, 1997.

Levenson, Jay A., ed. *Circa 1492. Art in the Age of the Exploration*. National Gallery of Art of Washington. New Haven, CT: Yale University Press, 1991.

Lévi-Strauss, Claude. *The Savage Mind*. Chicago: University of Chicago Press, 1966.

Lienhard, John H. *How Invention Begins: Echoes of Old Voices in the Rise of New Machines*. Oxford: Oxford University Press, 2006.

Limberger, Michael. "'No town in the world provides more advantages': Economies of agglomeration and the golden age of Antwerp." In *Urban Achievement in Early Modern Europe*, edited by Patrick O'Brien et al., 39–62. Cambridge: Cambridge University Press, 2001.

Linschoten, Jan Huyghen van. *Voyage . . . to the East Indies, from the Old English Translation of 1598*. Edited by Arthur Coke Burnell and P. A. Tiele. 2 vols. Hakluyt Society, 70–71. 1885. New Delhi: Asian Educational Services, 1988 (reprint).

_____. *Journael van de derthien-jarighe reyse, te water en te lande*. Amsterdam, 1663[?]. Sabin Americana 1500–1926.

Lodrick, Deryck O. *Sacred Cows, Sacred Places: Origins and Survivals of Animal Homes in India*. Berkeley: University of California Press, 1981.

Lombaerde, Piet. "Antwerp in its golden age: 'one of the largest cities in the Low Countries' and 'one of the best fortified in Europe'." In *Urban Achievement in Early Modern Europe: Golden Ages in Antwerp, Amsterdam and London*, edited by Patrick O'Brien et al., 99–127. Cambridge: Cambridge University Press, 2001.

Lucretius. *De rerum natura*. Translated by W. H. D. Rowse. Revised by Martin Ferguson Smith. Cambridge, MA: Harvard University Press, 1975.

Lukes, Stephen. *Individualism*. Oxford: Blackwell, 1973.

MacIagan, Edward. *The Jesuits and the Great Mogul*. London: Burns, Oates & Washbourne, 1932.

Maffei, Sonia. "La fama di Laocoonte nei testi del Cinquecento." In Salvatore Settis, ed., *Laocoönte: fama e stile*, 85–230. Rome: Donzelli Editore, 1999.

Magi, Filippo. *Il Ripristino del Laocoonte*. Memorie della Pontificia Accademia Romana di Archeologia IX, I. Rome: Tipografia Poliglotta Vaticana, 1960.

Magnaghi, Alberto. *Amerigo Vespucci. Studio critico con speciale riguardo ad una nuova valutazione delle fonti e con documenti inediti tratti dal Codice Vaglienti (Riccardiano 1910)*. 2 vols. Rome, 1924. Revised and augmented edition. Rome, 1926.

Mahānāma. The Mahāvaṃsa. Translated by Ananda W. P. Guruge. Madras: The M. P. Birla Foundation, 1990.

Mali, Joseph. *Mythistory: The Making of a Modern Historiography*. Chicago: University of Chicago Press, 2003.

Mallin, Eric. *Inscribing the Time: Shakespeare and the End of Elizabethan England*. Berkeley: University of California Press, 1995.

Manuel, Frank. *Utopias and Utopian Thought*. Boston: Houghton Mifflin, 1966.

Marc'hadour, Germain. "A Name for All Seasons." In *Essential Articles for the Study of Thomas More*, edited by R. S. Sylvester and G. P. Marc'hadour, 539–562. Hamden, CT: Archon Books, 1977.

Mardia, K. V. *The Scientific Foundations of Jainism*. Delhi: Motilal Banarsidass Publishers, 1990.

Marius, Richard. *Thomas More: A Biography*. New York: Knopf, 1984.

Martin, John Jeffries. *Myths of Renaissance Individualism*. New York: Palgrave Macmillan, 2004.

Martin, Michael R., and Richard Harrier. *The Concise Encyclopedic Guide to Shakespeare*. New York: Horizon Press, 1971.

Mason, Peter. *Deconstructing America: Representations of the Other*. New York: Routledge, Chapman, and Hall, 1990.

Maturana, Humberto R., and Francisco J. Varela, *Autopoiesis and Cognition: The Realization of the Living*. Boston: D. Reidel Publishing Company, 1980.

———. *Tree of Knowledge: The Biological Roots of Human Understanding*. 1984; Boston: Shambala, 1987.

Mauro, Frédéric, and Maria de Souza, *Le Brésil du XVe à la Fin du XVIIIe Siècle*. Paris: SEDES 1997.

Mayr, Otto. *Authority, Liberty & Automatic Machinery in Early Modern Europe*. Baltimore: Johns Hopkins University Press, 1986.

Mazlish, Bruce. *The Fourth Discontinuity: The Co-Evolution of Humans and Machines*. New Haven, CT: Yale University Press, 1993.

McAdams, Dan P. *The Redemptive Self: Stories Americans Live By*. Oxford: Oxford University Press, 2005.

McClellan, James E., and Harold Dorn. *Science and Technology in World History: An Introduction*. Baltimore: Johns Hopkins University Press, 1999.

McCutcheon, Elizabeth. "Puns, Paradoxes, and Heuristic Inquiry: The 'De Servis' Section of More's *Utopia*." In *Acta Conventus Neo-Latini Torontonensis: Proceedings of the Seventh International Congress of Neo-Latin Studies; Toronto, 8 August to 13 August 1988*, edited by Alexander Dalzell, Charles Fantazzi, and Richard J. Schoeck, 91–99. Binghamton, NY: Medieval & Renaissance Texts & Studies, 1991.

Mendes Pinto, Fernão. *The Travels of Mendes Pinto*. Edited and translated by Rebecca D. Catz. Chicago: University of Chicago Press, 1989.

Metcalf, Alida C. *Go-Betweens and the Colonization of Brazil: 1500–1600*. Austin: University of Texas Press, 2001.

Métraux, Alfred. *La Religion de Tupinambá et ses rapports avec celle des autres tribus Tupi-Guarani*. Paris: Librairie Ernest Leroux, 1928.

Micheli, Gianni. *Le origini del concetto di macchina*. Florence: Leo S. Olschki Editore, 1995.

Migiel, Marilyn. "Faltering on Demand: Freud's Dream of Irma." *Diacritics* **20**, no. 2 (1990): 20–39.

Mignolo, Walter. *The Darker Side of the Renaissance: Literacy, Territoriality, and Colonization*. Ann Arbor: University of Michigan Press, 1995.

Mintz, Stanley W. *Sweetness and Power: The Place of Sugar in Modern History*. New York: Viking Penguin, 1985.

Mittal, Kewal Krishan. *Materialism in Indian Thought*. Delhi: Munshiram Manoharlal Publishers, 1974.

Mocquet, Jean. *Voyages en Afrique, Asie, Indes Orientales & Occidentales*. Paris, 1617.

Montaigne, Michel de. *The Complete Essays of Montaigne*. Edited and translated by Donald M. Frame. Stanford, CA: Stanford University Press, 1958.

Montrose, Louis. "The Work of Gender in the Discourse of Discovery." In *New World Encounters*, edited by Stephen Greenblatt, 177–217. Berkeley: University of California Press, 1993.

More, Thomas. *Utopia*. Edited by Edward Surtz, S. J., and J. H. Hexter. Vol. 4 of *The Complete Works of St. Thomas More*. New Haven, CT: Yale University Press, 1965.

———. *Utopia: Latin Text and English Translation*. Edited by George M. Logan, Robert M. Adams, and Clarence H. Miller. Cambridge: Cambridge University Press, 1995.

Morison, Samuel Eliot. *The European Discovery of America*. New York: Oxford University Press, 1971–1974.

Mumford, Lewis. *The Myth of the Machine: Technics and Human Development*. 2 vols. New York: Harcourt, Brace & World, Inc., 1967–1990.

Murray, John J. *Antwerp in the Age of Plantin and Brueghel*. Norman: University of Oklahoma Press, 1970.

Navarro, Eduardo de Almeida. *Método moderno de Tupi Antigo: A língua do Brasil dos primeiros séculos*. Petrópolis, Brasil: Editora Vozes, 1999.

Nave, Francine de. "William Tyndale and the Antwerp Printers: An introduction to the exhibition." In *Tyndale's Testament*, edited by Paul Arblaster, Gergely Juhász, and Guido Latré, 3–9. Turnhout, Belgium: Brepols, 2002.

Nell, Andreas. *The Annals of the Tooth-Relic*. Kandy: Miller, 1928.

Ng, Su Fang. "Global Renaissance: Alexander the Great and Early Modern Classicism from the British Isles to the Malay Archipelago." *Comparative Literature* **58**, no. 4 (2006): 293–312.

Niederland, William G. "The Naming of America." In *The Unconscious Today: Essays in Honor of Max Schur*, edited by M. Kanzer, 459–472. New York: International Universities Press, 1971.

———. "River Symbolism, Part II." *Psychoanalytic Quarterly* **26** (1957): 50–75.

Nietzsche, Friedrich Wilhelm. *Die fröhliche Wissenschaft*. Frankfurt-am-Main: Insel, 1968.

———. *The Portable Nietzsche*. Translated by Walter Kaufmann. New York: Viking, 1968.

Nizami, Khaliq Ahmad. *Akbar and Religion.* Delhi: Adarahi-Adabiyat-i-Delli, 1989.

Nowak, Andrzej, and Robin R. Vallacher. *Dynamical Social Psychology.* New York: The Guilford Press, 1998.

O'Brien, Patrick, Keene Derek, Marjolein 'T. Hart, and Herman van der Wee, eds. *Urban Achievement in Early Modern Europe: Golden Ages in Antwerp, Amsterdam and London.* Cambridge: Cambridge University Press, 2001.

Obeyesekere, Donald. *Outlines of Ceylon History.* New Delhi: Asian Educational Services, 1999.

Obeyesekere, Gananath. "Anthropological Studies in Theravada Buddhism." Edited by Adrienne Suddard. Cultural Report Series 13. New Haven, CT: Yale University Press, 1966.

Ogilvy, John. *Asia, the First Part being An Accurate Description of Persia and the Several Provinces thereof. The Vast Empire of the Great Mogol, and other Parts of India: And their Several Kingdoms and Regions.* . . . London, 1673.

O'Gorman, Edmundo. *The Invention of America: An Inquiry into the Historical Nature of the New World and the Meaning of Its History.* Bloomington: Indiana University Press, 1961.

Olearius, Adam. *The Voyages and Travels of the Ambassadors sent by Frederick Duke of Holstein, to the Great Duke of Muscovy, and the King of Persia. Begun in the year MDCXXXIII. And finish'd in MDCXXXIX. . . . whereunto are added the Travels of John Albert de Mandelslo . . . into the East Indies.* Translated by John Davies. London, 1662.

Onions, C. T. *A Shakespeare Glossary.* Revised by Robert Eagleson. Oxford: Clarendon, 1986.

Ovington, John. *A Voyage to Suratt in the Year, 1689.* . . . London, 1696.

Pacey, Arnold. *Technology in World Civilization: A Thousand-Year History.* Cambridge, MA: MIT Press, 1990.

Pagden, Anthony. *Lords of All the World: Ideologies of Empire in Spain, France, and Britain, c. 1500–c. 1800.* New Haven, CT: Yale University Press, 1995.

Palencia-Roth, Michael. "Cannibalism and the New Man of Latin America in the Fifteenth and Sixteenth Century European Imagination." *Comparative Civilization Review* **12** (Spring 1985): 1–27.

Pal, Pratapaditya, ed. *The Peaceful Liberators: Jain Art from India.* Los Angeles: Los Angeles County Museum of Art; New York: Thames and Hudson, 1994.

Palla, Maria José. *Traje e Pintura: Grão Vasco e o Retábulo da Sé de Viseu.* Lisbon: Editorial Estampa, 1999.

Paré, Ambroise. *Dix livres de la chirurgie avec le magasin des instrumens necessaires à icelle.* Facsimile of the 1564 Paris edition. Paris: L'Editeur Claude Tchou, 1964.

Parker, Charles H. *Global Interactions in the Early Modern Age: 1400–1800.* Cambridge: Cambridge University Press, 2010.

Parr, Charles McKew. *Jan van Linschoten: The Dutch Marco Polo.* New York: Thomas Y. Crowell Company, 1964.

Passavant, Johann David. *Raphael of Urbino and His Father Giovanni Santi.* Reprint of the 1872 edition. New York: Garland, 1978.

Pastor, Ludwig. *History of the Popes from the Close of the Middle Ages.* 40 vols. London: Kegan Paul, 1923–1953.

Patrides, C. A. "The Microcosm of Man." *Notes and Queries* **CCV** (1960): 54–56, and **CCVIII** (1963): 282–286.

Pearson, M. N. *Merchants and Rulers in Gujarat: The Response to the Portuguese in the Sixteenth Century.* Berkeley: University of California Press, 1976.
———. *The Portuguese in India.* New York: Cambridge University Press, 1987.
Pereira, Moacyr Soares. *A navegação de 1501 ao Brasil e Américo Vespúcio.* Rio de Janeiro: ASA Artes Gráficas Ltda., 1984.
Peruschi, Giovanni Battista, S. J., *Informatione del regno, e stato del gran Rè di Mogor, della sua persona, qualita, e costumi, e delli buoni segni, e congietture della sua conuersione alla nostra santa fede.* Brescia, 1597.
Petrarca, Francesco. *Rime, trionfi, e poesie latine.* Edited by F. Neri et al. Milan: Ricciardi, 1951.
Petrosillo, Orazio. *The City of St. Peter: History, Art and Treasures.* Vatican City: Edizioni Musei Vaticani, 2003.
Pimenta, Nicholas, S. J. *Indian Observations. . . .* Vol. 9 of *Purchas His Pilgrims.* London: Hakluyt Society, 1906.
Piper, Anson C. "Jorge Ferreira de Vasconcellos and the Spirit of Empire." *Hispania* 50, no. 1 (1967): 44–48.
Pires, Maria Laura Bettencourt. "A América no imaginário europeu." In *Estudos de Arte e História: Homenagem a Artur Nobre de Gusmão,* edited by Artur Nobre de Gusmão, 425–429. Lisbon: Vega, 1995.
Plato. *Lysis. Symposium, Gorgias.* Translated by W. R. M. Lamb. New York: G. P. Putnam's Sons, 1925.
Pliny the Elder. *Natural History.* Translated by D. E. Eichholz. 10 vols. Cambridge, MA: Harvard University Press, 1962.
Pohl, Frederick Julius. *Amerigo Vespucci, Pilot Major.* New York: Columbia University Press, 1944.
Poliziano, Angelo. *Poesie volgari.* Edited by Francesco Bausi. 2 vols. Rome: Vecchiarelli Editore, 1997.
Portuondo, Maria M. *Secret Science: Spanish Cosmography and the New World.* Chicago: University of Chicago Press, 2009.
Prado, Décio de Almeida. *Teatro de Anchieta a Alencar.* São Paulo, Brasil: Editora Perspectiva, 1993.
Pratt, Mary Louise. *Imperial Eyes: Travel Writing and Transculturation.* New York: Routledge, 1992.
Price, Merrall Llewelyn. *Consuming Passions: The Uses of Cannibalism in Late Medieval and Early Modern Europe.* New York: Routledge, 2003.
Priolkar, Anant Kakba. *The Goa Inquisition.* Bombay: Bombay University Press, 1961.
Pyrard de Laval, François. *The Voyage of François Pyrard of Laval to the East Indies, the Maldives, the Moluccas and Brazil.* Edited and translated by Albert Gray. 3 vols. London: Hakluyt Society, 1887, 1890.
Queyroz, Fernão de. *The Temporal and Spiritual Conquest of Ceylon.* Translated by S. G. Perera, S. J. 3 vols. Colombo: A. C. Richards, 1930.
Rabasa, José. *Inventing A-M-E-R-I-C-A: Spanish Historiography and the Formation of Eurocentrism.* Norman: University of Oklahoma Press, 1993.
Rabelais, François. *Oeuvres Complètes.* Paris: Editions du Seuil, 1973.
Rahman, A., ed. *History of Indian Science, Technology and Culture AD 1000–1800.* New Delhi: Oxford University Press, 1999.

Ramachandran, V. S. *The Emerging Mind: The B.B.C. Reith Lectures 2003*. London: Profile Books, 2003.

Ramelli, Agostino. *Le Diverse et artificiose machine del Capitano Agostino Ramelli dal Ponte della Tresia Ingegniero del Christianissimo Re di Francia et di pollonia, Nellequali si contengono varii et industriosi Movimenti, degni di grandissima Speculatione, per cavarne beneficio infinito in ogni sorte d'operatione*. Paris, 1588.

Raminelli, Ronald. *Imagens da colonização: A representação do índio de Caminha a Vieira*. Rio de Janeiro: Jorge Zahar Editor, 1996.

Rao, Katti Padma. *Charvaka Darshan: Ancient Indian Dalit Philosophy*. Translated by D. Anjaneyulu. Madras: The Gurukul Lutheran Theological College & Research Institute, 1997.

Redig de Campos, Deoclecio. *Raffaello nelle Stanze*. Milan: Aldo Martello Editore, 1965.

Ricardo, Carlos A. *Povos indígenas no Brasil. 2001/2005*. São Paulo: CEDI, 2006.

Richter, Simon. *Laocoön's Body and the Aesthetics of Pain: Winckelmann, Lessing, Herder, Moritz, Goethe*. Detroit, MI: Wayne State University Press, 1992.

Riedweg, Christoph. *Pythagoras: His Life, Teaching, and Influence*. Translated by Steven Rendall. Ithaca, NY: Cornell University Press, 2005.

Rizzolatti, Giacomo, and Corrado Sinigaglia. *Mirrors in the Brain: How Our Minds Share Actions, Emotions, and Experiences*. Translated by Frances Anderson. New York, Oxford: Oxford University Press, 2008.

Rocchi, Girolamo. *Funerale della Signora Sitti Maani Goerida della Valle*. Rome: Zanetti, 1627.

Rodrigues, Dalila. *Grão Vasco, pintura portuguesa do Renascimento*. Salamanca: Consorcio Salamanca, 2002.

——. "Vasco Fernandes, Esboço Biográfico." In *Grão Vasco e a pintura europeia do Renascimento*. Lisbon: Comissão Nacional para as Comemorações dos Descobrimentos Portugueses, 1992.

Rosenfield, Leonora Cohen. *From Beast-Machine to Man-Machine: Animal Soul in French Letters from Descartes to La Mettrie*. New York: Octagon Books, 1968.

Rosheim, Mark Elling. *Leonardo's Lost Robots*. New York: Springer 2006.

Rossi, Paolo. *I filosofi e le macchine (1400–1700)*. Milan: Feltrinelli, 1962.

Rowland, Ingrid D. "The Intellectual Background of the *School of Athens*: Tracking Divine Wisdom in the Rome of Julius II." In *Raphael's "School of Athens*," edited by Marcia Hall, 131–175. Cambridge, Cambridge University Press, 1997.

Roy, M. N. *Materialism: An Outline of the History of Scientific Thought*. 1940. Delhi: Ajanta Publications, 1982 (reprint).

Rubiés, Joan-Pau. *Travel and Ethnology in the Renaissance: South India through European Eyes; 1250–1625*. Cambridge: Cambridge University Press, 2000.

Ruggiero, Guido, ed. *A Companion to the Worlds of the Renaissance*. Oxford: Blackwell Publishing, 2002.

Sangave, Vilas. *Le jaïnisme: philosophie et religion de l'Inde*. Translated by Pierre Amiel. 1990. Paris: Guy Trédaniel Éditeur, 1999.

Saraiva, António José. *The Marrano Factory: The Portuguese Inquisition and its New Christians; 1536–1765*. Translated, revised, and augmented by H. P. Salomon and I. S. D. Sassoon. Leiden: Brill, 2001.

Sarasohn, Lisa T. *Gassendi's Ethics: Freedom in a Mechanistic Universe.* Ithaca, NY: Cornell University Press, 1996.

Saunders, A. C. de C. M. *A Social History of Black Slaves and Freedmen in Portugal: 1441–1555.* Cambridge: Cambridge University Press, 1982.

Saussure, Ferdinand de. *Course in General Linguistics.* Edited by Charles Bally and Albert Sechehaye, with Albert Riedlinger. Translated by Wade Baskin. New York: McGraw-Hill Book Co., 1966.

Sawday, Jonathan. *Engines of the Imagination: Renaissance Culture and the Rise of the Machine.* London: Routledge, 2007.

———. "'Forms Such as Never Were in Nature': The Renaissance Cyborg." In *At the Borders of the Human: Beasts, Bodies and Natural Philosophy in the Early Modern Period*, ed. Erica Fudge, Ruth Gilbert, and Susan Wiseman, 171–195. Basingstoke, England: Palgrave Macmillan, 2002.

Schuhmacher, Stephan, and Gert Woerner, eds. *The Encyclopedia of Eastern Philosophy and Religion.* Boston: Shambala, 1994.

Schurhammer, Georg, S. J. *Francis Xavier: His Life, His Times.* Translated by M. Joseph Costelloe, S. J. 4 vols. Rome: The Jesuit Historical Institute, 1980.

Schwartz, Seymour I. *The Mismapping of America.* Rochester, NY: University of Rochester Press, 2003.

Seneviratne, H. L. *Rituals of the Kandyan State.* Cambridge Studies in Social Anthropology 22. Cambridge: Cambridge University Press, 1978.

Settis, Salvatore, ed. *Laocoönte: fama e stile.* Rome: Donzelli Editore, 1999.

Shah, Natubhai. *Jainism: The World of Conquerors.* 2 vols. Brighton, England: Sussex Academic Press, 1998.

Shakespeare, William. *The Complete Works of Shakespeare.* Edited by David Bevington. 5th edition. New York: Pearson Longman, 2004.

Sheppey, Thomas. *Several weighty considerations humbly recommended to the serious perusal of all, but more especially to the Roman Catholicks of England to which is prefix'd, An epistle from one who was lately of that communion to Dr. Stillingfleet, Dean of St. Pauls, declaring the occasion of the following discourse.* London, 1679. Early English Books Online. ftp://eebo.chadwyck.com/home.

Sheth, Chimanlal Bhailal. *Jainism in Gujarat (A.D. 1100 to 1600).* Bhavnagar: Shree Mohodaya P. Press, 1953.

Shewmaker, Eugene. *Shakespeare's Language: A Glossary of Unfamiliar Words in His Plays and Poems.* New York: Facts on File, 1996.

Shirodkar, P. P. "Socio-Cultural Life in Goa during the 16th and 17th Centuries." In *Researches in Indo-Portuguese History.* 2 vols. Jaipur: Publication Scheme, 1998.

Siegel, Daniel J. *The Mindful Brain: Reflection and Attunement in the Cultivation of Well-Being.* New York: Norton, 2007.

Sigurdson, Richard Franklin. *Jacob Burckhardt's Social and Political Thought.* Toronto: University of Toronto Press, 2004.

Silva, Chandra R. de, ed. *Portuguese Encounters with Sri Lanka and the Maldives: Translated Texts from the Age of the Discoveries.* Farnham, Surrey: Ashgate, 2009.

Simmel, Georg. *Conflict and The Web of Group-Affiliations.* Translated by Kurt H. Wolff and Reinhard Bendix. New York: Free Press, 1955.

————. *Sociology: inquiries into the construction of social forms.* Translated and edited by Anthony J. Blasi, Anton K. Jacobs, and Mathew Kanjirathinkal. With an introduction by Horst J. Helle. Leiden: Brill, 2009.

————. *Soziologie: Untersuchungen über die Formen der Vergesellsschaftung.* Edited by Otthein Rammstedt. Frankfurt am Main: Suhrkamp Verlag, 1992.

Singh, Jyotsna, ed. *A Companion to the Global Renaissance: English Literature and Culture in the Era of Expansion.* Malden, MA: Wiley-Blackwell, 2009.

Skinner, Quentin. *The Renaissance.* Vol. 1 of *The Foundations of Modern Political Thought.* Cambridge: Cambridge University Press, 1978.

Slavin, Arthur J. "The American Principle from More to Locke." In vol. 1 of *First Images of America: The Impact of the New World on the Old,* ed. Fredi Chiappelli, 139–164. Berkeley: University of California Press, 1976.

Soderini, Giovanvettorio. *I due trattati dell'agricoltura e della coltivazione delle viti.* 4 vols. Bologna: Romagnoli dall'Acqua, 1902.

Solerti, Angelo ed. *Le origini del melodramma: testimonianze dei contemporanei.* Torino: Fratelli Bocca, 1903.

Sousa, Francisco de, S. J. *Oriente conquistado a Jesus Christo pelos padres da Companhia de Jesus da Província de Goa.* Tesouros da Literatura e da História. Ed. M. Lopes de Almeida. Porto: Lello & Irmão Editores, 1978.

Soyer, François. "King João II of Portugal 'O Príncipe Perfeito' and the Jews (1481–1495)." *Sefarad* **69**, no. 1 (2009): 75–99.

Spencer, Colin. *The Heretic's Feast: A History of Vegetarianism.* Hanover, NH: University Press of New England, 1995.

Spolsky, Ellen. *Word vs. Image: Cognitive Hunger in Shakespeare's England.* Basingstoke, England: Macmillan, 2007.

Spragens, Thomas. *Politics of Motion: The World of Thomas Hobbes.* London: Croom Helms, 1973.

Staden, Hans. *Hans Staden's True History: An Account of Cannibal Captivity in Brazil.* Edited and translated by Neil L. Whitehead and Michael Harbsmeier. Durham, NC: Duke University Press, 2008.

Stadtner, Donald Martin. *Sacred Sites of Burma: Myth and Folklore in an Evolving Spiritual Realm.* Bangkok: River Books, 2010.

Strada, Famiano. *An account of the famous siege of Antvverp by Alexander prince of Parma, in the year 1584. Being the most memorable siege that was ever laid to any city.* London, 1672. Early English Books Online. ftp://eebo.chadwyck.com/home.

————. *De bello belgico, Decas secunda.* Rome, 1658.

Strauss, Leo. *The Political Philosophy of Hobbes: Its Basis and Its Genesis.* Translated by Elsa M. Sinclair. Clarendon Press, 1936. Chicago: University of Chicago Press, 1963 (reprint).

Strong, John. *Relics of the Buddha.* Princeton University Press, 2004. Delhi: Motilal Banarsidass Publishers Private Limited, 2007 (reprint).

Stuart, Tristam. *The Bloodless Revolution: A Cultural History of Vegetarianism from 1600 to Modern Times.* New York: W. W. Norton: 2007.

Subrahmanyam, Sanjay. *The Portuguese Empire in Asia, 1500–1700: A Political and Economic History.* New York: Longman, 1993.

Surtz, Edward J. *The Praise of Wisdom: A Commentary on the Religious and Moral Problems and Background of St. Thomas More's Utopia.* Chicago: Loyola University Press, 1957.

Sweet, James. "The Iberian Roots of American Racist Thought." *The William and Mary Quarterly*, 3rd ser., **54**, no. 1 (1997): 143–166.

Tasso, Torquato. *Discorsi dell'arte poetica* (1587). In *Scritti sull'arte poetica*. Edited by Ettore Mazzali. 2 vols. 1959. Turin: Einaudi, 1977 (reprint).

Taylor, Charles. *Sources of the Self: The Making of Modern Identity*. Cambridge, MA: Harvard University Press, 1989.

Tennant, James E. *Ceylon: An Account of the Island: Physical, Historical, and Topographical. . . .* 2 vols. London, 1860.

Teixeira, José. "Adoration of the Magi." In *Circa 1492: Art in the Age of the Exploration*, edited by Jay A. Levenson, 152–153. National Gallery of Art of Washington. New Haven, CT: Yale University Press, 1992.

Texeira, Pedro. *The History of Persia . . . .* Translated by John Stevens. London, 1715.

Thijs, A. K. L. "De Geschiedenis van de Suikernijverheid te Antwerpen (16de–19de eeuw): Een Terreinverkenning." *Bijdragen tot de geschiedenis* **62**, nos. 1–2 (1979): 23–50.

Tilly, Charles. *Stories, Identities, and Political Change*. Lanham, MD: Rowman & Littlefield Publishers, Inc., 2002.

———. *Coercion, Capital, and European States, AD 990–1992*. Cambridge, MA: Blackwell, 1992.

Tillyard, E. M. W. *The Elizabethan World Picture*. New York: MacMillan, 1944.

Tobias, Michael. *Life Force: The World of Jainism*. Berkeley, CA: Asian Humanities Press, 1991.

Todorov, Tzvetan. *The Conquest of America: The Question of the Other*. Translated by Richard Howard. 1982; New York: Harper & Row, 1984.

Tomlinson, Gary. *The Singing of the New World: Indigenous Voice in the Era of European Contact*. Cambridge: Cambridge University Press, 2007.

Toussaint-Samat, Maguelonne. *A History of Food*. Translated by Anthea Bell. Oxford: Blackwell, 1992.

Trainor, Kevin, ed., *Buddhism: The Illustrated Guide*. Oxford: Oxford University Press, 2004.

———. *Relics, Ritual, and Representation in Buddhism: Rematerializing the Sri Lanka Theravāda Tradition*. Cambridge: Cambridge University Press, 1997.

Trexler, Richard, ed. *Persons in Groups: Social Behavior as Identity Formation in Medieval and Renaissance Europe*. Binghamton, NY: Medieval and Renaissance Texts & Studies, 1985.

Trinkaus, Charles. *In Our Image and Likeness: Humanity and Divinity in Italian Humanist Thought*. 2 vols. Chicago: University of Chicago Press, 1970.

Turner, Henry S. "Toward an Analysis of the Corporate Ego: The Case of Richard Hakluyt." *Differences: A Journal of Feminist Cultural Studies* **20**, nos. 2 and 3 (2009): 103–147.

Turner, Mark. *Cognitive Dimensions of Social Science*. Oxford: Oxford University Press, 2001.

———, and Gilles Fauconnier. *The Way We Think: Conceptual Blending and the Mind's Hidden Complexities*. New York: Basic Books, 2002.

Turquet, P. M. "Menaces à l'identité personnelle dans le groupe large." In *Groupes, psychologie sociale et psychanalyse*, unnumbered special issue of *Bulletin de psychologie* (1974): 135–158.

Vainfas, Ronaldo. *A heresia dos indios: catolicismo e rebeldia no Brasil colonial*. São Paulo: Companhia das Letras, 1995.

Valignano, Alessandro, S. J., *Historia del principio y progresso de la Compañía de Jesús en las indias orientales (1542–64)*, ed. Josef Wicki, S. J. Biblioteca Instituti Historici S. I., vol. 2. Rome: Institutum Historicum S. I., 1944.

———, ed. *Monumenta xaveriana*. 2 vols. Monumenta Historica Societatis Iesu 16, no. 43. Madrid: Typis Augustini Avrial, 1899–1912.

Vallacher, Robin R., and Andrzej Nowak, eds. *Dynamical Systems in Social Psychology*. New York: Academic Press, Inc., 1994.

Vallavanthara, Antony, ed. *India in 1500 A.D.: The Narratives of Joseph, the Indian*. Mannanam: Research Institute for Studies in History, 1984.

Van der Wee, Hermann. *The Growth of the Antwerp Market and the European Economy (14th–16th Centuries)*. Recueil de travaux d'histoire et de philologie 4, nos. 28–30. Louvain: Université de Louvain, 1963.

Van Essen, C. C. "La découverte du Laocoön." *Mededelingen der Koninklijke Nederlandse Akademie van Wetenschappen, AFD. Letterkunde* **18**, no. 12 (1955): 291–305.

Vanpaemel, Geert. "Science for sale: The metropolitan stimulus for scientific achievements in sixteenth-century Antwerp." In *Urban Achievement in Early Modern Europe*, edited by Patrick O'Brien et al., 287–304. Cambridge: Cambridge University Press, 2001.

Varela, Francisco J., Evan Thompson, and Eleanor Rosch. *The Embodied Mind: Cognitive Science and Human Experience*. Cambridge, MA: MIT Press, 1993.

Varela Marcos, Jesús, and Maria Montserrat León Guerrero. *Colón, su tesis "pezonoidal"del globo terráqueo y el itinerario del tercer viaje: La fantasía del paraíso terrenal*. Valladolid: Instituto Interuniversitario de Estudios de Iberoamérica y Portugal, 2002.

Vasari, Giorgio. *Le vite de' più eccellenti pittori scultori e architettori nelle redazioni del 1550 e 1568*. Edited by Rosanna Bettarini. Commentary by Paola Barocchi. 6 vols. Florence: Sansoni, 1966.

———. *Lives of the Most Eminent Painter Sculptors & Architects*. Translated by Gaston Du C. de Vere. 10 vols. London: MacMillan and Co. and The Medici Society, 1912–14.

Vaz de Caminha, Pero. "A Carta de Pero Vaz de Caminha." In *As Cartas do Brasil*, edited by Henrique Campos Simões, 47–139. Illhéus: Editora da UESC, Editus, 1999.

Velayudhan, P. S., et al., eds. *Cochin Synagogue Quatercentenary Celebrations: December 15, 16, 18, & 19, 1968*. Cochin: The Kerala History Association and the Cochin Synagogue Quatercentenary Celebration Committee, 1971.

Verlinden, Charles. "Encore sure les origines de sclavus-esclave." *Cultus et Cognitio* (1976): 599–609.

———. "L'origine de 'sclavus'-esclave." *Archivum latinitatis medii aevi* **XVII** (1943): 97–128.

Vermeylen, F. *Painting for the Market: Commercialization of Art in Antwerp's Golden Age*. Turnhout, Belgium: Brepols, 2003.

Vesalius, Andreas. *On the Fabric of the Human Body*. Translated by William Frank Richardson and John Burd Carman. San Francisco: Norman Publishing, 1998.

Vespucci, Amerigo. *Lettera al Piero Soderini*. Edited by Giuseppe Sergio Martini. Florence: Leo S. Olschki, Editore, 1957.

———. *Letters from a New World: Amerigo Vespucci's Discovery of America*. Edited by Luciano Formisano. Translated by David Jacobson. 1985. New York: Marsilio, 1992.

Vico, Giambattista. *The New Science of Giambattista Vico*. Translated by Thomas Goddard Bergin and Max Harold Fisch. Ithaca, NY: Cornell University Press, 1948.

Virgil. *Eclogues, Georgics, Aeneid I–VI*. Translated by H. Rushton Fairclough. Revised by G. P. Gould. 2 vols. 1916. Cambridge, MA: Harvard University Press, 1999 (reprint).

Visconti, Ennio Quirino. *Statue del Museo Pio-Clementino*. 7 vols. Rome: L. Mirri, 1784.

Viveiros de Castro, Eduardo. *From the Enemy's Point of View: Humanity and Divinity in an Amazonian Society*. Translated by Catherine V. Howard. Chicago: University of Chicago Press, 1992.

Vlieghe, Hans. "The fine and decorative arts in Antwerp's Golden Age." In *Urban Achievements in Early Modern Europe*, edited by Patrick O'Brien et al., 173–185. Cambridge: Cambridge University Press, 2001.

Voet, Leon. *Antwerp: The Golden Age; The Rise and Glory of the Metropolis in the Sixteenth Century*. Antwerp: Mercatorfonds, 1973.

Vogt, John L. "The Early São Tome-Principe Slave Trade with Mina, 1500–1540." *The International Journal of African Studies* **6**, no. 3 (1973): 453–467.

Volkan, Vamik. *Bloodlines: From Ethnic Pride to Ethnic Terrorism*. New York: Farrar, Strauss, and Giroux, 1997.

———. "Large-Group Identity, Large-Group Regression and Massive Violence." Lecture presented at Molde, Norway (July 2, 2005). Electronic.

———. *The Need to Have Enemies and Allies: From Clinical Practice to International Relationships*. London: Jason Aronson, 1988.

Wallace, David. *Chaucerian Polity: Absolutist Lineages and Associational Forms in England and Italy*. Stanford, CA: Stanford University Press, 1997.

Wallerstein, Immanuel. *The Modern World-System I: Capitalist Agriculture and the Origins of the European World-Economy in the Sixteenth Century*. New York: Academic Press, Inc./Harcourt Brace Jovanovich Publishers, 1974.

Walter, E. V. "Simmel's Sociology of Power: The Architecture of Politics." In *Essays on Sociology, Philosophy & Aesthetics*, edited by Kurt H. Wolff, 139–166. New York: Harper & Row Publishers, 1959.

Wasserman, Renata. "The Theater of José de Anchieta and the Definition of Brazilian Literature." *Luso-Brazilian Review* **36**, no. 1 (1999): 71–85.

Waterschoot, Werner. "Antwerp: Books, publishing, and cultural production before 1585." In *Urban Achievement in Early Modern Europe*, edited by Patrick O'Brien et al., 233–248. Cambridge: Cambridge University Press, 2001.

Weerasooria, N. E. *Ceylon and Her People*. 4 vols. Colombo: Lake House Investments Limited Publishers, 1971.

Wegg, Jervis. *Antwerp 1477–1559: From the Battle of Nancy to the Treaty of Cateau Cambrésis*. London: Methuen, 1916.

Wellman, Barry, and S. D. Berkowitz, eds. *Social Structures: A Network Approach*. Cambridge: Cambridge University Press, 1988.

Westrup, J. A., and F. Ll. Harrison. *The New College Encyclopedia of Music*. Revised by Conrad Wilson. New York: W. W. Norton, 1976.

Wey Gómez, Nicolás. *The Tropics of Empire: Why Columbus Sailed South to the Indies*. Transformations: Studies in the History of Science and Technology. Cambridge, MA: MIT Press, 2008.

White, Hayden. "The Noble Savage Theme as Fetish." In Vol. 1 of *First Images of America*, edited by Fredi Chiappelli, 121–135. Berkeley: University of California Press, 1976.

White, Lynn. *Medieval Technology and Social Change*. Oxford: Oxford University Press, 1962.

Whitney, Charles. "The Naming of America as the Meaning of America: Vespucci, Publicity, Festivity, Modernity." *Clio* **22**, no. 3 (1993): 195–220.

Wicki, Joseph, S. J., ed. *Documenta indica*. 17 vols. Monumenta Historica Societatis Iesu. Rome: MHSI, 1948.

Williams, Eric. *Capitalism and Slavery*. Chapel Hill: University of North Carolina Press, 1944.

Williams, Gordon. *A Glossary of Shakespeare's Sexual Language*. London: Athlone, 1997.

Williams, Raymond. *Keywords: A Vocabulary of Culture and Society*. Oxford: Oxford University Press, 1976.

Wilson, Robert A. *Boundaries of the Mind: The Individual in the Fragile Sciences – Cognition*. Cambridge: Cambridge University Press, 2004.

Wilson, Samuel M. *The Archaeology of the Caribbean*. Leiden: Cambridge University Press, 2007. Electronic.

———. "The Cultural Mosaic of the Indigenous Caribbean." *Proceedings of the British Academy* **81** (1993): 37–66.

Winius, George D. *The Black Legend of Portuguese India: Diogo do Couto, His Contemporaries and the Soldado Prático*. Xavier Center for Historical Research Studies Series 3. New Delhi: Concept Publishing Company, 1985.

Wojciehowski, D. A. *Old Masters, New Subjects: Early Modern and Poststructuralist Theories of Will*. Palo Alto, CA: Stanford University Press, 1995.

Wolfe, Jessica. *Humanism, Machinery, and Renaissance Literature*. Cambridge: Cambridge University Press, 2004.

Woolf, Kurt, ed. *Essays on Sociology, Philosophy & Aesthetics*. New York: Harper & Row, Publishers, 1959.

Xavier, P. A. "The Role of Pinjrapoles in the Animal Welfare Work of India." *Animal Citizen* **4**, no. 3 (1967): 35–38.

Xavier, P. D. *Goa: A Social History (1510–1640)*. Panaji, Goa: Rajhauns Vitaran, 1993.

Yang, Ching-ming. "Gross Metempsychosis and Eastern Soul." In *Humans and Other Animals in Eighteenth-Century British Culture: Representation, Hybridity, Ethics*, edited by Frank Palmeri, 13–30. Aldershot, England: Ashgate, 2006.

Yule, Henry, and A. C. Burnell. *Hobson-Jobson: A Glossary of Colloquial Anglo-Indian Words and Phrases, and of Kindred Terms, Etymological, Historical, Geographical and Discursive*. London: John Murray, 1903.

Zamora, Margarita. *Reading Columbus*. Berkeley: University of California Press, 1993.

Zonca, Vittorio. *Novo teatro di machine et edificii*. Padua, 1656.

Županov, Ines G. *Missionary Tropics: The Catholic Frontier in India (16th–17th Centuries)*. Ann Arbor: University of Michigan Press, 2005.

———. "'The Wheel of Torments': Mobility and Redemption in Portuguese Colonial India (sixteenth century)." In *Cultural Mobility: A Manifesto*. Edited by Stephen Greenblatt et al., 24–74. Cambridge: Cambridge University Press, 2010.

INDEX